A Summa of the *Summa*

PETER KREEFT

A Summa
of the *Summa*

The Essential Philosophical Passages of
St. Thomas Aquinas' *Summa Theologica*
Edited and Explained for Beginners

IGNATIUS PRESS   SAN FRANCISCO

Passages from the *Summa Theologica*
are taken from the translation done in 1920 by
The Fathers of the English Dominican Province.
Used with permission.

Cover art credit: SCALA/Art Resource, New York
Detail of St. Thomas Aquinas from a work entitled
Trionfa di S. Tommaso d'Aquino
by Andrea di Buonaiuto
in the Spanish chapel of
St. Maria Novella, Florence

Cover design by Roxanne Mei Lum

© 1990 Ignatius Press, San Francisco
With ecclesiastical approval
All rights reserved
ISBN 978-0-89870-317-7 (HB)
ISBN 978-0-89870-300-9 (PB)
Library of Congress catalogue number 90–81772
Printed in the United States of America

To W. Norris Clark, S.J.

More than a great Thomist;
A little Thomas

CONTENTS

Introduction

INTRODUCTION

I couldn't make any judgment on the *Summa*, except to say this: I read it every night before I go to bed. If my mother were to come in during the process and say, "Turn off that light. It's late," I with lifted finger and broad bland beatific expression, would reply, "On the contrary, I answer that the light, being eternal and limitless, cannot be turned off. Shut your eyes," or some such thing. In any case I feel I can personally guarantee that St. Thomas loved God because for the life of me I cannot help loving St. Thomas.

— Flannery O'Connor, *The Habit of Being*

I. On St. Thomas

St. Thomas Aquinas is certainly one of the greatest philosophers who ever lived (to my mind he is *the* greatest), for at least eight reasons: truth, common sense, practicality, clarity, profundity, orthodoxy, medievalism, and modernity.

First, and most simply, he told the truth—that simple and unfashionable purpose of philosophy that is so often fudged ("nuanced") or forgotten today. The following quotation should be chiseled on the doorposts of every philosophy department in the world: "The study of philosophy is not the study of what men have opined, but of what is the truth."

2. Descartes says that the one thing he learned about philosophy in the university that stuck with him was that one could not imagine any doctrine so bizarre or unbelievable that it has not been seriously taught by some philosopher or other. What was true already in 1637 is triply true today. St. Thomas, however, is the master of common sense. He has an uncanny knack of sniffing out the obviously right position amid a hundred wrong ones. This holds true especially in ethics, the real test of a philosopher. Some great philosophers, like Descartes, Hegel, and Heidegger, have no

philosophical ethics at all. Others, like Hobbes and Hume and Kant and Nietzsche, have ethics that are simply unlivable. St. Thomas is as practical and plain and reasonable in ethics as Aristotle, or Confucius, or your uncle.

3. St. Thomas was a master of metaphysics and technical terminology; yet he was also such a practical man that as he lay dying he was talking about three things: a commentary on *The Song of Songs*, a treatise on aqueducts, and a dish of herring. Ordinary people, Popes, and kings wrote to him for advice and always got back sound wisdom. I know of no one since St. Paul who is so full of both theoretical *and* practical wisdom.

4. Those who love truth passionately usually also love simplicity and clarity of style so that as many people as possible can benefit from this precious thing, Truth. Fr. Norris Clarke, S.J. of Fordham University, the most Aquinas-like mind I know of all men living, says there are three kinds of philosophers: those who at first seem clear, but upon further readings become more and more obscure; those who at first may seem obscure but become clearer and clearer upon each reading (St. Thomas is the prime example of this kind), and those who seem obscure at first and remain obscure.

St. Thomas aimed only for light, not heat. There is almost never anything personal in the *Summa*, no rhetoric, no appeal to the irrational; nothing but lucidity.

5. And depth—no philosopher since St. Thomas has ever so successfully combined the two fundamental ideals of philosophical writing: clarity and profundity. Continental European philosophy in this century has sought and sometimes found depth, by focusing on the truly fundamental issues, but at the expense of clarity. English philosophy has sought and often found clarity, but at the expense of depth, concentrating on second-order linguistic questions rather than on those the average person wonders at: God, man, life, death, good, and evil.

6. A sixth reason for St. Thomas' greatness is decisive only for Catholics, but it should at least be decisive for *all* Catholics: according to the Church's own teaching authority (and to be a Catholic *means* to believe in such a thing), St. Thomas is the primary theological Doctor (Teacher) of the Church. During its proceedings, the Council of Trent placed the *Summa* on the high altar in second place only to the Bible. Pope Leo XIII in *Aeterni Patris* (1879) told all Catholic teachers to "restore the golden

wisdom of St. Thomas . . . and let them clearly point out its solidity and excellence above all other teaching".

Even non-Catholics must go to St. Thomas to understand Catholic theology and philosophy. You can never understand a philosophy from its critics or dissenters. In four colleges and universities, I have never had a good course on any philosopher (including many philosophers I disagree with) from a critic, and never a worthless one from a disciple.

7. St. Thomas was crucial for the medieval era. He fulfilled more than anyone else the essential medieval program of a marriage of faith and reason, revelation and philosophy, the Biblical and the classical inheritances. In so doing, he held together for another century the medieval civilization's intellectual soul, which in his century was threatening to break up like a ship battered by huge waves of division, caused mainly by the rediscovery of the works of Aristotle and the polarization of reactions into the fearful heresy-hunting of traditionalists, and the fashionable compromising of modernists. Aquinas stands as a shining example of an alternative to both the fundamentalists and the liberals of his day and of any day.

You may not agree that St. Thomas is history's greatest philosopher, but he was certainly the greatest philosopher for the two thousand years between Aristotle and Descartes. He represents the medieval mind par excellence, and the Middle Ages are the parent and source of all the divergent streams in the modern world, like a mother whose many children went their own various ways.

Not only does St. Thomas represent a unity of ingredients that were later to separate, but also a unity of ingredients that existed separately before him. In reading St. Thomas you also meet Thales, Parmenides, Heraclitus, Socrates, Plato, Aristotle, Plotinus, Proclus, Justin, Clement, Augustine, Boethius, Dionysius, Anselm, Abelard, Albert, Maimonides, and Avicenna. For one brief, Camelot-like moment it seemed that a synthesis was possible. Our fractured world has been praying "Forgive us our syntheses" ever since.

8. Finally, St. Thomas is important for us today precisely because of our lack. Timeless truth is always timely, of course, but some aspects of truth are especially needed at some times, and it seems that our times badly need seven Thomistic syntheses: (1) of faith and reason, (2) of the Biblical and the classical, the Judeo-Christian and the Greco-Roman heritages, (3) of the ideals of clarity and

profundity, (4) of common sense and technical sophistication, (5) of theory and practice, (6) of an understanding, intuitive vision and a demanding, accurate logic, and (7) of the one and the many, a cosmic unity or "big picture" and carefully sorted out distinctions. I think it a safe judgment that no one in the entire history of human thought has ever succeeded better than St. Thomas in making not just one but all seven of these marriages which are essential to mental health and happiness.

For some reason, many people seem so threatened by St. Thomas that they instantly label any admiration for, use of, or learning from him as slavish, unoriginal, and authoritarian—something that they do with no other thinker. Of course St. Thomas cannot be the be-all and end-all of our thought. He cannot be an end, but he can be a beginning, like Socrates. Of course we must go beyond him and not slavishly confine our thought to his. But there is no better bottom story to our edifice of thought.

II. On the *Summa Theologica*

Many theologians and philosophers in St. Thomas' time wrote Summas. A Summa is simply a summary. It is more like an encyclopedia than a textbook, and it is meant to be used more as a reference library than as a book. There is extreme economy in the use of words. There are no digressions and few illustrations. Everything is "bottom line". Such a style should appeal to us busy moderns.

The medievals had a passion for order, because they believed that *God* had a passion for order when He designed the universe. So a Summa is ordered and outlined with loving care. Yet, though very systematic, a Summa is not *a system* in the modern sense, a closed and deductive system like that of Descartes, Spinoza, Leibnitz, or Hegel. It uses induction as well as deduction, and its data come from ordinary experience and divine revelation as well as philosophical axioms ("first principles").

A Summa is really a summarized debate. To the medieval mind, debate was a fine art, a serious science, and a fascinating entertainment, much more than it is to the modern mind, because the medievals believed, like Socrates, that dialectic could uncover truth. Thus a "scholastic disputation" was not a personal contest in cleverness, nor was it "sharing opinions"; it was a shared journey of discovery. The "objections" from the other side are to be taken seriously in a Summa. They are not straw men to be knocked down easily, but live options to be considered and learned from. St. Thomas almost always finds some important truth hidden in each objection, which he carefully distinguishes from its error. For he believed not only that there was all truth Somewhere but also that there was some truth everywhere.

The structural outline of the *Summa Theologica* is a mirror of the structural outline of reality. It begins in God, Who is "in the beginning". It then proceeds to the act of creation and a consideration of creatures, centering on man, who alone is created in the image of God. Then it moves to man's return to God through his life of moral and religious choice, and culminates in the way or means to that end: Christ and His Church. Thus the overall scheme of the *Summa*, like that of the universe, is an *exitus-redditus*, an exit from and a return to God, Who is both Alpha and Omega. God is the ontological heart that pumps the blood of being through the arteries of creation into the body of the universe, which wears a human face, and receives it back through the veins of man's life of love and will. The structure of the *Summa*, and of the universe, is dynamic. It is not like information in a library, but like blood in a body.

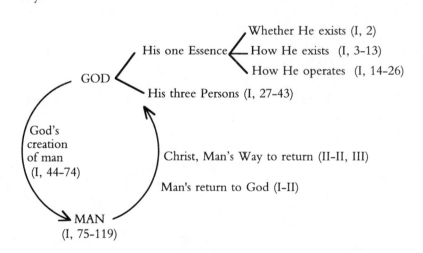

It is essential to keep this "big picture" in mind when reading the *Summa* because there are so many details that it is tempting to focus on them and lose the sense of their place and order. St. Thomas never does that. His style is atomistic and "choppy" but his vision is continuous and all-encompassing.

Why is the style so choppy? St. Thomas chops his prose into bite-sized segments for the same reason Mommy cuts Baby's meat into bite-sized chunks. The *Summa* would lose much of its clarity and digestibility if it were homogenized into continuous, running prose, like watery stew. (A current British version has done just that.)

The best preparation for reading the *Summa* is a review of basic, common sense logic, i.e., Aristotelian logic, especially the "Three Acts of the Mind", as the medievals labeled them: understanding, judging, and reasoning, with their respective logical expressions: terms, propositions, and arguments. The reader will be constantly confused if he does not first have in his mind a very clear idea of the differences between terms (which are either clear or unclear), propositions (which are either true or false), and arguments (which are either logically valid or invalid). He should also have a clear idea of the structure of a syllogism, the basic form of deductive argument, which connects the subject and predicate terms of its conclusion through the middle term in its two premises, the first of which (the major premise) states a general principle and the second (the minor premise) brings a particular case under that principle. The conclusion then demonstrates the result of applying the general principle to the particular case.

A knowledge of the basic ideas and technical terms of Aristotle's philosophy, which St. Thomas used as his philosophical language, is also essential. For beginners I recommend Mortimer Adler's amazingly clear *Aristotle for Everybody*, and for intermediate students W. D. Ross' one-volume *Aristotle*.

The *Summa Theologica* is divided into four overall Parts (I, I–II, II–II, and III). Each Part is divided into Treatises (e.g., On the Creation, On Man, On Law). Each Treatise is divided into numbered "Questions", or general issues within the topic of the treatise (e.g., "Of the Simplicity of God", "Of the Angels in Comparison with Bodies", "Of the Effects of Love"). Finally, each "Question" is divided into numbered "Articles". The

"Article" is the basic thought-unit of the *Summa*. What we mean in modern English by an "article"—an essay— is what St. Thomas means by a "Question", and what we mean by a "question"—a specific, single interrogative sentence—is what he means by an "Article", e.g., "Whether God Exists?", "Whether the Inequality of Things Is from God?", "Whether Sorrow Is the Same as Pain?"

Each Article begins by formulating in its title a single question in such a way that only two answers are possible: yes or no. St. Thomas does this, not because he thinks philosophy or theology is as simple as a true-false exam, but because he wants to make an issue finite and decidable, just as debaters do in formulating their "resolution". There are an indefinite number of possible answers to a question like "What is God?" If he had formulated his questions that way, the *Summa* might be three million pages long instead of three thousand. Instead, he asks, for example, "Whether God Is a Body?" It is possible to decide and demonstrate that one of the two possible answers (yes) is false and therefore that the other (no) is true.

Each "Article" has five structural parts. First, the question is formulated in a yes or no format, as explained above, beginning with the word "Whether" (*Utrum*).

Second, St. Thomas lists a number of Objections (usually three) to the answer he will give. The Objections are apparent proofs of this opposite answer, the other side to the debate. These objections begin with the formula: "It seems that . . ." (*Oportet*). These Objections must be *arguments*, not just *opinions*, for one of the basic principles of any intelligent debate (woefully neglected in all modern media) is that each debater *must* give relevant *reasons* for every controvertible opinion he expresses. The Objections are to be taken seriously, as *apparent* truth. One who is seeking the strongest possible arguments against any idea of St. Thomas will rarely find any stronger ones, any more strongly argued, than those in St. Thomas himself. He is extremely fair to all his opponents. I think he descends to name-calling only once in the entire *Summa*, when he speaks of the "really stupid" idea of David of Dinant that God is indistinguishable from prime matter, or pure potentiality —an idea not very far from that of Hegel and modern "process theologians"! Cf. p. 81, n. 21 and I, 3, 8 (p. 84).

Third, St. Thomas indicates his own position with the formula

"On the contrary . . ." (*Sed contra*). The brief argument that follows the statement of his position here is usually an argument from authority, i.e., from Scripture, the Fathers of the Church, or recognized wise men. The medievals well knew their own maxim that "the argument from authority is the weakest of all arguments" (see S.T. I, 1, 8, obj. 2). But they also believed in doing their homework and in learning from their ancestors—two habits we would do well to cultivate today.

The fourth part, "I answer that" (*Respondeo dicens*), is the body of the Article. In it, St. Thomas proves his own position, often adding necessary background explanations and making needed distinctions along the way. The easiest (but not the most exciting) way to read a *Summa* Article is to read this part first.

Fifth and finally, each Objection must be addressed and answered —not merely by repeating an argument to prove the opposite conclusion, for that has already been done in the body of the Article, but by explaining where and how the Objection went wrong, i.e., by distinguishing the truth from the falsity in the Objection.

No one of these five steps can be omitted if we want to have good grounds for settling a controverted question. If our question is vaguely or confusedly formulated, our answer will be, too. If we do not consider opposing views, we spar without a partner and paw the air. If we do not do our homework, we only skim the shallows of our selves. If we do not prove our thesis, we are dogmatic, not critical. And if we do not understand and refute our opponents, we are left with nagging uncertainty that we have missed something and not really ended the contest.

Like Socratic dialogue for Plato, this medieval method of philosophizing was very fruitful in its own day—and then subsequently neglected, especially in our day. That is one of the unsolved mysteries of Western thought. Surely both the Socratic and the Thomistic methodological trees can still bear much good fruit. Perhaps what stands in the way is our craze for originality and our proud refusal to be anyone's apprentice. I for one would be very happy to be Aquinas' apprentice, or Socrates'.

III. On This Book

A. Its Need. This book differs from all other books on St. Thomas because it has all four of the following characteristics: it is (1) an anthology of St. Thomas' own words, not a secondary source textbook. (2) It is one that uses the old, *literal* Dominican translation, originally published in America by Benziger Brothers, rather than the hubristic paraphrases of some subsequent non-literal translators who succumb to the itch to insert their own interpretative mind and style between the author and the reader. I hope the modern reader is more charmed than annoyed at the old-fashioned formal literalness of the translation and at the old-fashioned punctuation. (3) It is one that confines itself to the *Summa* alone (for a single book is a unit like a work of art); and, most importantly, (4) it is one that is replete with explanatory footnotes (more on this feature below).

There are some excellent books *about* St. Thomas by the likes of Chesterton, Gilson, Maritain, Pieper, and McInerney, but nothing can substitute for the primary source itself. Secondary source books without St. Thomas always miss something crucial; St. Thomas without them does not.

It is even easier to understand St. Thomas than to understand some books about St. Thomas. Thomas is clearer than Thomists. I have read some fifty or sixty books about St. Thomas, but I never really understood or appreciated him until I read a lot of St. Thomas himself. I find it easier to understand Thomists through Thomas than to understand Thomas through Thomists. The primary source illuminates the secondary sources more than the secondary sources illuminate the primary source.

Part of the reason for this is that St. Thomas' *habits* of mental clarity rub off best from long and direct contact with his writings. I noticed a remarkable improvement in my mental sharpness and order after doing long and slow readings of St. Thomas. The Master's habits rub off on his apprentices, if they have the good sense to stay close to him.

More doctoral dissertations have been written on St. Thomas than on any other philosopher or theologian who ever lived. Thomism was taught extensively in all Catholic and some non-Catholic schools until the Silly Sixties, when everything older than thirty fell prey to the jaws of Woodstockism. Over 99 percent of the books written on St. Thomas in this century have gone out of print. But we are now seeing a modest but steady revival of interest in and books about this philosopher—a development to which this book is very happy to contribute.

B. *Its Format.* Good anthologies, unlike good surgery, have to cut away much healthy tissue. To keep this volume manageably small, I had to be severely selective with the *Summa*'s three thousand pages. The principle for choosing which passage to include was its likely use, both in class by students and teachers, and by the independent reader with general intelligence but without the professional background of the philosopher or the theologian. To this end, I included only passages that are both (1) intrinsically important and (2) non-technical enough to be intelligible to modern readers. If a passage was important yet technical, I included it but also included explanatory footnotes.

Many, but not all, of the *Objections* St. Thomas lists and replies to are omitted because they are no longer live options or they no longer worry philosophers today. The Objections were real, actually debated questions in St. Thomas' day, and some should be the same for us. Not all are omitted because not all are dead issues by any means and also because it is essential to see the form of the *Summa* as a real, living dialogue, a structured and summarized debate, rather than a monologue or one-sided intellectual armory.

I also omitted all topics suitable for theology but not philosophy classes, i.e., the revealed as distinct from the rational, philosophical theology. This meant omitting all of Part III. The *Summa*, of course, is a work of theology rather than of philosophy, but it is appropriate to study it in a philosophy class because (1) it covers many other topics than God (e.g., man, knowledge, and morality), and because (2) even when it is about God, it uses many strictly rational, philosophical arguments based on logical principles and empirical data as well as often using appeals to the data of divine revelation accepted by faith; and St. Thomas is always quite clear about the distinction between these two methods of knowing.

The most important feature of the format is the *footnotes*. These are an attempt to bridge the gap between a secondary source textbook which is a substitute for the primary text, on the one hand, and a mere, unadorned anthology on the other hand. They are the printed equivalent of the traditional classroom technique so often used on classics, *explicatio texti*.

I know no reason why this simple and obvious device of many footnotes has not been used much more, except for an irrational prejudice against the atomistic, choppy prose style that a plethora of footnotes produces. But that is the style of the *Summa* in the first place. Remember, Mommy cuts up your meat into bite-sized chunks. Beginners would do well to copy A. A.'s slogan "One Day at a Time" and study the *Summa* One Point at a Time.

Why so *many* footnotes instead of longer, more general introductory essays for each section? (1) Because with St. Thomas general ideas are not adequate, though they are necessary; we need to understand him in specific detail; (2) because we need help understanding specific passages, which general introductions cannot supply; and (3) because this technique trains our minds, which all too often are accustomed to be satisfied with vague generalities, especially in philosophy and theology. St. Thomas thought of philosophy and theology as *sciences*. As a philosophy teacher I repeatedly discover that science majors find St. Thomas easier (at least at first) than humanities majors (especially sociology, psychology, and communications majors).

There are two different kinds of footnotes. Some explain the meaning of a difficult or technical idea. Others highlight the *importance* of an idea.

If a passage has no footnotes, that does not mean it is not important. Perhaps its meaning and importance are both very considerable, but clear.

There are more footnotes toward the beginning, for two reasons: (1) to prime the pump, to start the reader securely; and (2) because the first two Questions of the *Summa* are crucially important, both in themselves and as the foundation for the rest of the *Summa*; they are justly famous, and they need extra "unpacking".

Using the footnotes should not be felt as an onerous responsibility, but as a helpful aid, to be used only as needed and wanted. If they become a distraction from St. Thomas' text, ignore them.

If you as a reader get to the point in your reading of this book where the many footnotes begin to seem alien and intrusive, that is either a very good sign or a bad one. To find out which it is, ask yourself: "Alien and intrusive" *to what*? To the mind of the medieval author, or to the preconceptions of the modern reader? To St. Thomas or to yourself?

The whole purpose of these footnotes, as of all secondary source literature, is to serve as a crutch: to help you to walk yourself into the mind of the primary source, just as the purpose of a crutch is to become superfluous.

In any case, you should read the whole article in St. Thomas first, without reading the footnotes. Then read it a second time, more carefully and analytically, using the footnotes. A third reading can also dispense with the footnotes because they are now in the mind that is doing the reading.

Technical terms have been defined in the Glossary. The Glossary is very important because nearly all students' difficulties with St. Thomas are with the *terminology*, rather than with the *vision* (or content) or with the logical *form* (or style) of argument. The Glossary is put first because if it were put last, the reader would be tempted to ignore it except in emergencies. Placed first, it stands as a gate or door: a plain, dull door to a great, golden mansion.

GLOSSARY

abstract (opposite: *concrete*): not necessarily "spiritual" as vs. "material", but some property, quality, or essence considered apart from the subject, thing, or substance that possesses it (e.g., justice, redness).

abstraction: the mental act of apprehending some form, quality, or essence without the rest of the object; considering a form without considering the whole, concrete material object or the image (*phantasm*) of it; e.g., abstracting the essential treeness, or the accidental bigness, of a tree from everything else in the concrete individual tree or what we see of it.

accident (opposite: *substance*): that mode of being which can exist only in another being, as a modification or attribute of a substance (thing); e.g. the redness of a rose.

accidental: non-essential; non-substantial.

actual (opposite: *potential*): fully real, complete, perfect. (1) "*first act*": existence, being, actuality; (2) "*second act*": operation, doing, activity.

agent: efficient cause.

agent intellect: the intellect in the act of abstracting form from matter; the intellect that informs and determines the potential, passive, or possible (receptive) intellect with this form.

analogical: the relationship between two things or terms which are partly the same and partly different, neither *univocal* (wholly the same) nor *equivocal* (wholly different); the relationship of similarity but not identity between the meaning of a term when predicated of one subject (e.g., "milk is good") and the

23

meaning of that term when predicated of another subject (e.g., "God is good").

appetite: in the widest sense, any inclination or tendency to some good or suitable object, or away from some bad or unsuitable object; more narrowly, in living things, the tendency to growth and health; still more narrowly, in animals, the senses' desire for their natural object (see *concupiscible appetite* and *irascible appetite*); most narrowly, in man, the will's desire for its proper good, *happiness*.

argument: a proof that a certain proposition (the conclusion) is true by showing (demonstrating) that it follows logically and necessarily from other propositions (premises) being true.

being: (1) that which is, whether actual or potential and whether in the mind (a "being of reason") or in objective reality (a "being in nature"); (1A) *ens:* entity, thing, substance, that-which is; (1B) *esse:* the act of existing; (1C) *essentia:* essence, *what* a thing is; (2) the affirmative predicate "is" stating that the subject is, or is something (the predicate).

body: not just a human body, or an animal body, but any material thing that occupies space.

causality: influence of one being on another; responsibility of one being for some feature in another (the effect), such as its existence, its essence, its matter, its accidents, or its changes. See *final cause*, *formal cause*, *efficient cause*, *material cause*. In modern parlance "cause" usually means only "efficient cause", i.e., that which produces existence or change in another.

change: actualization of a potency.

charity: the will to do good to another for his own sake.

common (opposite: *proper*): present in two or more individuals or species.

concrete (opposite: *abstract*): not necessarily material or sensible, but individual and actual.

contemplative: see *speculative*.

concupiscence: sense appetite seeking pleasure.

corporeal: pertaining to the body as distinct from the soul.

cosmos: the universe as ordered.

creation: the act of bringing a being into existence from non-existence; production of being from no pre-existing material.

deduction: argument from a more universal premise to a more particular conclusion, from a general principle to an instance or application of it.

demonstration: logically valid argument from premises that are true and evident, thus proving the conclusion with certainty.

determine: to cause some definite perfection; to specify, to make particular.

efficient cause: agent which by its acting produces existence or change in another.

emanation: flowing forth from a source.

end: good, goal, purpose, aim, objective.

epistemology: the science of knowing.

equivocal term: a term used with two wholly different meanings.

essence: in the broad sense, *what* a thing is, all its "intelligible notes" (characteristics) (as contrasted with its *existence*); in the narrow sense, as vs. *accidents*, the definition, or genus plus specific difference of a thing, that without which it cannot be conceived.

eternity: mode of existence without beginning, end, or succession; "the whole and perfect simultaneous possession of limitless life" (Boethius).

existence: the actuality of an essence, that act by which something *is*.

faculty: inherent power or ability.

final cause: end or purpose of a thing.

finite: limited.

form: the essential nature of a thing, that which specifies it to be this rather than that.

formal cause: form as determining matter.

genus: the aspect of a thing's essence which is common to it and other members of its species; a broader class to which a thing essentially belongs (e.g., "animal" for man, "plane figure" for triangle).

grace: that which comes from God's free will, as distinct from natural necessity.

habit: disposition toward certain operations; inclination to an end. A "habit" is not a "rut", but is freely made, in man, by repeated acts.

happiness: satisfaction of desire in really possessing its true and proper good. (Note that there is both a subjective and an objective element in happiness; thus neither a stone nor an evil man can be happy.)

idea: concept.

image: representation or likeness.

imagination: internal sense which produces images of sensible, material things even when they are absent.

incorporeal: immaterial, without body.

incorruptible: incapable of decay or destruction.

individual: that which cannot be divided without losing its identity.

induction: reasoning from individual cases to general principles, from more particular premises to more universal conclusions.

infallible: incapable of error, thus certain.

inference: reasoning from some truths (premises) to others (conclusions).

infinite: unlimited.

infused: received from without.

innate: inborn, given by nature.

irascible appetite: sense desire to fight a danger.

judgment: act of the mind comparing two concepts (subject and predicate) in an affirmative or negative proposition.

life: the power of a substance to move itself.

locomotion: motion in space.

matter: the principle in a thing's being by which it is able to be determined by form; potency as vs. actuality. In modern parlance, the word refers to actual, visible, formed things (e.g., chemicals, molecules); but in Thomistic and Aristotelian parlance "matter" is not of itself observable or even of itself actual. It is not a thing but a metaphysical principle or aspect of things, which together with form explains change, as the actualization (in-form-ing) of potency (matter).

material cause: that (potency) from which a thing is produced— e.g., the clay of a pot.

mean: something in the middle between two extremes.

metaphysics: that division of philosophy which studies being as such, and the universal truths, laws, or principles of all beings; "the science of being qua being".

motion: broadly, any change; more narrowly, change of place, or locomotion.

natural: (1) as vs. *artificial*: found in nature, what a being has from birth, what happens by itself without outside interference (art or violence); (2) as vs. *supernatural*: what is or happens without direct, divine intervention; (3) as vs. *rational*: without intelligence (e.g., "natural bodies"); (4) as vs. *arbitrary* or *conventional*: what flows from a thing's essence; necessary.

nature: (1) the origin of growth and activity in a thing; (2) the totality of objects in the universe apart from human or divine modifications of them.

necessary: what cannot be otherwise.

nominal (as vs. *real*): pertaining to a name only. "Nominalism" is the theory that universal terms like "justice" or "man" are only names, not real essences; it is perhaps the most pervasive and destructive error in modern philosophy.

participation: sharing in, possessing some perfection of.

passion: in general, receptivity, being acted on by another; in particular, intense movement of the sensitive appetite.

passive: in potency to be determined by another agent.

patient: any being that is changed by an agent.

perfection: most generally, any definite actuality in a being; more particularly, any definite *good* suitable to a being; most particularly, complete good attained by a being.

phantasm: sense image.

philosophy: literally, the love of wisdom; the science that seeks to understand all things by knowing their causes by natural reason.

possible: that which can be.

potency, or *potentiality:* the principle of change; capacity or ability to be actualized in some way.

predicate: (noun): term that says something about the subject; (verb): to state something about a subject.

principle: source; that from which something proceeds.

proper: distinctive, special, specific (as vs. *common*).

property: "proper accident", an attribute that is not the very essence of the subject but results from its essence (e.g., speech in man or greenness in chlorophyll).

proposition: declarative sentence, affirmative or negative.

providence: intelligent plan by which things are ordered to an end.

prudence: practical wisdom, knowing how to choose good means to good ends, what to do and how to do it. It has none of the prudish, prune-like, over-careful connotations of the word in modern parlance.

quiddity: whatness, essence.

reason: (1) most generally, that which distinguishes man from brute animals: intelligence; (2) more specifically, the power of reasoning (all three "acts of the mind": conceiving, judging, and arguing); (3) most specifically, the power to argue or prove (the "third act of the mind").

reduction: the mental act of bringing something complex back to a more fundamental or elementary form or principle, or seeing it within a general principle or class.

science: intellectual knowledge by means of causes or general principles. In one way, "scientific" meant something narrower and tougher in pre-modern times: certain knowledge of real causes. In another way, it meant something broader and looser than the modern scientific method, for it did not always require experimentation or mathematical measurement.

sensation: act of one of the five senses.

simple: not composed of parts.

sin: any human act (deed, word, or deliberate desire) in disobedience to divine law.

soul: generally, the first intrinsic (inner, natural) principle of life in a living body; specifically, the human soul is the first principle of human, rational life, i.e., of knowing and willing.

species: (1) in logic, the class to which a thing essentially belongs, expressing both the genus and the specific difference (e.g., "man is a rational animal"); (2) in epistemology, a likeness or representation of an object, the form of an object known.

specify: to determine to a definite form or class.

speculative (opposite of *practical*): contemplative; knowledge for the sake of knowledge, seeking the truth for its own sake rather than for action (doing something with it) or production (making something by it). "Speculative" does not necessarily mean "uncertain" or "hypothetical".

subject: (1) in logic, the term in a proposition about which something is said in the predicate; (2) in metaphysics, a substance in relation to attributes; (3) in epistemology, a knower as distinct from an object known.

substance: a being that exists in itself rather than in another (as vs. *accident*).

supernatural: beyond the power of nature, caused by God alone without secondary (natural) causes.

syllogism: (1) logical argument; (2) especially a deductive argument; (3) especially a certain deductive argument, with three terms, two premises, and one conclusion.

term: (1) in metaphysics, the first or last point of a series; (2) in logic, the subject or predicate of a proposition, expressing a concept.

transcendent: greater than, superior to.

transcendental: universally common to all things. The five transcendental properties of all being are: something, one, true, good, beautiful.

truth: conformity of the mind to real things.

universal: general, common to many.

univocal: having the same meaning when predicated of different things.

virtual: having an active, positive potency to some perfection; more than merely passively potential, but less than actual.

virtue: good habit.

will: rational appetite; power of the soul to desire or choose a good known by the intellect.

ONE

Methodology:
Theology as a Science

PROLOGUE

Because the Master[1] of Catholic Truth ought not only to teach the proficient, but also to instruct beginners (according to the Apostle: As Unto Little Ones in Christ, I Gave You Milk to Drink, Not Meat—I Cor 3:1, 2), we purpose in this book to treat of whatever belongs to the Christian Religion, in such a way as may tend to the instruction of beginners.[2] We have considered that students in this Science have not seldom been hampered by what they have found written by other authors, partly on account of the multiplication of useless questions, articles, and arguments; partly also because those things that are needful for them to know are not taught according to the order of the subject-matter, but according as the plan of the book might require, or the occasion of the argument offer; partly, too, because frequent repetition brought weariness and confusion to the minds of the readers.

---

[1] "Master" (Latin, *doctor*) means "teacher", not "lord". A "master" of Catholic Truth is its *servant*.

[2] It may shock the reader to discover that the *Summa* was designed for "beginners", but it should encourage beginners to begin it.

Here is how St. Thomas described his *Summa* when explaining why he could not finish it, after he had had a "mystical experience" (the correct description is "infused contemplation"): "I can write no more; compared with what I have seen, all I have written seems to me as straw."

St. Thomas' close friend, Brother Reginald, testified under oath after St. Thomas' death that he had heard a voice from the crucifix in chapel saying to St. Thomas, "You have written well of Me, Thomas. What will you have as your reward?" And he heard Thomas reply, "Only Thyself, Lord." This reply tells us two things: one, why Thomas was *Saint* Thomas; and two, why he called Socrates the greatest philosopher (S.T. III, 42, 4): because, like St. Thomas, Socrates knew he was always a beginner. (See *Apology* 20d–23b.)

Endeavoring to avoid these and other like faults, we shall try, by God's help, to set forth whatever is included in this Sacred Science as briefly and clearly as the matter itself may allow.[3]

---

[3] Note how St. Thomas practices what he preaches in this Prologue even as he preaches it.

Question I

The Nature and Extent of Sacred Doctrine[4]

To place our purpose within proper limits, we first endeavor to investigate the nature and extent of this sacred doctrine. Concerning this there are ten points of inquiry: *theology*

(1) Whether it is necessary? (2) Whether it is a science? (3) Whether it is one or many? (4) Whether it is speculative or practical? (5) How it is compared with other sciences? (6) Whether it is the same as wisdom? (7) Whether God is its subject-matter? (8) Whether it is a matter of argument? (9) Whether it rightly employs metaphors and similes? (10) Whether the Sacred Scripture of this doctrine may be expounded in different senses?

FIRST ARTICLE

Whether, besides Philosophy, Any Further Doctrine Is Required?

Objection 1. It seems that, besides philosophical science, we have no need of any further knowledge. For man should not seek to know what is above reason:[5] *Seek not the things that are too high for thee* (Sir 3:22). But whatever is not above reason is fully treated of in philosophical science. Therefore any other knowledge besides philosophical science is superfluous.

---

[4] "Sacred doctrine" = theology. Scripture is its data, or material cause. God's act of revealing Himself is the source, or efficient cause, of its data. Its species or formal cause is "science" (an ordered body of knowledge through causes). And its end or final cause is, speculatively, the truth about God, and, practically, salvation through this truth.

[5] I.e., more than what can be (a) discovered, (b) understood, or (c) proved by human reason alone.

Objection 2. Further, knowledge can be concerned only with being, for nothing can be known, save what is true; and all that is, is true.[6] But everything that is, is treated of in philosophical science—even God Himself; so that there is a part of philosophy called theology,[7] or the divine science, as Aristotle has proved (*Metaph.* 6). Therefore, besides philosophical science, there is no need of any further knowledge.

On the contrary, It is written (2 Tim 3:16): *All Scripture*[8] *inspired of God is profitable to teach, to reprove, to correct, to instruct in justice.* Now Scripture, inspired of God, is no part of philosophical science, which has been built up by human reason. Therefore it is useful that besides philosophical science there should be other knowledge —*i.e.,* inspired of God.

I answer that, It was necessary for man's salvation[9] that there should be a knowledge revealed by God, besides philosophical science built up by human reason.

Firstly, indeed, because man is directed to God, as to an end that surpasses the grasp of his reason: *The eye hath not seen, O God, besides Thee, what things Thou hast prepared for them that wait for Thee* (Is 66:4). But the end must first be known by men who are to direct their thoughts and actions to the end. Hence it was necessary for the salvation of man that certain truths which exceed human reason should be made known to him by divine revelation.

Even as regards those truths about God which human reason could have discovered, it was necessary that man should be taught by a divine revelation; because the truth about God such as reason could discover, would only be known by a few, and that after a

---

[6] Cf. S.T. I, 16, 3.

[7] This is "natural theology" (or "rational theology" or "philosophical theology") as distinct from "revealed theology". It is known by reason alone, not by faith in divine revelation.

[8] Note how closely St. Thomas' theology is identified with Scripture, its data. The common Protestant objection that this theology is more rationalistic and Greek than believing and biblical is a radical inaccuracy.

[9] Note that although St. Thomas is a theoretical philosopher, and although theology is primarily a theoretical science (S.T. I, 1, 4), St. Thomas sees God's reason for revealing theology's data as primarily a practical one: our salvation.

long time, and with the admixture of many errors.[10] Whereas man's whole salvation, which is in God, depends upon the knowledge of this truth. Therefore, in order that the salvation of men might be brought about more fitly and more surely,[11] it was necessary that they should be taught divine truths by divine revelation. It was therefore necessary that, besides philosophical science built up by reason there should be a sacred science learned through revelation.

Reply Obj. 1. Although those things which are beyond man's knowledge may not be sought for by man through his reason, nevertheless, once they are revealed by God they must be accepted by faith. Hence the sacred text continues, *For many things are shown to thee above the understanding of man* (Sir 3:25). And in this the sacred science consists.

Reply Obj. 2. Sciences are differentiated according to the various means through which knowledge is obtained. For the astronomer and the physicist both may prove the same conclusion—that the earth, for instance, is round:[12] the astronomer by means of mathematics (*i.e.*, abstracting from matter), but the physicist by means of matter itself. Hence there is no reason why those things which may be learned from philosophical science, so far as they can be known by natural reason, may not also be taught us by another science so far as they fall within revelation. Hence theology included in sacred doctrine differs in kind from that theology which is part of philosophy.

SECOND ARTICLE

Whether Sacred Doctrine Is a Science?

I answer that, Sacred doctrine is a science. We must bear in mind that there are two kinds of sciences. There are some which proceed

---

[10] Cf. St. Thomas' *Summa contra Gentiles* I, 4 for a fuller treatment of this point.

[11] N.b.: this seems to imply that pagans too can be saved, though less "fitly" and "surely".

[12] N.b.: the Middle Ages did *not* believe the myth of a flat earth; modernity believes the myth of an ignorant Middle Ages.

from a principle known by the natural light of the intelligence, such as arithmetic and geometry and the like. There are some which proceed from principles known by the light of a higher science: thus the science of perspective proceeds from principles established by geometry, and music from principles established by arithmetic. So it is that sacred doctrine is a science, because it proceeds from principles established by the light of a higher science, namely, the science of God and the blessed.[13] Hence, just as the musician accepts on authority[14] the principles taught him by the mathematician, so sacred science is established on principles revealed by God. . . .

THIRD ARTICLE

Whether Sacred Doctrine Is One Science?

I answer that, Sacred doctrine is one science. The unity of a faculty or habit is to be gauged by its object, not indeed, in its material aspect, but as regards the precise formality under which it is an object. For example, man, ass, stone agree in the one precise formality of being colored; and color is the formal object of sight. Therefore, because Sacred Scripture considers things precisely under the formality of being divinely revealed, whatever has been divinely revealed possesses the one precise formality of the object of this science; and therefore is included under sacred doctrine as under one science.

---

[13] I.e., the knowledge that God and the blessed in Heaven have, not our knowledge of them.

[14] N.b.: nearly all our knowledge begins with our accepting some principles (starting points) on the authority of parents, teachers, newspapers, textbooks, or society. But it does not *end* there. "Authority" does not mean to St. Thomas *unquestionableness.* Cf. S.T. I, 1, 8 on the great difference between human and divine authority.

FOURTH ARTICLE

Whether Sacred Doctrine Is a Practical Science?

Objection 1. It seems that sacred doctrine is a practical science; for a practical science is that which ends in action according to the Philosopher (*Metaph.* ii). But sacred doctrine is ordained to action: *Be ye doers of the word, and not hearers only* (James 1:22). Therefore sacred doctrine is a practical science.

Objection 2. Further, sacred doctrine is divided into the Old and the New Law. But law implies a moral science, which is a practical science. Therefore sacred doctrine is a practical science.

On the contrary, Every practical science is concerned with human operations; as moral science is concerned with human acts, and architecture with buildings. But sacred doctrine is chiefly concerned with God, whose handiwork is especially man. Therefore it is not a practical but a speculative science.

I answer that, Sacred doctrine, being one, extends to things which belong to different philosophical sciences, because it considers in each the same formal aspect, namely so far as they can be known through divine revelation. Hence, although among the philosophical sciences one is speculative and another practical, nevertheless sacred doctrine includes both; as God, by one and the same science, knows both Himself and His works. Still, it is speculative rather than practical, because it is more concerned with divine things than with human acts; though it does treat even of these latter, inasmuch as man is ordained by them to the perfect knowledge of God, in which consists eternal bliss.[15] This is a sufficient answer to the Objections.

---

[15] Theology, the (primarily speculative) science of God, includes *moral* theology, the (practical) science of human acts as means to the (speculative) end of the knowledge of God (the Beatific Vision).

FIFTH ARTICLE

Whether Sacred Doctrine Is Nobler[16] Than Other Sciences?

Objection 1. It seems that sacred doctrine is not nobler than other sciences; for the nobility of a science depends on the certitude[17] it establishes. But other sciences, the principles of which cannot be doubted,[18] seem to be more certain than sacred doctrine; for its principles[19]—namely, articles of faith—can be doubted.[20] Therefore, other sciences seem to be nobler.

Objection 2. Further, it is the sign of a lower science to depend upon a higher; as music depends upon arithmetic. But sacred doctrine does in a sense depend upon the philosophical sciences; for Jerome observes, in his Epistle to Magnus, that *the ancient doctors so enriched their books with the ideas and phrases of the philosophers, that thou knowest not what more to admire in them, their profane erudition or*

---

[16] "Nobler"—a favorite medieval concept almost totally abandoned in our time—does not refer to a social class system ("nobles") but to what is objectively greater, more perfect, or worthy of respect.

[17] This ("certitude") is a typically modern concern, beginning with Descartes.

It was a medieval commonplace, taken from Aristotle and repeated by Augustine, that the human mind is related to ultimate realities as a bat's or owl's eyes are related to the sun; and that we must therefore choose between (a) more perfect (certain) knowledge of less perfect (noble) things—i.e., the human sciences—or (b) less perfect (certain) knowledge of more perfect (noble) things—i.e., theology. The former is more perfect subjectively, the latter is more perfect objectively. The objectively-oriented medieval mind naturally emphasized (b) over (a), while the more subjectively-oriented modern mind naturally emphasizes (a) over (b), because of the subjectively more perfect (certain) nature of this knowledge of human things.

[18] This is because they are either self-evident, like the axioms of mathematics and logic, or immediately evident to anyone's senses, like the data of the physical sciences.

[19] N.b.: theology ("sacred doctrine") has data (principles, starting points) just as the physical sciences do, namely the "articles of faith", the truths revealed to us by God in Scripture and summarized in the Creeds of the Church.

[20] This is because they are neither of the two things in note 18.

their scriptural learning. Therefore sacred doctrine is inferior to other sciences.

On the contrary, Other sciences are called the handmaidens of this one: *Wisdom sent her maids to invite to the tower* (Prov 9:3).

I answer that, Since this science is partly speculative and partly practical, it transcends all others speculative and practical.

Now one speculative science is said to be nobler than another, either by reason of its greater certitude, or by reason of the higher worth of its subject-matter. In both these respects this science surpasses other speculative sciences; in point of greater certitude, because other sciences derive their certitude from the natural light of human reason, which can err; whereas this derives its certitude from the light of the divine knowledge, which cannot be misled:[21] in point of the higher worth of its subject-matter, because this science treats chiefly of those things which by their sublimity transcend human reason; while other sciences consider only those things which are within reason's grasp.

Of the practical sciences, that one is nobler which is ordained to a further purpose, as political science is nobler than military science; for the good of the army is directed to the good of the State. But the purpose of this science, in so far as it is practical, is eternal bliss; to which as to an ultimate end the purposes of every practical science are directed.[22] Hence it is clear that from every standpoint it is nobler than other sciences.

---

[21] I.e., we have the *objective right* to be more certain of theology's principles (data) than of any products of human reason, which can err, for theology's data have been revealed by God, Who can neither deceive nor be deceived; but the data God revealed can be (and are) doubted with more *subjective, psychological* ease than the data of the human sciences. Perhaps we should use two different words for these two different dimensions of certainty, the objective ("certain-*ness*", or certainty) and the subjective (*certitude*, or intellectual confidence).

[22] It may sound strange to imply, as St. Thomas does here, that the ultimate end of every practical science, even economics or cooking, is heavenly bliss. But unless heavenly bliss is *not* in fact our final end, everything we do must be, in some way, by some route, a means to that end—or else it is meaningless, "vanity" (as in Ecclesiastes). Note the unified vision of human life here: the sacred and the secular, the supernatural and the natural, are not kept safely apart from each other.

Reply Obj. 1. It may well happen that what is in itself the more certain may seem to us the less certain[23] on account of the weakness of our intelligence, "which is dazzled by the clearest objects of nature;[24] as the owl is dazzled by the light of the sun" (*Metaph.* ii lect. i). Hence the fact that some happen to doubt about articles of faith is not due to the uncertain nature of the truths, but to the weakness of human intelligence; yet the slenderest knowledge that may be obtained of the highest things is more desirable than the most certain knowledge obtained of lesser things, as is said in *de Animalibus* xi.[25]

Reply Obj. 2. This science can in a sense depend upon the philosophical sciences, not as though it stood in need of them, but only in order to make its teaching clearer. For it accepts its principles not from other sciences; but immediately from God, by revelation. Therefore it does not depend upon other sciences as upon the higher, but makes use of them as of the lesser, and as hand-maidens:[26] even so the master sciences make use of the sciences that supply their materials, as political of military science. That it thus uses them is not due to its own defect or insufficiency, but to the

---

[23] Many students today find quite unintelligible this simple distinction because the notion of that which is "in itself more certain" presupposes an epistemological objectivism and realism which modern post-Kantian "critical" or skeptical thought has ceased to assume, to believe, or even sometimes to comprehend. Yet the notion is commonsensical; e.g., it is objectively more certain that it will not snow today in Bermuda than that it *will* snow today in Greenland; yet a Greenlander who knows nothing about Bermuda feels subjectively *less* certain that it will not snow today in Bermuda than that it will in Greenland.

[24] "The clearest objects of nature" here means not physical objects that are not dark to the eye, but those objects which by their own nature are the most clear and rational, like the mind of God and angels.

[25] Cf. the last paragraph of n. 17.

[26] The medieval formula "philosophy the handmaid of theology" (*philosophia ancilla theologiae*) and the associated idea of theology as "the queen of the sciences" are seldom taken seriously today, even in most "Catholic" universities. Yet neither philosophy nor science have ever refuted that claim during the past seven hundred years. It has been dismissed by fashion, not by reason. If God is, and is our ultimate end, then the science of God must indeed be the queen of the sciences.

defect of our intelligence, which is more easily led by what is known through natural reason (from which proceed the other sciences), to that which is above reason, such as are the teachings of this science.

Whether This Doctrine Is the Same As Wisdom?

I answer that, This doctrine is wisdom above all human wisdom; not merely in any one order, but absolutely. For since it is the part of a wise man to arrange and to judge, and since lesser matters should be judged in the light of some higher principle, he is said to be wise in any one order who considers the highest principle in that order: thus in the order of building he who plans the form of the house is called wise and architect, in opposition to the inferior laborers who trim the wood and make ready the stones: *As a wise architect I have laid the foundation* (1 Cor 3:10). Again, in the order of all human life, the prudent man is called wise, inasmuch as he directs his acts to a fitting end: *Wisdom is prudence to a man* (Prov 10:23). Therefore he who considers absolutely the highest cause of the whole universe, namely God, is most of all called wise. Hence wisdom is said to be the knowledge of divine things, as Augustine says (*De Trin.* xii. 14). But sacred doctrine essentially treats of God viewed as the highest cause—not only so far as He can be known through creatures just as philosophers knew Him—*That which is known of God is manifest in them* (Rom 1:19)—but also so far as He is known to Himself alone and revealed to others. Hence sacred doctrine is especially called wisdom. . . .

Whether God Is the Object of This Science?

I answer that, . . . in sacred science all things are treated of under the aspect of God; either because they are God Himself; or because they refer to God as their beginning and end. Hence it follows that God is in very truth the object of this science. . . .

EIGHTH ARTICLE

Whether Sacred Doctrine Is a Matter of Argument?

Objection 2. Further, if it is a matter of argument, the argument is either from authority or from reason. If it is from authority, it seems unbefitting its dignity, for the proof from authority is the weakest form of proof.[27] But if from reason, this is unbefitting its end, because, according to Gregory (*Homil.* 26), *faith has no merit in those things of which human reason brings its own experience.*[28] Therefore sacred doctrine is not a matter of argument. . . .

I answer that, As other sciences do not argue in proof of their principles,[29] but argue from their principles to demonstrate other truths in these sciences: so this doctrine does not argue in proof of its principles, which are the articles of faith, but from them it goes on to prove something else; as the Apostle from the resurrection of Christ argues in proof of the general resurrection (1 Cor 15). However, it is to be borne in mind, in regard to the philosophical sciences, that the inferior sciences neither prove their principles nor dispute with those who deny them, but leave this to a higher science; whereas the highest of them, viz., metaphysics,[30] can dispute with one who denies its principles, if only the opponent will make some concession; but if he concede nothing, it can have

---

[27] This was a medieval commonplace. The popular modern notion that the medieval mind was uncritical, blindly fideistic, and authoritarian is simply an ignorant cavil.

[28] I.e., if I know x by reason, I cannot be rightly praised for believing x by faith (assuming faith is praiseworthy) because I cannot believe x by faith at the same time as I know it by reason. E.g., first I *believe* that running into the street is dangerous because my parents tell me, but once I prove it for myself I no longer know it by faith.

[29] No science or set of sciences can prove everything, for every proof presupposes some principle(s) or starting point(s) or assumption(s) as its data. Theology's principles and data = divine revelation, i.e., Scripture.

[30] Metaphysics is the philosophical science of being qua being, i.e., the science of the most universal principles that hold true of everything that is. Every other science implicitly presupposes some principles of metaphysics, e.g., that nothing can both be and not be at the same time; or that whatever comes to be, needs a cause; or that being is intelligible.

no dispute with him, though it can answer his objections.[31] Hence Sacred Scripture, since it has no science above itself, can dispute with one who denies its principles only if the opponent admits some at least of the truths obtained through divine revelation; thus we can argue with heretics from texts in Holy Writ, and against those who deny one article of faith we can argue from another. If our opponent believes nothing of divine revelation, there is no longer any means of proving the articles of faith by reasoning, but only of answering his objections—if he has any—against faith.[32]

---

[31] St. Thomas is here following Aristotle's refutation of the skepticism of Protagoras the Sophist (*Metaphysics*, Bk. Γ, chap. 3, 1005b8–end of chap. 4). The point is that a metaphysical principle like "nothing can both be and not be at the same time" cannot be proved by any prior principle (because there *is* no prior principle; every other principle presupposes this one); but its opposite (contradictory proposition) can be *dis*proved if anyone utters that opposite as a proposition, or even any proposition at all. For to say "S is" is to say that it is *not* true that "S is not" at the same time; thus the speaker does (and must) actually assume and use the metaphysical principle he denies, viz., that S cannot both be and not be at the same time. Universal skepticism is self-contradictory for it amounts to saying that it is true that there is no truth. But if the skeptic "concede nothing", i.e., utter no proposition at all, he cannot be refuted, for he has said nothing to refute. But he cannot refute the nonskeptic either. And if he tries, all his skeptical objections to nonskepticism can be answered.

[32] The "articles of faith" are not simply coextensive with divine revelation but consist in only those truths within divine revelation which cannot be discovered or proved by human reason alone. Cf. S.T. I, 2, 2, ad 2. The last sentence of this "*I answer that*" is a summary of *Summa contra Gentiles* I, 7, where St. Thomas proves that even though not every doctrine of revelation can be proved by unaided human reason, yet every possible argument against every doctrine of revelation can be answered by unaided human reason alone without appeal to faith or revelation, because the same God Who is the ultimate source of human reason is also the source of divine revelation, and this God never contradicts Himself, since He never teaches anything untrue but only what is true, and truth cannot contradict truth. Thus even the doctrine of the Trinity, which is an article of faith and not provable by reason, is not *dis*provable by reason either; and all objections to it (e.g., that to call God both one and three is logically self-contradictory) are answerable by reason (e.g., that God is one in nature, not three, and three in Persons, not one).

Since faith rests upon infallible truth, and since the contrary of a truth can never be demonstrated, it is clear that the arguments brought against faith cannot be demonstrations, but are difficulties that can be answered. . . .

Reply Obj. 2. This doctrine is especially based upon arguments from authority, inasmuch as its principles are obtained by revelation: thus we ought to believe on the authority of those to whom the revelation has been made. Nor does this take away from the dignity of this doctrine, for although the argument from authority based on human reason is the weakest, yet the argument from authority based on divine revelation is the strongest.[33] But sacred doctrine makes use even of human reason, not, indeed, to prove faith (for thereby the merit of faith would come to an end), but to make clear other things that are put forward in this doctrine. Since therefore grace does not destroy nature, but perfects it, natural reason should minister to faith as the natural bent of the will ministers to charity.[34] Hence the Apostle says: *Bringing into captivity*

In most places in St. Thomas, e.g., in the next sentence, "faith" refers not to the psychological *act* of believing but to "*the* faith", i.e., the content believed, viz., the teachings of divine revelation.

[33] The medieval mind, typically expressed here, was *not* more "authoritarian" than the modern mind but *less* so, because of its clear distinction between divine authority (which is infallible) and human authority (which is fallible and weak, and the weakest of all bases for an argument). Surely, people in modern secular societies base their beliefs on human authorities (intellectual fashions, peer pressure, media propaganda, etc.) much *more* than people did in medieval Christendom. Even medieval *theology* was far more rationalistic than modern theology. Note the last paragraph of St. Thomas' Reply here as an example of how the medieval mind was far from naively and dogmatically authoritarian even with regard to the greatest of all merely human, fallible authorities, viz., the Fathers of the Church.

[34] Still another typically modern cavil against the medievals is that they ignored or denigrated nature because they believed so strongly in the supernatural. The argument is a non sequitur, for the maxim that "grace [the supernatural] perfects nature" was universally believed. Two applications of this maxim that St. Thomas mentions here are (1) that natural goodness in a human will helps and is helped by supernatural charity (divine love), and (2) that divine revelation both helps human reason

every understanding unto the obedience of Christ (2 Cor 10:5). Hence sacred doctrine makes use also of the authority of philosophers in those questions in which they were able to know the truth by natural reason, as Paul quotes a saying of Aratus: *As some also of your own poets said: For we are also His offspring* (Acts 17:28).

Nevertheless, sacred doctrine makes use of these authorities as extrinsic and probable arguments; but properly uses the authority of the canonical Scriptures as an incontrovertible proof, and the authority of the doctors of the Church as one that may properly be used, yet merely as probable. For our faith rests upon the revelation made to the apostles and prophets, who wrote the canonical books, and not on the revelations (if any such there are) made to other doctors. Hence Augustine says (*Epist. ad Hieron.* xix. 1): *Only those books of Scripture which are called canonical have I learned to hold in such honor as to believe their authors have not erred in any way in writing them. But other authors I so read as not to deem anything in their works to be true, merely on account of their having so thought and written, whatever may have been their holiness and learning.*

NINTH ARTICLE

Whether Holy Scripture Should Use Metaphors?

I answer that, It is befitting Holy Writ to put forward divine and spiritual truths by means of comparisons with material things. For God provides for everything according to the capacity of its nature. Now it is natural to man to attain to intellectual truths through sensible objects, because all our knowledge originates from sense. Hence in Holy Writ spiritual truths are fittingly taught under the likeness of material things. This is what Dionysius says (*Coel. Hier.* i): *We cannot be enlightened by the divine rays except they be hidden within the covering of many sacred veils.* It is also befitting Holy Writ, which is proposed to all without distinction of persons—*To the wise and to the unwise I am a debtor* (Rom 1:14)—that spiritual truths

---

(completing, clarifying, instructing, and fulfilling it) and is helped by it (as a tool of communicating it), though sacred doctrine does not *depend on* human reason.

be expounded by means of figures taken from corporeal things, in order that thereby even the simple who are unable by themselves to grasp intellectual things may be able to understand it. . . .

Whether in Holy Scripture a Word May Have Several Senses?[35]

Objection 1. It seems that in Holy Writ a word cannot have several senses, historical or literal, allegorical, tropological or moral, and anagogical. For many different senses in one text produce confusion and deception and destroy all force of argument. Hence no argument, but only fallacies, can be deduced from a multiplicity of propositions. But Holy Writ ought to be able to state the truth without any fallacy. Therefore in it there cannot be several senses to a word.

---

[35] This article, seemingly out of place, is included here because it concerns the way in which we interpret theology's data, Scripture.

Modern hermeneutics (the science of interpretation) tends to create a great divide between the Modernist Demythologizers, who interpret as merely symbolic whatever passages are too miraculous or supernaturalistic for their philosophy to stomach, and the Fundamentalists, who in reaction to the Modernists tend to be suspicious of all symbolism and confine themselves to literal interpretation of every passage (*except* Jn 6:48–56).

St. Thomas cuts across this either/or and maintains that a passage could rightly be interpreted both literally ("historically") and symbolically ("spiritually"), because God writes history as man writes words. That is, behind this hermeneutic is a metaphysic: the sacramental view of nature and history, according to which things and events as well as words can be *signs* as well as *things*, can be means by which other things are signified and known as well as being things known themselves.

This view of nature and history as signs and not only things, and therefore as objectively *sign*ificant, implicitly presupposes theism; for only God, not man, could be the author of this significance in nature and history which comes to us as given rather than from us as contrived. This sacramental view of nature has been abandoned correctly in modern science (for methodological purposes), unnecessarily in modern philosophy, and disastrously in modern consciousness.

On the contrary, Gregory says, (*Moral.* xx. 1): *Holy Writ by the manner of its speech transcends every science, because in one and the same sentence, while it describes a fact, it reveals a mystery.*

I answer that, The author of Holy Writ is God, in whose power it is to signify His meaning, not by words only (as man also can do), but also by things themselves. So, whereas in every other science things are signified by words, this science has the property, that the things signified by the words have themselves also a signification. Therefore that first signification whereby words signify things belongs to the first sense, the historical or literal. That signification whereby things signified by words have themselves also a signification is called the spiritual sense, which is based on the literal, and presupposes it [A].[36] Now this spiritual sense has a threefold division. For as the Apostle says (Heb 10:1) the Old Law is a figure of the New Law, and Dionysius says (*Coel. Hier.* i) *the New Law itself is a figure of future glory.* Again, in the New Law, whatever our Head has done is a type of what we ought to do. Therefore, so far as the things of the Old Law signify the things of the New Law, there is the allegorical sense; so far as the things done in Christ, or so far as the things which signify Christ, are types of what we ought to do, there is the moral sense. But so far as they signify what relates to eternal glory, there is the anagogical sense.[37] Since the literal

---

[36] These three principles (see Reply to Objection 1 for B and C) prevent the spiritual, symbolic interpretation from becoming uncontrolled and irresponsible. They put a sober and scientific control on this imaginative aspect of interpretation, like putting a strong rider on a strong horse. This imaginative aspect is neglected or scorned today partly because of the false notion that such controls were not known or practiced in medieval theology. Sometimes they were not. But sometimes (as in St. Thomas) they were.

[37] "Old Law" = "Old Testament"; "New Law" = "New Testament"; "future glory" = Heaven. An example of allegorical sense would be Moses (symbolic of Christ) leading the Hebrews (symbolic of the Church, Christ's Body) through the exodus (symbolic of salvation) from slavery (symbolic of sin) to Pharaoh (symbolic of Satan), ruler of Egypt (symbolic of this fallen world), across the Red Sea (symbolic of death), through the wilderness (symbolic of Purgatory), to the Promised Land (symbolic of Heaven). An example of the moral sense would be Christ's washing of

49

sense is that which the author intends, and since the author of Holy Writ is God, Who by one act comprehends all things by His intellect, it is not unfitting, as Augustine says (*Confess.* xii), if, even according to the literal sense, one word in Holy Writ should have several senses.

Reply Obj. 1. The multiplicity of these senses does not produce equivocation or any other kind of multiplicity, seeing that these senses are not multiplied because one word signifies several things; but because the things signified by the words can be themselves types of other things. Thus in Holy Writ no confusion results, for all the senses are founded on one—the literal—from which alone can any argument be drawn, and not from those intended in allegory [B], as Augustine says (*Epist.* xlviii). Nevertheless, nothing of Holy Scripture perishes on account of this, since nothing necessary to faith is contained under the spiritual sense which is not elsewhere put forward by the Scripture in its literal sense [C]. . . .

His disciples' feet (Jn 13), symbolizing our obligation to serve our neighbors humbly. An example of the anagogical, or eschatological, sense would be Christ's miracles of healing blind men symbolizing His complete healing of our spiritual blindness in Heaven's Beatific Vision.

TWO

Proofs for
The Existence of God

Question 2

The Existence of God

Because the chief aim of sacred doctrine is to teach the knowledge of God, not only as He is in Himself, but also as He is the beginning of things and their last end, and especially of rational creatures, as is clear from what has been already said, therefore, in our endeavor to expound this science, we shall treat: (1) Of God; (2) Of the rational creature's advance towards God; (3) Of Christ, Who as man, is our way to God.

In treating of God there will be a threefold division:

For we shall consider (1) Whatever concerns the Divine Essence; (2) Whatever concerns the distinctions of Persons; (3) Whatever concerns the procession of creatures from Him.

Concerning the Divine Essence, we must consider:

(1) Whether God exists? (2) The manner of His existence, or, rather, what is *not* the manner of His existence; (3) Whatever concerns His operations—namely, His knowledge, will, power.

Concerning the first, there are three points of inquiry:

(1) Whether the proposition "God exists" is self-evident? (2) Whether it is demonstrable? (3) Whether God exists?[1]

---

[1] If the existence of God is self-evident, it is superfluous to try to demonstrate (prove) it. No one *proves* "2 + 2 = 4" or "something exists". In Article 1, St. Thomas shows that God's existence is not so obvious that it needs no proof; and in Article 2 he shows that it is not so obscure that it cannot be proved. Thus he refutes both extremes of "dogmatism" and "skepticism" about the existence of God.

FIRST ARTICLE

Whether the Existence of God is Self-Evident?

Objection 1. It seems that the existence of God is self-evident. Now those things are said to be self-evident to us the knowledge of which is naturally implanted in us, as we can see in regard to first principles. But as Damascene says (*De Fid. Orth.* i. 1, 3), *the knowledge of God is naturally implanted in all.*[2] Therefore the existence of God is self-evident.

Objection 2.[3] Further, those things [propositions] are said to be self-evident which are known [to be true] as soon as the terms are known [understood], which the Philosopher (1 *Poster.* iii) says is true of the first principles of demonstration. Thus, when the nature of a whole and of a part is known, it is at once recognized that every whole is greater than its part. But as soon as the signification of the word "God" is understood, it is at once seen that God exists. For by this word is signified that thing than which nothing greater can be conceived. But that which exists actually and mentally is greater than that which exists only mentally.[4] Therefore, since as soon as the word "God" is understood it exists mentally, it also follows that it exists actually. Therefore the proposition "God exists" is self-evident.

---

[2] For the vast majority of all humans who have ever lived have believed in some God. Children (or societies) have to be educated out of theism into atheism, not vice versa. Atheism always comes later.

[3] St. Thomas here rephrases St. Anselm's famous "ontological argument" (*Proslogion* chap. 2), interpreting it as an attempt to demonstrate not only that God exists but that God's existence is self-evident, i.e., that the proposition "God exists" is a self-evident proposition, like "Bachelors are males" or "Wholes are greater than their parts". St. Thomas includes St. Anselm's argument as an *objection* to his thesis that the existence of God is *not* self-evident. St. Thomas disagrees with St. Anselm's argument (cf. Reply to Objection 2), but not, of course, with its conclusion (that God exists).

[4] I.e., "that which exists actually" (objectively, outside man's mind) is a greater concept than "that which exists only mentally" (subjectively, within man's mind). Therefore, "God does not exist" becomes a self-contradictory proposition (and its opposite, "God exists", thus becomes a self-evident proposition). "God lacks existence" means "The greatest conceivable being lacks one conceivable perfection, viz., objective existence."

Objection 3. Further, the existence of truth is self-evident. For whoever denies the existence of truth grants that truth does not exist: and, if truth does not exist, then the proposition "Truth does not exist" is true: and if there is anything true, there must be truth. But God is truth itself: *I am the way, the truth, and the life* (Jn 14:6). Therefore "God exists" is self-evident.

On the contrary, No one can mentally admit the opposite of what is self-evident; as the Philosopher (*Metaph.* iv. lect. vi) states concerning the first principles of demonstration. But the opposite of the proposition "God is" can be mentally admitted: *The fool said in his heart, There is no God* (Ps 52:1). Therefore, that God exists is not self-evident.

I answer that, A thing can be self-evident in either of two ways; on the one hand, self-evident in itself, though not to us; on the other, self-evident in itself, and to us.[5] A proposition is self-evident

---

[5] A proposition that is "self-evident in itself" is one whose predicate is logically identical with or contained in the meaning of its subject. A proposition that is "self-evident to us" must first be self-evident in itself, and it is also self-evident to us if it contains only terms which we can define, by knowing their essences. The following chart may be useful:

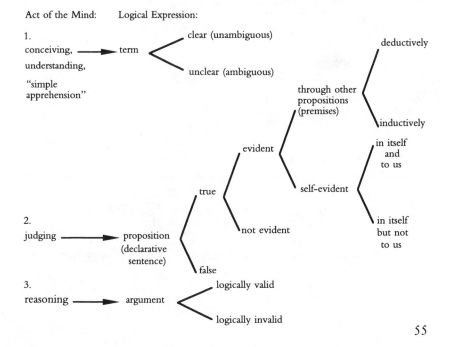

because the predicate is included in the essence of the subject, as "Man is an animal," for animal is contained in the essence of man. If, therefore the essence of the predicate and subject be known to all, the proposition will be self-evident to all; as is clear with regard to the first principles of demonstration, the terms of which are common things that no one is ignorant of, such as being and non-being, whole and part, and such like. If, however, there are some to whom the essence of the predicate and subject is unknown, the proposition will be self-evident in itself, but not to those who do not know the meaning of the predicate and subject of the proposition. Therefore, it happens, as Boëthius says (*Hebdom.*, the title of which is: *"Whether all that is, is good"*), "that there are some mental concepts self-evident only to the learned, as that incorporeal substances are not in space." Therefore I say that this proposition, "God exists," of itself is self-evident, for the predicate is the same as the subject: because God is His own existence as will be hereafter shown (Q. 3, A. 4). Now because we do not know the essence of God, the proposition is not self-evident to us; but needs to be demonstrated by things that are more known to us, though less known in their nature[6]—namely, by effects.

Reply Obj. 1. To know that God exists in a general and confused way is implanted in us by nature, inasmuch as God is man's beatitude. For man naturally desires happiness, and what is naturally desired by man must be naturally known to him. This, however, is not to know absolutely[7] that God exists; just as to know that someone is approaching is not the same as to know that Peter is approaching, even though it is Peter who is approaching; for many there are who imagine that man's perfect good which is happiness,

---

[6] I.e., the nature of God is perfectly intelligible, clear, rational, and like light in itself, while the nature of a creature (e.g., a stone) is a mixture of form (which is the intelligible object of knowledge) and matter (which of itself is formless potentiality and is thus not knowable in itself). Yet creatures are more easily known by us than God is, for our minds are proportioned to them more than to God, as the eyes of the owl are proportioned to dim night light, not bright day light.

[7] I.e., explicitly as vs. implicitly, and specifically and clearly as vs. "in a general and confused way".

consists in riches, and others in pleasures, and others in something else.

Reply Obj. 2. Perhaps not everyone who hears this word "God" understands it to signify something than which nothing greater can be thought, seeing that some have believed God to be a body. Yet, granted that everyone understands that by this word "God" is signified something than which nothing greater can be thought, nevertheless, it does not therefore follow that he understands that what the word signifies exists actually, but only that it exists mentally. Nor can it be argued that it actually exists, unless it be admitted that there actually exists something than which nothing greater can be thought; and this precisely is not admitted by those who hold that God does not exist.[8]

Reply Obj. 3. The existence of truth in general is self-evident but the existence of a Primal Truth is not self-evident to us.

SECOND ARTICLE

Whether It Can Be Demonstrated That God Exists?

Objection 1. It seems that the existence of God cannot be demonstrated. For it is an article of faith that God exists. But what is of faith cannot be demonstrated, because a demonstration produces scientific knowledge; whereas faith is of the unseen (Heb 11:1). Therefore it cannot be demonstrated that God exists.

Objection 2. Further, the essence is the middle term of demonstration.[9] But we cannot know in what God's essence consists, but

---

[8] St. Thomas' refutation of St. Anselm's argument here is essentially that it begs the question by implicitly assuming the point to be proved, viz., that there is a referent or denotation (real being) corresponding to the meaning or connotation of the term "that than which nothing greater can be conceived".

[9] A true "demonstration" is not merely any deductive argument, but a proof that a certain property necessarily follows from the essence. Euclid's geometry is full of such demonstrations. "Rational animals are mortal; Socrates is a rational animal; therefore Socrates is mortal" is a demonstration, using "rational animal" as the middle term:

solely in what it does not consist; as Damascene says (*De Fid. Orth.* i. 4). Therefore we cannot demonstrate that God exists.

Objection 3. Further, if the existence of God were demonstrated, this could only be from His effects. But His effects are not proportionate to Him, since He is infinite and His effects are finite; and between the finite and infinite there is no proportion. Therefore, since a cause cannot be demonstrated by an effect not proportionate to it, it seems that the existence of God cannot be demonstrated.

On the contrary, The Apostle says: *The invisible things of Him are clearly seen, being understood by the things that are made* (Rom 1:20).[10] But this would not be unless the existence of God could be demonstrated through the things that are made; for the first thing we must know of anything is, whether it exists.

I answer that, Demonstration can be made in two ways: One is through the cause, and is called *a priori*, and this is to argue from what is prior absolutely. The other is through the effect, and is called a demonstration *a posteriori*; this is to argue from what is prior relatively only to us. When an effect is better known to us than its cause, from the effect we proceed to the knowledge of the cause.[11] And from every effect the existence of its proper cause can

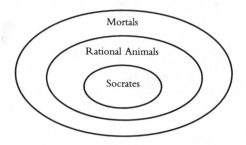

[10] Note the irony here: it is sacred Scripture, and faith in it, that says the existence of God is "clearly seen" by natural reason, not just by faith and Scripture.

[11] Demonstration can be either a priori (from the cause as premise to its effect as conclusion) or a posteriori (from the effect as premise to its cause as conclusion). A cause is prior to its effect objectively, in itself ("absolutely"). A premise is prior to the conclusion subjectively, in our knowledge ("relatively to us"). Thus in an a posteriori demonstration, that which is posterior in itself (the effect) is prior in our knowledge, as the premise.

be demonstrated, so long as its effects are better known to us; because since every effect depends upon its cause, if the effect exists, the cause must pre-exist. Hence the existence of God, in so far as it is not self-evident to us, can be demonstrated from those of His effects which are known to us.

Reply Obj. 1. The existence of God and other like truths about God, which can be known by natural reason, are not articles of faith,[12] but are preambles to the articles; for faith presupposes natural knowledge, even as grace presupposes nature, and perfection supposes something that can be perfected. Nevertheless, there is nothing to prevent a man, who cannot grasp a proof, accepting, as a matter of faith, something which in itself is capable of being scientifically known and demonstrated.

Reply Obj. 2. When the existence of a cause is demonstrated from an effect, this effect takes the place of the definition of the cause in proof of the cause's existence.[13] This is especially the case in regard to God, because, in order to prove the existence of anything, it is necessary to accept as a middle term the meaning of the word, and not its essence,[14] for the question of its essence follows on the question of its existence. Now the names given to God are derived from His effects; consequently, in demonstrating the existence of God from His effects, we may take for the middle term the meaning of the word "God."

Reply Obj. 3. From effects not proportionate to the cause no perfect knowledge of that cause can be obtained. Yet from every

---

[12] I.e., they are not objectively, or in themselves, articles of faith. "Article of faith" is used here in the technical sense: cf. n. 32 of chap. I.

[13] The definition or essence of the cause is the middle term in an a priori demonstration, e.g., "All animals are mortal, and all men are animals, therefore all men are mortal." "Animal" is part of man's definition (essence) and the cause of man's mortality.

The existence of the effect is the middle term in an a posteriori demonstration, e.g., "Where there are footprints, there were feet, and there are footprints on this beach, therefore there were feet on this beach." Footprints = the middle term here, and is the effect (of feet).

[14] In the example above (n. 13), we need not know the *essence* of footprints for the demonstration to be valid, but we do need to know the meaning of the word.

effect the existence of the cause can be clearly demonstrated, and so we can demonstrate the existence of God from His effects; though from them we cannot perfectly know God as He is in His essence.[15]

THIRD ARTICLE

Whether God Exists?

Objection 1.[16] It seems that God does not exist; because if one of two contraries be infinite, the other would be altogether destroyed. But the word "God" means that He is infinite goodness. If, therefore, God existed, there would be no evil discoverable; but there is evil in the world. Therefore God does not exist.

---

[15] Similarly to n. 14, from knowing a footprint we do not yet know the essence of feet, or have perfect or adequate knowledge of feet. Or, from an artefact we cannot know the essence of the arteficer, but we can know his existence. Note how severely St. Thomas restricts the extent of our rational knowledge of God. He is closer in spirit to agnosticism than to dogmatism.

[16] N.b.: St. Thomas can find only two objections to the existence of God in the whole history of human thought! There are numerous alternative psychological explanations for belief in God (fear, folly, fallacy, or fantasy), and there are objections to each of the many arguments for the existence of God. But there are only two arguments that even claim to *disprove* the existence of God. And the second only claims to show that the existence of God is an unnecessary hypothesis, like the existence of leprechauns or Martians: disappearing Irish gold can be adequately explained without leprechauns, and the "canals" on Mars without Martians. The second Objection does not prove that God cannot possibly exist. Only the first Objection, the Problem of Evil, remains as an apparent *proof* of atheism.

St. Augustine had two famous formulations of the Problem of Evil that were similar, and similarly condensed: (1) "If there is God, how can there be evil? But if there is no God, how can there be good?" (2) "If God is all-good, He wants His creatures to be happy, and if He is all-powerful, He can do whatever He wants. But His creatures are not happy. Therefore He lacks either goodness or power or both." See C. S. Lewis' *The Problem of Pain* for the best answer to this formulation.

Objection 2. [17] Further, it is superfluous to suppose that what can be accounted for by a few principles has been produced by many. But it seems that everything we see in the world can be accounted for by other principles, supposing God did not exist. For all natural things can be reduced to one principle, which is nature; and all voluntary things can be reduced to one principle, which is human reason, or will. Therefore there is no need to suppose God's existence.

On the contrary, It is said in the person of God: *I am Who am* (Ex 3:14). [18]

I answer that, The existence of God can be proved in five ways. [19]

---

[17] Objection 2 tries to prove, not that God does not exist, but that the existence of God is like Martians, or Santa Claus, or the conspiracy theory of history: a hypothesis that is superfluous to a scientific explanation of all the phenomena we observe. Since all five of St. Thomas' proofs ("ways") begin with sense data and try to prove that a God, or First Cause, is the only possible adequate rational explanation of this data, Objection 2 is very serious and relevant to St. Thomas' empirical, scientific arguments. N.b.: medieval science, like modern science, used the principle of simplicity, or "Ockham's Razor": always prefer the simpler hypothesis. St. Thomas' objection appeals to this in the first sentence. But medieval science, unlike modern science, did not exclude questions (and answers) about first, ultimate causes. Therefore both philosophy and physics come under the heading of "science" for the Middle Ages, and are not kept strictly separated, as they are in modern times.

[18] Note the irony and humor here: the "on the contrary" is usually an argument from authority; so what authority does St. Thomas appeal to on the question of whether God exists? God Himself! God cuts through our discussion about Him in the third person and announces, in the first person, "I am here!"

[19] Three important notes about the "five ways":

I

These five are not the *proofs* themselves but *ways*, i.e., indications or summaries of proofs. The proofs themselves are elsewhere worked out in much greater detail; e.g., in the *Summa contra Gentiles* the first way takes thirty-one paragraphs (Bk I, chap. 13); here, it takes only one.

II

These five ways are really essentially one way: the "cosmological argument",
or argument from the cosmos. The logical structure of all five proofs is the
same:

1. There are really three premises:
   a. an implicit logical principle: the tautology that either there is a First
      Cause or there is not. (The proofs prove there is a First Cause by
      showing that the alternative entails a contradiction; this pre-
      supposes the Law of Excluded Middle: that there can be no middle
      alternative between two mutually contradictory propositions; thus,
      to disprove one is to prove the other.)
   b. an explicit empirical datum (motion, causality, etc.)
   c. a metaphysical principle, which is neither tautological, like (a),
      nor empirical, like (b), but known by metaphysical insight or
      understanding: e.g., "If there is no First Cause, there can be no
      second causes", or "nothing can cause itself to be".
2. There are two possible hypotheses to explain the empirical data:
   a. that there is a God (First Mover, Uncaused Cause, etc.)
   b. that there is no God.
   St. Thomas shows in each of the five "ways" that the metaphysical
   principle (1c) coupled with the empirical data (1b) makes 2b impossible.
   Thus only 2a is left, if we admit 1a to begin with.
3. However, two "weakening" qualifications must be added:
   a. Each proof individually, and all five together, prove only a thin
      slice of God, a few attributes of God. More attributes are deduced
      later in the *Summa*, and much that is known by Revelation is not
      provable by reason at all (e.g., the Trinity, the Incarnation, and
      Redemption).
   b. Each proof ends with a sentence like "And this is what everyone
      calls God"—an observation about linguistic usage which answers
      Pascal's complaint that "the God of the philosophers is not the
      God of Abraham, Isaac, and Jacob" by saying in effect that the God
      proved here by philosophy, though "thinner" than the God
      revealed in the Bible, is "thick" enough to refute an atheist. There
      are simply no other candidates for the position of First Cause,
      Unmoved Mover, Perfect Being, Cosmic Designer, etc.

III

These five ways are not by any means the only ways of proving the existence of God in the history of philosophy. There have been at least two dozen very different sorts of attempts to prove the existence of God (below). St. Thomas carefully and modestly confines himself to the most scientific proofs alone.

(An Extremely Brief Summary of 24 Arguments for God's Existence)

    I. Ontological (Anselm): "God" means "that which has all conceivable perfections"; and it is more perfect to exist really than only mentally; therefore God exists really. The most perfect conceivable being cannot lack any conceivable perfection.

   II. Cosmological
     A. Motion: Since no thing (or series of things) can move (change) itself, there must be a first, Unmoved Mover, source of all motion.
     B. Efficient Causality: Nothing can cause its own existence. If there is no first, uncaused cause of the chain of causes and effects we see, these second causes could not exist. They do, so It must.
     C. Contingency and Necessity: Contingent being (beings able not to be) depend on a Necessary Being (a being not able not to be).
     D. Degrees of Perfection: Real degrees of real perfections presuppose the existence of that perfection itself (the Perfect Being).
     E. Design: Design can be caused only by an intelligent Designer. Mindless nature cannot design itself or come about by chance.
     F. The *Kalam* (Time) Argument: Time must have a beginning, a first moment (creation) to give rise to all other moments. (The "Big Bang" seems to confirm this: time had an absolute beginning fifteen to twenty billion years ago.) And the act of creation presupposes a Creator.

  III. Psychological
     A. from mind and truth
       1. Augustine: Our minds are in contact with eternal, objective, and absolute truth superior to our minds (e.g. $2 + 2 = 4$), and the eternal is divine, not human.
       2. Descartes: Our *idea* of a perfect being (God) could not have come from any imperfect source (cause), for the effect cannot be greater than the cause. Thus it must have come from God.

B. from will and good
    1. Kant: Morality requires a perfect ideal, and requires that this ideal be actual and real, somewhere.
    2. Newman: Conscience speaks with absolute authority, which could come only from God.
C. from emotions and desire
    1. C. S. Lewis: Innate desires correspond to real objects, and we have an innate desire (at least unconsciously) for God, and Heaven.
    2. Von Balthasar: Beauty reveals God. There is Mozart, therefore there must be God.
D. from experience
    1. Existential Argument: If there is no God (and no immortality) life is ultimately meaningless.
    2. Mystical experience meets God.
    3. Ordinary religious experience (prayer) meets God. (Prayer of the Skeptic: "God, if you exist, show me"—a real experiment.)
    4. Love argument: If there is no God of Love, no Absolute that is love, then love is not absolute. Or, the eyes of love reveal the infinite value of the human person as the image of God.

IV. The argument from the analogy of other minds, which are no harder to prove than God (Plantinga).

V. The practical argument: Pascal's Wager: To bet on God is your only chance of winning eternal happiness, and to bet against Him is your only chance of losing. It is the most reasonable bet in life.

VI. Historical
    A. from miracles: If miracles exist, a supernatural miracle-worker exists.
    B. from Providence, perceivable in history (e.g., in Scripture) and in one's own life.
    C. from authority: Most good, wise, reliable people believe in God.
    D. from saints: You see God through them. Where do they get their joy and power?
    E. from Jesus: If God is unreal, Jesus was history's biggest fool or fake.

(This list is not exhaustive, but illustrative. Maritain and Marcel, for example, have formulated other, more complex arguments for God.)

64

The first and more manifest[20] way is the argument from motion. It is certain, and evident to our senses, that in the world some things are in motion. Now whatever is in motion is put in motion by another, for nothing can be in motion except it is in potentiality to that towards which it is in motion; whereas a thing moves inasmuch as it is in act. For motion is nothing else than the reduction of something from potentiality to actuality. But nothing can be reduced from potentiality to actuality, except by something in a state of actuality. Thus that which is actually hot, as fire, makes wood, which is potentially hot, to be actually hot, and thereby moves and changes it. Now it is not possible that the same thing should be at once in actuality and potentiality in the same respect, but only in different respects. For what is actually hot cannot simultaneously be potentially hot; but it is simultaneously potentially cold. It is therefore impossible that in the same respect and in the same way a thing should be both mover and moved, *i.e.*, that it should move itself. Therefore, whatever is in motion must be put in motion by another. If that by which it is put in motion be itself put in motion, then this also must needs be put in motion by another, and that by another again. But this cannot go on to infinity, because then there would be no first mover, and, consequently, no other mover; seeing that subsequent movers move only inasmuch as they are put in motion by the first mover; as the staff moves only because it is put in motion by the hand. Therefore it is necessary to arrive at a first mover, put in motion by no other; and this everyone understands to be God.[21]

---

[20] St. Thomas is not saying that the first of the five ways is easier to follow logically (in fact it is more complex than any of the other four), but that its premise, or data is the most obvious data. This is *motion*, i.e., not just locomotion (motion through space), but any change. Each of the five ways begins with a different datum (motion, causality, possibility, degrees of perfection, and order) and arrives at the same conclusion: God, under five different attributes: Prime Mover, Uncaused Cause, Necessary Being, Most Perfect Being, Ordering Mind.

[21] The difficult half of this proof is the first half, which proves the commonsensical proposition: "Whatever is in motion, must be put in motion by another." The second half of the proof, which then proves that there can be no infinite regress in movers, is a simple syllogism: If there is

The second way is from the nature of the efficient cause.[22] In the world of sense we find there is an order of efficient causes. There is no case known (neither is it, indeed, possible) in which a thing is

---

no first (un-moved) mover, then there can be no second (moved) movers; but there are second movers; therefore there is a First Mover (cf. *Summa contra Gentiles* I, 13 for an expanded version of this whole argument).

Infinite *progress* in *effects* is possible without contradiction, but infinite *regress* in *causes* is not. For that would be like a train composed of an infinite number of boxcars all moving uphill without a locomotive, or like a stairway with an infinite number of steps each resting on the one below it but with no first step. "Infinite regress" means *indefinite* regress, without a term, or first step. It does not mean a positive, actual infinity like God's attributes.

And "first" in this proof does not necessarily mean first in *time*, only in causality. Sometimes a cause comes temporally before its effect, as parents are born before their children, and the bat swings before the ball is hit; but at other times, the cause and effect are simultaneous, as when the stories of a building, or rungs on a ladder, or books in a pile each rest on the one below it. There too, there must be a first cause (the bottom story, rung, or book *causes* the others to stand), though it is not prior in time.

St. Thomas believed, of course (because he read it in Genesis), that God was prior in time to the universe—not in the sense that God is *in* time or that time existed before the universe existed (like Einstein and unlike Newton, St. Thomas regarded time not as an absolute, prior background to the universe but as co-created with the universe; for him, as for Einstein, time was relative to matter and motion, i.e., to the universe, not vice versa), but in the sense that there is no infinite regress of time, but only a finite regress of time: the universe has existed for only a finite time. (This fact has recently been confirmed by astrophysics in the form of the "Big Bang" as vs. the "Steady State" and "Oscillating" models of the universe.) But St. Thomas did not think that philosophical reason without divine revelation could prove the universe had only a finite time span, as the "kalam" (time) argument used by some medieval Muslim and Christian philosophers tried to prove, because God *could* have created a universe with infinite time, co-eternal with Himself. That is not *logically* impossible, and therefore cannot be logically disproved. The universe is finite in time only because God's free will chose to create it that way.

[22] "Efficient cause" for Aristotle meant only cause of *change*, cause of form informing matter. But for St. Thomas it means also the cause of the very *existence* of its effect. Thus the second way goes beyond the first: the

found to be the efficient cause of itself; for so it would be prior to itself, which is impossible. Now in efficient causes it is not possible to go on to infinity, because in all efficient causes following in order, the first is the cause of the intermediate cause, and the intermediate is the cause of the ultimate cause, whether the intermediate cause be several, or one only. Now to take away the cause is to take away the effect. Therefore, if there be no first cause among efficient causes, there will be no ultimate, nor any intermediate cause. But if in efficient causes it is possible to go on to infinity, there will be no first efficient cause, neither will there be an ultimate effect, nor any intermediate efficient causes; all of which is plainly false. Therefore it is necessary to admit a first efficient cause, to which everyone gives the name of God.

The third way is taken from possibility and necessity, and runs thus. We find in nature things that are possible to be and not to be,[23] since they are found to be generated, and to corrupt, and consequently, they are possible to be and not to be. But it is impossible for these always to exist, for that which is possible not to be at some time is not.[24] Therefore, if everything is possible not to be, then at

---

first proved God as cause of universal change; the second proves God as cause of the very existence of the universe.

The argument here is similar to that in the last half of the first way: if no First (Uncaused) Cause, no second causes; but there are second causes; therefore there is a First Cause. "Infinite regress" is impossible because it means "no First Cause".

[23] "Things that are possible to be and not to be" = "things whose existence is contingent", "things that have a potentiality to not-be as well as to be", "things that can go out of existence or fail to come into existence". "Generation" = "coming into existence"; "corruption" = "going out of existence".

[24] I.e., given infinite time, every possibility is eventually actualized. N.b.: this proof, like the others, is a *reductio ad absurdum*, which examines the hypothesis of atheism (no God, no Necessary Being) and perceives that this hypothesis logically entails a conclusion which is evidently false (thus the hypothesis must be false), viz., that nothing exists now. For if there has been infinite time (which there must have been if there is no Creator), then every possibility must have already had enough time to have been actualized, including the possibility of simultaneous non-existence for all contingent beings.

one time there could have been nothing in existence. Now if this were true, even now there would be nothing in existence, because that which does not exist only begins to exist by something already existing. Therefore, if at one time nothing was in existence, it would have been impossible for anything to have begun to exist; and thus even now nothing would be in existence—which is absurd. Therefore, not all beings are merely possible, but there must exist something the existence of which is necessary.

But every necessary thing[25] either has its necessity caused by another, or not. Now it is impossible to go on to infinity in necessary things which have their necessity caused by another, as has been already proved in regard to efficient causes. Therefore we cannot but postulate the existence of some being having of itself its own necessity, and not receiving it from another, but rather causing in others their necessity. This all men speak of as God.

The fourth way is taken from the gradation to be found in things.[26] Among beings there are some more and some less good, true, noble, and the like. But "more" and "less" are predicated of different things, according as they resemble in their different ways something which is the maximum, as a thing is said to be hotter according as it more nearly resembles that which is hottest; so that there is something which is truest, something best, something noblest, and, consequently, something which is uttermost being; for those things that are greatest in truth are greatest in being, as it is written in *Metaph*. ii.[27] Now the maximum in any genus is the

---

[25] The last half of the proof, which speaks of a plurality of necessary beings, refers to changeless angels (in biblical terms) or bodiless "intelligences" (in Aristotelian terms).

[26] The fourth way presupposes something which everyone except a few Sophists in ancient Greece and Skeptics in ancient Rome accepted until modern times, but which the modern mind tends to find incomprehensible: viz., that "values" are objective, that value judgments are judgments of fact—e.g., that a man *really* has more value than an ape.

[27] The concept of degrees of being as well as of goodness, and of an "uttermost being" as well as a "greatest good", will probably seem very strange to the modern reader. But a thing must first *be* before it can be good (thus whatever has goodness must also have being), and every thing that has being also has some goodness (cf. S.T. I, 5, 3); therefore goodness

cause of all in that genus; as fire, which is the maximum of heat, is the cause of all hot things. Therefore there must also be something which is to all beings the cause of their being, goodness, and every other perfection; and this we call God.[28]

The fifth way is taken from the governance of the world. We see that things which lack intelligence, such as natural bodies, act for an end, and this is evident from their acting always, or nearly always, in the same way, so as to obtain the best result. Hence it is plain that not fortuitously, but designedly, do they achieve their end. Now whatever lacks intelligence cannot move towards an end, unless it be directed by some being endowed with knowledge and intelligence; as the arrow is shot to its mark by the archer. Therefore some intelligent being exists by whom all natural things are directed to their end; and this being we call God.[29]

Reply Obj. 1. As Augustine says (*Enchir.* xi): *Since God is the highest good, He would not allow any evil to exist in His works, unless His omnipotence and goodness were such as to bring good even out of evil.* This is part of the infinite goodness of God, that He should allow evil to exist, and out of it produce good.[30]

---

and being are coextensive. The concept of degrees of being can be understood if we remember that "being" means not simply existence ("to be or not to be") but also essence (*what* a thing is, its nature), and this latter aspect of being admits of degrees.

[28] The point of the argument is that "better" implies "best". Put dynamically, progress presupposes an unchanging standard to judge the progress. If the standard also progressed, how could we progress to it? How could we reach or even approach a goal line that moved with us?

St. Thomas' example of this principle (fire) is, of course, bad science. But the invalid illustration does not invalidate the principle.

[29] This is often called the "argument from design". It is probably the most popular and instinctively obvious of all arguments for the existence of God. As Paley said, if we find a watch, it is reasonable to conclude there is a watchmaker.

[30] Like Scripture, St. Augustine and St. Thomas answer the problem of evil not with some timeless formula but with a dramatic promise for the future: since evil occurs in history, its solution also occurs in history. The greatest example in history of both evil and of God producing good from it is the Crucifixion.

Reply Obj. 2. Since nature works for a determinate end under the direction of a higher agent, whatever is done by nature must needs be traced back to God, as to its first cause. So also whatever is done voluntarily must also be traced back to some higher cause other than human reason or will, since these can change and fail; for all things that are changeable and capable of defect must be traced back to an immovable and self-necessary first principle, as was shown in the body of the *Article*.[31]

---

[31] The natural and human sciences of themselves need not raise questions of ultimate origin. But philosophy must. Once the philosophical question is raised of the ultimate origin of the data of the natural and human sciences, the five ways prove that God is the only adequate answer to that question.

THREE

The Nature of God

Question 3

Of the Simplicity of God

When the existence of a thing has been ascertained there remains the further question of the manner of its existence, in order that we may know its essence.[1] Now, because we cannot know what God is, but rather what He is not, we have no means for considering how God is, but rather how He is not.[2]

Therefore, we must consider (1) How He is not; (2) How He is known by us; (3) How He is named.[3]

Now it can be shown how God is not, by denying of Him

---

[1] N.b.: for St. Thomas "essence" = ultimately "manner (mode, way) of existence". Essence is relative to existence, as potency to act. Existence (*esse*) is the ultimate actuality and is therefore also the nature (essence) of God. In Him alone essence and existence are identical.

[2] Note how scrupulously St. Thomas confines our knowledge of God and how fruitfully he develops that knowledge within those bounds. Cf. S.T. I, 13, 5: we must choose between positive but analogical knowledge of God (what God is *like*, not what He *is*) or univocal but negative knowledge of God (what He is *not*).

[3] N.b.: these three questions correspond to the three meanings of *logos* in the Greek language and Greek philosophy: (1) intelligible being, (2) intelligence, and (3) communication; or (1) essence, (2) concept, and (3) word. Gorgias the Sophist formulated a philosophy of total skepticism with his three theses that (1) there is no Being (i.e., intelligible being, *logos*), (2) if there were, we could not have knowledge (*logos*) of it, and (3) if we could know it, we could not have communication (*logos*) of it. The history of Western philosophy has also passed through three corresponding stages: (1) the ancient and medieval period, which concentrated on metaphysics (being), (2) the classical modern period, which concentrated on epistemology (knowledge), and (3) the contemporary period, which concentrates on philosophy of language and communication of meaning.

whatever is opposed to the idea of Him—viz., composition, motion, and the like. Therefore (1) we must discuss His simplicity,[4] whereby we deny composition in Him; and because whatever is simple in material things is imperfect and a part of something else, we shall discuss (2) His perfection; (3) His infinity; (4) His immutability; (5) His unity.

Concerning His simplicity, there are eight points of inquiry: (1) Whether God is a body? (2) Whether He is composed of matter and form? (3) Whether in Him there is composition of quiddity, essence or nature, and subject? (4) Whether He is composed of essence and existence? (5) Whether He is composed of genus and difference? (6) Whether He is composed of subject and accident? (7) Whether He is in any way composite, or wholly simple? (8) Whether He enters into composition with other things?

FIRST ARTICLE

Whether God Is a Body?

Objection 1. It seems that God is a body.[5] For a body is that which has the three dimensions. But Holy Scripture attributes the three dimensions to God, for it is written: *He is higher than Heaven, and what wilt thou do? He is deeper than Hell, and how wilt thou know? The measure of Him is longer than the earth and broader than the sea* (Job 11:8, 9). Therefore God is a body.

Objection 2. Further, everything that has figure is a body, since figure is a quality of quantity. But God seems to have figure, for it

---

[4] St. Thomas deduces many other (negative) attributes of God from the one attribute of simplicity (noncomposedness), for there are many kinds of composition to be denied (see next paragraph).

In *this* (footnoted) paragraph, note that divine attributes 2–5 are all negative to our understanding, though positive in themselves. Our idea of God's perfection, infinity, immutability, and unity is negative because it comes from our experience of imperfection, finitude, temporality, and plurality: we deny that these apply to God. We do not have a positive understanding of God's perfection, infinity, immutability, and unity.

[5] Who thinks so? Children, who cannot yet understand abstractly, and pagans, whose gods (like Zeus) had bodies.

is written: *Let us make man to our image and likeness* (Gen 1:26).[6]
Now a figure is called an image, according to the text: *Who being the
brightness of His glory and the figure, i.e.,* the image, *of His substance*
(Heb 1:3). Therefore God is a body. . . .

On the contrary, It is written in the Gospel of St. John (4:24): *God
is a spirit.*

I answer that, It is absolutely true that God is not a body; and this
can be shown in three ways.

First, because no body is in motion unless it be put in motion, as
is evident from induction. Now it has been already proved (Q. 2,
A. 3), that God is the First Mover, and is Himself unmoved.
Therefore it is clear that God is not a body.

Secondly, because the first being must of necessity be in act, and
in no way in potentiality. For although in any single thing that
passes from potentiality to actuality, the potentiality is prior in
time to the actuality; nevertheless, absolutely speaking, actuality is
prior to potentiality; for whatever is in potentiality can be reduced
into actuality only by some being in actuality. Now it has been
already proved that God is the First Being. It is therefore impossible
that in God there should be any potentiality. But every body is in
potentiality, because the continuous, as such, is divisible to infinity;[7]
it is therefore impossible that God should be a body.

Thirdly, because God is the most noble [perfect] of beings. Now
it is impossible for a body to be the most noble of beings; for a body
must be either animate [living] or inanimate; and an animate body is
manifestly nobler than any inanimate body. But an animate body is
not animate precisely as body; otherwise all bodies would be
animate. Therefore its animation depends upon some other thing,
as our body depends for its animation on the soul. Hence that by
which a body becomes animated must be nobler than the body.
Therefore it is impossible that God should be a body.

Reply Obj. 1. As we have said above (Q. 1, A. 9), Holy Writ
puts before us spiritual and divine things under the comparison of

---

[6] Who thinks the image of God refers to the body? Many people, even
intelligent but not religiously educated people, like the young Augustine
in the *Confessions.*

[7] I.e., a body occupies extended, continuous space and therefore has the
potentiality to be divided.

corporeal things. Hence, when it attributes to God the three dimensions under the comparison of corporeal quantity, it implies His virtual quantity; thus, by depth, it signifies His power of knowing hidden things; by height, the transcendence of His excelling power; by length, the duration of His existence; by breadth, His act of love for all. Or, as says Dionysius (*Div. Nom.* ix), by the depth of God is meant the incomprehensibility of His essence; by length, the procession of His all-pervading power; by breadth, His overspreading all things, inasmuch as all things lie under His protection.[8]

Reply Obj. 2. Man is said to be after the image of God, not as regards his body, but as regards that whereby he excels other animals. Hence, when it is said, *Let us make man to our image and likeness*, it is added, *And let him have dominion over the fishes of the sea* (Gen 1:26). Now man excels all animals by his reason and intelligence; hence it is according to his intelligence and reason, which are incorporeal, that man is said to be according to the image of God. . . .

SECOND ARTICLE

Whether God Is Composed of Matter and Form?[9]

Objection 1. It seems that God is composed of matter and form. For whatever has a soul is composed of matter and form; since the soul is the form of the body. But Scripture attributes a soul to God; for it is mentioned in Hebrews (10:38), where God says: *But My just man liveth by faith; but if he withdraw himself, he shall not please My soul.* Therefore God is composed of matter and form.

---

[8] Note how the symbolism is not arbitrary and subjective but subject to a right and proper interpretation. Yet right interpretations can be diverse, as in this paragraph, where St. Thomas gives two different right interpretations of the same four symbols. This is also relevant to I, 1, 9 on Scripture's proper use of metaphor.

[9] N.b.: Question Two is not the same as Question One, for *matter* is a broader term than *body*. E.g., the subject and predicate terms are *matter* for a proposition, which can be affirmative or negative, universal or particular in *form*; yet this matter (potentiality) is not *corporeal* matter (body).

Objection 2. Further, anger, joy, and the like are passions of the [matter-form] composite. But these are attributed to God in Scripture: *The Lord was exceedingly angry with His people* (Ps 105:40). Therefore God is composed of matter and form.

Objection 3. Further, matter is the principle of individualization.[10] But God seems to be individual, for He cannot be predicated of many. Therefore He is composed of matter and form. . . .

I answer that, It is impossible that matter should exist in God.

First, because matter is in potentiality. But we have shown (Q. 2, A. 3) that God is pure act, without any potentiality. Hence it is impossible that God should be composed of matter and form.

Secondly, because everything composed of matter and form owes its perfection and goodness to its form; therefore its goodness is participated, inasmuch as matter participates the form. Now the first good and the best—viz. God—is not a participated good, because the essential good is prior to the participated good. Hence it is impossible that God should be composed of matter and form.

Thirdly, because every agent acts by its form; hence the manner in which it has its form is the manner in which it is an agent. Therefore whatever is primarily and essentially an agent must be primarily and essentially form. Now God is the first agent, since He is the first efficient cause. He is therefore of His essence a form; and not composed of matter and form.

Reply Obj. 1. A soul is attributed to God because His acts resemble the acts of a soul; for, that we will anything, is due to our soul. Hence what is pleasing to His will is said to be pleasing to His soul.[11]

Reply Obj. 2. Anger and the like are attributed to God on

---

[10] Why are there many dogs? Because though each dog has the same form (dogginess), each has its own matter. Thus matter is the principle (source) of individuation within a species.

[11] God is *spirit* but not *soul*. Both are more than body, and immaterial, but a soul is the form and life of a body. We tend to use the word *soul* both more broadly (as including God and angels and anything immaterial) *and* more narrowly (as *not* including the principle of life in a plant or animal) than the medievals did, because we think in terms of the simple and absolute Cartesian dualism between "thinking substance" (immaterial spirit) and "extended substance" (matter). So we try to conceive of God's essence through an analogy to our own souls.

account of a similitude of effect. Thus, because to punish is properly the act of an angry man, God's punishment is metaphorically spoken of as His anger.[12]

Reply Obj. 3. Forms which can be received in matter are individualized by matter, . . . But that form which cannot be received in matter, but is self-subsisting, is individualized precisely because it cannot be received in a subject; and such a form is God. Hence it does not follow that matter exists in God.

THIRD ARTICLE

Whether God Is the Same As His Essence or Nature?

On the contrary, It is said of God that He is life itself, and not only that He is a living thing: *I am the way, the truth, and the life* (Jn 14:6). Now the relation between Godhead and God is the same as the relation between life and a living thing. Therefore God is His very Godhead.[13] . . .

FOURTH ARTICLE

Whether Essence and Existence Are the Same in God?

Objection 2. Further, we can know *whether* God exists as said above (Q. 2, A. 2); but we cannot know *what* He is. Therefore God's existence is not the same as His essence—that is, as His quiddity[14] or nature.

---

[12] I.e., though God's love is a literal objective reality in God, God's wrath, or anger, is not. For God is purely actual, not potential, and love can be active, but anger is a passion, i.e., passive, reactive. Therefore, God's love is not just a metaphor, an anthropomorphic projection of something proper to us onto God, but God's wrath is.

[13] I.e., in creatures, an individual substance is the subject that *has* an essence (e.g., Socrates has humanness); but God does not *have* Godhead, or divinity, but He *is* divinity, He is His own Godhead. St. Thomas does not mean that God is merely divinity, a universal essence. Nor is God an individual that *has* an essence. God transcends the distinction between individual and universal; He is neither.

[14] "Quid" = "what". "Quiddity" = "whatness".

On the contrary, Hilary says (*Trin.* vii): *In God existence is not an accidental quality, but subsisting truth.* Therefore what subsists in God is His existence.

I answer that, God is not only His own essence, as shown in the preceding article, but also His own existence. This may be shown in several ways.

First, whatever a thing has besides its essence must be caused either by the constituent principles of that essence (like a property that necessarily accompanies the species—as the faculty of laughing is proper to a man—and is caused by the constituent principles of the species), or by some exterior agent,—as heat is caused in water by fire. Therefore, if the existence of a thing differs from its essence, this existence must be caused either by some exterior agent or by its essential principles. Now it is impossible for a thing's existence to be caused by its essential constituent principles, for nothing can be the sufficient cause of its own existence, if its existence is caused.[15] Therefore that thing, whose existence differs from its essence, must have its existence caused by another.[16] But this cannot be true of God; because we call God the first efficient cause. Therefore it is impossible that in God His existence should differ from His essence.

Secondly, existence is that which makes every form or nature actual; for goodness and humanity are spoken of as actual, only because they are spoken of as existing. Therefore, existence must be compared to essence, if the latter is a distinct reality, as actuality to potentiality.[17] Therefore, since in God there is no potentiality, as

---

[15] Even God is not *self*-caused, but *un*-caused. St. Thomas would call Spinoza's definition of God as "cause of itself" (*causa sui*) a confusion. Nothing can be the *efficient* cause of itself. (See S.T. I, 2, 3, the second "way".) God's essence might be said to be the sufficient *formal* cause of itself, however, since His essence is identical with His being.

[16] The *essence*, or nature, of a unicorn or a horse does not determine whether either one *exists*. Therefore something else must cause its existence. Since this something else is not its own essence or existence, it must be another being which works as an efficient cause. Everything except God needs a cause of its existence. God needs no cause of His existence because that (His existence) is His essence—as a triangle needs no cause of its three-sidedness because that is its essence.

[17] Essence is actual qua form in relation to matter, but it is potential in

shown above (A. 1), it follows that in Him essence does not differ from existence. Therefore His essence is His existence.

Thirdly, because, just as that which has fire, but is not itself fire, is on fire by participation; so that which has existence but is not existence, is a being by participation. But God is His own essence, as shown above (A. 3); if, therefore, He is not His own existence

---

relation to existence. The form determines the matter in the order of formal causality (e.g., horseness makes "animal" to be "horse" rather than "lion"), but the resulting essence *may* exist (a horse does) or *may* not exist (a unicorn does not), therefore it is still potential to existence. See the diagram below.

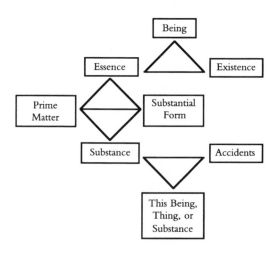

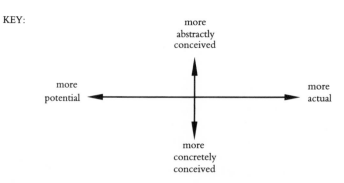

He will be not essential, but participated being. He will not therefore be the first being—which is absurd. Therefore God is His own existence, and not merely His own essence. . . .

Reply Obj. 2. To be can mean either of two things. It may mean the act of essence, or it may mean the composition of a proposition effected by the mind in joining a predicate to a subject.[18] Taking *to be* in the first sense, we cannot understand God's existence nor His essence; but only in the second sense. We know that this proposition which we form about God when we say *God is*, is true; and this we know from His effects (Q. 2, A. 2).[19]

FIFTH ARTICLE

Whether God Is Contained in a Genus?

I answer that, . . . That He cannot be a species of any genus may be shown in three ways. First, because a species is constituted of genus and difference. Now that from which the difference constituting the species is derived, is always related to that from which the genus is derived, as actuality is related to potentiality.[20] . . . Hence since in God actuality is not added to potentiality, it is impossible that He should be in any genus as a species.

Secondly, since the existence of God is His essence, if God were in any genus, He would be the genus "being," because, since genus is predicated as an essential it refers to the essence of a thing. But the Philosopher has shown (*Metaph.* iii) that being cannot be a genus, for every genus has differences distinct from its generic essence. Now no difference can exist distinct from being; for non-being cannot be a difference.[21] It follows then that God is not in a genus.

---

[18] The first meaning of "being" is actual, ontological, objective reality, e.g., "Tom *exists*." The second meaning of "being" is the *logical* "being" of an affirmative copula in a proposition, e.g., "Tom *is* the hero of *Tom Sawyer*."

[19] A remote parallel: if we found Martian artefacts on Mars, we would know *that* Martian arteficers *existed*, as the necessary causes of these effects, but we would not yet know *what* the Martians were.

[20] E.g., "animal" is potential to "rational" or "irrational".

[21] Being is not a genus because there is nothing outside it. A genus

Thirdly, because all in one genus agree in the quiddity or essence of the genus which is predicated of them as an essential, but they differ in their existence. For the existence of man and of horse is not the same; as also of this man and that man: thus in every member of a genus, existence and quiddity—*i.e.*, essence—must differ. But in God they do not differ, as shown in the preceding article. Therefore it is plain that God is not in a genus as if He were a species.

From this it is also plain that He has no genus nor difference, nor can there be any definition of Him; . . . for a definition is from genus and difference. . . .

SIXTH ARTICLE

Whether in God There Are Any Accidents? [22]

Objection 1. It seems that there are accidents in God. For . . . wisdom, virtue, and the like, which are accidents in us, are attributes of God. Therefore in God there are accidents. . . .

I answer that, From all we have said, it is clear there can be no accident in God. . . . Because a subject is compared to its accidents as potentiality to actuality; for a subject is in some sense made actual by its accidents. But there can be no potentiality in God, as was shown (Q. 2, A. 3). . . .

Reply Obj. 1. Virtue and wisdom are not predicated of God and of us univocally. [23] Hence it does not follow that there are accidents in God as there are in us. . . .

(e.g., "animal") has specific differences (e.g., "rational") distinct from its generic essence. Rationality is not *an animal* (i.e., you cannot predicate a genus of its differences), but all real differences *are* real, are being (i.e., you *do* predicate "being" of all real specific differences); therefore being is not a genus. The common but mistaken idea of being as the most abstract genus reduces metaphysics to empty abstraction and accounts for errors like Hegel's, who identified being with nothing, both of which were equally indeterminate, and Nietzsche's, who declared being "a vapor and a fallacy". (Contrast Heidegger, *Introduction to Metaphysics*, chap. 1.) Because being is not just essence but existence for St. Thomas, it is not empty but full, supremely *actual*.

[22] This article clearly distinguishes God from a Los Angeles freeway.

[23] What St. Thomas is pointing out here as not univocal, or the same, in

SEVENTH ARTICLE

Whether God Is Altogether Simple?

Objection 2. . . . Whatever is best must be attributed to God. But with us that which is composite is better than that which is simple; thus, chemical compounds are better than simple elements, and animals than the parts that compose them. Therefore it cannot be said that God is altogether simple. . . .

I answer that, The absolute simplicity of God may be shown in many ways. First, from the previous articles of this question. For there is neither composition of quantitative parts in God, since He is not a body; nor composition of form and matter; nor does His nature differ from His *suppositum* [person-substance]; nor His essence from His existence; neither is there in Him composition of genus and difference, nor of subject and accident. Therefore, it is clear that God is nowise composite, but is altogether simple. [24]

Secondly, because every composite is posterior to its component parts, and is dependent on them; but God is the first being, as shown above (Q. 2, A. 3).

Thirdly, because every composite has a cause, for things in themselves different cannot unite unless something causes them to unite. But God is uncaused, as shown above (*loc. cit.*), since He is the first efficient cause.

Fourthly, because in every composite there must be potentiality and actuality; but this does not apply to God; for either one of the parts actuates another, or at least all the parts are potential to the whole. . . .

Reply Obj. 2. With us composite things are better than simple things, because the perfections of created goodness cannot be found in one simple thing, but in many things. But the perfection of divine goodness is found in one simple thing (QQ. 4, A. 1, and 6, A. 2).

---

both God and creatures, is not only the meaning of each of these attributes, but also the meaning of "attribute" as such, i.e., the relation between attributes and the subject that has them. Creatures *have* attributes (Peter is alive), but God *is* His attributes (God *is* life).

[24] This is an inductive argument by complete enumeration. Each of the six kinds of composition cannot exist in God, therefore no composition can exist in God.

EIGHTH ARTICLE

Whether God Enters Into the Composition of Other Things?

Objection 3. Further, whatever things exist, in no way differing from each other, are the same.[25] But God and primary matter exist, and in no way differ from each other. Therefore they are absolutely the same. But primary matter enters into the composition of things. Therefore also does God. Proof of the minor—whatever things differ, they differ by some differences, and therefore must be composite. But God and primary matter are altogether simple. Therefore they nowise differ from each other. . . .

I answer that, On this point there have been three errors. Some have affirmed that God is the world-soul,[26] as is clear from Augustine (*De Civit. Dei* vii. 6). This is practically the same as the opinion of those who assert that God is the soul of the highest heaven. Again, others have said that God is the formal principle of all things;[27] and this was the theory of the Almaricians. The third error is that of David of Dinant, who most absurdly[28] taught that God was primary matter. Now all these contain manifest untruth; since it is not possible for God to enter into the composition of anything, either as a formal or a material principle. First, because God is the first efficient cause. Now the efficient cause is not identical numerically with the form of the thing caused, but only specifically: for man begets man.[29] But primary matter can be neither numerically nor specifically identical with an efficient cause; for the former [prime matter] is merely potential, while the

---

[25] This is Hegel's (more properly, Schelling's) argument to prove the identity of Being and Nonbeing. Being and Nonbeing, like God and prime matter, are both infinite and without determinate limits, so they do not differ by *form*.

[26] This is essentially the view of Taoism and many of its Western imitators, e.g., the "New Age Movement".

[27] This is essentially the view of Spinoza.

[28] This is essentially the argument of Objection 3. St. Thomas hardly ever uses such rhetoric or personal insult in this way, thus making it all the more effective (like judicious profanity).

[29] The causing parent belongs to the same *species* as the caused child but is not *numerically* one and the same with the child, not the same *entity*.

latter [efficient cause] is actual. Secondly, because, since God is the first efficient cause, to act belongs to Him primarily and essentially. But that which enters into composition with anything does not act primarily and essentially, but rather the composite so acts; for the hand does not act, but the man by his hand; and, fire warms by its heat. Hence God cannot be part of a compound. . . .

Reply Obj. 1. The Godhead is called the being of all things, as their efficient and exemplar cause, but not as being their essence.

Reply Obj. 2. The Word is an exemplar form; but not a form that is part of a compound.

Reply Obj. 3. Simple things do not differ by added differences, —for this is the property of compounds. Thus man and horse differ by their differences, rational and irrational; which differences, however, do not differ from each other by other differences. Hence, to be quite accurate, it is better to say that they are not different, but diverse. Hence, according to the Philosopher (*Metaph.* x), *things which are diverse are absolutely distinct, but things which are different differ by something.* Therefore, strictly speaking, primary matter and God do not differ, but are by their very being diverse. Hence it does not follow they are the same.

Question 4

The Perfection of God

Whether God Is Perfect?

Objection 1. It seems that perfection does not belong to God. For we say a thing is perfect if it is completely made.[30] But it does not befit God to be made. Therefore He is not perfect.

Objection 2. Further, God is the first beginning of things. But the beginnings of things seem to be imperfect, as seed is the beginning of animal and vegetable life.[31] Therefore God is imperfect.

Objection 3. Further, as shown above (Q. 3, A. 4), God's essence is existence. But existence seems most imperfect, since it is most universal and receptive of all modification. Therefore God is imperfect.[32]

On the contrary, It is written: *Be you perfect as also your heavenly Father is perfect* (Mt 5:48).

I answer that, As the Philosopher relates (*Metaph.* xii), some ancient philosophers, namely, the Pythagoreans, and Leucippus, did not predicate *best* and *most perfect* of the first principle. The

---

[30] "Perfect" = *per-factum*, "completely made".

[31] St. Thomas would allow for evolution, or growth, to be a universal principle of *nature*, but not of all being universally. Cf. Reply to Objection 2.

[32] This objection is very important for it expresses a common misunderstanding of "existence" and of St. Thomas' identification of God ('s essence) with existence: the false notion that existence is the most empty and abstract of concepts, since it has no finite, specific, determinate, formal perfection like dogginess or humanness. But that does not mean it has no perfection at all. In itself it has infinite perfection. Furthermore, it is not an abstract concept because it is not a concept at all, but is expressed in a judgment.

reason was that the ancient philosophers[33] considered only a material principle; and a material principle is most imperfect. For since matter as such is merely potential, the first material principle must be simply potential, and thus most imperfect. Now God is the first principle, not material, but in the order of efficient cause, which must be most perfect. For just as matter, as such, is merely potential, an agent, as such, is in the state of actuality. Hence, the first active principle must needs be most actual, and therefore most perfect; for a thing is perfect in proportion to its state of actuality, because we call that perfect which lacks nothing of the mode of its perfection.

Reply Obj. 1. As Gregory says (*Moral.* v, 26, 29): *Though our lips can only stammer, we yet chant the high things of God.* For that which is not made is improperly called perfect. Nevertheless because created things are then called perfect, when from potentiality they are brought into actuality, this word *perfect* signifies whatever is not wanting in actuality, whether this be by way of perfection, or not.[34]

Reply Obj. 2. The material principle which with us is found to be imperfect, cannot be absolutely primal; but must be preceded by something perfect.[35] For seed, though it be the principle of animal life reproduced through seed, has previous to it, the animal or plant from which it came. Because, previous to that which is potential, must be that which is actual; since a potential being can only be reduced into act by some being already actual.

Reply Obj. 3. Existence is the most perfect of all things, for it is compared to all things as that by which they are made actual; for nothing has actuality except so far as it exists. Hence existence is

---

[33] These are the pre-Socratics as interpreted by Aristotle in Book Alpha of the *Metaphysics*—e.g., Thales' "water", Anaximander's "air", Heraclitus' "fire", Anaxagoras' "seeds".

[34] God is not literally "perfect" (*per-factum*, completely made) because what is not made at all cannot be perfectly made. One of the two features of "perfection" in creatures is properly predicated of God, viz., actuality, but the other is not, viz., being made perfect.

[35] In terms of the following diagram, St. Thomas affirms A, B1, and B4. He does not affirm B2 or B3, as philosophies of universal evolutionism do, but he could do so if the evolution were preceded by generation (A) and an already-actual First Cause (1).

that which actuates all things, even their forms.[36] Therefore it is not compared to other things as the receiver is to the received; but rather as the received to the receiver. When therefore I speak of the existence of man, or horse, or anything else, existence is considered a formal principle, and as something received; and not as that which exists.

SECOND ARTICLE

Whether the Perfections of All Things Are in God?

I answer that, All created perfections are in God.[37] Hence He is spoken of as universally perfect, because He lacks not (says the Commentator, *Metaph.* v) any excellence which may be found in any genus. This may be seen from two considerations. First, because whatever perfection exists in an effect must be found in the effective cause. . . . Secondly, from what has been already proved, God is existence itself, of itself subsistent (Q. 3, A. 4). Consequently, He must contain within Himself the whole perfection of being. . . .

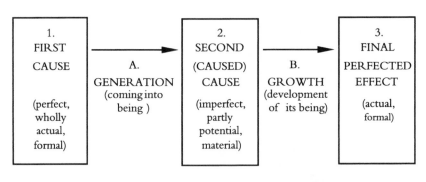

B1: individual
B2: species
B3: cosmos
B4: history of philosophy

[36] See (a) the diagram in note 17, (b) note 32, and (c) the next Article in the *Summa* to properly understand *esse* in St. Thomas.

[37] Cf. St. Anselm's *Proslogion*, the last two chapters, for an immensely moving and practical treatment of this truth.

THIRD ARTICLE

Whether Any Creature Can Be Like God?

Objection 2. . . . Likeness implies comparison. But there can be no comparison between things in a different *genus*. Therefore neither can there be any likeness. Thus we do not say that sweetness is like whiteness. But no creature is in the same *genus* as God: since God is no *genus*, as shown above (Q. 3, A. 5). Therefore no creature is like God. . . .

Objection 4. . . . Among like things there is mutual likeness; for like is like to like. If therefore any creature is like God, God will be like some creature, which is against what is said by Isaias: *To whom have you likened God* (40:18)?

On the contrary, It is written: *Let us make man to our image and likeness* (Gen 1:26), and: *When He shall appear we shall be like to Him* (1 Jn 3:2).

I answer that, . . . since every agent reproduces itself so far as it is an agent, and everything acts according to the manner of its form, the effect must in some way resemble the form of the agent. If therefore the agent is contained in the same species as its effect, there will be a likeness in form between that which makes and that which is made, according to the same formality of the species; as man reproduces man. If, however, the agent and its effect are not contained in the same species, there will be a likeness, but not according to the formality of the same species; as things generated by the sun's heat may be in some sort spoken of as like the sun, not as though they received the form of the sun in its specific likeness, but in its generic likeness. Therefore if there is an agent not contained in any *genus*, its effects will still more distantly reproduce the form of the agent, not, that is, so as to participate in the likeness of the agent's form according to the same specific or generic formality, but only according to some sort of analogy; as existence is common to all. In this way all created things, so far as they are beings, are like God as the first and universal principle of all being.[38] . . .

---

[38] If the cause and the effect share the same species, there is specific likeness, and the only differences between the two are accidental, not specific (essential). If the cause and the effect share the same genus but not

Reply Obj. 2. God is not related to creatures as though belonging to a different *genus*, but as transcending every *genus*, and as the principle of all *genera*.[39]. . .

Reply Obj. 4. Although it may be admitted that creatures are in some sort like God, it must nowise be admitted that God is like creatures: because, as Dionysius says (*Div. Nom.* ix): *A mutual likeness may be found between things of the same order, but not between a cause and that which is caused.* For, we say that a statue is like a man, but not conversely; so also a creature can be spoken of as in some sort like God; but not that God is like a creature.

---

the same species, there is generic likeness, and the differences between them are specific (essential), i.e., differences between two species, but not generic (not differences between two genera). Finally, if the cause and the effect do not even share the same genus (which is the case with Creator and creatures), there is an even greater difference between them, for there is not even a generic likeness. The only likeness is then an analogy of being: we *have* being and God *is* being.

[39] Since God is in no genus, no general class at all, but transcends all genera, He therefore transcends all creatures *more* than any creature in one genus can transcend any creature in another genus. But He is also immanent for the same reason that He is transcendent: viz., He is not in a genus, but is the principle (source) of all genera. A parallel: existence is not any essence at all, it transcends all essence; therefore it can be the actualization of all essences, somewhat as light, which is no color, can be with and actualize and reveal all colors.

Question 5

Of Goodness in General[40]

FIRST ARTICLE

Whether Goodness Differs Really from Being?

On the contrary, Augustine says (*De Doctr. Christ.* i. 42) that, *inasmuch as we exist we are good.*

I answer that, Goodness and being are really the same, and differ only in idea; which is clear from the following argument. The essence of goodness consists in this, that it is in some way desirable.[41] Hence the Philosopher says (*Ethic.* i): *Goodness is what all desire.* Now it is clear that a thing is desirable only in so far as it is perfect; for all desire their own perfection. But everything is perfect so far as it is actual. Therefore it is clear that a thing is perfect so far as it exists; for it is existence that makes all things actual, as is clear from the foregoing (Q. 3, A. 4; Q. 4, A. 1). Hence it is clear that goodness and being are the same really. But goodness presents the aspect of desirableness, which being does not present.[42]. . .

---

[40] This question is preliminary to the question of the goodness of God (Question 6). Goodness is one of the five "transcendentals", or universal properties of all being: all that is, is something, is one, is good, is true, and is beautiful.

[41] N.b.: the (objectively) desirable is not necessarily the same as the (subjectively) desired; real needs are not identical to felt wants.

[42] I.e., whatever is, is good (desirable) in some way (see I, 5, 3). "Good" adds nothing to the content of "being" not already in that content, but adds only a relation to a desiring will.

SECOND ARTICLE

Whether Goodness Is Prior in Idea to Being?

I answer that, In idea being is prior to goodness. For the meaning signified by the name of a thing is that which the mind conceives of the thing and intends by the word that stands for it. Therefore, that is prior in idea, which is first conceived by the intellect. Now the first thing conceived by the intellect is being;[43] because everything is knowable only inasmuch as it is in actuality. Hence, being is the proper object of the intellect, and is primarily intelligible; as sound is that which is primarily audible. Therefore in idea being is prior to goodness. . . .

THIRD ARTICLE

Whether Every Being Is Good?

On the contrary, Every being that is not God, is God's creature. Now every creature of God is good (1 Tim 4:4): and God is the greatest good. Therefore every being is good.

I answer that, Every being, as being, is good. For all being, as being, has actuality and is in some way perfect; since every act implies some sort of perfection; and perfection implies desirability and goodness, as is clear from A. 1. Hence it follows that every being as such is good.[44]. . .

---

[43] As an explicit idea, "being" is the highest, hardest, and last: the mind's Ultima Thule. As an implicit idea, "being" is the least, easiest, and first idea, the mind's preliminary, confused notion, the infant's "buzzing, blooming confusion". The first certainty is that there *is something* there.

[44] This article is a good example of the difference between the kind of argument St. Thomas uses in his *"On the contrary"*, viz., an argument from authority, and the kind of argument he uses in the *"I answer that"*, viz., a rational demonstration. (The demonstration is the same as the one in I, 5, 1: Being = actuality = perfection = desirability = goodness.)

FOURTH ARTICLE

Whether Goodness Has the Aspect of a Final Cause?

Objection 1. It seems that goodness has not the aspect of a final cause, but rather of the other causes. For, as Dionysius says (*Div. Nom.* iv), *Goodness is praised as beauty.* But beauty has the aspect of a formal cause. Therefore goodness has the aspect of a formal cause.

Objection 2. Further, goodness is self-diffusive; for Dionysius says (*loc. cit.*) that goodness is that whereby all things subsist, and are. But to be self-giving implies the aspect of an efficient cause. Therefore goodness has the aspect of an efficient cause.

Objection 3. Further, Augustine says (*De Doctr. Christ.* i, 31) that *we exist, because God is good.* But we owe our existence to God as the efficient cause. Therefore goodness implies the aspect of an efficient cause.

On the contrary, The Philosopher says (*Physic.* ii) that *that is to be considered as the end and the good of other things, for the sake of which something is.* Therefore goodness has the aspect of a final cause.

I answer that, Since goodness is that which all things desire, and since this has the aspect of an end, it is clear that goodness implies the aspect of an end. . . .

Reply Obj. 1. Beauty and goodness in a thing are identical fundamentally; for they are based upon the same thing, namely, the form; and consequently goodness is praised as beauty.[45] But they differ logically, for goodness properly relates to the appetite (goodness being what all things desire[46]); and therefore it has the aspect of an end (the appetite being a kind of movement towards a thing). On the other hand, beauty relates to the cognitive faculty; for beautiful things are those which please when seen. Hence beauty consists in due proportion; for the senses delight in things duly proportioned, as in what is after their own kind—because even sense is a sort of reason, just as is every cognitive faculty. Now,

---

[45] Goodness is a kind of beauty: there is beauty in virtue, in effectiveness, and in the pleasant. Beauty is also a kind of goodness: beauty is a good to the eyes, and to the desires. Only in modern times has there been a sharp separation and even opposition between goodness and beauty in popular thinking and culture: artists are expected to be immoral social outcasts and virtuous people are expected to be hokey, graceless nerds.

[46] Cf. I, 6, 1, Reply 2.

since knowledge is by assimilation, and similarity relates to form, beauty properly belongs to the nature of a formal cause.

Reply Obj. 2. Goodness is described as self-diffusive in the sense that an end is said to move.[47]

Reply Obj. 3. He who has a will is said to be good, so far as he has a good will; because it is by our will that we employ whatever powers we may have. Hence a man is said to be good, not by his good understanding; but by his good will.[48] Now the will relates to the end as to its proper object. Thus the saying, *we exist because God is good* has reference to the final cause. . . .

SIXTH ARTICLE

Whether Goodness Is Rightly Divided into the Virtuous, the Useful, and the Pleasant?[49]

I answer that, . . . in the movement of the appetite, the thing desired that terminates the movement of the appetite relatively, as a means by which something tends towards another, is called the useful; but that sought after as the last thing absolutely terminating the movement of the appetite, as a thing towards which for its own sake the appetite tends, is called the virtuous; for the virtuous is that which is desired for its own sake; but that which terminates the movement of the appetite in the form of rest in the thing desired, is called the pleasant. . . .

---

[47] I.e., not to move itself but to move other things to itself by being attractive.

[48] N.b.: Kant was not the first to understand this (cf. the beginning of *The Foundations of the Metaphysic of Morals*). St. Thomas clearly distinguishes moral virtues from intellectual virtues, but includes both under "virtues", unlike Kant, who limits "good in itself" to "a good *will*".

[49] "The virtuous" (*bonum honestum*) means the right, the intrinsically valuable, the fitting and proper. The thesis that there are only these three kinds of good is radical and practical, for it means that there are only three reasons why anyone should ever do anything: because it is morally virtuous, practically necessary, or fun. How much of what we do is not good by this standard? (E.g., doing things just because "everyone is doing it", or because it is "expected".) St. Thomas' classification of goods is a philosophical justification for a wonderful simplification of our lives.

Question 6

The Goodness of God

Whether God Is Good?

Objection 2. . . . The good is what all things desire. But all things do not desire God, because all things do not know Him; and nothing is desired unless it is known. Therefore to be good does not belong to God. . . .

Reply Obj. 2. All things, by desiring their own perfection, desire God Himself, inasmuch as the perfections of all things are so many similitudes of the divine being; as appears from what is said above (Q. 4, A. 3). And so of those things which desire God, some know Him as He is Himself, and this is proper to the rational creature; others know some participation of His goodness, and this belongs also to sensible knowledge; others have a natural desire without knowledge, as being directed to their ends by a higher intelligence.[50] . . .

---

[50] A whole cosmic vision, now lost, is implied here. Of course, acorns do not consciously desire God when they desire to grow into oak trees, because acorns' desire is not conscious. But it *is* a kind of desire, a determinate movement from within, and therefore a desire for something good, and therefore a desire for that which God is. Why is it so unfamiliar and even shocking to the modern mind to admit that acorns desire God? Perhaps because we do not naturally look at the thing acorns desire (the perfection of being an oak tree) as a reflection or similitude of the divine being; or perhaps because we look at desire as only a conscious, human thing and not as present in all living things. But even a particle of inanimate matter "desires" and "loves" (is attracted to) another particle. Gravity is very low-level love; love is very high-level gravity.

THIRD ARTICLE

Whether to Be Essentially Good Belongs to God Alone?

I answer that, God alone is good essentially. For everything is called good according to its perfection. Now perfection of a thing is threefold: first, according to the constitution of its own being; secondly, in respect of any accidents being added as necessary for its perfect operation; thirdly, perfection consists in the attaining to something else as the end. . . . This triple perfection belongs to no creature by its own essence; it belongs to God only, in Whom alone essence is existence; in Whom there are no accidents; since whatever belongs to others accidentally belongs to Him essentially; . . . and He is not directed to anything else as to an end, but is Himself the last end of all things. Hence it is manifest that God alone has every kind of perfection by His own essence; therefore He Himself alone is good essentially. . . .

FOURTH ARTICLE

Whether All Things Are Good by the Divine Goodness?

On the contrary, All things are good, inasmuch as they have being. But they are not called beings through the divine being [act of existing], but through their own being: therefore all things are not good by the divine goodness, but by their own goodness.[51] . . .

I answer that, . . . Everything is therefore called good from the divine goodness, as from the first exemplary effective and final principle of all goodness. Nevertheless, everything is called good by reason of the similitude of the divine goodness belonging to it, which is formally its own goodness, whereby it is denominated good. And so of all things there is one goodness, and yet many goodnesses.[52] . . .

---

[51] Note how St. Thomas relates everything to *being*. Note also how he carefully preserves the ontological rights of creatures.

[52] Note how St. Thomas' mind balances likenesses and differences, the one and the many, divine transcendence and divine immanence. All truths are set out in their proper order, place, balance, and relations.

Question 7

The Infinity of God

Whether God Is Infinite?

I answer that, All the ancient philosophers attribute infinitude to the first principle, as is said (*Physic.* iii), and with reason; for they considered that things flow forth infinitely from the first principle. But because some erred concerning the nature of the first principle, as a consequence they erred also concerning its infinity; forasmuch as they asserted that matter was the first principle; consequently they attributed to the first principle a material infinity, to the effect that some infinite body was the first principle of things.

We must consider therefore that a thing is called infinite because it is not finite. Now matter is in a way made finite by form, and the form by matter. Matter indeed is made finite by form, inasmuch as matter, before it receives its form, is in potentiality to many forms; but on receiving a form, it is terminated by that one. Again, form is made finite by matter, inasmuch as form, considered in itself, is common to many; but when received in matter, the form is determined to this one particular thing. Now matter is perfected by the form by which it is made finite; therefore infinite as attributed to matter, has the nature of something imperfect; for it is as it were formless matter. On the other hand form is not made perfect by matter, but rather is contracted by matter; and hence the infinite, regarded on the part of the form not determined by matter, has the nature of something perfect. Now being is the most formal [actual] of all things, as appears from what is shown above (Q. 4, A. 1, *Obj. 3*). Since therefore the divine being is not a being received in anything, but He is His own subsistent being as was shown above (Q. 3, A. 4), it is clear that God Himself is infinite and perfect. . . .

SECOND ARTICLE

Whether Anything but God Can Be Essentially Infinite?

Objection 1. It seems that something else besides God can be essentially infinite. For the power of anything is proportioned to its essence. Now if the essence of God is infinite, His Power must also be infinite. Therefore He can produce an infinite effect, since the extent of a power is known by its effect. . . .

I answer that, Things other than God can be relatively infinite, but not absolutely infinite. For . . . those things, the forms of which are in matter, are absolutely finite, and in no way infinite. If, however, any created forms are not received into matter, but are self-subsisting, as some think is the case with the angels, these will be relatively infinite, inasmuch as such kinds of forms are not terminated, nor contracted by any matter. But because a created form thus subsisting has being [existence], and yet is not [by its essence] its own being [existence], it follows that its being [existence] is received and contracted to a determinate nature [essence]. Hence it cannot be absolutely infinite.[53]

Reply Obj. 1. It is against the nature of a made thing for its essence to be its existence; because subsisting being is not a created being; hence it is against the nature of a made thing to be absolutely infinite. Therefore, as God, although He has infinite power, cannot make a thing to be not made (for this would imply that two contradictories are true at the same time), so likewise He cannot make anything to be absolutely infinite. . . .

---

[53] Infinity is not a single, univocal absolute. The notion of relative infinities is a commonplace of modern mathematics. E.g., the number of all odd positive integers is infinite, but is only half the number of all positive integers, which is also infinite.

THIRD ARTICLE

Whether an Actually Infinite Magnitude Can Exist?[54]

On the contrary, Every body has a surface. But every body which has a surface is finite; because surface is the term of a finite body. Therefore all bodies are finite. The same applies both to surface and to a line. Therefore nothing is infinite in magnitude. . . .

FOURTH ARTICLE

Whether an Infinite Multitude Can Exist?

I answer that, . . . it is impossible for an actually infinite multitude to exist, even accidentally. But a potentially infinite multitude is possible; because the increase of multitude follows upon the division of magnitude; since the more a thing is divided, the greater number of things result. . . .

---

[54] In this article and the next, the infinity of God is distinguished from two false infinities which the human imagination easily believes: infinite magnitude (size, in space) and infinite multitude (actual number).

Question 8

The Existence of God in Things[55]

FIRST ARTICLE

Whether God Is in All Things?

Objection 1. It seems that God is not in all things. For what is above all things is not in all things. But God is above all, according to the Psalm (112:4), *The Lord is high above all nations*, etc. Therefore God is not in all things.[56]

Objection 2. Further, what is in anything is thereby contained. Now God is not contained by things, but rather does He contain them. Therefore God is not in things; but things are rather in Him. Hence Augustine says (*Octog. Tri. Quaest., qu.* 20), that *in Him things are, rather than He is in any place.*

Objection 3. Further, the more powerful an agent is, the more extended is its action. But God is the most powerful of all agents. Therefore His action can extend to things which are far removed from Him; nor is it necessary that He should be in all things.

Objection 4. Further, the demons are beings. But God is not in the demons; for there is no fellowship between light and darkness (2 Cor 6:14). Therefore God is not in all things.

---

[55] The previous question explored God's transcendence and difference from all things: Christianity is not pantheism. This question explores God's *presence* in all things: Christianity is not deism either.

[56] Objection 1 assumes, in effect (in the second sentence) that deism and pantheism are the only two possibilities, because it works within sensory-imaginative categories of "inside" and "outside" (or "above"). The Reply interprets these two prepositions metaphysically rather than physically. The same is true of Objection and Reply 2.

On the contrary, A thing is wherever it operates.[57] But God operates in all things, according to Isaiah 26:12, *Lord . . . Thou hast wrought all our works in* [Vulg., *for*] *us.* Therefore God is in all things.

I answer that, God is in all things; not, indeed, as part of their essence, nor as an accident; but as an agent is present to that upon which it works. For an agent must be joined to that wherein it acts immediately, and touch it by its power; hence it is proved in *Physic.* vii that the thing moved and the mover must be joined together. Now since God is very being by His own essence, created being must be His proper effect; as to ignite is the proper effect of fire. Now God causes this effect in things not only when they first begin to be, but as long as they are preserved in being;[58] as light is caused in the air by the sun as long as the air remains illuminated. Therefore as long as a thing has being, God must be present to it, according to its mode of being. But being is innermost in each thing and most fundamentally inherent in all things since it is formal [actual] in respect of everything found in a thing, as was shown above (Q. 7, A. 1). Hence it must be that God is in all things, and innermostly.[59]

---

[57] We, too! Our being is not confined to our skin—that is epidermiolatry, idolatry of the epidermis—but is like a magnetic field. The footnoted sentence is the essence of Einstein's Field Theory of matter too, as vs. Newton's notion of matter as existing only inside its surface boundaries. Einstein defined a physical body as existing wherever it produced an effect.

[58] This sharply distinguishes Christianity from deism. A carpenter does not cause the very being of the house he builds, only its form; therefore when he stops working, the house continues to exist. But if God stopped "working" (cf. Jn 5:17), the very existence of all things would perish, for this is His work.

[59] Gilson calls this "the Great Syllogism":
  1. Being is innermost in each thing;
  2. But God is Being (His essence is existence);
  3. Therefore God is innermost in each thing.
Nothing is more inner, present, and intimate to every being than God. God activates every being from within, so to speak. N.b.: God can be thus supremely present and immanent only because He is supremely

Reply Obj. 1. God is above all things by the excellence of His nature; nevertheless, He is in all things as the cause of the being of all things; as was shown above in this article.

Reply Obj. 2. Although corporeal things are said to be in another as in that which contains them, nevertheless spiritual things contain those things in which they are; as the soul contains the body.[60] Hence also God is in things as containing them: nevertheless by a certain similitude to corporeal things, it is said that all things are in God; inasmuch as they are contained by Him.

Reply Obj. 3. No action of an agent, however powerful it may be, acts at a distance, except through a medium. But it belongs to the great power of God that He acts immediately in all things. Hence nothing is distant from Him, as if it could be without God in itself. But things are said to be distant from God by the unlikeness to Him in nature or grace; as also He is above all by the excellence of His own nature.[61]

Reply Obj. 4. In the demons there is their nature which is from God, and also the deformity of sin which is not from Him; therefore, it is not to be absolutely conceded that God is in the demons, except with the addition, *inasmuch as they are beings*. But in things not deformed in their nature, we must say absolutely that God is.

---

transcendent, i.e., He is pure, infinite existence, not existence limited by a finite essence. If He were one of many essences, He could not be present in opposite essences. Blue cannot be present in red because it is a different essence, but colorless light can be present in red and blue and all colors. God (and existence) is like light in this analogy. Cf. also Article 2.

[60] A remote physical analogy might be the sea being "in" a sunken ship. St. Thomas' analogy is better: the body is *in* the soul rather than vice versa, as we usually think. (How materialistic our usual thinking is!) Even Descartes was victimized by this sensory-imaginative picture-thinking when he struggled with the mind-body problem. He thought, for a time, that the soul might be "in" the pineal gland! And we still often think the mind is "in" the brain. That is like thinking a computer programmer is "in" his hardware. He transcends even his software, how much more his hardware!

[61] God is transcendent in *nature*, not in *place*. He is here, now, present to this place and time and to all places and times. God is transcendent in His *nature* and immanent in His *presence*.

SECOND ARTICLE

Whether God Is Everywhere?

On the contrary, It is written, *I fill heaven and earth* (Jer 23:24).

I answer that, . . . God fills every place; not, indeed, like a body, for a body is said to fill place inasmuch as it excludes the co-presence of another body; whereas by God being in a place, others are not thereby excluded from it; indeed, by the very fact that He gives being to the things that fill every place, He Himself fills every place.[62]. . .

THIRD ARTICLE

Whether God Is Everywhere by Essence, Presence, and Power?

I answer that, God is said to be in a thing in two ways;[63] in one way after the manner of an efficient cause; and thus He is in all things created by Him; in another way He is in things as the object of operation is in the operator; and this is proper to the operations of the soul, according as the thing known is in the one who knows; and the thing desired in the one desiring. In this second way God is especially in the rational creature, which knows and loves Him actually or habitually. And because the rational creature possesses this prerogative by grace, as will be shown later (Q. 12), He is said to be thus in the saints by grace.

---

[62] The famous question about how many angels could dance on the head of a pin was never debated in the Middle Ages, but it could have been, for it is a very good question, and those who use it to mock medieval philosophy show who the pinheads really are. The question concerns the difference between matter and spirit, and their different ways of being present. Two bodies cannot be present at the same time and place; they are essentially competitive, like all material things (e.g., money); while two minds or spirits *can* be co-present, and spirit can be co-present with matter, as God and the world, and (in a different way) my soul and my body.

[63] Cf. C. S. Lewis, *Miracles*, chap. 11, contrasting the complexity of Christianity with the simplicity of pantheism: "God is present in a good many modes: not present in matter as He is in man, not present in all men as in some; not present in any other man as in Jesus."

But how He is in other things created by Him, may be considered from human affairs. A king, for example, is said to be in the whole kingdom by his power, although he is not everywhere present. Again a thing is said to be by its presence in other things which are subject to its inspection; as things in a house are said to be present to anyone, who nevertheless may not be in substance in every part of the house. Lastly a thing is said to be by way of substance or essence in that place in which its substance may be.

Now there were some (the Manichees) who said that spiritual and incorporeal things were subject to the divine power; but that visible and corporeal things were subject to the power of a contrary principle. Therefore against these it is necessary to say that God is in all things by His power.

But others, though they believed that all things were subject to the divine power, still did not allow that divine providence extended to these inferior bodies, and in the person of these it is said, *He walketh about the poles of the heavens; and He doth not consider our things* (Job 22:14). Against these it is necessary to say that God is in all things by His presence.

Further, others said that, although all things are subject to God's providence, still all things are not immediately created by God; but that He immediately created the first creatures, and these created the others. Against these it is necessary to say that He is in all things by His essence.

Therefore, God is in all things by His power, inasmuch as all things are subject to His power; He is by His presence in all things, as all things are bare and open to His eyes; He is in all things by His essence, inasmuch as He is present to all as the cause of their being. . . .

Question 9

The Immutability of God

Whether God Is Altogether Immutable?

Objection 3. . . . To approach and to recede signify movement. But these are said of God in Scripture, *Draw nigh to God, and He will draw nigh to you* (James 4:8). Therefore God is mutable.[64]

On the contrary, It is written, *I am the Lord, and I change not* (Mal 3:6).

I answer that, From what precedes, it is shown that God is altogether immutable.

First, because it was shown above that there is some first being, whom we call God; and that this first being must be pure act, without the admixture of any potentiality, for the reason that, absolutely, potentiality is posterior to act. Now everything which is in any way changed, is in some way in potentiality. Hence it is evident that it is impossible for God to be in any way changeable.

Secondly, because everything which is moved, remains as it was in part, and passes away in part; as what is moved from whiteness to blackness, remains the same as to substance; thus in everything which is moved, there is some kind of composition to be found. But it has been shown above (Q. 3, A. 7) that in God there is no composition, for He is altogether simple. Hence it is manifest that God cannot be moved.

Thirdly, because everything which is moved acquires something

---

[64] The main *religious* argument for modern "process theology" is that a mutable and changing God is necessary to theologically ground the experienced changing relationship with God that this verse designates. It is alleged that an immutable God would make such a real, lived relationship of change impossible.

by its movement, and attains to what it had not attained previously. But since God is infinite, comprehending in Himself all the plenitude of perfection of all being, He cannot acquire anything new, nor extend Himself to anything whereto He was not extended previously. Hence movement in no way belongs to Him.[65]. . .

Reply Obj. 3. These things are said of God in Scripture metaphorically. For as the sun is said to enter a house, or to go out, according as its rays reach the house, so God is said to approach to us, or to recede from us, when we receive the influx of His goodness, or decline from Him.[66]

SECOND ARTICLE

Whether to Be Immutable Belongs to God Alone?

On the contrary, Augustine says (*De Nat. Boni.* i), *God alone is immutable; and whatever things He has made, being from nothing, are mutable.*

I answer that, God alone is altogether immutable; whereas, every creature is in some way mutable. . . . For all creatures before they existed, were possible, not by any created power, since no creature is eternal, but by the divine power alone, inasmuch as God could produce them into existence. Thus, as the production of a thing into existence depends on the will of God, so likewise it depends on His will that things should be preserved; for He does not preserve them otherwise than by ever giving them existence; hence if He took away His action from them, all things would be reduced to nothing,[67] as appears from Augustine (*Gen. ad lit.* iv. 12). Therefore as it was in the Creator's power to produce them before they existed in themselves; so likewise it is in the Creator's power when they exist in themselves to bring them to nothing. In this way therefore, by the power of another—namely, of God—they are mutable, inasmuch as they are producible from nothing by Him, and are by Him reducible from existence to non-existence. . . .

---

[65] As usual, the only recourse for one who would deny the conclusion (God's immutability) is to deny the premise (that God is actual, one, and infinite, not potential, compound, or finite).

[66] Thus the experience of a changing *relationship* is accounted for.

[67] Cf. I, 8, 1, and note 58.

Question 10

The Eternity of God

Whether This Is a Good Definition of Eternity,
"The Simultaneously-Whole and Perfect Possession
of Interminable Life"?[68]

I answer that, As we attain to the knowledge of simple things
[e.g., forms] by way of compound things [e.g., substances], so we
must reach to the knowledge of eternity by means of time, which is
nothing but the numbering of movement by *before* and *after*.[69] For
since succession occurs in every movement, and one part comes
after another, the fact that we reckon before and after in movement, makes us apprehend time, which is nothing else but the
measure of before and after in movement. Now in a thing bereft of
movement, which is always the same, there is no before and after.
As therefore the idea of time consists in the numbering of before
and after in movement; so likewise in the apprehension of the
uniformity of what is outside of movement, consists the idea of
eternity.

Further, those things are said to be measured by time which have
a beginning and an end in time, because in everything which is

---

[68] Cf. Boethius, *The Consolation of Philosophy*, Book V. Eternity is not
the same as immutability because immutability is only unending and
changeless but not simultaneous and without duration.

[69] St. Thomas here comes down on the side of Einsteinian relativity
of time rather than the Newtonian absolute time, in two ways: (1) time
is relative to movement rather than vice versa (cf. sentence 3); and
(2) time is the product of the mind measuring ("numbering", quanti-
fying) movement (sentence 1). Yet time is not wholly subjective and
determined by the mind for St. Thomas, as it is for Kant.

moved there is a beginning, and there is an end. But as whatever is wholly immutable can have no succession, so it has no beginning, and no end.

Thus eternity is known from two sources: first, because what is eternal is interminable—that is, has no beginning nor end (that is, no term either way); secondly, because eternity has no succession, being simultaneously whole. . . .

SECOND ARTICLE

Whether God Is Eternal?

Objection 4. . . . In eternity there is no present, past, nor future, since it is simultaneously whole; as was said in the preceding article. But words denoting present, past, and future time are applied to God in Scripture. Therefore God is not eternal. . . .

Reply Obj. 1. The *now* that stands still, is said to make eternity according to our apprehension. As the apprehension of time is caused in us by the fact that we apprehend the flow of the *now*; so the apprehension of eternity is caused in us by our apprehending the *now* standing still.[70]. . .

Reply Obj. 4. . . . His eternity includes all times; not as if He Himself were altered through present, past, and future.[71]

---

[70] N.b.: only *now* is actual, whether the "now flowing" (*nunc fluens*) or the "now standing still" (*nunc stans*). The past is no longer actual, the future is not yet actual. The "now flowing" (the present moment in the life of a temporal creature) is more akin to eternity (the "now standing still") than it is akin to past or future. Eternity touches time only in the present.

[71] We *think* of eternity as negative, as *excluding* time (for "e-ternal" means, after all, "*not*-temporal"); but in objective fact, God's eternity is positive and *includes* all times, for it can lack nothing actual, positive, and perfect that time contains. A remote parallel: the mind of an author contains, at once, all his characters and the events of his plot.

THIRD ARTICLE

Whether to Be Eternal Belongs to God Alone?

On the contrary, Jerome says (*Ep. ad Damasum*, xv) that *God is the only one who has no beginning.* Now whatever has a beginning, is not eternal. Therefore God is the only one eternal.[72]. . .

FOURTH ARTICLE

Whether Eternity Differs from Time?

On the contrary, Eternity is simultaneously whole. But time has a *before* and an *after*. Therefore time and eternity are not the same thing.

I answer that, It is manifest that time and eternity are not the same. Some have founded this difference on the fact that eternity has neither beginning nor an end; whereas time has a beginning and an end. This, however, makes a merely accidental, and not an absolute difference; because, granted that time always was and always will be, according to the idea of those who think the movement of the heavens goes on for ever, there would yet remain a difference between eternity and time, as Boëthius says (*De Consol.* v), arising from the fact that eternity is simultaneously whole. . . .

---

[72] This teaching is distinctive to Judaism, Christianity, and Islam, with their doctrine of *creatio ex nihilo* (creation out of nothing). Plato, e.g., in the *Timaeus*, thought *four* things were eternal: the "Demiurge" (the efficient cause of the cosmos), the Forms (the formal causes), the spatial "receptacle" (matter, the material cause), and the Good (the final cause).

FIFTH ARTICLE

The Difference of Aeviternity[73] and Time

I answer that, Aeviternity differs from time, and from eternity, as the mean between them both. This difference is explained by some to consist in the fact that eternity has neither beginning nor end, aeviternity, a beginning but no end, and time both beginning and end. This difference, however, is but an accidental one. . . . This [aeviternity] appears in the heavenly bodies, the substantial being of which is unchangeable; and yet with unchangeable being they have changeableness of place.[74] The same applies to the angels, who have an unchangeable being as regards their nature with changeableness as regards choice; moreover they have changeableness of intelligence, of affections, and of places, in their own degree. Therefore these are measured by aeviternity, which is a mean between eternity and time. But the being that is measured by eternity is not changeable, nor is it annexed to change. In this way time has *before* and *after*; aeviternity in itself has no *before* and *after*, which can, however, be annexed to it; while eternity has neither *before* nor *after*, nor is it compatible with such at all. . . .

Reply Obj. 2. Aeviternity is simultaneously whole; yet it is not eternity, because *before* and *after* are compatible with it. . . .

---

[73] Aeviternity is the mode of existence or duration of angels. Medieval astronomy taught it was also the mode of existence of the changeless heavenly bodies.

[74] St. Thomas, like all thinkers, certainly including present ones such as the present writer and the present reader, occasionally failed to free himself from the intellectual fashions and scientific "authorities" of his day, e.g., the medieval astronomical authorities according to whom the heavenly bodies were unchangeable and composed of a radically different kind of matter (the "quintessence", or fifth essence, over and above earth, air, fire, and water). In effect, stars are here confused with angels.

Question 11

The Unity of God

FIRST ARTICLE

Whether One Adds Anything to Being?

On the contrary, Dionysius says (*Div. Nom.* 5, *ult.*): *Nothing which exists is not in some way one,* which would be false if *one* were an addition to *being,* in the sense of limiting it. Therefore *one* is not an addition to *being.*

I answer that, One does not add any reality to *being;* but is only a negation of division: for *one* means undivided *being.* . . . And hence it is that everything guards its unity as it guards its being. . . .

THIRD ARTICLE

Whether God Is One?

On the contrary, It is written, *Hear, O Israel, the Lord our God is one Lord* (Deut 6:4).

I answer that, It can be shown from these three sources that God is one. First from His simplicity. For it is manifest that the reason why any singular thing is *this particular thing* is because it cannot be communicated to [shared with] many: since that whereby Socrates is a man [human nature], can be communicated to many; whereas, what makes him this particular man, is only communicable to one. Therefore, if Socrates were a man by what makes him to be this particular man, as there cannot be many Socrates, so there could not in that way be many men. Now this belongs to God alone; for God Himself is His own nature, as was shown above (Q. 3, A. 3). Therefore, in the very same way God is God, and He is this God. Impossible is it therefore that many Gods should exist.

Secondly, this is proved from the infinity of His perfection. For it was shown above (Q. 4, A. 2) that God comprehends in Himself the whole perfection of being. If then many gods existed, they would necessarily differ from each other. Something therefore would belong to one, which did not belong to another. And if this were a privation, one of them would not be absolutely perfect; but if a perfection, one of them would be without it. So it is impossible for many gods to exist. . . .

Thirdly, this is shown from the unity of the world. For all things that exist are seen to be ordered to each other since some serve others. But things that are diverse do not harmonize in the same order, unless they are ordered thereto by one. . . .

FOURTH ARTICLE

Whether God Is Supremely One?

On the contrary, Bernard says (*De Consid.* v): *Among all things called one, the unity of the Divine Trinity holds the first place.*[75] . . .

---

[75] N.b.: surprisingly, it is the Trinity that is the *most* unified! Far from God's trinity lessening His unity, it increases it; for the oneness of love, which is the glue that holds the Trinity together, is a closer and more perfect union than the oneness of mere quantitative, arithmetical oneness.

Question 12

How God Is Known by Us

FIRST ARTICLE

Whether Any Created Intellect Can See the Essence of God?

Objection 2. . . . Everything infinite, as such, is unknown. But God is infinite, as was shown above (Q. 7. A. 1). Therefore in Himself He is unknown.

On the contrary, It is written: *We shall see Him as He is* (1 Jn 2:2).

I answer that, Since everything is knowable according as it is actual, God, Who is pure act without any admixture of potentiality, is in Himself supremely knowable. But what is supremely knowable in itself, may not be knowable to a particular intellect, on account of the excess of the intelligible object above the intellect; as, for example, the sun, which is supremely visible, cannot be seen by the bat by reason of its excess of light.

Therefore some who considered this, held that no created intellect can see the essence of God. This opinion, however, is not tenable. For as the ultimate beatitude of man consists in the use of his highest function, which is the operation of the intellect; if we suppose that the created intellect could never see God, it would either never attain to beatitude,[76] or its beatitude would consist in something else beside God; which is opposed to faith. . . . Further the same opinion is also against reason. For there resides in every man a natural desire to know the cause of any effect which he sees; and thence arises wonder in men. But if the intellect of the rational

---

[76] N.b.: St. Thomas considers that alternative self-evidently impossible (contrast modern nihilism) for "no natural desire can be in vain". Man never attaining beatitude, his end, is to St. Thomas as absurd as rabbits never reproducing or deer never drinking or plants never growing or stones never falling.

creature could not reach so far as to the first cause of things, the natural desire would remain void.[77]

Hence it must be absolutely granted that the blessed see the essence of God. . . .

Reply Obj. 2. The infinity of matter not made perfect by form, is unknown in itself, because all knowledge comes by the form; whereas the infinity of the form not limited by matter, is in itself supremely known. God is Infinite in this way, and not in the first way.[78] . . .

THIRD ARTICLE

Whether the Essence of God Can Be Seen with the Bodily Eye?

Objection 2. Augustine says (*De Civ. Dei* xxix. 29); *Those eyes* [namely of the glorified] *will therefore have a greater power of sight, not so much to see more keenly, as some report of the sight of serpents or of eagles (for whatever acuteness of vision is possessed by these creatures, they can see only corporeal things) but to see even incorporeal things.* Now whoever can see incorporeal things, can be raised up to see God. Therefore the glorified eye can see God. . . .

Reply Obj. 2. Augustine speaks as one inquiring, and conditionally. This appears from what he says previously: *Therefore they will have an altogether different power* [*viz., the glorified eyes*]*, if they shall see that incorporeal nature*; and afterwards he explains this, saying: *It is very credible, that we shall so see the mundane bodies of the new heaven and the new earth, as to see most clearly God everywhere*

---

[77] N.b.: this "natural desire to know the First Cause" includes especially the desire to know the First *Final* Cause, the ultimate *purpose* of everything in the world and in our lives. The principle that "no natural desire is in vain" coupled with the truth that we have a natural desire for God seem to form a proof for God's existence. Cf. P. Kreeft, *Heaven, the Heart's Deepest Longing* (San Francisco: Ignatius Press, 1989), esp. Appendix A.

[78] Greek philosophers knew only the first kind of infinity. They therefore never thought of God as infinite. Aristotle came the closest with his notion of God as pure actuality with no potency or matter. Pantheism, ancient or modern, tends to think of God in this first way, as infinite matter, rather than as infinite form; thus its God is formless. Cf. C. S. Lewis, *Miracles*, chap. 11.

present, governing all corporeal things, not as we now see the invisible things of God as understood by what is made; but as when we see men among whom we live, living and exercising the functions of human life, we do not believe they live, but see it. Hence it is evident how the glorified eyes will see God, as now our eyes see the life of another. But life is not seen with the corporeal eye, as a thing in itself visible, but as the indirect object of the sense; which indeed is not known by sense, but at once, together with sense, by some other cognitive power.[79] But that the divine presence is known by the intellect immediately on the sight of, and through, corporeal things, happens from two causes—viz., from the perspicuity of the intellect, and from the refulgence of the divine glory infused into the body after its renovation. . . .

FOURTH ARTICLE

Whether Any Created Intellect by Its Natural Powers Can See the Divine Essence?

I answer that, It is impossible for any created intellect to see the essence of God by its own natural power. For knowledge is regulated according as the thing known is in the knower.[80] But the thing known is in the knower according to the mode of the knower.[81]

---

[79] This cuts across the usual dualism between abstract, rational argument and concrete sense experience. Our awareness of the *life* of another person already escapes that dualism, for life is not in itself visible, nor is it abstract and inferred by reason. The same applies to other people's *minds*. (Cf. Alvin Plantinga, *God and Other Minds*.) St. Thomas is saying here that we will probably see God *in* the concrete, bodily things in Heaven as we now see life in persons, or mind in speech, or happiness in a smile: by our "inner eye" ("some other cognitive power").

[80] As we shall see when we get to the Epistemology section of the *Summa*, St. Thomas' epistemology is very realistic compared with most modern epistemologies: instead of a *correspondence* between mind and object, he teaches a real presence. The thing known *is* (exists) in the knower, i.e., *the same form* exists first individuated by matter in the object and then abstracted from matter, as a universal, in the mind of the knower.

[81] Water in a bucket takes the shape and quantity of the bucket. A form

Hence the knowledge of every knower is ruled according to its own nature. If therefore the mode of anything's being exceeds the mode of the knower, it must result that the knowledge of that object is above the nature of the knower.[82]. . .

Reply Obj. 3. The sense of sight, as being altogether material, cannot be raised up to immateriality. But our intellect, or the angelic intellect, inasmuch as it is elevated above matter in its own nature, can be raised up above its own nature to a higher level by grace. The proof is, that sight cannot in any way know abstractedly what it knows concretely; for in no way can it perceive a nature except as this one particular nature; whereas our intellect is able to consider abstractedly what it knows concretely. Now although it knows things which have a form residing in matter, still it resolves the composite into both of these elements; and it considers the form separately by itself. Likewise, also, the intellect of an angel, although it naturally knows the concrete in any nature, still it is able to separate that existence by its intellect; since it knows that the thing itself is one thing, and its existence is another. Since therefore the created intellect is naturally capable of apprehending the concrete form, and the concrete being abstractedly, by way of a kind of resolution of parts; it can by grace be raised up to know separate subsisting substance, and separate subsisting existence.

FIFTH ARTICLE

Whether the Created Intellect Needs Any Created Light in Order to See the Essence of God?

Objection 2. . . . If God is seen through a medium, He is not seen in His essence. But if seen by any created light, He is seen through a medium. Therefore He is not seen in His essence. . . .

(e.g., red) in the mind takes the mode of existence of the mind: abstract and immaterial, not the mode of existence of red things: concrete and material. When we know the world, we give it a second, spiritual life in our mind. We "humanize" the world as God "divinizes" us. (The analogy is remote but real.)

[82] Therefore a worm cannot, by its nature, understand an ape; an ape, a man; the body, the soul; or man, God.

On the contrary, It is written: *In Thy light we shall see light* (Ps 35:10).

I answer that, Everything which is raised up to what exceeds its nature, must be prepared by some disposition above its nature. . . .

Reply Obj. 2. This light is required to see the divine essence, not as a similitude in which God is seen, but as a perfection of the intellect, strengthening it to see God. Therefore it may be said that this light is to be described not as a medium in which God is seen, but as one by which He is seen; and such a medium does not take away the immediate vision of God. . . .

SIXTH ARTICLE

Whether of Those Who See the Essence of God, One Sees More Perfectly Than Another?[83]

On the contrary, Eternal life consists in the vision of God, according to John 27:3: *This is eternal life, that they may know Thee the only true God,* etc. Therefore, if all saw the essence of God equally in eternal life, all would be equal; the contrary to which is declared by the Apostle: *Star differs from star in glory* (1 Cor 15:41).

I answer that, Of those who see the essence of God, one sees Him more perfectly than another . . . because one intellect will have a greater power or faculty to see God than another. The faculty of seeing God, however, does not belong to the created intellect naturally, but is given to it by the light of glory, which establishes the intellect in a kind of *deiformity,* as appears from what is said above, in the preceding article.

Hence the intellect which has more of the light of glory will see God the more perfectly; and he will have a fuller participation of the light of glory who has more charity; because where there is the greater charity, there is the more desire; and desire in a certain degree makes the one desiring apt and prepared to receive the object desired. Hence he who possesses the more charity, will see God the more perfectly, and will be the more beatified.[84]. . .

---

[83] The thesis is unarguably biblical, but often comes as a great shock to many Americans whose real religion is Equality.

[84] N.b.: this is an intrinsic, natural, and necessary causality, not an

SEVENTH ARTICLE

Whether Those Who See the Essence of God Comprehend Him?

Reply Obj. 1. Comprehension is twofold: in one sense it is taken strictly and properly, according as something is included in the one comprehending; and thus in no way is God comprehended either by intellect, or in any other way; forasmuch as He is infinite and cannot be included in any finite being; so that no finite being can contain Him infinitely, in the degree of His own infinity. In this sense we now take comprehension. But in another sense *comprehension* is taken more largely as opposed to *non-attainment*; for he who attains to anyone is said to comprehend him when he attains to him. And in this sense God is comprehended by the blessed, according to the words, *I held him, and I will not let him go* (Song 3:4); in this sense also are to be understood the words quoted from the Apostle concerning comprehension. And in this way *comprehension* is one of the three prerogatives of the soul, responding to hope, as vision responds to faith, and fruition responds to charity. . . .

EIGHTH ARTICLE

Whether Those Who See the Essence of God See All in God?

Objection 4. . . . The rational creature naturally desires to know all things. Therefore, if in seeing God it does not know all things, its natural desire will not rest satisfied; thus, in seeing God it will not be fully happy; which is incongruous. Therefore, he who sees God knows all things.

On the contrary, The angels see the essence of God; and yet do not know all things. . . . No created intellect can comprehend God wholly, as shown above (A. 7). Therefore no created intellect in seeing God can know all that God does or can do, for this would be to comprehend His power. . . .

---

extrinsic, supernatural reward. Charity itself opens the eye of understanding: cf. Mt 5:8; Jn 7:17. In lesser things too: I know by twenty-eight years of teaching that love of the subject very powerfully increases understanding of it.

Reply Obj. 4. The natural desire of the rational creature is to know everything that belongs to the perfection of the intellect, namely, the species and genera of things and their types, and these everyone who sees the divine essence will see in God. But to know other singulars, their thoughts and their deeds does not belong to the perfection of the created intellect nor does its natural desire go out to these things;[85] neither, again, does it desire to know things that exist not as yet, but which God can call into being. Yet if God alone were seen, Who is the fount and principle of all being and of all truth, He would so fill the natural desire of knowledge that nothing else would be desired, and the seer would be completely beatified. Hence Augustine says (*Confess.* v): *Unhappy the man who knoweth all these* (that is, all creatures) *and knoweth not Thee! but happy whoso knoweth Thee although he know not these. And whoso knoweth both Thee and them is not the happier for them, but for Thee alone.*[86] . . .

ELEVENTH ARTICLE

Whether Anyone in This Life Can See the Essence of God?

Objection 3. . . . That wherein we know all other things, and whereby we judge of other things, is known in itself to us. But even now we know all things in God; for Augustine says (*Confess.* viii): *If we both see that what you say is true, and we both see that what I say is true; where, I ask, do we see this? neither I in thee, nor thou in me;*

---

[85] We may think that in Heaven we would want to know everything, even the details of the intrigues of King Henry VIII; but our present curiosities are not to be taken as the measure of our real and natural needs to know.

[86] The reader is invited and challenged to read this quotation two or three times and ask himself whether he really believes it is true, and what a revolution in his life it would make if he did. In his sermon "On the Pure Love of God", St. Augustine asks his congregation to test themselves by the following thought experiment: Suppose God offered you anything and everything you wanted, anything you could imagine, with nothing forbidden, nothing sinful, nothing impossible—but added this one "catch": "—but you will never see My face". Would you accept this "deal"?

but both of us in the very incommutable truth itself above our minds.[87] He also says (*De Vera Relig.* xxx) that, *We judge of all things according to the divine truth*; and (*De Trin.* xii) that, *it is the duty of reason to judge of these corporeal things according to the incorporeal and eternal ideas; which unless they were above the mind could not be incommutable.* Therefore even in this life we see God Himself. . . .

On the contrary, It is written, *Man shall not see Me, and live* (Ex 33:20), and a gloss upon this says: *In this mortal life God can be seen by certain images, but not by the likeness itself of His own nature.*

I answer that, God cannot be seen in His essence by a mere human being, except he be separated from this mortal life. The reason is, because, as was said above (A. 4), the mode of knowledge follows the mode of the nature of the knower. But our soul, as long as we live in this life, has its being in corporeal matter;[88] hence naturally it knows only what has a form in matter, or what can be known by such a form. Now it is evident that the divine essence cannot be known through the nature of material things.[89] For it was shown above (AA. 2, 9) that the knowledge of God by means of any created similitude is not the vision of His essence. Hence it is impossible for the soul of man in this life to see the essence of God. . . .

Reply Obj. 3. All things are said to be seen in God and all things are judged in Him, because by the participation of His light we know and judge all things; for the light of natural reason itself is a participation of the divine light; as likewise we are said to see and judge of sensible things in the sun, that is, by the sun's light. Hence Augustine says (*Soliloq.* i. 8), *The lessons of instruction can only be seen as it were by their own sun*, namely God. As therefore in order to see a sensible object it is not necessary to see the substance of the sun, so

---

[87] This is Augustine's epistemological argument for the existence of God (as eternal Truth) from our experience of knowing. For the reason why St. Thomas does not use this argument, see I, 2, 1, Objection and Reply 3.

[88] This does not mean that the soul's essence is material, but that it exists as the form of a material body.

[89] God's *existence* can be known by deduction from sensory data, but not God's *essence*.

in like manner to see any intelligible object, it is not necessary to see the essence of God.[90] . . .

Whether God Can Be Known in This Life by Natural Reason?[91]

On the contrary, It is written (Rom 1:19), *That which is known of God,* namely, what can be known of God by natural reason, *is manifest in them.*

I answer that, Our natural knowledge begins from sense. Hence our natural knowledge can go as far as it can be led by sensible things. But our mind cannot be led by sense so far as to see the essence of God; because the sensible effects of God do not equal the power of God as their cause. Hence from the knowledge of sensible

---

[90] "In Thy light we see light" (Ps 36:9), but we do *not* see God's light itself, as we see the mirror in which we see other things. In terms of St. Thomas' metaphor, we cannot see the sun itself; if we stare directly at it, we will be blinded.

N.b.: there is a strong Platonic and Augustinian dimension to St. Thomas in addition to his more generally recognized Aristotelianism. "Participation" is a typical Platonic theme, especially intellectual participation; and "divine illumination" is a typical Augustinian theme. Both find their place in St. Thomas' philosophy. Platonic *anamnesis*, transformed by Augustine's Christianity into divine illumination, is further transformed by St. Thomas' Aristotelianism into "the first principle of knowledge".

[91] N.b.: St. Thomas is severely agnostic about how adequately we can know God, for all our knowledge depends on a very thin base of sense experience and intellectual abstraction and deduction from it; yet from this narrow foundation, he constructs a remarkably high building, with many stories. The "*I answer that*" mentions at least five: (1) His existence, (2) His relation to creatures as their cause, (3) attributes which the First Cause must have (St. Thomas deduces quite a few in I, 3–10), (4) how He differs from creatures, what He is *not*; and (5) that these differences, though expressed in negative words (since the meanings of these words come from creatures, which God is *not*) are nevertheless due to God's positive perfections.

things the whole power of God cannot be known; nor therefore can His essence be seen. But because they are His effects and depend on their cause, we can be led from them so far as to know of God [1] *whether He exists*, and to know of Him [2] what must necessarily belong to Him, as the first cause of all things, exceeding all things caused by Him.

Hence we know [3] His relationship with creatures so far as to be the cause of them all; also [4] that creatures differ from Him, inasmuch as He is not in any way part of what is caused by Him; and [5] that creatures are not removed from Him by reason of any defect on His part, but because He superexceeds them all. . . .

Question 13

The Names of God

After the consideration of those things which belong to the divine knowledge, we now proceed to the consideration of the divine names. For everything is named by us according to our knowledge of it.

Whether a Name Can Be Given to God?

I answer that, Since according to the Philosopher (*Peri Herm.* i), words are signs of ideas, and ideas the similitude of things,[92] it is evident that words relate to the meaning of things signified through the medium of the intellectual conception. It follows therefore that we can give a name to anything in as far as we can understand it. Now it was shown above (Q. 12, AA. 11, 12) that in this life we cannot see the essence of God; but we know God from creatures as their principle, and also by way of excellence and remotion.[93] In

---

[92] Note this simple, commonsensical, and realistic theory of language: language is not a world of its own (as in Derrida) but the expression of the world of thought, which in turn is also not a world of its own (as in Kant) but the expression of the real world. Note also how St. Thomas always prefers to think and speak concretely and specifically rather than abstractly and generically; thus he says "words are signs of ideas, and ideas the similitude of things" rather than "language expresses thought and thought expresses reality". Note also the close connection and distinction between the three meanings of *logos* here: cf. n. 3.

[93] I.e., we know God (1) as "principle" (cause) of creatures, (2) as more "excellent" (perfect) than creatures, (3) and by removing from our concept of God all qualities of creatures that are due to imperfections (e.g.,

this way therefore He can be named by us from creatures, yet not so that the name which signifies Him expresses the divine essence in itself. . . .

SECOND ARTICLE

Whether Any Name Can Be Applied to God Substantially?

I answer that, [1] Negative names applied to God or [2] signifying His relation to creatures manifestly do not at all signify His substance, but rather express the distance of the creature from Him, or His relation to something else, or rather, the relation of creatures to Himself.

But as regards [3] absolute and affirmative names of God, as *good*, *wise*, and the like, various and many opinions have been given. For some have said that [a] all such names, although they are applied to God affirmatively, nevertheless have been brought into use more to express some remotion from God, rather than to express anything that exists positively in Him. Hence they assert that when we say that God lives, we mean that God is not like an inanimate thing; and the same in like manner applies to other names; and this was taught by Rabbi Moses. Others say that [b] these names applied to God signify His relationship towards creatures: thus in the words, *God is good*, we mean, God is the cause of goodness in things; and the same rule applies to other names.

Both of these opinions, however, seem to be untrue for three reasons. First because in neither of them can a reason be assigned why some names more than others are applied to God. For He is assuredly the cause of bodies in the same way as He is the cause of good things; therefore if the words *God is good*, signified no more than, *God is the cause of good things*, it might in like manner be said that God is a body, inasmuch as He is the cause of bodies. So also to say that He is a body implies that He is not a mere potentiality, as is

---

finitude, temporality, and composition). St. Thomas has a simple yet sophisticated answer here and in the following articles to the question frequently posed today by skeptical philosophers of religion: How can the word "God" have acceptable meaning for us if God is not an object of our ordinary experience? Cf. Kal Nielsen and J. Moreland, *Does God Exist?* (Nashville: Nelson, 1990).

primary matter. Secondly, because it would follow that all names applied to God would be said of Him by way of being taken in a secondary sense, as healthy is secondarily said of medicine, forasmuch as it signifies only the cause of health in the animal which primarily is called healthy. Thirdly, because this is against the intention of those who speak of God. For in saying that God lives, they assuredly mean more than to say that He is the cause of our life, or that He differs from inanimate bodies.

Therefore we must hold a different doctrine—viz., [c] that these names signify the divine substance, and are predicated substantially of God, although they fall short of a full representation of Him. . . . The aforesaid names signify the divine substance, but in an imperfect manner, even as creatures represent it imperfectly. So when we say, *God is good*, the meaning is not, *God is the cause of goodness*, or, *God is not evil*; but the meaning is, *Whatever good we attribute to creatures, pre-exists in God*, and in a more excellent and higher way. . . .

FOURTH ARTICLE

Whether Names Applied to God Are Synonymous?

I answer that, These names spoken of God are not synonymous. . . . Our intellect, since it knows God from creatures, in order to understand God, forms conceptions proportional to the perfections flowing from God to creatures, which perfections pre-exist in God unitedly and simply, whereas in creatures they are received, divided and multiplied.[94]. . . Therefore, although the names applied to God signify one thing, still because they signify that under many and different aspects, they are not synonymous. . . .

---

[94] God's perfections are all one objectively, ontologically, in God; but they are many subjectively, conceptually, in our mind—somewhat as white light refracted through a prism appears as many colors. E.g., to us, mercy is contrasted with justice, as a relaxation of justice; and truth is distinguished from goodness, for truth is a relation to intellect and goodness is a relation to will. We cannot *understand how* these are one in God, but we can *know that* they are, for it has already been proved that God is absolutely simple, without any divisions.

FIFTH ARTICLE

*Whether What Is Said of God and of Creatures
Is Univocally Predicated of Them?*

On the contrary, Whatever is predicated of various things under the same name but not in the same sense, is predicated equivocally.[95] But no name belongs to God in the same sense that it belongs to creatures; for instance, wisdom in creatures is a quality, but not in God.[96] Now a different genus changes an essence, since the genus is part of the definition; and the same applies to other things. Therefore whatever is said of God and of creatures is predicated equivocally.

Further, God is more distant from creatures than any creatures are from each other. But the distance of some creatures makes any univocal predication of them impossible, as in the case of those things which are not in the same genus. Therefore much less can anything be predicated univocally of God and creatures; and so only equivocal predication can be applied to them.[97]

---

[95] If St. Thomas held that terms could be univocally predicated of God and creatures (i.e., mean the same thing when used to describe God and creatures, as predicates), he would have an anthropomorphic conception of God and a rationalistic conception of the human mind. If he held that all terms predicated of God and creatures were equivocal, he would be agnostic about God and skeptical about the human mind. Analogical predication fits between these two popular extremes. Univocal terms about God are negative, and positive terms about God are analogical.

"Equivocal" is used in this Article in a broad sense, meaning simply not-univocal. "Equivocal" here can include "analogical". Later, in the body of this Article, he uses "equivocal" in a narrower sense as distinct from "analogical" as well as from "univocal".

[96] The attributes of God are not accidents, qualities added to His substance. God *is* His wisdom, and truth, and righteousness, etc. Cf. Jn 11:25; 14:6. Therefore although "wise" in "that man is wise" is in the the genus *quality*, "wise" in "God is wise" is not. If it were in any genus, it would be substance, for everything in God is His substance or essence.

[97] Compare the meaning of "good" in "good doggie", "good man", and "good God". The goodness of a man is closer to the goodness of a dog, even though the dog lacks reason and morality, than to the goodness

I answer that, . . . as said in the preceding article, all perfections existing in creatures divided and multiplied, pre-exist in God unitedly. Thus, when any term expressing perfection is applied to a creature, it signifies that perfection distinct in idea from other perfections; as, for instance, by this term *wise* applied to a man, we signify some perfection distinct from a man's essence, and distinct from his power and existence, and from all similar things; whereas when we apply it to God, we do not mean to signify anything distinct from His essence, or power, or existence. Thus also this term *wise* applied to man in some degree circumscribes and comprehends the thing signified; whereas this is not the case when it is applied to God; but it leaves the thing signified as incomprehended;[98] and as exceeding the signification of the name. Hence it is evident that this term *wise* is not applied in the same way to God and to man. The same rule applies to other terms. Hence no name is predicated univocally of God and of creatures.

Neither, on the other hand, are names applied to God and creatures in a purely equivocal sense, as some have said. Because if that were so, it follows that from creatures nothing could be known or demonstrated about God at all; for the reasoning would always be exposed to the fallacy of equivocation. Such a view is against the philosophers, who proved many things about God, and also against what the Apostle says: *The invisible things of God are clearly seen being understood by the things that are made* (Rom 1:20). Therefore it must be said that these names are said of God and creatures in an analogous sense, that is, according to proportion.[99]

Now names are thus [analogously] used in two ways: either according as many things are proportionate to one, thus for example

---

of God; for any two finite things are closer to each other than either is to the infinite.

[98] "Uncomprehended" does not mean "totally unknown" but "not surrounded or controlled", not *adequately* known. Cf. I, 12, 7, Reply 1 for what St. Thomas means by "comprehension".

[99] I.e., wisdom in God is infinite and one with God's essence because it is proportionate to God's being, which is infinite and one with His essence; while wisdom in man is finite and distinct from his essence because it is proportionate to man's being, which is finite and composed of essence plus existence.

healthy is predicated of medicine and urine in relation and in proportion to health of a body, of which the former is the sign and the latter the cause: or according as one thing is proportionate to another, thus *healthy* is said of medicine and animal, since medicine is the cause of health in the animal body. And in this way some things are said of God and creatures analogically, and not in a purely equivocal nor in a purely univocal sense. For we can name God only from creatures (A. 1). Thus, whatever is said of God and creatures, is said according to the relation of a creature to God as its principle and cause, wherein all perfections of things pre-exist excellently. Now this mode of community of idea is a mean between pure equivocation and simple univocation. For in analogies the idea is not, as it is in univocals, one and the same, yet it is not totally diverse as in equivocals.[100]. . .

SIXTH ARTICLE

Whether Names Predicated of God Are Predicated Primarily of Creatures?

On the contrary, It is written, *I bow my knees to the Father of our Lord Jesus Christ, of Whom all paternity in heaven and earth is named* (Eph 3:14, 15); and the same applies to the other names applied to God and creatures.[101] Therefore these names are applied primarily to God rather than to creatures.

I answer that, . . . all names applied metaphorically to God, are applied to creatures primarily rather than to God, because when said of God they mean only similitudes to such creatures. For as

---

[100] Thus, to summarize, all names of God and all terms predicable of God designate either (1) God's essence (Being, existence, I AM WHO AM), (2) what God is *not* (univocal negative terms like "eternal" (not-temporal) and "immaterial"), (3) what God is *like* (analogical positive terms like "wise" and "good"), (4) *relationships* to God (e.g., "Creator", "Lord", "Redeemer"), or (5) mere metaphors ("Rock", "Lion").

[101] Scripture thus reverses our usual thinking. God the Father is not the analogy; human fatherhood is. What "father" primarily means is the relation between the Father and the Son in the Trinity. We are, after all, made in God's image, not vice versa. Cf. also "food" in Jn 4:31–34; 6:55.

smiling applied to a field means only that the field in the beauty of its flowering is like to the beauty of the human smile by proportionate likeness, so the name of *lion* applied to God means only that God manifests strength in His works, as a lion in his. . . . But to other names not applied to God in a metaphorical sense, . . . as regards what the name signifies, these names are applied primarily to God rather than to creatures, because these perfections flow from God to creatures; but as regards the imposition of the names, they are primarily applied by us to creatures which we know first. Hence they have a mode of signification which belongs to creatures, as said above (A. 3). . . .

SEVENTH ARTICLE

Whether Names Which Imply Relation to Creatures Are Predicated of God Temporally?

I answer that, The names which import relation to creatures are applied to God temporally, and not from eternity.

. . . They are called relative, not forasmuch as they are related to other things, but as others are related to them. Likewise for instance, *on the right* is not applied to a column, unless it stands as regards an animal on the right side; which relation is not really in the column, but in the animal.

Since therefore God is outside the whole order of creation, and all creatures are ordered to Him, and not conversely, it is manifest that creatures are really related to God Himself; whereas in God there is no real relation [relativity] to creatures, but a relation only in idea, inasmuch as creatures are referred to Him. Thus there is nothing to prevent these names which import relation to the creature from being predicated of God temporally, not by reason of any change in Him, but by reason of the change of the creature; as a column is on the right of an animal, without change in itself, but by change in the animal.[102]. . .

---

[102] Thus when Scripture speaks of God getting angry after man sins, this does not designate a passion or change in God, as if man could change God, but only a change in the *relationship* between man and God. Similarly, we speak of the sun "coming out" or "shining again" when there was no change in the sun but only in our relation to it when a cloud has passed

NINTH ARTICLE

Whether This Name "God" Is Communicable [Shareable]?

On the contrary, It is written: *They gave the incommunicable name to wood and stones* (Wis 14:21), in reference to the divine name. Therefore this name *God* is incommunicable.

I answer that, . . . Since . . . this name *God* is given to signify the divine nature as stated above (A. 8), and since the divine nature cannot be multiplied as shown above (Q. 11, A. 3), it follows that this name *God* is incommunicable in reality, but communicable in opinion; just in the same way as this name *sun* would be communicable according to the opinion of those who say there are many suns. Therefore, it is written: *You served them who by nature are not gods* (Gal 4:8), and a gloss adds, *Gods not in nature, but in human opinion.* Nevertheless this name *God* is communicable, not in its whole signification, but in some part of it by way of similitude; so that those are called gods who share in divinity by likeness, according to the text, *I have said, You are gods* (Ps 81:6).

But if any name were given to signify God not as to His nature but as to His *suppositum* [substance], accordingly as He is considered as *this something*, that name would be absolutely incommunicable; as, for instance, perhaps the Tetragrammaton among the Hebrews [JHWH, "I AM"]; and this is like giving a name to the sun as signifying this individual thing. . . .

ELEVENTH ARTICLE

Whether This Name, HE WHO IS, Is
the Most Proper Name of God?

On the contrary, It is written that when Moses asked, *If they should say to me, What is His name? what shall I say to them?* the Lord

---

away; or of the sun "rising" when in fact it was the earth that moved relative to the sun rather than the sun relative to the earth. Even God's act of creating the universe was not a change in God, for the God who creates the universe, of which time is an aspect, is not in time, any more than Shakespeare is somewhere in Hamlet's Denmark. Time, like matter, is an aspect of the creation, not of the Creator.

answered him, *Thus shalt thou say to them, HE WHO IS hath sent me to you* (Ex 3:13, 14). Therefore this name *HE WHO IS*, most properly belongs to God.

I answer that, This name *HE WHO IS*, is most properly applied to God, for three reasons:

First, because of its signification. For it does not signify form, but simply existence itself.[103] Hence since the existence of God is His essence itself, which can be said of no other (Q. 3, A. 4), it is clear that among other names this one specially denominates God, for everything is denominated by its form.

Secondly, on account of its universality.[104] For all other names are either less universal, or, if convertible with it, add something above it at least in idea; hence in a certain way they inform and determine it. Now our intellect cannot know the essence of God itself in this life, as it is in itself, but whatever mode it applies in determining what it understands about God, it falls short of the mode of what God is in Himself. Therefore the less determinate the names are, and the more universal and absolute they are, the more properly they [are] applied to God. Hence Damascene says (*De Fid. Orth.* i) that, *HE WHO IS, is the principal of all names applied to God; for comprehending all in itself, it contains existence itself as an infinite and indeterminate sea of substance.*[105] Now by any other name some mode of substance is determined, whereas this name *HE WHO IS*, determines no mode of being, but is indeterminate to all; and therefore it denominates the *infinite ocean of substance*.

Thirdly, from its consignification, for it signifies present existence; and this above all properly applies to God, whose existence knows not past or future, as Augustine says (*De Trin.* v). . . .

---

[103] Cf. Etienne Gilson, *The Elements of Christian Philosophy*, *Being and Some Philosophers*, and "Haec Sublimas Veritas" in *A Gilson Reader*. Gilson's voluminous work on St. Thomas centered on the claim that the primacy of existence is the most important and distinctive discovery in St. Thomas and, in fact, in the whole history of metaphysics.

[104] However, St. Thomas does not hold that God is a universal, like humanness or divinity. Nor is He a particular, like Socrates or Zeus.

[105] This metaphor is not meant to indicate pantheism, but infinity.

TWELFTH ARTICLE

Whether Affirmative Propositions Can Be Formed About God?

Objection 3. . . . . Every intellect is false which understands a thing otherwise than as it is. But God has existence without any composition as shown above (Q. 3, A. 7). Therefore since every affirmative intellect understands something as compound,[106] it follows that a true affirmative proposition about God cannot be made. . . .

I answer that, True affirmative propositions can be formed about God. To prove this we must know that in every true affirmative proposition the predicate and the subject signify in some way the same thing in reality, and different things in idea.[107] . . .

God, however, as considered in Himself, is altogether one and simple, yet our intellect knows Him by different conceptions because it cannot see Him as He is in Himself. Nevertheless, although it understands Him under different conceptions, it knows that one and the same simple object corresponds to its conceptions. Therefore the plurality of predicate and subject represents the plurality of idea; and the intellect represents the unity by composition.[108] . . .

Reply Obj. 3. This proposition, *The intellect understanding anything otherwise than it is, is false,* can be taken in two senses, accordingly as this adverb *otherwise* determines the word *understanding* on the part of the thing understood, or on the part of the one who understands. Taken as referring to the thing understood,

---

[106] I.e., an affirmative proposition distinguishes its predicate from its subject in the very act of identifying the two, by predicating the predicate of the subject. This technical point is important because many "mystical" thinkers answer the question of this Article "No" because of this objection, which, St. Thomas shows, is based on a technical, logical confusion, as pointed out in the Reply.

[107] E.g., in "Spot is a dog", the same substance is signified by the subject and by the predicate; the subject tells its individual name and the predicate tells its species. In "Spot is wet", the predicate signifies an accident that exists only in its subjects (wet things).

[108] I.e., by the affirmative copula composing (or affirming the ontological unity of) the subject and the predicate.

the proposition is true, and the meaning is: Any intellect which understands that the thing is otherwise than it is, is false. But this does not hold in the present case; because our intellect, when forming a proposition about God, does not affirm that He is composite, but that He is simple. But taken as referring to the one who understands, the proposition is false. For the mode of the intellect in understanding is different from the mode of the thing in its essence. Since it is clear that our intellect understands material things below itself in an immaterial manner; not that it understands them to be immaterial things; but its manner of understanding is immaterial, likewise, when it understands simple things above itself, it understands them according to its own mode, which is in a composite manner; yet not so as to understand them to be composite things. And thus our intellect is not false in forming composition in its ideas concerning God. . . .

Question 14

Of God's Knowledge

Whether There Is Knowledge [Scientia] in God?

On the contrary, The Apostle says, *O the depth of the riches of the wisdom and of the knowledge of God* (Rom 11:33).

I answer that, In God there exists the most perfect knowledge. To prove this, we must note that intelligent beings are distinguished from non-intelligent beings in that the latter possess only their own form; whereas the intelligent being is naturally adapted to have[109] also the form of some other thing; for the idea of the thing known is in the knower. Hence it is manifest that the nature of a non-intelligent being is more contracted and limited; whereas the nature of intelligent beings has a greater amplitude and extension; therefore the Philosopher says (*De Anima* iii) that *the soul is in a sense all things.*[110] Now the contraction of the form comes from the matter.[111] Hence, as we have said above (Q. 7, A. 1) forms according as they are the more immaterial, approach more nearly to a kind of infinity. Therefore it is clear that the immateriality of a thing is

---

[109] Distinguish two ways of *having* a form. Only knowers *have* forms in both ways. A knower has the form of his species (humanity) in his *substance*; and he also has other forms, which he knows (e.g., treeness, abstracted from trees) in his *intellect*.

[110] For the (intellectual) soul can know (thus possess in its intellect) any and all forms.

[111] I.e., dogginess as a whole, dogginess as a form, is contracted and limited to Spot by being received into the particular matter of Spot. Spot is less than all dogginess because in addition to the form dogginess Spot has his own individual matter.

the reason why it is cognitive; and according to the mode of immateriality is the mode of knowledge. Hence, it is said in *De Anima* ii that plants do not know, because they are wholly material.[112] But sense is cognitive because it can receive images free from matter, and the intellect is still further cognitive, because it is more separated from matter and unmixed, as said in *De Anima* iii. Since therefore God is in the highest degree of immateriality as stated above (Q. 7, A. 1), it follows that He occupies the highest place in knowledge. . . .

---

[112] St. Thomas uses "soul" in a broader way than modernity does, for animals and even plants are said to have souls (sources of life). But the plant soul is wholly material and non-cognitive: a hill of beans does not know a hill of beans. Animals do know, but only sensorially and imagistically. The whole cosmic hierarchy may be set out as follows:

	Name	Science	Matter & Form	Potency & Act	Kind of Knowledge
8	God	theology	pure form	pure act	knowledge = one with being
7	angels	angelology	pure form	essence (potency) & existence (act)	intuitive
6	men	anthropology psychology	rational soul = form of body	essence & existence and matter & form	rational
5	animals	zoology	sensitive soul	"	sensory
4	plants	botany	vegetative soul	"	none
3	things	physics	no soul; purely material forms	"	"
2	chemical elements	chemistry	first rudimentary forms (wet/dry, hot/cold)	"	"
1	prime matter	none	formless matter	pure potency	"

Reply Obj. 2. Whatever is divided and multiplied in creatures exists in God simply and unitedly (Q. 13, A. 4). Now man has different kinds of knowledge, according to the different objects of His knowledge.[113] He has *intelligence* as regards the knowledge of principles; he has *science* as regards knowledge of conclusions; he has *wisdom*, according as he knows the highest cause; he has *counsel* or *prudence*, according as he knows what is to be done. But God knows all these by one simple act of knowledge. . . .

FOURTH ARTICLE

Whether the Act of God's Intellect Is His Substance?

I answer that, It must be said that the act of God's intellect is His substance. For if His act of understanding were other than His substance, then something else, as the Philosopher says (*Metaph.* xii), would be the act and perfection of the divine substance, to which the divine substance would be related, as potentiality is to act, which is altogether impossible. . . .

Thus it follows from all the foregoing that in God, intellect, and the object understood, and the intelligible species, and His act of understanding are entirely one and the same. Hence, when God is said to be understanding, no kind of multiplicity is attached to His substance.[114]. . .

---

[113] This simple principle distinguishes the Aristotelian, Realist concept of the sciences from the Cartesian, Idealist conception of a single, ideal, mathematically perfect science for all reality. For Aristotle and St. Thomas, sciences, and their methods, differ depending on the real objects to be known.

[114] Mystics reach this conclusion by a different route, one that is intuitive and experiential rather than rational and scientific: that at the summit or heart of reality there is absolute unity, without even the dualism between subject and object, knower and known. If the mystic lacks the doctrine of creation, he will probably become a pantheist, unless, like Plotinus, he raises The One *above* Intelligence (Plotinus' *Nous*) which contains a subject-object dualism. Of all pagan mystics, Plotinus came closest to Christian mysticism; perhaps that explains why in God's providence Plotinus was the mystic most available and influential to medieval Christian philosophers, beginning with Augustine. The

FIFTH ARTICLE

Whether God Knows Things Other Than Himself?[115]

Objection 2. . . . . The object understood is the perfection of the one who understands. If therefore God understands other things besides Himself, something else will be the perfection of God, and will be nobler than He; which is impossible.

Objection 3. . . . . The act of understanding is specified [determined] by the intelligible object, as is every other act from its own object. Hence the intellectual act is so much the nobler, the nobler the object understood. But God is His own intellectual act. If therefore God understands anything other than Himself, then God Himself is specified [determined] by something else than Himself; which cannot be. Therefore He does not understand things other than Himself.

On the contrary, It is written: *All things are naked and open to His eyes* (Heb 4:13).

I answer that, God necessarily knows things other than Himself. For it is manifest that He perfectly understands Himself; otherwise His existence would not be perfect, since His existence is His act of understanding. Now if anything is perfectly known, it follows of necessity that its power is perfectly known. But the power of anything can be perfectly known only by knowing to what its power extends. Since therefore the divine power extends to other things by the very fact that it is the first effective cause of all things,

---

creationist theist, however, knows that the absolute unity of subject and object, and transcendence of the subject-object dualism, is true only of God's knowledge, not of the natural knowledge of any creature.

[115] The issue is critical for the Middle Ages, since Aristotle, who seemed to be speaking for reason, contradicted faith and divine revelation here. Aristotle taught that God, being perfect, knew only that object perfectly worth knowing, viz., Himself, and did not know or love or providentially care for things other than Himself. To preserve the synthesis of faith and reason and show the reasonableness of the Christian faith, St. Thomas had to show Aristotle's rational mistake here. In the body of the article St. Thomas validates God's knowledge of objects other than Himself without compromising His perfection or unity or lowering Him to the human, subject-object mode of knowing, by appealing again, as he does so often, to the fact of *creation*.

as is clear from the aforesaid (Q. 2, A. 3), God must necessarily know things other than Himself. . . .

Reply Obj. 2. The object understood is a perfection of the one understanding not by its substance, but by its image, according to which it is in the intellect, as its form and perfection, as is said in *De Anima* iii. For *a stone is not in the soul, but its image.* Now those things which are other than God are understood by God, inasmuch as the essence of God contains their images as above explained; hence it does not follow that there is any perfection in the divine intellect other than the divine essence.

Reply Obj. 3. The intellectual act is . . . specified . . . by the principal object understood in which other things are understood. . . . This . . . in God is nothing but His own essence in which all images of things are comprehended. Hence it does not follow that the divine intellectual act, or rather God Himself, is specified by anything else than the divine essence itself.

SIXTH ARTICLE

Whether God Knows Things Other Than Himself by Proper Knowledge?

I answer that, Some have erred on this point, saying that God knows things other than Himself only in general.[116] . .

But this cannot be. For to know a thing in general and not in particular, is to have an imperfect knowledge of it. . . .

---

[116] This is another thesis typical of Plato and Aristotle and Aristotle's medieval Muslim commentators, especially Averroes, "The Commentator" ("Latin Averroism" in the West). The Greeks tended to a Gnostic notion of perfection as incompatible with materiality and particularity. St. Thomas' reply is a good example of how the substance of his philosophy is biblical rather than Greek when push comes to shove.

EIGHTH ARTICLE

Whether the Knowledge of God Is the Cause of Things?

On the contrary, Augustine says (*De Trin.* xv), *Not because they are, does God know all creatures spiritual and temporal, but because He knows them, therefore they are.* [117]

I answer that, The knowledge of God is the cause of things. For the knowledge of God is to all creatures what the knowledge of the artificer is to things made by his art. Now the knowledge of the artificer is the cause of the things made by his art, . . . [but] the intelligible form does not denote a principle of action in so far as it resides in the one who understands unless there is added to it the inclination to an effect, which inclination is through the will. . . .

Reply Obj. 3. Natural things are midway between the knowledge of God and our knowledge: for we receive knowledge from natural things, of which God is the cause by His knowledge. Hence, as the natural objects of knowledge are prior to our knowledge, and are its measure, so, the knowledge of God is prior to natural things, and is the measure of them; as, for instance, a house is midway between the knowledge of the builder who made it, and the knowledge of the one who gathers his knowledge of the house from the house already built. [118]

NINTH ARTICLE

Whether God Has Knowledge of Things That Are Not?

I answer that, . . . Whatever therefore can be made, or thought, or said by the creature, as also whatever He Himself can do, all are

---

[117] Cf. Ps 1:6. The "Copernican revolution" of Kantian epistemology (man's mind imposing form rather than discovering it), and, even more, the epistemology of his successor Fichte, in which the mind (ego) creates (posits) the matter as well as the form, is quite incorrect for man but quite correct for God.

[118] Cf. 16, 1. A whole world view is implied here. It sees human science as reading God's art (for "God wrote two books, nature and scripture", according to the medieval maxim). This view was as habitual and natural to medieval man as the positivistic-materialistic-empiricistic-

known to God, although they are not actual. And in so far as it can be said that He has knowledge even of things that are not.[119]. . .

Whether God Knows Evil Things?

I answer that, . . . a thing is knowable in the degree in which it is; hence, since this is the essence of evil that it is the privation of good, by the very fact that God knows good things, He knows evil things also; as by light is known darkness.

Whether God Knows Singular Things? [120]

I answer that, God knows singular things. For all perfections found in creatures preexist in God in a higher way, as is clear from the foregoing (Q. 4, A. 2). Now to know singular things is part of

---

scientific-secular world view is to modern man. The medieval world view includes, surrounds, and expands the modern one:

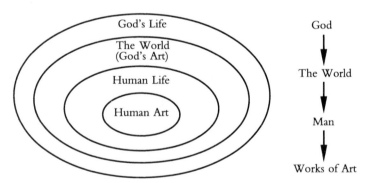

In these two diagrams, both the arrows and the enclosing circles represent the relationship of determining, forming, or making. The lower level, or smaller circle, is relative to the higher or larger one.

[119] We do not know "what would have been if . . .". God does. The very practical consequences of this apparently highly theoretical truth in the area of our trust in God's all-wise providence are obvious.

[120] Cf. notes 115 and 116.

our perfection. Hence God must know singular things. Even the Philosopher considers it incongruous that anything known by us should be unknown to God. . . .

. . . Since God is the cause of things by His knowledge, as stated above (A. 8), His knowledge extends as far as His causality extends. Hence as the active power of God extends not only to forms, which are the source of universality, but also to matter, as we shall prove further on (Q. 44, A. 2), the knowledge of God must extend to singular things, which are individualized by matter. . . .

TWELFTH ARTICLE

Whether God Can Know Infinite Things?

I answer that, Since God knows not only things actual but also things possible to Himself or to created things, as shown above (A. 9), and as these must be infinite, it must be held that He knows infinite things. . . . If we consider more attentively, we must hold that God knows infinite things even by the knowledge of vision. For God knows even the thoughts and affections of hearts, which will be multiplied to infinity as rational creatures go on for ever. . . .

THIRTEENTH ARTICLE

Whether the Knowledge of God Is of Future Contingent Things?

On the contrary, It is written (Ps 32:15), *He Who hath made the hearts of every one of them; Who understandeth all their works,* that is, of men. Now the works of men are contingent, being subject to free will. Therefore God knows future contingent things.

I answer that, Since as was shown above (A. 9), God knows all things; not only things actual but also things possible to Him and the creature; and since some of these are future contingent to us, it follows that God knows future contingent things.[121] . . .

---

[121] "Future contingent" things are things which will be in the future if and only if other things happen; they are contingent on these other things. For the classic answer to the oft-asked question why God's infallible and therefore necessarily true foreknowledge of all things actual and possible

Question 15

Of Ideas

Whether There Are Ideas? [122]

I answer that, It is necessary to suppose ideas in the divine mind. For the Greek word Ἰδέα is in Latin *Forma*. Hence by ideas are understood the forms of things, existing apart from the things themselves. [123] . . .

SECOND ARTICLE

Whether Ideas Are Many?

I answer that, . . . there cannot be an idea of any whole, unless particular ideas are had of those parts of which the whole is made; just as a builder cannot conceive the idea of a house unless he has the

---

does not remove their contingency, especially their contingency on human free will, see Boethius, *The Consolation of Philosophy*, Bk. 5. Briefly, his point is that God is not in time, therefore He does not *fore*see events *before* they happen but eternally and all at once sees all things *as* they happen temporally and one by one.

[122] Note St. Thomas' Platonism here. Most medieval philosophers, including St. Thomas, thought of themselves as inheritors and users of many past traditions, not just one, and especially of Plato and Aristotle. As St. Augustine found, Christianity undergirds Platonic metaphysics by giving Plato's Ideas a home in God's mind.

[123] Aristotle's objection to Plato was against Plato's separation (*chorismos*) of the Forms from natural things. St. Thomas agrees with Aristotle rather than Plato as far as nature is concerned: there are no separately existing forms in nature. But he agrees with Plato as far as God is con-

idea of each of its parts. So, then, it must needs be that in the divine mind there are the proper ideas of all things. Hence Augustine says (*Octog. Tri. Quaest.*; *qu.* xlvi), *that each thing*[124] *was created by God according to the idea proper to it*, from which it follows that in the divine mind ideas are many. . . . Now, it is not repugnant to the simplicity of the divine mind that it understand many things; though it would be repugnant to its simplicity were His understanding to be formed by a plurality of images. Hence many ideas exist in the divine mind, as things understood by it. . . .

---

cerned, following Augustine here: there are Forms (Ideas) in the divine mind.

[124] Here St. Thomas approximates Duns Scotus' notion of *hecceitas*, or "thisness" (and Gerard Manley Hopkins' notion of "inscape" derived from it). God "calls each star by name" (Ps 147:4).

Question 16

Of Truth[125]

Since knowledge is of things that are true, after the consideration of the knowledge of God, we must inquire concerning truth. About this there are eight points of inquiry: (1) Whether truth resides in the thing, or only in the intellect? (2) Whether it resides only in the intellect composing and dividing? (3) On the comparison of the true to being. (4) On the comparison of the true to the good. (5) Whether God is truth? (6) Whether all things are true by one truth, or by many? (7) On the eternity of truth. (8) On the unchangeableness of truth.

FIRST ARTICLE

Whether Truth Resides Only in the Intellect?

On the contrary, The Philosopher says (*Metaph.* vi), *The true and the false reside not in things, but in the intellect.*

I answer that, As the good denotes that towards which the appetite tends, so the true denotes that towards which the intellect tends. Now there is this difference between the appetite and the intellect, or any knowledge whatsoever, that knowledge is according as the thing known is in the knower, whilst appetite is according as the desirer tends towards the thing desired. Thus the term of the appetite, namely good, is in the object desirable, and the term of the intellect, namely true, is in the intellect itself. . . . Natural things are said to be true in so far as they express the

---

[125] For a classic advanced treatment of Truth, see St. Thomas' *De Veritate*.

likeness of the species that are in the divine mind. For a stone is called true, which possesses the nature proper to a stone, according to the preconception in the divine intellect. Thus, then, truth resides primarily in the intellect, and secondarily in things according as they are related to the intellect as their principle.[126]. . . The definition that *Truth is the equation of thought and thing* is applicable to it under either aspect. . . .

THIRD ARTICLE

Whether the True and Being Are Convertible Terms?

I answer that, As good has the nature of what is desirable, so truth is related to knowledge. Now everything, in as far as it has being, so far is it knowable.[127] Wherefore it is said in *De Anima* iii that *the soul is in some manner all things*, through the senses and the intellect. And therefore, as good is convertible with being, so is the true. But as good adds to being the notion of desirable, so the true adds relation to the intellect. . . .

FOURTH ARTICLE

Whether Good Is Logically Prior to the True?

Objection 1. It seems that good is logically prior to the true. For what is more universal is logically prior, as is evident from *Physic.* i. But the good is more universal than the true, since the true is a kind of good, namely, of the intellect. Therefore the good is logically prior to the true.

---

[126] Truth exists, then, in three places: in God's mind as the measure and design of things; in things measured by and conforming to the divine mind; and in the human mind as measured by and conforming to things (and through them to the divine mind that designed them). (Cf. n. 118.)

[127] In itself (*in se*), not necessarily in relation to us (*quoad nos*). Nothing is unknowable to God, or to an ideal intellect. But many obstacles may impair the knowledge of a particular thing by a particular intellect.

Objection 2. Further, good is in things, but the true is in the intellect composing and dividing, as said before (A. 2). But that which is in things is prior to that which is in the intellect. Therefore good is logically prior to the true. . . .

Reply Obj. 1. The will and the intellect mutually include one another: for the intellect understands the will, and the will wills the intellect to understand.[128] So then, among things directed to the object of the will, are comprised also those that belong to the intellect; and conversely. Whence in the order of things desirable, good stands as the universal, and the true as the particular;[129] whereas in the order of intelligible things the converse is the case.[130] From the fact, then, that the true is a kind of good, it follows that the good is prior in the order of things desirable; but not that it is prior absolutely.

Reply Obj. 2. A thing is prior logically in so far as it is prior to the intellect. Now the intellect apprehends primarily being itself; secondly, it apprehends that it understands being; and thirdly, it apprehends that it desires being. Hence the idea of being is first, that of truth second, and the idea of good third. . . .

FIFTH ARTICLE

Whether God Is Truth?

On the contrary, Our Lord says, *I am the Way, the Truth and the Life* (Jn 14:6).

I answer that, . . . He Himself is His own . . . act of understanding. Whence it follows not only that truth is in Him, but that He is truth itself.[131] . . .

---

[128] N.b.: St. Thomas is not a simple rationalist or intellectualist like Plato; nor is he a voluntarist like Scotus or Luther.

[129] I.e., truth is one particular good: the good sought by the intellect.

[130] I.e., good is one particular truth: the truth about the object of the will.

[131] Not that God is nothing but the abstraction "truth", but that there is

Whether Created Truth Is Eternal?

I answer that, . . . it has been already said that things are called true from the truth of the intellect. Hence, if no intellect were eternal, no truth would be eternal. Now because only the divine intellect is eternal, in it alone truth has eternity.[132]. . .

EIGHTH ARTICLE

Whether Truth Is Immutable?

I answer that, Truth, properly speaking, resides only in the intellect, as said before (A. 1); but things are called true in virtue of the truth residing in an intellect. Hence the mutability of truth must be regarded from the point of view of the intellect. . . . If, then, there is an intellect wherein there can be no alternation of opinions, and the knowledge of which nothing can escape, in this is immutable truth.[133] Now such is the divine intellect, as is clear from what has been said before (Q. 14, A. 15). Hence the truth of the divine intellect is immutable. But the truth of our intellect is mutable; not because it is itself the subject of change, but in so far as our intellect changes from truth to falsity.[134]. . .

---

in God no distinction between Him and His act of understanding, as between substance and accident. There are no accidents in God; in God all is substance.

[132] St. Thomas here argues from the eternity of the divine intellect to the eternity of truth. (Cf. also Article 8.) Augustine argued from the eternity of truth to the existence of an eternal divine intellect.

[133] Cf. Jean-Paul Sartre in "Existentialism and Humanism": "There can be no eternal truth since there is no divine mind to think it."

[134] N.b.: even the truth *we* know ("objective truth") is not a changing *truth* if it is a truth about unchanging things, like "justice is a virtue" or "2 + 2 = 4" rather than about changing things like "Caesar crossed the Rubicon"; but our *knowledge* of it is a changing *knowledge* or opinion ("subjective truth").

Question 17

Concerning Falsity

Whether Falsity Exists in Things?

I answer that, . . . natural things depend on the divine intellect, as artificial things on the human. Wherefore artificial things are said to be false simply and in themselves, in so far as they fall short of the form of the art; whence a craftsman is said to produce a false work, if it falls short of the proper operation of his art.

In things that depend on God, falseness cannot be found, in so far as they are compared with the divine intellect; since whatever takes place in things proceeds from the ordinance of that intellect, unless perhaps in the case of voluntary agents only, who have it in their power to withdraw themselves from what is so ordained; wherein consists the evil of sin.[135] Thus sins themselves are called untruths and lies in the Scriptures, according to the words of the text, *Why do you love vanity, and seek after lying?* (Ps 4:3): as on the other hand virtuous deeds are called the *truth of life* as being obedient to the order of the divine intellect. Thus it is said, *He that doth truth, cometh to the light* (Jn 3:21).

But in relation to our intellect, natural things which are compared thereto accidentally, can be called false; not simply, but relatively. . . . And whereas it is innate in us to judge things by external appearances, since our knowledge takes its rise from sense, which principally and naturally deals with external accidents, therefore those external accidents, which resemble things other than themselves, are said to be false with respect to those things; thus gall is falsely honey; and

---

[135] Note the ontological horror of sin: it alone in all the universe escapes the universal truth of conformity to the creative plan.

tin, false gold. Regarding this, Augustine says (*ibid.* 6): *We call those things false that appear to our apprehension like the true.* . . .

Reply Obj. 2. Things do not deceive by their own nature, but by accident. For they give occasion to falsity, by the likeness they bear to things which they actually are not. . . .

SECOND ARTICLE

Whether There Is Falsity in the Senses?

I answer that, . . . Sense . . . has no false knowledge about its proper objects,[136] except accidentally and rarely, and then, because of the unsound organ it does not receive the sensible form rightly. . . . Hence, for instance, it happens that on account of an unhealthy tongue sweet seems bitter to a sick person. . . .

THIRD ARTICLE

Whether Falsity Is in the Intellect?

I answer that, Just as . . . natural things cannot fall short of the being that belongs to them by their form [essence], but may fall short of accidental or consequent qualities, even as a man may fail to possess two feet, but not fail to be a man; so the faculty of knowing cannot fail in knowledge of the thing with the likeness of which it is informed; but may fail with regard to something consequent upon that form, or accidental thereto.[137] For it has been said (A. 2), that sight is not deceived in its proper sensible. . . .

---

[136] I.e., sight perceives color, hearing perceives sound, touch perceives hardness, etc. Contrast the natural common sense of these two Articles (2 and 3) with the *artificiality* of the radical skepticism ("universal methodic doubt") with which modern philosophy begins, in Descartes.

[137] E.g., when I know a triangle, I do not mistake it for a circle, but I may mistake its properties (e.g., the number of degrees in its interior angles) or its accidents (e.g., its size). I cannot know a triangle and mistake it for a circle, because if I mistook it for a circle, I would not be knowing a *triangle*.

Now as the sense is directly informed by the likeness of its proper object, so is the intellect by the likeness of the essence of a thing.[138] Hence the intellect is not deceived about the essence of a thing, as neither the sense about its proper object. But in affirming and denying, the intellect may be deceived, by attributing to the thing of which it understands the essence, something which is not consequent upon it, or is opposed to it. . . .

But because falsity of the intellect is concerned essentially only with the composition of the intellect [judgment], falsity occurs also accidentally in that operation of the intellect whereby it knows the essence of a thing, in so far as composition of the intellect [judgment] is mixed up in it. This can take place in two ways. In one way, by the intellect applying to one thing the definition proper to another; as that of a circle to a man.[139] Wherefore the definition of one thing is false of another. In another way, by composing a definition of parts which are mutually exclusive. For thus the definition is not only false of the thing, but false in itself. A definition such as "a reasonable four-footed animal" would be of this kind, and the intellect false in making it; for such a statement as "some reasonable animals are four-footed" is false in itself. For this reason the intellect cannot be false in its knowledge of simple essences; but it is either true, or it understands nothing at all. . . .

Reply Obj. 2. The intellect is always right as regards first principles; since it is not deceived about them for the same reason that it is not deceived about what a thing is. For self-known principles are such as are known as soon as the terms are understood, from the fact that the predicate is contained in the definition of the subject.

---

[138] Cf. I, 85, 2. The sense image is not the object known but the means whereby the real object is known. St. Thomas is an epistemological realist. Since the essence of the object is directly known, error and falsehood come in the second act of the mind, judgment, not yet in the first act of the mind, conception of an essence or form. Only propositions can be false, not terms. The concept or term may be *rudimentary* or *inadequate*, but it cannot be *false*. "Justice" is neither true nor false, but "Justice is more profitable than injustice" is true, and "Justice is wholly relative to human law" is false.

[139] For the *definition* of a concept (e.g., "man") is a proposition (e.g., "Man is a rational animal"), which can be true or false.

Question 18

The Life of God

Whether to Live Belongs to All Natural Things?

I answer that, We can gather to what things life belongs, and to what it does not, from such things as manifestly possess life.[140] Now life manifestly belongs to animals, for it is said in *De Vegetab.* i [*De Plantis* i. 1] that in animals life is manifest. We must, therefore, distinguish living from lifeless things, by comparing them to that by reason of which animals are said to live: and this it is in which life is manifested first and remains last. We say then that an animal begins to live when it begins to move of itself:[141] and as long as such movement appears in it, so long is it considered to be alive. When it no longer has any movement of itself, but is only moved by another power, then its life is said to fail, and the animal to be dead. Whereby it is clear that those things are properly called living that move themselves by some kind of movement. . . . Accordingly all things are said to be alive that determine themselves to movement or operation of any kind: whereas those things that cannot by their nature do so, cannot be called living, unless by a similitude. . . .

---

[140] The question "What is life?" is not as impossibly mysterious as we often think, if only we approach it with the commonsensical method stated here.

[141] Even plants grow by their own inner life, as distinct from a crystal or a sand castle, which grow only by external accidental additions. In higher animals this self-movement is manifest especially in the motion of moving *air* by breathing. Thus in many languages, such as Greek and Hebrew, the same word means "life" (or "soul" or "spirit") and "breath" (or "wind" or "air"): *pneuma* in Greek, *ruah'* in Hebrew.

THIRD ARTICLE

Whether Life Is Properly Attributed to God?

Objection 1. It seems that life is not properly attributed to God. For things are said to live inasmuch as they move themselves, as previously stated (A. 2). But movement does not belong to God. Neither therefore does life. . . .

I answer that, Life is in the highest degree properly in God. In proof of which it must be considered that since a thing is said to live in so far as it operates of itself and not as moved by another, the more perfectly this power is found in anything, the more perfect is the life of that thing. In things that move and are moved a threefold order is found. In the first place . . . are plants, which move themselves according to their inherent nature, with regard only to executing the movements of growth and decay.

Other things have self-movement in a higher degree. . . . Of this kind are animals, in which the principle of movement is not a naturally implanted form; but one received through sense. Hence the more perfect is their sense, the more perfect is their power of self-movement. Such as have only the sense of touch, as shellfish, move only with the motion of expansion and contraction; and thus their movement hardly exceeds that of plants. Whereas such as have the sensitive power in perfection, so as to recognize not only connection and touch, but also objects apart from themselves, can move themselves to a distance by progressive movement. Yet although animals of the latter kind receive through sense the form that is the principle of their movement, nevertheless they cannot of themselves propose to themselves the end of their operation, or movement; for this has been implanted in them by nature; and by natural instinct they are moved to any action through the form apprehended by sense. Hence such animals as move themselves in respect to an end they themselves propose are superior to these. This can only be done by reason and intellect. . . .

But although our intellect moves itself to some things, yet others are supplied by nature, as are first principles, which it cannot doubt; and the last end, which it cannot but will. Hence, although with respect to some things it moves itself, yet with regard to other things it must be moved by another. Wherefore that being whose act of understanding is its very nature, and which, in what it naturally possesses, is not determined by another, must have life in the most perfect degree. Such is God; and hence in Him principally is life. . . .

Reply Obj. 1. As stated in *Metaph.* ix. 16, action is two-fold. Actions of one kind pass out to external matter, as to heat or to cut; whilst actions of the other kind remain in the agent, as to understand, to sense, and to will. The difference between them is this, that the former action is the perfection not of the agent that moves, but of the thing moved; whereas the latter action is the perfection of the agent. . . . [The former] movement is an act of the imperfect, that is, of what is in potentiality; while this kind of act is an act of the perfect, that is to say, of what is in act. . . .

Question 19

The Will of God

Whether There Is Will in God?

Objection 2. . . . Will is a kind of appetite. But appetite, as it is directed to things not possessed, implies imperfection, which cannot be imputed to God. Therefore there is not will in God.[142] . . .

I answer that, There is will in God, as there is intellect: since will follows upon intellect. For as natural things have actual existence by their form, so the intellect is actually intelligent by its intelligible form. Now everything has this aptitude towards its natural form, that when it has it not it tends towards it; and when it has it, it is at rest therein. It is the same with every natural perfection, which is a natural good. This aptitude to good in things without knowledge is called natural appetite. Whence also intellectual natures have a like aptitude as apprehended through its intelligible form; so as to rest therein when possessed, and when not possessed to seek to possess it, both of which pertain to the will. Hence in every intellectual being there is will, just as in every sensible being there is animal appetite. And so there must be will in God, since there is intellect in Him. And as His intellect is His own existence, so is His will. . . .

Reply Obj 2. Will in us belongs to the appetitive part, which, although named from appetite, has not for its only act the seeking what it does not possess; but also the loving and delighting in what it does possess. In this respect will is said to be in God, as having

---

[142] This is probably one of the major reasons (at least implicitly) why the notion of God as mere "cosmic consciousness" without personal *will* is so popular, and why the Judeo-Christian belief in a God with a will is so unusual and unpopular.

always good which is its object, since, as already said, it is not distinct from His essence.[143]. . .

SECOND ARTICLE

Whether God Wills Things Apart from Himself?

I answer that, God wills not only Himself, but other things apart from Himself. This is clear from the comparison which we made above (A. 1). For natural things have a natural inclination not only towards their own proper good, to acquire it if not possessed, and if possessed, to rest therein; but also to spread abroad their own good amongst others, so far as possible. Hence we see that every agent, in so far as it is perfect and in act, produces its like. It pertains, therefore, to the nature of the will to communicate as far as possible to others the good possessed; and especially does this pertain to the divine will, from which all perfection is derived in some kind of likeness. Hence, if natural things, in so far as they are perfect, communicate their good to others, much more does it appertain to the divine will to communicate by likeness its own good to others as much as possible. Thus, then, He wills both Himself to be, and other things to be;[144] but Himself as the end, and other things as ordained to that end; inasmuch as it befits the divine goodness that other things should be partakers therein. . . .

---

[143] Thus God is always active, dynamic, and willing, yet not in process and time and potentiality. "Process theology" argues that God must be in time and process for Him to be dynamic and active and personal. St. Thomas would reply that a temporally active God may be more perfect than an eternally static God, but an eternally active God is the most perfect of all.

[144] This is the only possible motive for a Being with no needs or imperfections to create a world: sheer generosity, "spreading the wealth" of His own goodness. To create naturally follows from His nature as goodness (*naturally* but not *necessarily*; freely—cf. Article 3), for "goodness is naturally diffusive of itself." N.b.: the act of creation is both natural and free.

THIRD ARTICLE

Whether Whatever God Wills He Wills Necessarily?

I answer that, . . . He wills something of absolute necessity: but this is not true of all that He wills. For the divine will has a necessary relation to the divine goodness, since that is its proper object. Hence God wills His own goodness necessarily, even as we will our own happiness necessarily, and as any other faculty has necessary relation to its proper and principal object, for instance the sight to color, since it tends to it by its own nature. But God wills things apart from Himself in so far as they are ordered to His own goodness as their end. Now in willing an end we do not necessarily will things that conduce to it, unless they are such that the end cannot be attained without them; as, we will to take food to preserve life, or to take ship in order to cross the sea. But we do not necessarily will things without which the end is attainable, such as a horse for a journey which we can take on foot,[145] for we can make the journey without one. The same applies to other means. Hence, since the goodness of God is perfect, and can exist without other things inasmuch as no perfection can accrue to Him from them, it follows that His willing things apart from Himself is not absolutely necessary.[146]. . .

FOURTH ARTICLE

Whether the Will of God Is the Cause of Things?

Objection 2. . . . God is the first agent. Therefore He acts by His essence; and that is His nature. He acts then by nature, and not by will. Therefore the divine will is not the cause of things. . . .

---

[145] St. Thomas himself travelled thousands of miles across Europe on foot rather than on horseback.

[146] St. Thomas opposes the "necessitarianism" of theologians too strongly influenced by Greek philosophers, especially by Plotinus; for he knows from divine revelation that God created the world freely and that He has a will—two truths the Greeks did not know and two truths which Scotus and Ockham later took to antirationalistic extremes. Cf. the next two Articles, 3 and 4 (Reply 2).

Reply Obj. 2. Because the essence of God is His intellect and will, from the fact of His acting by His essence, it follows that He acts after the mode of intellect and will.[147] . . .

Whether Any Cause Can Be Assigned to the Divine Will?

Objection 1. It seems that some cause can be assigned to the divine will. For Augustine says (Qq. lxxxiii. 46): *Who would venture to say that God made all things irrationally?* But to a voluntary agent, what is the reason of operating, is the cause of willing. Therefore the will of God has some cause.[148]

Objection 2. . . . If . . . there is no cause of His will, we cannot seek in any natural things any cause, except the divine will alone. Thus all science would be in vain. . . .

I answer that, In no wise has the will of God a cause. In proof of which we must consider that, since the will follows from the intellect, there is a cause of the will in the person that wills, in the same way as there is a cause of the understanding, in the person that understands. The case with the understanding is this: that if the premiss and its conclusion are understood separately from each other, the understanding of the premiss is the cause that the conclusion is known. If the understanding perceive the conclusion in the premiss itself, apprehending both the one and the other at the same glance, in this case the knowing of the conclusion would not be caused by understanding the premisses, since a thing cannot be its own cause; and yet, it would be true that the thinker would understand the premisses to be the cause of the conclusion. It is the same with the will, with respect to which the end stands in the same relation to the means to the end, as do the premisses to the conclusion with regard to the understanding.

---

[147] Thus Greek intellectualism and biblical voluntarism are united.

[148] Cf. Socrates' question in the *Euthyphro*: "Is a thing pious because the gods love it, or do the gods love it because it is pious?" The problem is to avoid both the intellectual imperfection of arbitrariness (the first alternative in Socrates' question) and the volitional imperfection of God's will being formed, determined, and judged by anything outside Himself (Socrates' second alternative).

Hence, if anyone in one act wills an end, and in another act the means to that end, his willing the end will be the cause of his willing the means. This cannot be the case if in one act he wills both end and means; for a thing cannot be its own cause. Yet it will be true to say that he wills to order to the end the means to the end. Now as God by one act understands all things in His essence, so by one act He wills all things in His goodness. Hence, as in God to understand the cause is not the cause of His understanding the effect, for He understands the effect in the cause, so, in Him, to will an end is not the cause of His willing the means, yet He wills the ordering of the means to the end. Therefore, He wills this to be as means to that; but does not will this on account of that.[149]

Reply Obj. 1. The will of God is reasonable, not because anything is to God a cause of willing, but in so far as He wills one thing to be on account of another.

Reply Obj. 2. . . . God wills effects to proceed from definite causes, for the preservation of order in the universe. . . .

SIXTH ARTICLE

Whether the Will of God Is Always Fulfilled?

I answer that, . . . an effect cannot possibly escape the order of the universal cause. . . . Hence that which seems to depart from the divine will in one order, returns into it in another order; as does the sinner, who by sin falls away from the divine will as much as lies in

---

[149] It may help to think of the analogy of a human novelist conceiving and willing, all at once, the entire plot of his novel, *in* which perfect order demands that one event take place because of and after another.

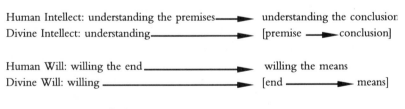

(arrows represent causality)

him, yet falls back into the order of that will, when by its justice he is punished.[150]

Reply Obj. 1. The words of the Apostle, *God will have all men to be saved*, etc., . . . are understood of the antecedent will of God; not of the consequent will. This distinction must not be taken as applying to the divine will itself, in which there is nothing antecedent nor consequent, but to the things willed.

To understand this we must consider that everything, in so far as it is good, is willed by God. A thing taken in its primary sense, and absolutely considered, may be good or evil, and yet when some additional circumstances are taken into account, by a consequent consideration may be changed into the contrary. Thus that a man should live is good; and that a man should be killed is evil, absolutely considered. But if in a particular case we add that a man is a murderer or dangerous to society, to kill him is a good; that he live is an evil. Hence it may be said of a just judge, that antecedently he wills all men to live; but consequently wills the murderer to be hanged. In the same way God antecedently wills all men to be saved, but consequently wills some to be damned, as His justice exacts. . . .

SEVENTH ARTICLE

Whether the Will of God Is Changeable?

Objection 1. It seems that the Will of God is changeable. For the Lord says (Gen 6:7): *It repenteth Me that I have made man.* But whoever repents of what he has done, has a changeable will. Therefore God has a changeable will. . . .

Objection 3. Further, whatever God does, He does voluntarily. But God does not always do the same thing, for at one time He

---

[150] The laws of God are no more escapable in the long run by any creature than the law of gravity is escapable by any body, for the laws of God encompass all reality, as gravity encompasses all physical reality. Those who defy gravity in the short run, by jumping off a cliff, illustrate it in the long run, by falling. This uncompromising doctrine of objective law is complemented by an uncompromising doctrine of human subjective free will in Article 8.

ordered the law to be observed, and at another time forbade it. Therefore He has a changeable will. . . .

On the contrary, It is said: *God is not as a man, that He should lie, nor as the son of man, that He should be changed* (Num 23:19).

I answer that, The will of God is entirely unchangeable. On this point we must consider that to change the will is one thing; to will that certain things should be changed is another. It is possible to will a thing to be done now, and its contrary afterwards; and yet for the will to remain permanently the same:[151] whereas the will would be changed, if one should begin to will what before he had not willed; or cease to will what he had willed before. This cannot happen, unless we presuppose change either in the knowledge or in the disposition of the substance of the willer. For since the will regards good, a man may in two ways begin to will a thing. In one way when that thing begins to be good for him, and this does not take place without a change in him. Thus when the cold weather begins, it becomes good to sit by the fire; though it was not so before. In another way when he knows for the first time that a thing is good for him, though he did not know it before; hence we take counsel in order to know what is good for us. Now it has already been shown that both the substance of God and His knowledge are entirely unchangeable (QQ. 9, A. 1; 14, A. 15). Therefore His will must be entirely unchangeable.

Reply Obj. 1. These words of the Lord are to be understood metaphorically, and according to the likeness of our nature. . . .

Reply Obj. 3. It does not follow from this argument that God has a will that changes, but that He sometimes wills that things should change. . . .

EIGHTH ARTICLE

Whether the Will of God Imposes Necessity on the Things Willed?

On the contrary, All good things that exist God wills to be. If therefore His will imposes necessity on things willed, it follows

---

[151] Cf. n. 149. In the sentence footnoted, "now" modifies "done", not "will".

that all good happens of necessity; and thus there is an end of free will, counsel, and all other such things.[152]

I answer that, The divine will imposes necessity on some things willed but not on all. . . . This happens on account of the efficacy of the divine will. For when a cause is efficacious to act, the effect follows upon the cause, not only as to the thing done, but also as to its manner of being done or of being. . . . Since then the divine will is perfectly efficacious, it follows not only that things are done, which God wills to be done, but also that they are done in the way that He wills. Now God wills some things to be done necessarily, some contingently, to the right ordering of things, for the building up of the universe. Therefore to some effects He has attached necessary causes, that cannot fail; but to others defectible and contingent causes, from which arise contingent effects.[153]

NINTH ARTICLE

Whether God Wills Evils?

Objection 3. . . . That evil should exist, and should not exist, are contradictory opposites. But God does not will that evil should not exist; otherwise, since various evils do exist, God's will would not always be fulfilled. Therefore God wills that evil should exist.

---

[152] Today, the popular versions of this deterministic denial of free will are subhuman, naturalistic determinisms (Freudian instinctualism, evolutionary genetic programming, environmental "behavior modification", cultural conditioning, Marxist economic historical necessity, etc.) rather than the superhuman divine determinism of Luther and Calvin and their predecessors, especially among some medieval Muslim philosophers. The logical results of both are equally absurd to common sense and practice: there is no point to praising, blaming, counseling, encouraging, or commanding a machine.

[153] N.b.: in the body of the article, St. Thomas fits human free will in with divine infallibility, not by compromising either but by seeing human free will as a *result* of divine infallibility. Man is free precisely *because* God's will is totally efficacious and infallible, not in spite of this fact. Again, the analogy of the novelist may help: he decrees that the hero be killed, not by lightning, for example, but by a freely chosen murder; *that is why* it is done freely. Instead of writing a story about machines or trees, God writes a story also about free-willed human beings. That divine efficacy is why we are free. God's Omnipotence decrees our freedom.

On the contrary, Augustine says (Qq. 83, 3): *No wise man is the cause of another man becoming worse. Now God surpasses all men in wisdom. Much less therefore is God the cause of man becoming worse: and when He is said to be the cause of a thing, He is said to will it.* Therefore it is not by God's will that man becomes worse. Now it is clear that every evil makes a thing worse. Therefore God wills not evil things.

I answer that, . . . evil may be sought accidentally,[154] so far as it accompanies a good. . . . [God] in no way wills the evil of sin, which is the privation of right order towards the divine good. The evil of natural defect, or of punishment, He does will, by willing the good to which such evils are attached. Thus in willing justice He wills punishment; and in willing the preservation of the natural order, He wills some things to be naturally corrupted. . . .

Reply Obj. 3. The statements that evil exists, and that evil exists not, are opposed as contradictories; yet the statements that anyone wills evil to exist and that he wills it not to be, are not so opposed; since either is affirmative. God therefore neither wills evil to be done, nor wills it not to be done, but wills to permit evil to be done; and this is a good.[155]. . .

ELEVENTH ARTICLE

Whether the Will of Expression Is to Be Distinguished in God?

I answer that, Some things are said of God in their strict sense; others by metaphor, as appears from what has been said before (Q. 13, A. 3). When certain human passions are predicated of the Godhead metaphorically, this is done because of a likeness in the effect. Hence a thing that is in us a sign of some passion, is signified metaphorically in God under the name of that passion. Thus with

---

[154] Punishment is an "accident" of justice not in the modern sense that it is unforeseen or mistaken, but in the Aristotelian, logical sense that it is *attached* to justice. Corruption and death are also "attached to" nature; if plants and animals did not die, new ones could not be born.

[155] The logical point here should be clear through careful rereading and a little effort.

us it is usual for an angry man to punish, so that punishment becomes an expression of anger. Therefore punishment itself is signified by the word anger, when anger is attributed to God. . . . There is, however, this difference between will and anger, that anger is never attributed to God properly, since in its primary meaning it includes passion; whereas will is attributed to Him properly.[156] . . .

---

[156] When Lady Julian of Norwich asked God to show her His wrath, she said of the divine "shewing", "I saw no wrath but on man's part." God's love is not a human projection, but God's wrath is. The sun does not hate us when it burns us if we neglect proper protection. God's justice is similar in punishing sins.

God *wills* justice, but God does not have the *passion* of anger. What St. Thomas means by "passion" is the *category* of "passion", i.e., receptivity, which involves potentiality. The modern meaning of "passion" is often the opposite: a "passionately" strong will is active and actual, not passive and potential. What is supremely present in God is *act*, but not action in time. The doctrine that God has no passions must not be confused with the idea of God as a sort of divine dishrag or cosmic wimp. As C. S. Lewis put it, the idea that the love of God is any less burning and dynamic than our temporary and derivative passions is "a most disastrous fantasy".

Question 20

God's Love

Whether Love Exists in God?

Objection 1. It seems that love does not exist in God. For in God there are no passions. Now love is a passion. Therefore love is not in God. . . .

On the contrary, It is written: *God is love* (1 Jn 4:16).

I answer that, We must needs assert that in God there is love: because love is the first movement of the will and of every appetitive faculty.[157] For since the acts of the will and of every appetitive faculty tend towards good and evil, as to their proper objects: and since good is essentially and especially the object of the will and the appetite, whereas evil is only the object secondarily and indirectly, as opposed to good; it follows that the acts of the will and appetite that regard good must naturally be prior to those that regard evil; thus, for instance, joy is prior to sorrow, love to hate: because what exists of itself is always prior to that which exists through another. Again, the more universal is naturally prior to what is less so. Hence the intellect is first directed to universal truth; and in the second place to particular and special truths. Now there are certain acts of the will and appetite that regard good under some special condition, as joy and delight regard good present and possessed; whereas desire and hope regard good not as yet possessed. Love, however, regards good universally, whether possessed or not. Hence love is naturally the first act of the will and appetite; for which reason all the other appetite movements presuppose love, as

---

[157] St. Thomas learned this psychology from St. Augustine: *amor meus, pondus meum,* "my love is my gravity."

their root and origin. For nobody desires anything nor rejoices in anything, except as a good that is loved: nor is anything an object of hate except as opposed to the object of love. Similarly, it is clear that sorrow, and other things like to it, must be referred to love as to their first principle. Hence, in whomsoever there is will and appetite, there must also be love: since if the first is wanting, all that follows is also wanting. Now it has been shown that will is in God (Q. 19, A. 1), and hence we must attribute love to Him.

Reply Obj. 1. . . . Acts of the sensitive appetite, inasmuch as they have annexed to them some bodily change, are called passions; whereas acts of the will are not so called. Love, therefore, and joy and delight are passions, in so far as they denote acts of the sensitive appetite. But in so far as they denote acts of the intellective appetite, they are not passions. It is in this latter sense that they are in God. Hence the Philosopher says (*Ethic.* vii): *God rejoices by an operation that is one and simple*, and for the same reason He loves without passion.[158] . . .

SECOND ARTICLE

Whether God Loves All Things?

Objection 4. . . . It is written (Ps 5:7): *Thou hatest all the workers of iniquity.* Now nothing is at the same time hated and loved. Therefore God does not love all things.

On the contrary, It is said (Wis 11:25): *Thou lovest all things that are, and hatest none of the things which Thou hast made.*

I answer that, God loves all existing things. For all existing things, in so far as they exist, are good, since the existence of a thing is itself a good; and likewise, whatever perfection it possesses. Now it has been shown above (Q. 19, A. 4) that God's will is the cause of all things. It must needs be, therefore, that a thing has existence, or any kind of good, only inasmuch as it is willed by God. To every existing thing, then, God wills some good. Hence, since to love anything is nothing else than to will good to that thing, it is manifest that God loves everything that exists. Yet not

---

[158] Cf. n. 156.

as we love. Because since our will is not the [active] cause of the goodness of things, but is [passively] moved by it as by its object, our love, whereby we will good to anything, is not the cause of its goodness; but conversely its goodness, whether real or imaginary, calls forth our love, by which we will that it should preserve the good it has, and receive besides the good it has not, and to this end we direct our actions: whereas the love of God infuses and creates goodness.[159] . . .

Reply Obj. 4. Nothing prevents one and the same thing being loved under one aspect, while it is hated under another. God loves sinners in so far as they are existing natures; for they have existence, and have it from Him. In so far as they are sinners, they have not existence at all, but fall short of it; and this in them is not from God. Hence under this aspect, they are hated by Him.[160]

THIRD ARTICLE

Whether God Loves All Things Equally?

On the contrary, Augustine says (*Tract. in Joan.* cx): *God loves* [1] *all things that He has made, and amongst them* [2] *rational creatures more, and of these especially* [3] *those who are members of his only-begotten Son; and much more than all,* [4] *His only-begotten Son Himself.*

I answer that, Since to love a thing is to will it good, in a twofold way anything may be loved more, or less. In one way on the part of the act of the will itself, which is more or less intense. In this way God does not love some things more than others, because He loves all things by an act of the will that is one, simple, and always the

---

[159] For God is pure act, without potentiality, and therefore without being caused or moved (changed) by other things. God does not fall in love for the same reason water does not get wet.

[160] God practices what He preaches to us: love the sinner and hate the sin. God loves even the being He created in the devil, but not the lack of being in the devil's sin. St. Thomas is not saying that sinners have no existence, but that they lack the fullness of existence that comes from loving the good. Vice and virtue have an ontological dimension as well as a moral one; we diminish our being when we sin and augment it by the virtues.

same. In another way on the part of the good itself that a person
wills for the beloved. In this way we are said to love that one more
than another, for whom we will a greater good, though our will is
not more intense. In this way we must needs say that God loves
some things more than others. For since God's love is the cause of
goodness in things, as has been said (A. 2), no one thing would be
better than another, if God did not will greater good for one than
for another.[161]. . .

FOURTH ARTICLE

Whether God Always Loves More the Better Things?

I answer that, God's will is the cause of goodness in things; and
the reason why some things are better than others, is that God wills
for them a greater good. Hence it follows that He loves more the
better things. . . .
Reply Obj. 2. . . . As to natural condition an angel is better than a
man. God therefore did not assume human nature because He
loved man, absolutely speaking, more; but because the needs of
man were greater; just as the master of a house may give some
costly delicacy to a sick servant, that he does not give to his own
son in sound health.

---

[161] It may shock those whose real religion is Americanism, but God is
not an American. God's love is hierarchically ordered, as ours should be.
(Does anyone really think we should love people no more than animals?)
The argument in the last sentence of the Article seems simple and decisive.

Question 21

The Justice and Mercy of God

Whether There Is Justice in God?

On the contrary, It is said (Ps 10:8): *The Lord is just, and hath loved justice.*

I answer that, There are two kinds of justice. The one consists in mutual giving and receiving, as in buying and selling, and other kinds of intercourse and exchange. This the Philosopher (*Ethic.* v. 4) calls commutative justice, that directs exchange and the intercourse of business. This does not belong to God, since, as the Apostle says: *Who hath first given to Him, and recompense shall be made him?* (Rom 11:35). The other consists in distribution, and is called distributive justice; whereby a ruler or a steward gives to each what his rank deserves. As then the proper order displayed in ruling a family or any kind of multitude evinces justice of this kind in the ruler, so the order of the universe, which is seen both in effects of nature and in effects of will, shows forth the justice of God. Hence Dionysius says (*Div. Nom.* viii. 4): *We must needs see that God is truly just, in seeing how He gives to all existing things what is proper to the condition of each; and preserves the nature of each one in the order and with the powers that properly belong to it. . . .*

SECOND ARTICLE

Whether the Justice of God Is Truth?

On the contrary, it is said (Ps 84:11): *Mercy and truth have met each other*: where truth stands for justice.

I answer that, Truth consists in the equation of mind and thing, as said above (Q. 16, A. 1). Now the mind that is the cause of the thing, is related to it as its rule and measure: whereas the converse is the case with the mind that receives its knowledge from things. When therefore things are the measure and rule of the mind, truth consists in the equation of the mind to the thing, as happens in ourselves. For according as a thing is, or is not, our thoughts or our words about it are true or false. But when the mind is the rule or measure of things, truth consists in the equation of the thing to the mind; just as the work of an artist is said to be true, when it is in accordance with his art.

Now as works of art are related to the art, so are works of justice related to the law with which they accord. Therefore God's justice, which establishes things in the order conformable to the rule of His wisdom, which is the law of His justice, is suitably called truth. Thus we also in human affairs speak of the truth of justice.

THIRD ARTICLE

Whether Mercy Can Be Attributed to God?

Objection 2. . . . . Mercy is a relaxation of justice. But God cannot remit what appertains to His justice. For it is said (2 Tim 2:13): *If we believe not, He continueth faithful: He cannot deny Himself.* But He would deny Himself, as a gloss says, if He should deny His words. Therefore mercy is not becoming to God. . . .

Reply Obj. 2. God acts mercifully, not indeed by going against His justice, but by doing something more than justice; thus a man who pays another two hundred pieces of money, though owing him only one hundred, does nothing against justice, but acts liberally or mercifully. The case is the same with one who pardons an offence committed against him, for in remitting it he may be said to bestow a gift. Hence the Apostle calls remission a forgiving:[162]

---

[162] Mercy is expressed in forgiveness. In the word "forgive" is the word "give". For forgiveness is not primarily an attitude or feeling, but a gift, remitting a debt, and therefore it costs the giver something. God's forgiveness of human sin cost Him dearly on Calvary. Both justice and mercy were satisfied there (see Ps 84:11).

Forgive one another, as Christ has forgiven you (Eph 4:32). Hence it is clear that mercy does not destroy justice, but in a sense is the fulness thereof. And thus it is said: *Mercy exalteth itself above judgment* (James 2:13).

FOURTH ARTICLE

Whether in Every Work of God There Are Mercy and Justice?

On the contrary, It is said (Ps 24:10): *All the ways of the Lord are mercy and truth.*

I answer that, Mercy and truth are necessarily found in all God's works, if mercy be taken to mean the removal of any kind of defect. Not every defect, however, can properly be called a misery; but only defect in a rational nature whose lot is to be happy; for misery is opposed to happiness. For this necessity there is a reason, because since a debt paid according to the divine justice is one due either to God, or to some creature, neither the one nor the other can be lacking in any work of God: because God can do nothing that is not in accord with His wisdom and goodness; and it is in this sense, as we have said, that . . . whatever is done by Him in created things, is done according to proper order and proportion wherein consists the idea of justice. Thus justice must exist in all God's works. Now the work of divine justice always presupposes the work of mercy; and is founded thereupon.[163] For . . . since we cannot go on to infinity, we must come to something that depends only on the goodness of the divine will—which is the ultimate end. We may say, for instance, that to possess hands is due to man on account of his rational soul; and his rational soul is due to him that he may be man; and his being man is on account of the divine goodness. So in every work of God, viewed at its primary source, there appears mercy. . . .

---

[163] We tend to reverse this formula. But mercy, as a property of love, is more primordial than justice. Justice is finite, and proportioned to desert; love can be infinite. Our very existence is due to mercy and generosity, not justice, for we were not even there to deserve anything, even existence, before God gave us the gift of existence.

Question 22

The Providence of God

Whether Providence Can Suitably Be Attributed to God?

I answer that, It is necessary to attribute providence to God. For all the good that is in created things has been created by God, as was shown above (Q. 6, A. 4). In created things good is found not only as regards their substance, but also as regards their order towards an end and especially their last end, which, as was said above, is the divine goodness (Q. 21, A. 4). This good of order existing in things created, is itself created by God. Since, however, God is the cause of things by His intellect, and thus it behooves that the type [model or plan] of every effect should pre-exist in Him, as is clear from what has gone before (Q. 19, A. 4), it is necessary that the type of the order of things towards their end should pre-exist in the divine mind: and the type of things ordered towards an end is, properly speaking, providence. . . .

Whether Everything Is Subject to the Providence of God? [164]

Objection 1. It seems that everything is not subject to divine providence. For nothing foreseen can happen by chance. If then everything was foreseen by God, nothing would happen by chance. And thus hazard and luck would disappear; which is against common opinion.

Objection 2. Further, a wise provider excludes any defect or evil,

---

[164] Here the Christian and Greek world views are radically contradictory, for there is ultimately no room for real chance in a universe created, designed, and providentially cared for by God.

as far as he can, from those over whom he has a care. But we see many evils existing. Either, then, God cannot hinder these, and thus is not omnipotent; or else He does not have care for everything.

On the contrary, It is said of Divine Wisdom: *She reacheth from end to end mightily, and ordereth all things sweetly* (Wis 8:1).

I answer that, . . . all things are subject to divine providence, not only in general, but even in their own individual selves. This is made evident thus. For since every agent acts for an end, the ordering of effects towards that end extends as far as the causality of the first agent extends. . . . It necessarily follows that all things, inasmuch as they participate existence, must likewise be subject to divine providence. . . .

Reply Obj. 1. There is a difference between universal and particular causes. A thing can escape the order of a particular cause; but not the order of a universal cause. For nothing escapes the order of a particular cause, except through the intervention and hindrance of some other particular cause; as, for instance, wood may be prevented from burning, by the action of water. Since then, all particular causes are included under the universal cause, it could not be that any effect should take place outside the range of that universal cause. So far then as an effect escapes the order of a particular cause, it is said to be casual or fortuitous in respect to that cause; but if we regard the universal cause, outside whose range no effect can happen, it is said to be foreseen. Thus, for instance, the meeting of two servants, although to them it appears a chance circumstance, has been fully foreseen by their master, who has purposely sent them to meet at the one place, in such a way that the one knows not about the other.

Reply Obj. 2. It is otherwise with one who has care of a particular thing, and one whose providence is universal, because a particular provider excludes all defects from what is subject to his care as far as he can; whereas, one who provides universally allows some little defect to remain, lest the good of the whole should be hindered. Hence, corruption and defects in natural things are said to be contrary to some particular nature; yet they are in keeping with the plan of universal nature; inasmuch as the defect in one thing yields to the good of another, or even to the universal good: for the corruption of one is the generation of another, and through this it is that a species is kept in existence. Since God, then, provides universally for all being, it belongs to His providence to permit certain defects in particular effects, that the perfect good of the universe may not be hindered, for if all evil were prevented, much good would be absent from the universe. A lion would cease to live, if there were no slaying of animals; and there would be no patience of martyrs if there were no tyrannical persecution. Thus Augustine says (*Enchir.* ii): *Almighty God would in no wise permit evil to exist in His works, unless He were so almighty and so good as to produce good even from evil.* It would appear that it was on account of these two arguments to which we have just replied, that some were persuaded to consider corruptible things—*e.g.*, casual and evil things—as removed from the care of divine providence.[165] . . .

THIRD ARTICLE

Whether God Has Immediate Providence over Everything?

I answer that, . . . there are certain intermediaries of God's providence; for He governs things inferior by superior, not on account of any defect in His power, but by reason of the abundance of His goodness; so that the dignity of causality is imparted even to creatures.[166] . . .

FOURTH ARTICLE

Whether Providence Imposes Any Necessity on Things Foreseen?

Objection 1. It seems that divine providence imposes necessity upon things foreseen . . . for divine providence cannot be frustrated.[167] .

---

[165] The idea that God does not control all events, especially evils, is still popular today (cf. Rabbi Kushner's best-selling book, *When Bad Things Happen to Good People*). Our natural negative *emotional* reaction to divine providence allowing evils into our lives does not, however, invalidate St. Thomas' *argument*.

[166] Cf. Pascal: "God instituted prayer to communicate to creatures the dignity of causality."

[167] St. Thomas answers the objection not by compromising the efficacy

On the contrary, Dionysius says that (*Div. Nom.* iv. 23) *to corrupt nature is not the work of providence*. But it is in the nature of some things to be contingent. Divine providence does not therefore impose any necessity upon things so as to destroy their contingency.

I answer that, Divine providence imposes necessity upon some things; not upon all, as some formerly believed. For to providence it belongs to order things towards an end. Now after the divine goodness, which is an extrinsic end to all things, the principal good in things themselves is the perfection of the universe; which would not be, were not all grades of being found in things. Whence it pertains to divine providence to produce every grade of being. And thus it has prepared for some things necessary causes, so that they happen of necessity; for others contingent causes, that they may happen by contingency, according to the nature of their proximate causes.

Reply Obj. 1. The effect of divine providence is not only that things should happen somehow; but that they should happen either by necessity or by contingency. Therefore whatsoever divine providence ordains to happen infallibly and of necessity happens infallibly and of necessity; and that happens from contingency, which the plan of divine providence conceives to happen from contingency. . . .

---

or infallibility of divine providence at all, but by deriving from it (and from the principle that grace perfects nature rather than corrupting it) the proper contingency of human events. (Cf. I, 19, 8.) Essentially, the objection is that because God's will is never frustrated, therefore all effects are necessary; and the answer is that precisely because God's will is never frustrated, therefore not all effects are necessary.

Question 23

Of Predestination[168]

Whether Men Are Predestined by God?

On the contrary, It is written (Rom 8:30): *Whom He predestined, them He also called.*

I answer that, It is fitting that God should predestine men. For all things are subject to His providence, as was shown above (Q. 22, A. 2). Now it belongs to providence to direct things towards their end, as was also said (Q. 22, AA. 1, 2). The end towards which created things are directed by God is twofold; one which exceeds all proportion and faculty of created nature; and this end is life eternal, that consists in seeing God which is above the nature of every creature, as shown above (Q. 12, 4). The other end, however, is proportionate to created nature, to which end created being can attain according to the power of its nature. Now if a thing cannot attain to something by the power of its nature, it must be directed thereto by another; thus, an arrow is directed by the archer towards a mark. Hence, properly speaking, a rational creature, capable of eternal life, is led towards it, directed, as it were, by God. . . .

THIRD ARTICLE

Whether God Reprobates [Damns] *Any Man?*

Objection 2. . . . If God reprobates any man, it would be necessary for reprobation to have the same relation to the reprobate as

---

[168] The "pre" in "predestination" is, of course (like the "first" in "First Cause") from our point of view only, since God is not in time. Time does not determine God; God determines time.

predestination has to the predestined. But predestination is the cause of the salvation of the predestined. Therefore reprobation will likewise be the cause of the loss of the reprobate. But this is false. For it is said (Hosea 13:9): *Destruction is thy own, O Israel; Thy help is only in Me.* God does not, then, reprobate any man. . . .

I answer that, . . . as men are ordained to eternal life through the providence of God, it likewise is part of that providence to permit some to fall away from that end; this is called reprobation.[169] . . .

Reply Obj. 2. Reprobation differs in its causality from predestination. This latter is the cause both of what is expected in the future life by the predestined—namely, glory—and of what is received in this life—namely, grace. Reprobation, however, is not the cause of what is in the present—namely, sin; but it is the cause of abandonment by God. It is the cause, however, of what is assigned in the future—namely, eternal punishment. But guilt proceeds from the free will of the person who is reprobated and deserted by grace. . . .

FIFTH ARTICLE

Whether the Foreknowledge of Merits Is the Cause of Predestination?

Objection 2. . . . Divine predestination includes the divine will, which by no means can be irrational; since predestination is *the purpose to have mercy*, as Augustine says (*De Praed. Sanct.* ii. 17). But there can be no other reason for predestination than the foreknowledge of merits. Therefore it must be the cause or reason of predestination. . . .

On the contrary, The Apostle says (Titus 3:5): *Not by the works of*

---

[169] Note the difference between the positive, causally efficacious "ordaining" in predestination and the purely negative *permitting* in reprobation. Cf. Article 1: God's causal activity is necessary to predestine men to a salvation above their natural capacity, but reprobation is not parallel to this. God saves the saved; the damned damn themselves (Cf. Reply 2). St. Thomas strongly affirmed both predestination and free will, like Augustine and unlike Luther and Calvin, who denied free will, and unlike Pelagius and Arminius, who denied predestination.

justice which we have done, but according to His mercy He saved us. But as He saved us, so He predestined that we should be saved. Therefore, foreknowledge of merits is not the cause or reason of predestination.

I answer that, . . . [Some] said that pre-existing merits in this life are the reason and cause of the effect of predestination. For the Pelagians taught that the beginning of doing well came from us; and the consummation from God: so that it came about that the effect of predestination was granted to one, and not to another, because the one made a beginning by preparing, whereas the other did not. But against this we have the saying of the Apostle (2 Cor 3:5), that *we are not sufficient to think anything of ourselves as of ourselves.* . . .

And so others said that merits following the effect of predestination are the reason of predestination; giving us to understand that God gives grace to a person, and pre-ordains that He will give it, because He knows beforehand that He will make good use of that grace, as if a king were to give a horse to a soldier because he knows he will make good use of it. But these seem to have drawn a distinction between that which flows from grace, and that which flows from free will, as if the same thing cannot come from both.[170] It is, however, manifest that what is of grace is the effect of predestination; and this cannot be considered as the reason of predestination. . . . Now there is no distinction between what flows from free will, and what is of predestination; as there is no distinction between what flows from a secondary cause and from a first cause. For the providence of God produces effects through the operation of secondary causes, as was above shown (Q. 22, A. 3). Wherefore, that which flows from free will is also of predestination [cf. n. 170]. . . .

Reply Obj. 2. Predestination has its foundation in the goodness of God.[171] . . .

---

[170] This is a key principle in solving the thorny old problem of grace and free will. Again the analogy of the novelist may help: the protagonist's choices come both wholly from his free will *and* wholly from the author.

[171] This is the ultimate reason, first cause, and sourceless source of all grace. St. Thomas is as strong as Calvin on the absolute sovereignty of God.

SEVENTH ARTICLE

Whether the Number of the Predestined Is Certain?

I answer that, . . . concerning the number of all the predestined, some say that so many men will be saved as angels fell; some, so many as there were angels left; others, as many as the number of angels who fell, added to that of all the angels created by God. It is, however, better to say that, *to God alone is known the number for whom is reserved eternal happiness.*[172] [From the *secret* prayer in the missal, *pro vivis et defunctis.*]

EIGHTH ARTICLE

Whether Predestination Can Be Furthered by the Prayers of the Saints?

I answer that, Concerning this question, there were different errors. Some, regarding the certainty of divine predestination, said that prayers were superfluous, as also anything else done to attain salvation; because whether these things were done or not, the predestined would attain, and the reprobate would not attain, eternal salvation. But against this opinion are all the warnings of Holy Scripture, exhorting us to prayer and other good works.

Others declared that the divine predestination was altered through prayer. . . . Against this also is the authority of Scripture. For it is said: *But the triumpher in Israel will not spare and will not be moved to repentance* (I Kings 15:29); and that *the gifts and the calling of God are without repentance* (Rom 11:29).

Wherefore we must say otherwise that in predestination two things are to be considered—namely, the divine preordination; and its effect. As regards the former, in no possible way can predestination be furthered by the prayers of the saints. For it is not due to their prayers that anyone is predestined by God. As regards the latter, predestination is said to be helped by the prayers of the

---

[172] A typically sober and reasonable Thomistic solution. Note his *habit* of mind here.

saints, and by other good works; because providence, of which predestination is a part, does not do away with secondary causes but so provides effects, that the order of secondary causes falls also under providence. So, as natural effects are provided by God in such a way that natural causes are directed to bring about those natural effects, without which those effects would not happen; so the salvation of a person is predestined by God in such a way, that whatever helps that person towards salvation falls under the order of predestination; whether it be one's own prayers, or those of another; or other good works, and suchlike, without which one would not attain to salvation. Whence, the predestined must strive after good works and prayer; because through these means predestination is most certainly fulfilled. For this reason it is said: *Labor the more that by good works you may make sure your calling and election* (2 Pet 1:10).[173] . . .

---

[173] "Prayer changes things." Prayer does not change *God*, but it changes *things*, and people. The reason to pray is not to change God's will, but to fulfill it. It is the same reason as the reason to work (cf. n. 166).

Question 25

The Power of God

FIRST ARTICLE

Whether There Is Power in God?

Objection 1. It seems that power is not in God. For as primary matter is to power, so God, who is the first agent, is to act. But primary matter, considered in itself, is devoid of all act. Therefore, the first agent—namely, God—is devoid of power. . . .

Reply Obj. 1. Active power is not contrary to act, but is founded upon it, for everything acts according as it is actual: but passive power is contrary to act; for a thing is passive according as it is potential. Whence this potentiality is not in God, but only active power.[174]. . .

SECOND ARTICLE

Whether the Power of God Is Infinite?

Objection 1. It seems that the power of God is not infinite. For everything that is infinite is imperfect according to the Philosopher (*Phys.* iii. 6).[175] But the power of God is far from imperfect. Therefore it is not infinite. . . .

I answer that, As stated above (A. 1), active power exists in God

---

[174] St. Thomas distinguishes *power* and *potentiality*, or active power and passive power. The Aristotelian and Thomistic category of "potentiality" means "passivity"; "potentiality" in modern English often means "active power".

[175] This is the Greek notion of infinity (e.g., in Anaxagoras) as infinite *potentiality*, or prime matter.

according to the measure in which He is actual. Now His existence is infinite, inasmuch as it is not limited by anything that receives it, as is clear from what has been said, when we discussed the infinity of the divine essence (Q. 7, A. 1). Wherefore, it is necessary that the active power in God should be infinite. For in every agent is it found that the more perfectly an agent has the form by which it acts the greater its power to act. For instance, the hotter a thing is, the greater power has it to give heat; and it would have infinite power to give heat, were its own heat infinite. Whence, since the divine essence, through which God acts, is infinite, as was shown above (l.c.), it follows that His power likewise is infinite.

Reply Obj. 1. The Philosopher is here speaking of an infinity in regard to matter not limited by any form; and such infinity belongs to quantity. But the divine essence is otherwise, as was shown above (l.c.); and consequently so also His power. It does not follow, therefore, that it is imperfect. . . .

THIRD ARTICLE

Whether God Is Omnipotent?

I answer that, All confess that God is omnipotent; but it seems difficult to explain in what His omnipotence precisely consists: for there may be doubt as to the precise meaning of the word "all" when we say that God can do all things. If, however, we consider the matter aright, since power is said in reference to possible things, this phrase, *God can do all things*, is rightly understood to mean that God can do all things that are possible; and for this reason He is said to be omnipotent. Now according to the Philosopher (*Metaph.* v. 17), a thing is said to be possible in two ways. First in relation to some power, thus whatever is subject to human power is said to be possible to man. Secondly absolutely, on account of the relation in which the very terms stand to each other.[176] Now God

---

[176] "Absolutely possible" means intrinsically possible, logically possible, possible in all worlds; not just physically possible, or possible under the laws of some particular world. God's power extends to miracles, which are exceptions to physical laws, but not to contradictions, which are

cannot be said to be omnipotent through being able to do all things that are possible to created nature; for the divine power extends farther than that. If, however, we were to say that God is omnipotent because He can do all things that are possible to His power, there would be a vicious circle in explaining the nature of His power. For this would be saying nothing else but that God is omnipotent, because He can do all that He is able to do.

It remains therefore, that God is called omnipotent because he can do all things that are possible absolutely; which is the second way of saying a thing is possible. For a thing is said to be possible or impossible absolutely, according to the relation in which the very terms stand to one another, possible if the predicate is not incompatible with the subject, as that Socrates sits; and absolutely impossible when the predicate is altogether incompatible with the subject, as, for instance, that a man is a donkey.

. . . Whatsoever has or can have the nature of being, is numbered among the absolutely possible things, in respect of which God is called omnipotent. Now nothing is opposed to the idea of being except non-being. Therefore, that which implies being and non-being at the same time is repugnant to the idea of an absolutely possible thing, within the scope of the divine omnipotence. For such cannot come under the divine omnipotence, not because of any defect in the power of God, but because it has not the nature of a feasible or possible thing. Therefore, everything that does not imply a contradiction in terms, is numbered amongst those possible things, in respect of which God is called omnipotent: whereas whatever implies contradiction does not come within the scope of divine omnipotence, because it cannot have the aspect of possibility. Hence it is better to say that such things cannot be done, than that God cannot do them. Nor is this contrary to the word of the angel,

---

exceptions to logical laws; for such a thing would be simply meaningless. God can create a universe out of nothing, but He cannot both create and not create at the same time. A meaningless set of words, like "a man who is at the same time not a man but a donkey", do not become meaningful just because someone says God can do them. God is not *subject* to the laws of logic, but the laws of logic and metaphysics are the laws of being, based on God's own absolute and unchangeable nature, and God cannot contradict His own nature.

saying: *No word shall be impossible with God.* For whatever implies a contradiction cannot be a word, because no intellect can possibly conceive such a thing. . . .

FOURTH ARTICLE

Whether God Can Make the Past Not to Have Been?

I answer that, As was said above (Q. 7, A. 2), there does not fall under the scope of God's omnipotence anything that implies a contradiction. Now that the past should not have been implies a contradiction. For as it implies a contradiction to say that Socrates is sitting, and is not sitting, so does it to say that he sat, and did not sit. But to say that he did sit is to say that it happened in the past. To say that he did not sit, is to say that it did not happen. Whence, that the past should not have been, does not come under the scope of divine power. . . .

Reply Obj. 1. . . . It is more impossible than the raising of the dead; in which there is nothing contradictory, because this is reckoned impossible in reference to some power, that is to say, some natural power; for such impossible things do come beneath the scope of divine power. . . .

SIXTH ARTICLE

Whether God Can Do Better Than What He Does?

Objection 3. . . . What is very good and the best of all cannot be bettered; because nothing is better than the best. But as Augustine says (*Enchir.* 10), *each thing that God has made is good, and, taken all together they are very good; because in them all consists the wondrous beauty of the universe.* Therefore the good in the universe could not be made better by God.[177] . . .

---

[177] This raises Leibnitz' question of whether this world is "the best of all possible worlds". St. Thomas' commonsensical answer is "Of course not." Possible finite worlds are like the finite number series: a higher and better one can always be conceived.

On the contrary, It is said (Eph 3:20): *God is able to do all things more abundantly than we desire or understand.*

I answer that, The goodness of anything is twofold; one, which is of the essence of it—thus, for instance, to be rational pertains to the essence of man. As regards this good, God cannot make a thing better than it is itself; although He can make another thing better than it; even as He cannot make the number four greater than it is; because if it were greater it would no longer be four, but another number. . . . Another kind of goodness is that which is over and above the essence; thus, the good of a man is to be virtuous or wise. As regards this kind of goodness, God can make better the things He has made. Absolutely speaking, however, God can make something else better than each thing made by Him. . . .

Reply Obj. 3. The universe, the present creation being supposed, cannot be better, on account of the most beautiful order given to things by God; in which the good of the universe consists. For if any one thing were bettered, the proportion of order would be destroyed; as if one string were stretched more than it ought to be, the melody of the harp would be destroyed. Yet God could make other things, or add something to the present creation; and then there would be another and a better universe. . . .

Question 26

Of the Divine Beatitude

FOURTH ARTICLE

Whether All Other Beatitude Is Included in the Beatitude of God?

On the contrary, Beatitude is a certain perfection. But the divine perfection embraces all other perfection, as was shown above (Q. 4, A. 2). Therefore the divine beatitude embraces all other beatitudes.

I answer that, Whatever is desirable in whatsoever beatitude, whether true or false, pre-exists wholly and in a more eminent degree in the divine beatitude. As to contemplative happiness, God possesses a continual and most certain contemplation of Himself and of all things else; and as to that which is active, he has the governance of the whole universe. As to earthly happiness, which consists in delight, riches, power, dignity, and fame, according to Boëthius (*De Consol.* iii. 10), He possesses joy in Himself and all things else for His delight; instead of riches He has that complete self-sufficiency, which is promised by riches; in place of power, He has omnipotence; for dignities, the government of all things; and in place of fame, He possesses the admiration of all creatures. . . .

FOUR

Cosmology:
Creation and Providence

Question 44

The Procession of Creatures from God, and of the First Cause of All Things

FIRST ARTICLE

Whether It Is Necessary[1] That Every Being Be Created by God?

Objection 1. It would seem that it is not necessary that every being be created by God. For there is nothing to prevent a thing from being without that which does not belong to its essence, as a man can be found without whiteness. But the relation of the thing caused to its cause does not appear to be essential to beings, for some beings can be understood without it; therefore they can exist without it,[2] and therefore it is possible that some beings should not be created by God. . . .

---

[1] The question is not whether the *being* of creatures is necessary. Obviously, if they are creatures, dependent on their Creator for their being, they are not necessary but contingent. The question is whether it is *logically* necessary that all beings be relative to and dependent on God's act of creating them (causing their very existence). Or could there possibly be, as the Greeks thought, a plurality of existentially independent beings in addition to God? For Plato there were *four* co-eternal beings: the maker-God, or "Demiurge"; matter, or the "Receptacle" of Form; the Forms, or "Ideas"; and the Good, or final cause and end of everything. (This is the source, from Plato's *Timaeus*, of Aristotle's doctrine of the "four causes".) Christianity reduces matter to a creature and the other three causes to the Creator. St. Thomas asks here whether this Creator–creature dualism is absolutely necessary, logically.

[2] Nothing can be understood without its essence. But creatures (e.g., water) can be understood without understanding their relation to their first cause (God). Therefore this relation to God is not part of creatures'

On the contrary, It is said (Rom 11:36) *Of Him, and by Him, and in Him are all things.*

I answer that, It must be said that every being in any way existing is from God. For whatever is found in anything by participation, must be caused in it by that to which it belongs essentially, as iron becomes ignited by fire.[3] Now it has been shown above (Q. 3, A. 4) when treating of the divine simplicity that God is the essentially self-subsisting Being; and also it was shown (Q. 11, AA. 3, 4) that subsisting being must be one. . . . Therefore all beings apart from God are not their own being, but are beings by participation.[4] Therefore it must be that . . . things which are diversified by the diverse participation of being, . . . are caused by one First Being. . . .

Reply Obj. 1. Though the relation to its cause is not part of the definition of a thing caused, still it follows, as a consequence, on what belongs to its essence; because from the fact that a thing has being by participation, it follows that it is caused. Hence such a being cannot be without being caused, just as man cannot be without having the faculty of laughing.[5] But, since to be caused does not enter into the essence of being as such, therefore is it possible for us to find a being uncaused. . . .

FOURTH ARTICLE

Whether God Is the Final Cause [End] *of All Things?*

Objection 1. It would seem that God is not the final cause of all things. For to act for an end seems to imply need of the end. But

---

essence. The Objection is not *deducing* existence from essence in this sentence, as St. Anselm did in his "ontological argument".

[3] A more scientifically accurate illustration might be that paper becomes wet by participation in water. The medievals *identified* heat with fire.

[4] I.e., they are not the source of their own being, but they receive their being from a cause. A cause of *being* (existence) = a creator.

[5] Being caused is not the *essence* of being-by-participation, but it is *essential* to it, i.e., it flows from the essence as an essential property, or "proper accident"—just as being able to laugh is not the essence of a man but flows from his essence as a *"proper accident"*, and *must* be present, rather than an *accidental* quality like baldness.

God needs nothing. Therefore it does not become Him to act for an end. . . .

Objection 3. Further, all things desire their end. But all things do not desire God, for all do not even know Him. Therefore God is not the end of all things. . . .

On the contrary, It is said (Prov 16:4): *The Lord has made all things for Himself.*

I answer that, Every agent acts for an end: otherwise one thing would not follow more than another from the action of the agent, unless it were by chance.[6]. . . But it does not belong to the First Agent, Who is agent only, to act for the acquisition of some end; He intends only to communicate His perfection, which is His goodness;[7] while every creature intends to acquire its own perfection, which is the likeness of the divine perfection and goodness. Therefore the divine goodness is the end of all things.

Reply Obj. 1. To act from need belongs only to an imperfect agent, which by its nature is both agent and patient. But this does not belong to God, and therefore He alone is the most perfectly liberal giver, because He does not act for His own profit, but only for His own goodness. . . .

Reply Obj. 3. All things desire God as their end, when they desire some good thing, whether this desire be intellectual or sensible, or natural, *i.e.,* without knowledge; because nothing is good and desirable except forasmuch as it participates in the likeness to God.[8]. . .

---

[6] Here is St. Thomas' (and Aristotle's) fundamental argument for a teleological view of nature—a view largely abandoned in modern philosophy and culture as well as in modern science. Teleology, or final causality, proved to be an unfruitful notion in physical science; but that fact does not prove the nonexistence of final causes. Nor does it entail their unfruitfulness in philosophy.

[7] Note how the very concrete and practical fact of the divine liberality, generosity, and unselfish love is grounded in the very abstract metaphysical principle that God is "agent only", i.e., pure act without potentiality, need, or process in time.

[8] Thus grass grows, stones fall, and stars shine out of their desire for God!

Question 45

The Mode of Emanation of Things
from the First Principle

Whether to Create Is to Make Something from Nothing?

On the contrary, On the text of Gen 1, *In the beginning God created,* etc., the gloss has *To create is to make something from nothing.*

I answer that, As said above (Q. 44, A. 2), we must consider not only the emanation of a particular being from a particular agent, but also the emanation of all being from the universal cause, which is God; and this emanation we designate by the name of creation. Now . . . when a man is generated, he was not before, but man is made from *not-man.* . . . Therefore as the generation of a man is from the *not-being* which is *not-man,* so creation, which is the emanation of all being, is from the *not-being* which is *nothing.* . . .

Reply Obj. 3. When anything is said to be made from nothing, this preposition *from* (*ex*) does not signify the material cause,[9] but only order; as when we say, *from morning comes midday*—*i.e.*, after morning is midday. . . .

Whether God Can Create Anything?

Objection 1. It would seem that God cannot create anything, because, according to the Philosopher (*Phys.* i, text 34), the ancient philosophers considered it as a commonly received axiom [self-

---

[9] "Nothing" is nothing at all, not something, as a material cause (e.g., space, or formless matter, or even potentiality). The only cause of creation is the Creator. He needs no aids.

evident first principle] that *nothing is made from nothing*. But the power of God does not extend to the contraries of first principles as, for instance, that God could make the whole to be less than its part, or that affirmation and negation are both true at the same time. Therefore God cannot make anything from nothing, or create. . . .

Objection 4. Further, infinite distance cannot be crossed. But infinite distance exists between being and nothing. Therefore it does not happen that something is made from nothing.

On the contrary, It is said (Gen 1:1): *In the beginning God created heaven and earth.*

I answer that, Not only is it possible that anything should be created by God, but it is necessary to say that all things were created by God, as appears from what has been said (Q. 44, A. 1). For when anyone makes one thing from another, this latter thing from which he makes [the material cause] is presupposed to his action, and is not produced by his action; thus the craftsman works from natural things, as wood or brass, which are caused not by the action of [his] art, but by the action of nature. So also nature itself causes natural things as regards their form, but presupposes matter.[10] If therefore God did only act from something presupposed, it would follow that the thing presupposed would not be caused by Him. Now it has been shown above (Q. 44, AA. 1, 2), that nothing can be, unless it is from God, Who is the universal cause of all being. Hence it is necessary to say that God brings things into being from nothing.

Reply Obj. 1. Ancient philosophers, as is said above (Q. 44, A. 2), considered only the emanation of particular effects from particular causes, which necessarily presuppose something in their action; whence came their common opinion that *nothing is made from nothing*. But this has no place in the first emanation from the universal principle of things. . . .

Reply Obj. 4. This objection proceeds from a false imagination, as if there were an infinite medium between nothing and being; which is plainly false. This false imagination comes from creation being taken to signify a change existing between two terms.[11]

---

[10] By nature, dogs are made from puppies, and puppies from dogs, as from a material cause.

[11] A. Creation is not a change in time from one state to another, for it is

FIFTH ARTICLE

Whether It Belongs to God Alone to Create?

I answer that, It sufficiently appears at the first glance, according to what precedes (A. 1), that to create can be the action of God alone. For the more universal effects must be reduced to [explained by] the more universal and prior causes. Now among all effects the most universal is being itself: and hence it must be the proper effect of the first and most universal cause, and that is God. . . .

And above all it is absurd to suppose that a body can create, for no body acts except by touching or moving; and thus it requires in its action some pre-existing thing, which can be touched or moved, which is contrary to the very idea of creation. . . .

SIXTH ARTICLE

Whether to Create Is Proper to Any Person?

I answer that, To create is, properly speaking, to cause or produce the being of things. And as every agent produces its like, the principle of action can be considered from the effect of the action; for it must be fire that generates fire.[12] And therefore to create belongs to God according to His being, that is, His essence, which is common to the three Persons. Hence to create is not proper to any one Person, but is common to the whole Trinity.

Nevertheless the divine Persons, according to the nature of their procession, have a causality respecting the creation of things.[13] For

---

not a process in time at all. God created time itself.

B. And there is no previous state in creation-out-of-nothing. "Nothing" is not a state out of which creation produced a second state; creation is thus not a relation "between two terms", or end points.

[12] I.e., the nature of the agent or source of any action can be inferred from the result of the action, since the effect must resemble the cause.

[13] I.e., the order and structure of the act of God creating creatures depends on the order and structure within God, i.e., the relationship among the three Persons in the Trinity. The Father creates through His Son, the *Logos* (Word, or Truth) and His Spirit (Love, or Goodness). The

as was said above (Q. 14, A. 8; Q. 19, A. 4), when treating of the knowledge and will of God, God is the cause of things by His intellect and will, just as the craftsman is cause of the things made by his craft. Now the craftsman works through the word conceived in his mind, and through the love of his will regarding some object. Hence also God the Father made the creature through His Word, which is His Son; and through His Love, which is the Holy Ghost. And so the processions of the Persons are the type [archetype, model] of the productions of creatures inasmuch as they include the essential attributes, knowledge and will. . . .

SEVENTH ARTICLE

Whether in Creatures Is Necessarily Found a Trace of the Trinity? [14]

On the contrary, Augustine says (*De Trin.* vi. 10) that *the trace of the Trinity appears in creatures.*

I answer that, Every effect in some degree represents its cause, but diversely. For some effects represent only the causality of the cause, but not its form; as smoke represents fire. Such a representation is called a *trace,* for a trace shows that someone has passed by but not who it is. Other effects represent the cause as regards the similitude of its form, as fire generated represents fire generating;

---

ultimate reason why all creatures are true and good is because *God* is Truth and Goodness, and He creates by His intellect (which is Truth) and His will (which is Goodness). This is also the reason why *we* create by our knowledge and will. See also the next Article.

[14] St. Thomas does not claim we can *deduce* or prove this threefold feature of creatures from the Trinity, nor that we can deduce or prove the Trinity from this threefold feature of creatures; but once we know, by divine revelation, the fact of the Trinity, we can see Its traces in all things and Its image in man. Finding Trinitarian echoes or traces was a favorite occupation of many medieval philosophers, following St. Augustine. It is rare today only because it is unfashionable, not because it has been shown to be unreasonable. Indeed, how could there *not* be ubiquitous Trinitarian resemblances if the Trinity is the true Designer and Design of all reality? Cf. Nathan R. Wood and G. Campbell Morgan, *The Trinity in the Universe* (Grand Rapids: Kregel, 1984).

and a statue of Mercury represents Mercury; and this is called the representation of *image*. Now the processions of the divine Persons are referred to the acts of intellect and will, as was said above (Q. 27). For the Son proceeds as the word of the intellect; and the Holy Ghost proceeds as love of the will. Therefore in rational creatures, possessing intellect and will, there is found the representation of the Trinity by way of image, inasmuch as there is found in them the [mental] word conceived, and the love proceeding.

But in all creatures there is found the trace of the Trinity, inasmuch as in every creature are found some things which are necessarily reduced to the divine Persons as to their cause. For every creature [1] subsists in its own being, and [2] has a form, whereby it is determined to a species, and [3] has relation to something else. Therefore [1] as it is a created substance, it represents the cause and principle; and so in that manner it shows the Person of the Father, Who is the *principle from no principle*. [2] According as it has a form and species, it represents the Word, as the form of the thing made by art is from the conception [mental word] of the craftsman. [3] According as it has relation of order, it represents the Holy Ghost, inasmuch as He is love, because the order of the effect to something else is from the will of the Creator. And therefore Augustine says (*De Trin.* vi, *loc. cit.*) that the trace of the Trinity is found in every creature, [1] according as *it is one individual*, and [2] according *as it is formed by a species*, and [3] according as it *has a certain relation of order*. . . .

Question 46

Of the Beginning of
the Duration of Creatures

Whether the Universe of Creatures Always Existed? [15]

Objection 1. It would seem that the universe of creatures, called the world, had no beginning, but existed from eternity. For everything which begins to exist, is a possible being before it exists: otherwise it would be impossible for it to exist. If therefore the world began to exist, it was a possible being before it began to exist. But possible being is matter. . . . If therefore the world began to exist, matter must have existed before the world. . . .

Objection 3. Further, what is unbegotten has no beginning. But

---

[15] The issue is important for the Middle Ages because Aristotle had apparently proved that the world was eternal, but Scripture had revealed that it had a beginning; thus philosophy and revealed theology, reason and faith, seemed to contradict each other, invalidating the central medieval enterprise of their marriage.

In modern scientific cosmology, the "Steady State theory" was the equivalent of the Aristotelian eternal universe theory, and the "Big Bang" theory, which gives the world a temporal beginning, fits in nicely with the idea of creation *of* time (rather than creation *in* time). The scientific evidence seems to have refuted the "Steady State" and confirmed the "Big Bang" pretty conclusively, thus also confirming once again that faith and reason never really contradict each other.

N.b.: Article 1 shows that we cannot prove that the world is eternal; Article 2 shows that we cannot prove by philosophy alone that it is not. Philosophical reasoning leaves both options as logical possibilities. Divine revelation (and today perhaps also scientific data) resolve the question; philosophy does not.

the Philosopher (*Phys.* i, text. 82) proves that matter is unbegotten, and also (*De Coelo et Mundo* i, text. 20) that the heaven [the firmament, "the heavens"] is unbegotten. Therefore the universe did not begin to exist.

Objection 4. Further, a vacuum is where there is not a body, but there might be. But if the world began to exist, there was first no body where the body of the world now is; and yet it could be there, otherwise it would not be there now. Therefore before the world there was a vacuum; which is impossible.[16]

Objection 5. Further, nothing begins anew to be moved except through being otherwise than it was before. . . . What is otherwise now than it was before, is moved. Therefore before every new movement there was a previous movement. Therefore movement always was;[17] and therefore also the thing moved always was, because movement is only in a movable thing.

Objection 6. . . . He who wills to make a house tomorrow, and not today, awaits something which will be tomorrow, but is not today; and at least awaits for today to pass, and for tomorrow to come; and this cannot be without change.[18] . . . Therefore before every new movement, there was a previous movement; and so the same conclusion follows as before. . . .

---

[16] It was a supposed truism of medieval physics that a vacuum is impossible.

[17] This is an argument of Aristotle (*Physics*, Bk. 8) for the eternity of the world. St. Thomas answers it in the Reply by distinguishing *creation* (of existence) from *change* (of state)—a distinction Aristotle did not use, for, not knowing that the world was created, he never wondered why it *existed* but took its existence for granted and wondered only about its *nature* and properties. The doctrine of creation, as an answer to a question the Greeks did not ask, led Christian philosophers to ask the new question, and thus to become aware of the distinction between existence and essence.

[18] This is similar to the question, Why did God create the world eighteen billion years ago, and not at some other time? What was He doing before He created? The reply is (1) that there *is* no "before creation" since time itself is a creature, and (2) the distinction between (a) an eternal will to create a temporal world, (b) an eternal will to create an eternal world, and (c) a temporal will to create a temporal world. The objector's question assumes that (c) is the truth, since the world is temporal. Aristotle would be closest to (b), minus "creation". St. Thomas teaches (a).

I answer that, Nothing except God can be eternal. And this statement is far from impossible to uphold: for it has been shown above (Q. 19, A. 4) that the will of God is the cause of things. Therefore things are necessary, according as it is necessary for God to will them, since the necessity of the effect depends on the necessity of the cause (*Metaph.* v, text. 6). Now it was shown above (Q. 19, A. 3), that, absolutely speaking, it is not necessary that God should will anything except Himself. It is not therefore necessary for God to will that the world should always exist; but the world exists forasmuch as God wills it to exist, since the being of the world depends on the will of God, as on its cause. It is not therefore necessary for the world to be always; and hence it cannot be proved by demonstration.

Nor are Aristotle's reasons (*Phys.* viii) simply, but relatively, demonstrative—viz., in order to contradict the reasons of some of the ancients who asserted that the world began to exist in some quite impossible manner. This appears in three ways. Firstly, because, both in *Phys.* viii and in *De Coelo* i, text. 101, he premises some opinions, as those of Anaxagoras, Empedocles and Plato, and brings forward reasons to refute them. Secondly, because wherever he speaks of this subject, he quotes the testimony of the ancients, which is not the way of a demonstrator, but of one persuading of what is probable. Thirdly, because he expressly says (*Topic.* i. 9), that there are dialectical problems, about which we have nothing to say from reason, as, *whether the world is eternal*.

Reply Obj. 1. Before the world existed it was possible for the world to be, not, indeed, according to a passive power which is matter, but according to the active power of God. . . .

Reply Obj. 3. Aristotle (*Phys.* i, text. 82) proves that matter is unbegotten from the fact that it has not a subject from which to derive its existence;[19] and (*De Coelo et Mundo* i, text. 20) he proves that heaven ["the heavens"] is ungenerated, forasmuch as it has no contrary from which to be generated. Hence it appears that no conclusion follows either way, except that matter and heaven did not begin by generation, as some said, especially about heaven. But

---

[19] This is *unimaginable*, for imagination requires space and time. A vacuum is imaginable, however. Thus we tend to think mistakenly of "nothing" as a vacuum, i.e., empty space, which is really *something*.

we say that matter and heaven were produced into being by creation, as appears above (Q. 44, A. 1 *ad* 2).

Reply Obj. 4. The notion of a vacuum is not only *in which is nothing*, but also implies a space capable of holding a body and in which there is not a body, as appears from Aristotle (*Phys.* iv, text. 60). Whereas we hold that there was no place or space before the world was.

Reply Obj. 5. The first mover was always in the same state: but the first movable thing was not always so, because it began to be whereas hitherto it was not. This, however, was not through change, but by creation, which is not change, as said above (Q. 45, A. 2 *ad* 2). . . .

Reply Obj. 6. The first agent is a voluntary agent. And although He had the eternal will to produce some effect, yet He did not produce an eternal effect. . . . But the universal agent who produces the thing and time also, is not correctly described as acting now, and not before, according to an imaginary succession of time succeeding time, as if time were presupposed to His action. . . .

SECOND ARTICLE

Whether It Is an Article of Faith[20] That the World Began?

Objection 1. It would seem that it is not an article of faith but a demonstrable conclusion that the world began. For everything that is made has a beginning of its duration. But it can be proved demonstratively that God is the effective cause of the world; indeed this is asserted by the more approved philosophers. Therefore it can be demonstratively proved that the world began. . . .

Objection 3. Further, everything which works by intellect, works from some principle [beginning], as appears in all kinds of craftsmen. But God acts by intellect: therefore His work has a principle. The world, therefore, which is His effect, did not always exist. . . .

---

[20] I.e., discoverable only by faith, not by unaided reason. After showing, in Article 1, that reason cannot *disprove* the doctrine of the creation of a world with a finite rather than an infinite time span, St. Thomas now shows that reason cannot *prove* it either. The first Article refutes the Latin Averroists; the second refutes the Augustinians.

Objection 6. Further, if the world always was, the consequence is that infinite days preceded this present day. But it is impossible to pass . . . through an infinite medium. Therefore we should never have arrived at this present day; which is manifestly false.[21]. . .

Objection 8. Further, if the world and generation always were, there have been an infinite number of men. But man's soul is immortal: therefore an infinite number of human souls would actually now exist, which is impossible. Therefore it can be known with certainty that the world began, and not only is it known by faith. . . .

I answer that, By faith alone do we hold, and by no demonstration can it be proved, that the world did not always exist, as was said above of the mystery of the Trinity (Q. 32, A. 1).

The reason of this is that the newness of the world cannot be demonstrated [1] on the part of the world itself. For the principle of demonstration is the essence of a thing. Now everything according to its species [essence] is abstracted from *here* and *now*. . . . Hence it cannot be demonstrated that man, or heaven, or a stone were not always.

Likewise neither can it be demonstrated [2] on the part of the efficient cause, which acts by will. For the will of God cannot be investigated by reason, except as regards those things which God must will of necessity; and what He wills about creatures is not among these, as was said above (Q. 19, A. 3). But the divine will can be manifested by revelation, on which faith rests. Hence that the world began to exist is an object of faith, but not of demonstration or science.

And it is useful to consider this, lest anyone, presuming to demonstrate what is of faith, should bring forward reasons that are not cogent, so as to give occasion to unbelievers to laugh, thinking that on such grounds we believe things that are of faith.[22]

Reply Obj. 1. As Augustine says (*De Civ. Dei* xi. 4), the opinion of philosophers who asserted the eternity of the world was twofold.

---

[21] This is the *kalam* (time) argument used by many medieval Muslim philosophers and taken over by Christian philosophers like St. Bonaventura.

[22] St. Thomas' tendency is always to be more critical, skeptical, and agnostic rather than credulous. He would rather give no argument than a weak one. This severe habit is often annoying to believers, but the opposite habit is often annoying to unbelievers.

For some said that the substance of the world was not from God, which is an intolerable error; and therefore it is refuted by proofs that are cogent.[23] Some, however, said that the world was eternal, although made by God. For they hold that the world has a beginning, not of time, but of creation, so that in a certain hardly intelligible way it was always made. And they try to explain their meaning thus (*De Civ. Dei* x. 31): *for as, if the foot were always in the dust from eternity, there would always be a footprint which without doubt was caused by him who trod on it, so also the world always was, because its Maker always existed.* To understand this we must consider that the efficient cause, which acts by motion, of necessity precedes its effect in time. . . . But if the action is instantaneous and not successive, it is not necessary for the maker to be prior to the thing made in duration, as appears in the case of illumination. Hence they say that it does not follow necessarily if God is the active cause of the world, that He should be prior to the world in duration; because creation, by which He produced the world, is not a successive change, as was said above (Q. 45, A. 2).[24]. . .

Reply Obj. 3. This is the argument of Anaxagoras (as quoted in *Phys.* viii, text. 15). But it does not lead to a necessary conclusion, except as to that intellect which deliberates in order to find out what should be done, which is like movement. Such is the human intellect, but not the divine intellect (Q. 14, AA. 7, 12). . . .

---

[23] Cf. I, 44, 1.

[24] Distinguish three kinds of efficient causes in regard to time:

1. The most usual kind precede their effects in time. E.g., the bat hitting the ball (the cause) occurs before the ball flies to the outfield (the effect).

2. Sometimes the cause and effect are simultaneous in duration. E.g., an iron ball making an impression in a pillow, or the act of thinking producing an idea in the mind.

3. With regard to the unique kind of efficient cause that is *creating*, the cause and effect can be simultaneous *and* instantaneous rather than durational, since creation is not a process in time (see I, 45, 2). This is impossible for us to imagine, since our image-making faculty can only imagine something in space and time; and it is difficult for us to conceive, but it is barely possible, or "hardly intelligible", as St. Thomas says. It is intelligible at least negatively, through what it is not.

Reply Obj. 6. Passage is always understood as being from term to term. Whatever bygone day we choose, from it to the present day there is a finite number of days which can be passed through. The objection is founded on the idea that, given two extremes, there is an infinite number of mean terms.[25] . . .

Reply Obj. 8. Those who hold the eternity of the world evade this reason in many ways. . . . One might say that the world was eternal, or at least some creature, as an angel, but not man. But we are considering the question in general, as to whether any creature can exist from eternity. . . .

---

[25] Cf. Zeno's famous paradoxes against motion, which assert the impossibility of passing through an infinite number of points in space in a finite time. The *kalam* argument makes a similar mistake, according to St. Thomas, in asserting the impossibility of passing through an infinite number of days in time. His point is that there *is* no actually infinite number of days, no matter how far back we think. The false premise common to both Zeno's paradoxes and the *kalam* argument is smoked out in the last sentence.

Question 47

Of the Distinction of Things in General

After considering the production of creatures, we come to the consideration of the distinction of things. This consideration will be threefold—first, of the distinction of things in general; secondly, of the distinction of good and evil; thirdly of the distinction of the spiritual and corporeal creature. . . .

FIRST ARTICLE

Whether the Multitude and Distinction of Things Come from God?[26]

I answer that, . . . we must say that the distinction and multitude of things come from the intention of the first agent, who is God. For He brought things into being in order that His goodness might be communicated to creatures, and be represented by them; and because His goodness could not be adequately represented by one creature alone, He produced many and diverse creatures, that what was wanting to one in the representation of the divine goodness might be supplied by another. For goodness, which in God is

---

[26] The belief that plurality, or differences between things, is not from God, or is evil, or illusion, is a surprisingly widespread belief, especially among pantheists of all kinds, e.g., most forms of Hinduism, Buddhism, and Taoism in the East, and Parmenides, Plotinus, and Origen in the ancient West, as well as many popular forms of mysticism in the modern West such as theosophy and the "New Age Movement". One feature common to all monisms and pantheisms is to deny that God has a will, and wills moral goodness; for to will one thing is to distinguish it from another: will is essentially discriminatory. Thus St. Thomas here derives the distinction among things from God's will and goodness.

simple and uniform, in creatures is manifold and divided; and hence the whole universe together participates the divine goodness more perfectly, and represents it better than any single creature whatever. . . .

SECOND ARTICLE

Whether the Inequality of Things Is from God?[27]

Objection 1. It would seem that the inequality of things is not from God. For it belongs to the best to produce the best. But among things that are best, one is not greater than another. Therefore, it belongs to God, Who is the Best, to make all things equal. . . .

On the contrary, It is said (Sir 33:7): *Why does one day excel another, and one light another, and one year another year, one sun another sun?* (Vulg.—*when all come of the sun*). *By the knowledge of the Lord they were distinguished.*

I answer that, When Origen wished to refute those who said that the distinction of things arose from the contrary principles of good and evil, he said that in the beginning all things were created equal by God. For he asserted that God first created only the rational creatures, and all equal; and that inequality arose in them from free will, some being turned to God more and some less, and others turned more and others less away from God. And so those rational creatures which were turned to God by free will, were promoted to the order of angels according to the diversity of merits. And those who were turned away from God were bound down to bodies according to the diversity of their sin, and he said this was the cause of the creation and diversity of bodies. But

---

[27] Article 2 differs from Article 1 as *inequality* differs from *multitude* and distinction in general. One might believe that creatures are diverse in quantity but equal in quality. The American reader is likely to object not to plurality (Article 1) but to inequality (Article 2), since equality is part of his political creed, and he often treats politics as religion and religion as politics. Of course there is no logical argument from Americans' love of political equality to God's love of cosmic equality.

according to this opinion, it would follow that the universality of bodily creatures would not be the effect of the goodness of God as communicated to creatures, but it would be for the sake of the punishment of sin, which is contrary to what is said: *God saw all the things that He had made, and they were very good* (Gen 1:31). And, as Augustine says (*De Civ. Dei* ii. 23): *What can be more foolish than to say that the divine Architect provided this one sun for the one world, not to be an ornament to its beauty, nor for the benefit of corporeal things, but that it happened through the sin of one soul; so that, if a hundred souls had sinned, there would be a hundred suns in the world?*

Therefore it must be said that as the wisdom of God is the cause of the distinction of things, so the same wisdom is the cause of their inequality. . . . In natural things species seem to be arranged in degrees; as the mixed things are more perfect than the elements, and plants than minerals, and animals than plants, and men than other animals; and in each of these one species is more perfect than others. Therefore, as the divine wisdom is the cause of the distinction of things for the sake of the perfection of the universe, so it is the cause of inequality. For the universe would not be perfect if only one grade of goodness were found in things.

Reply Obj. 1. It is the part of the best agent to produce an effect which is best in its entirety; but this does not mean that He makes every part of the whole the best absolutely, but in proportion to the whole; in the case of an animal, for instance, its goodness would be taken away if every part of it had the dignity of an eye. Thus, therefore, God also made the universe to be best as a whole, according to the mode of a creature; whereas He did not make each single creature best, but one better than another. And therefore we find it said of each creature, *God saw the light that it was good* (Gen 1:4); and in like manner of each one of the rest. But of all together it is said, *God saw all the things that He had made, and they were very good* (Gen 1:31). . . .

THIRD ARTICLE

Whether There Is Only One World?

Objection 2. Further, nature does what is best and much more does God. But it is better for there to be many worlds than one, because many good things are better than a few. Therefore many worlds have been made by God.[28]. . .

I answer that, The very order of things created by God shows the unity of the world. For this world is called one by the unity of order, whereby some things are ordered to others. But whatever things come from God, have relation of order to each other, and to God Himself, as shown above (Q. 11, A. 3; Q. 21, A. 1).[29] Hence it must be that all things should belong to one world. Therefore those only can assert that many worlds exist who do not acknowledge any ordaining wisdom, but rather believe in chance, as Democritus, who said that this world, besides an infinite number of other worlds, was made from a casual concourse of atoms. . . .

Reply Obj. 2. . . . For the same reason it might be said that if He had made two worlds, it would be better if He had made three; and so on to infinity.[30]. . .

---

[28] "World" here means not "planet" but "universe". Even the Middle Ages knew there was more than one planet; but is there more than one space-time universe? One may think so because just as it seems more perfect for an author to write many books rather than just one, it seems more perfect and Godlike to create many universes rather than one. (In that case, you could get from one universe to another only through the mind of the common author, or by "magic", but not by space-time travel.)

[29] Thus, however many worlds God made, they are all ordered to each other (and to God), thus constituting one world (universe). A "uni-verse" is a unity-of-diversity. Many worlds all created by God would be such a single uni-verse.

[30] Thus we have a *reductio ad absurdum* argument similar to the one in I, 25, 6 showing that no finite world can be the best of all possible worlds.

Question 48

The Distinction of Things in Particular

FIRST ARTICLE

Whether Evil Is a Nature?

On the contrary, Dionysius says (*Div. Nom.* iv), *Evil is neither a being nor a good.*

I answer that, One opposite is known through the other, as darkness is known through light. Hence also what evil is must be known from the nature of good.[31] Now, we have said above that good is everything appetible [desirable]; and thus, since every nature desires its own being and its own perfection, it must be said also that the being and the perfection of any nature is good. Hence it cannot be that evil signifies being, or any form or nature. Therefore it must be that by the name of evil is signified the absence of good.[32] And this is what is meant by saying that *evil is neither a*

---

[31] It does not follow that good must also be known only from the nature of evil. Evil is relative to good but good is not relative to evil. If good could not exist without evil, there can be no independently existing, wholly-good God; and if good cannot be *known* without evil, God either does not know good or does so only by being dependent on knowing evil. The point needs to be made because the contrary view, that good and evil are relative to each other, as yin and yang, is very popular today (as it was not in St. Thomas' day) among philosophies that deny the Fall and sin (pantheism, pop psychology, the New Age movement); for only because we are fallen creatures must we, unlike God, now notice and appreciate good, beauty, light, and pleasure only by contrast with evil, ugliness, darkness, and pain.

[32] St. Thomas does not see evil as illusory, but as negative; not as unreal, but as something other than a being, entity, essence, form, or nature. It is an absence—more exactly, a privation, or deprivation, of

being nor a good. For since being, as such, is good, the absence of one implies the absence of the other. . . .

Whether Evil Is Found in Things?

I answer that, As was said above (Q. 47, AA. 1, 2), the perfection of the universe requires that there should be inequality in things, so that every grade of goodness may be realized. Now, one grade of goodness is that of the good which cannot fail. Another grade of goodness is that of the good which can fail in goodness. And this grade is to be found in existence itself; for some things there are which cannot lose their existence, as incorruptible things, while some there are which can lose it, as things corruptible.

As, therefore, the perfection of the universe requires that there should be not only beings incorruptible, but also corruptible beings; so the perfection of the universe requires that there should be some which can fail in goodness, and thence it follows that sometimes they do fail. Now it is in this that evil consists, namely, in the fact that a thing fails in goodness. Hence it is clear that evil is found in things, as corruption also is found; for corruption is itself an evil. . . .

Whether Evil Is in Good As in Its Subject?

On the contrary, Augustine says (*Enchir.* 14) that *evil exists only in good.*

I answer that, As was said above (A. 1), evil imports the absence of good. But not every absence of good is evil. For absence of good

---

good (see Article 3). Darkness, blindness, and disease are not *illusions*, but they are the *absence* of light, sight, and health rather than things in their own right with positive natures or forms (essences), like light, or sight, or health. St. Thomas learned this doctrine of evil from St. Augustine. Evil is not a thing (Article 1) but it is in things (Article 2), not just in the mind.

can be taken [1] in a privative and [2] in a negative sense. Absence of good, taken negatively, is not evil; otherwise, it would follow that what does not exist is evil, and also that everything would be evil, through not having the good belonging to something else; for instance, a man would be evil who had not the swiftness of the roe, or the strength of a lion. But the absence of good, taken in a privative sense, is an evil; as, for instance, the privation of sight is called blindness. . . .

FOURTH ARTICLE

Whether Evil Corrupts the Whole Good?

I answer that, Evil cannot wholly consume good.[33] To prove this we must consider that good is threefold. One kind of good is wholly destroyed by evil, and this is the good opposed to the evil, as light is wholly destroyed by darkness, and sight by blindness. Another kind of good is neither wholly destroyed nor diminished by evil, and that is the good which is the subject of evil; for by darkness the substance of the air is not injured. And there is also a kind of good which is diminished by evil, but is not wholly taken away; and this good is the aptitude of a subject to some actuality. . . . If opaque bodies were interposed to infinity between the sun and the air, the aptitude of the air to light would be infinitely diminished, but still it would never be wholly removed while the air remained, which in its very nature is transparent. Likewise, addition in sin can be made to infinitude, whereby the aptitude of the soul to grace is more and more lessened; and these sins, indeed, are like obstacles interposed between us and God, according to Isaiah 59:2: *Our sins have divided between us and God.* Yet the aforesaid aptitude of the soul is not wholly taken away, for it belongs to its very nature. . . .

---

[33] St. Thomas bases his optimism (his confidence that good is stronger than evil) not on accidental and changeable factors like his feelings or his observation of how well things were going in his life or his society, but on the unchangeable essence of good and evil themselves (Cf. n. 43).

FIFTH ARTICLE

Whether Evil Is Adequately Divided Into Pain and Fault?

I answer that, Evil, as was said above (A. 3) is the privation of good, which chiefly and of itself consists in perfection and act [actuality]. Act, however, is twofold; first, and second. The first act is the form and integrity of a thing; the second act is its operation.[34] Therefore evil also is twofold. In one way it occurs by the subtraction of the form, or of any part required for the integrity of the thing, as blindness is an evil, as also it is an evil to be wanting in any member of the body. In another way evil exists by the withdrawal of the due operation, either because it does not exist, or because it has not its due mode and order.

But because good in itself is the object of the will, evil, which is the privation of good, is found in a special way in rational creatures which have a will. Therefore the evil which comes from the withdrawal of the form and integrity of the thing, has the nature of a pain; . . . for it is of the very nature of a pain to be against the will. But the evil which consists in the subtraction of the due operation in voluntary things has the nature of a fault; for this is imputed to anyone as a fault to fail as regards perfect action, of which he is master by the will. Therefore every evil in voluntary things is to be looked upon [either] as a pain or a fault. . . .

SIXTH ARTICLE

Whether Pain Has the Nature of Evil More Than Fault Has?

On the contrary, A wise workman chooses a less evil in order to prevent a greater,[35] as the surgeon cuts off a limb to save the whole

---

[34] "First act", form, is actual in relation to matter within a substance, for matter is potential to being formed. "Second act", operation or activity, is actual in relation to the substance, for the substance is potential to its own activities; it is able to act.

Pain and suffering come under a defect of first act; sin and wickedness come under a defect of second act. The term "evil" is thus analogical, not univocal. Pain is evil we suffer, sin is evil we do.

[35] St. Thomas is not saying here that it is wise or good to commit a

body. But divine wisdom inflicts pain to prevent fault. Therefore fault is a greater evil than pain.

I answer that, Fault has the nature of evil more than pain has; not only more than pain of sense, consisting in the privation of corporeal goods, which kind of pain appeals to most men; but also more than any kind of pain, thus taking pain in its most general meaning, so as to include privation of grace or glory.[36]

There is a twofold reason for this. The first is that one becomes evil by the evil of fault, but not by the evil of pain, as Dionysius says (*Div. Nom.* iv): *To be punished is not an evil; but it is an evil to be made worthy of punishment.* And this because, since good absolutely considered consists in act, and not in potentiality, and the ultimate act is operation, or the use of something possessed, it follows that the absolute good of man consists in good operation, or the good use of something possessed. Now we use all things by the act of the will. Hence from a good will, which makes a man use well what he has, man is called good, and from a bad will he is called bad. For a man who has a bad will can use ill even the good he has, as when a grammarian of his own will speaks incorrectly. Therefore, because the fault itself consists in the disordered act of the will, and the pain consists in the privation of something used by the will, fault has more of evil in it than pain has.[37]

---

lesser fault to prevent a greater one (for this is never necessary; our own faults are prevented by our own choices, and others' faults are others' faults, not ours), but that it is wise and good sometimes to inflict the lesser *kind* of evil, pain, to prevent the greater kind, fault. Thus punishment, which must be painful in some way, can be morally good if it is both deserved and is aimed at deterring the one punished from future faults. The principle of "the lesser of two evils" means (1) that we often must *tolerate* or allow the lesser evil to prevent the greater one, and (2) that we should sometimes inflict the lesser *kind* of evil to prevent the greater kind (above), but not (3) that we should commit little sins to prevent big sins.

[36] Therefore sin (the evil of fault) is an even greater evil than its punishment (the privation of God's life in the soul, which is present imperfectly in this life by grace and perfectly in the next by glory). In other words, the worst evil is not Hell but sin. The conclusion is startling to our sensibilities but demonstrated to our reason.

[37] St. Thomas here includes the fundamental moral insight of Socrates,

The second reason can be taken from the fact that God is the author of the evil of pain, but not of the evil of fault. And this is because the evil of pain takes away the creature's good, which may be either something created, as sight, destroyed by blindness, or something uncreated, as by being deprived of the vision of God, the creature forfeits its uncreated good. But the evil of fault is properly opposed to uncreated good: for it is opposed to the fulfillment of the divine will, and to divine love, whereby the divine good is loved for itself, and not only as shared by the creature. Therefore it is plain that fault has more evil in it than pain has.[38]

---

that it is better to suffer evil than to do it, and that of Kant, that the heart of good (Kant says the *only* intrinsic good) is a good will.

[38] Actively to oppose uncreated good (God Himself) is more evil than to be deprived of it passively.

Question 49

The Cause of Evil

Whether Good Can Be the Cause of Evil?

Objection 1. It would seem that good cannot be the cause of evil. For it is said (Mt 7:18): *A good tree cannot bring forth evil fruit.* . . .

On the contrary, Augustine says (*Contra Julian.* i. 9): *There is no possible source of evil except good.*

I answer that, It must be said that every evil in some way has a cause. For evil is the absence of the good, which is natural and due to a thing. But that anything fail from its natural and due disposition, can come only from some cause drawing it out of its proper disposition. For a heavy thing is not moved upwards except by some impelling force; nor does an agent fail in its action except from some impediment. But only good can be a cause; because nothing can be a cause except inasmuch as it is a being, and every being, as such, is good.[39]

And if we consider the special kinds of causes, we see that the agent, the form, and the end, import some kind of perfection which belongs to the notion of good. Even matter, as a potentiality

---

[39] Both the evil of pain and the evil of fault are caused by something real, therefore something at least *ontologically* good (see I, 5, 3). In the next paragraph, St. Thomas shows that all four causes, as such, are good; therefore insofar as evil has any of the four causes, its cause is something good. Though evil does not have a formal or final cause (for it is the deprivation of a being's form and end), it has a material cause, or subject, and an efficient cause, or agent, both of which must be ontologically good. To chop off your head, I need a good strong arm and a good stroke of the axe.

to good, has the nature of good. Now that good is the cause of evil by way of the material cause was shown above (Q. 48, A. 3). For it was shown that good is the subject of evil. But evil has no formal cause, rather is it a privation of form; likewise, neither has it a final cause, but rather is it a privation of order to the proper end; since not only the end has the nature of good, but also the useful, which is ordered to the end. Evil, however, has a cause by way of an agent [efficient cause]. . . .

Reply Obj. 1. As Augustine says (*Contra Julian.* i): *The Lord calls an evil will the evil tree, and a good will a good tree.* Now, a good will does not produce a morally bad act, since it is from the good will itself that a moral act is judged to be good. Nevertheless the movement itself of an evil will is caused by the rational creature, which is [ontologically] good; and thus good is the cause of evil. . . .

SECOND ARTICLE

Whether the Supreme Good, God, Is the Cause of Evil?

Objection 1. It would seem that the supreme good, God, is the cause of evil. For it is said (Is 45:5, 7): *I am the Lord, and there is no other God, forming the light, and creating darkness, making peace, and creating evil.* And (Amos 3:6), *Shall there be evil in a city, which the Lord hath not done?* . . .

On the contrary, Augustine says (QQ. 83, *qu.* 21), that, *God is not the author of evil because He is not the cause of tending to not-being.*

I answer that, As appears from what was said (A. 1), the evil which consists in the defect of action is always caused by the defect of the agent. But in God there is no defect, but the highest perfection, as was shown above (Q. 4, A. 1). Hence, the evil which consists in defect of action, or which is caused by defect of the agent, is not reduced to God as to its cause.

But the evil which consists in the corruption[40] of some things is

---

[40] "Corruption" here does not mean moral corruption, or wickedness (that is the evil of fault, not pain) but mortality in creatures. God designed leaves and cats to die.

reduced to God as the cause. And this appears as regards both natural things and voluntary things. For . . . the order of the universe requires, as was said above (Q. 22, A. 2 *ad* 2; Q. 48, A. 2), that there should be some things that can, and do sometimes, fail. And thus God, by causing in things the good of the order of the universe, consequently and as it were by accident, causes the corruptions of things. . . . The order of justice belongs to the order of the universe; and this requires that penalty should be dealt out to sinners. And so God is the author of the evil which is penalty, but not of the evil which is fault.[41] . . .

Reply Obj. 1. These passages refer to the evil of penalty, and not to the evil of fault. . . .

THIRD ARTICLE

Whether There Be One Supreme Evil Which Is the Cause of Every Evil?[42]

Objection 1. It would seem that there is one supreme evil which is the cause of every evil. For contrary effects have contrary causes. But contrariety is found in things, according to Sirach 33:15: *Good is set against evil, and life against death; so also is the sinner against a just man.* Therefore there are many [two] contrary principles [causes] one of good, the other of evil. . . .

Objection 3. Further, as we find good and better things, so we find evil and worse. But good and better are so considered in

---

[41] The modern reader is likely to doubt whether a wholly good God can be the author of any evil, even the evil of penalty, or punishment. If St. Thomas were writing to modern readers, he would surely add an article against those who believe that a God Who punishes sin is not wholly good. He would probably show that a God of love without justice is not as good or as loving as a God of perfect love *and* perfect justice; and also that punishing evil is not evil, since pain is not as great an evil as fault (I, 48, 6). The typically modern mind fears pain more than sin. (That is why modern martyrs and heroes are few.)

[42] Dualism—the idea that there are two supreme Powers, one good, one evil—is easy to imagine but hard to justify rationally. In effect it exalts a creature, the devil, to the status of a second Creator.

relation to what is best. Therefore evil and worse are so considered in relation to some supreme evil. . . .

On the contrary, The supreme good is the cause of every being, as was shown above (Q. 2, A. 3; Q. 6, A. 4). Therefore there cannot be any principle opposed to it as the cause of evils.

I answer that, It appears from what precedes that there is no one first principle of evil, as there is one first principle of good.

First, indeed, because the first principle of good is essentially good, as was shown above (Q. 6, AA. 3, 4). But nothing can be essentially bad. For it was shown above that every being, as such, is good (Q. 5, A. 3); and that evil can exist only in good as in its subject (Q. 48, A. 3).

Secondly, because the first principle of good is the highest and perfect good which pre-contains in itself all goodness, as shown above (Q. 6, A. 2). But there cannot be a supreme evil; because, as was shown above (Q. 48, A. 4), although evil always lessens good, yet it never wholly consumes it; and thus, while good ever remains, nothing can be wholly and perfectly bad. Therefore, the Philosopher says (*Ethic.* iv. 5) that *if the wholly evil could be, it would destroy itself;* because all good being destroyed (which it need be for something to be wholly evil), evil itself would be taken away, since its subject is good.[43]. . .

Those, however, who upheld two first principles, one good and the other evil, fell into this error from the same cause, whence also arose other strange notions of the ancients; namely, because they failed to consider the universal cause of all being, and considered only the particular causes of particular effects. For on that account,

---

[43] Evil is like a parasite which destroys its good host. If it could totally destroy its host, it would also destroy itself. Evil is inherently self-destructive. This metaphysical fact explains the otherwise puzzling empirical fact of humanity's amazing resiliancy. Time after time, after falling into some deadly evil (e.g., totalitarianism), we bounce back, the evil dissipates. This is one of history's great mysteries: the power of goodness. The other is the power of evil: how can the species that thinks like an angel behave like a beast? The mystery of goodness is explained by the metaphysical nature of evil in this article, and the mystery of evil is explained by the metaphysical nature of human goodness as free, thus contingent rather than necessary, in I, 83, 1.

if they found a thing hurtful to something by the power of its own nature, they thought that the very nature of that thing was evil; as, for instance, if one should say that the nature of fire was evil because it burnt the house of a poor man. The [true] judgment, however, of the goodness of anything does not depend upon its order [relation, relativity] to any particular thing, but rather upon what it is in itself, and on its order to the whole universe, wherein every part has its own perfectly ordered place, as was said above (Q. 47, A. 2 *ad* 1). . . .

Reply Obj. 1. Contraries agree in one genus,[44] and they also agree in the nature of being; and therefore, although they have contrary particular causes, nevertheless we must come at last to one first common cause. . . .

Reply Obj. 3. . . . Every form, perfection, and good is intensified by approach to the perfect term; but privation and evil by receding from that term. Hence a thing is not said to be evil and worse, by reason of access to the supreme evil, in the same way as it is said to be good and better, by reason of access to the supreme good. . . .

---

[44] E.g., life and death are both in the genus "states of an organism"; virtues and vices are both in the genus "moral habits"; hot and cold are both in the genus "temperature".

Question 65

The Work of Creation
of Corporeal Creatures

FIRST ARTICLE

Whether Corporeal Creatures Are from God?[45]

Objection 2. Further, it is said (Gen 1:31): *God saw all the things that He had made, and they were very good.* But corporeal creatures are evil, since we find them harmful in many ways; as may be seen in serpents, in the sun's heat, and other things. Now a thing is called evil, in so far as it is harmful. Corporeal creatures, therefore, are not from God.

Objection 3. Further, what is from God does not withdraw us from God, but leads us to Him. But corporeal creatures withdraw us from God. Hence the Apostle says (2 Cor 4:18): *While we look not at the things which are seen.* Corporeal creatures, therefore, are not from God.

On the contrary, It is said (Ps 145:6): *Who made heaven and earth, the sea, and all things that are in them.*

I answer that, Certain heretics maintain that visible things are not created by the good God, but by an evil principle, and allege in proof of their error the words of the Apostle (2 Cor 4:4), *The god of*

---

[45] St. Thomas here writes against those Gnostics and Neoplatonists who held that matter was evil (as if the devil had created the world when God turned His back). The Gnostic hatred of nature and matter is by no means dead. Though no longer expressed directly and theologically, the anti-natural attitude is surely still very popular, e.g., among all whose goal is not *sanctity* but "spirituality", and among those of the far, puritanical Right *or* the far, feminist Left who hate their own bodies and reproductive systems.

this world[46] *hath blinded the minds of unbelievers.* But this position is altogether[47] untenable. For, if things that differ agree in some point, there must be some cause for that agreement, since things diverse in nature cannot be united of themselves. Hence whenever in different things some one thing common to all is found, it must be that these different things receive that one thing from some one cause, as different bodies that are hot receive their heat from fire. But being is found to be common to all things, however otherwise different. There must, therefore, be one principle of being from which all things in whatever way existing have their being, whether they are invisible and spiritual, or visible and corporeal. But the devil is called the god of this world, not as having created it, but because worldlings serve him, of whom also the Apostle says, speaking in the same sense, *Whose god is their belly* (Phil 3:19). . . .

Reply Obj. 2. Corporeal creatures according to their nature are good, though this good is not universal, but partial and limited, the consequence of which is a certain opposition of contrary qualities, though each quality is good in itself. To those, however, who estimate things, not by the nature thereof, but by the good they themselves can derive therefrom, everything which is harmful to themselves seems simply evil. For they do not reflect that what is in some way injurious to one person, to another is beneficial, and that even to themselves the same thing may be evil in some respects, but good in others. And this could not be, if bodies were essentially evil and harmful.

Reply Obj. 3. Creatures of themselves do not withdraw us from God, but lead us to Him; for *the invisible things of God are clearly seen, being understood by the things that are made* (Rom 1:20). If, then, they withdraw men from God, it is the fault of those who use them

---

[46] If St. Thomas knew Greek, he would explicate this text by making clear that the Greek word for "world" here is not *gaia*, which means the *planet*, but *aion*, which means the *era* or age. Satan is not the god of God's good, green earth, but the god of the era begun by man's fall into sin.

[47] Notice the unusually extreme language St. Thomas uses against this error. He here stakes out a claim in the happy fields of Christian, incarnational optimism over against both the hatred *and* the idolatrous love of creatures. The former error was more fashionable in his day, the latter in ours.

foolishly. Thus it is said (Wis 14:11): *Creatures are turned into a snare to the feet of the unwise.* And the very fact that they can thus withdraw us from God proves that they came from Him, for they cannot lead the foolish away from God except by the allurements of some good that they have from Him. . . .

Question 103

Of the Government of Things in General

Whether the World Is Governed by Anyone?

Objection 1. It would seem that the world is not governed by anyone. For it belongs to those things to be governed, which move or work for an end. But natural things which make up the greater part of the world do not move, or work for an end; for they have no knowledge of their end. Therefore the world is not governed.[48]

Objection 2. Further, those things are governed which are moved towards some object. But the world does not appear to be so directed, but has stability in itself. Therefore it is not governed.

Objection 3. Further, what is necessarily determined by its own nature to one particular thing, does not require any external principle of government. But the principal parts of the world are by a certain necessity determined to something particular in their actions and movements. Therefore the world does not require to be governed.[49]

On the contrary, It is written (Wis 14:3): *But Thou, O Father, governest all things by Thy Providence.* And Boëthius says (*De Consol.* 3): *Thou Who governest this universe by mandate eternal.*

I answer that, Certain ancient philosophers denied the govern-

---

[48] This is essentially the modern, non-teleological view of nature. The two concepts of the universe as teleological (full of design) and of God as the cosmic designer obviously fit together and can be derived from one another.

[49] The "natural" means that which is born (*natus*), or arises spontaneously from within, as distinct from the artificial, which comes from an external agent. The point of the objection is that nature seems to determine itself, thus to need or admit no external God.

ment of the world, saying that all things happened by chance. But such an opinion can be refuted as impossible in two ways. First, by observation of things themselves: for we observe that in nature things happen always or nearly always for the best; which would not be the case unless some sort of providence directed nature towards good as an end; which is to govern. Wherefore the unfailing order we observe in things is a sign of their being governed; for instance, if we enter a well-ordered house we gather therefrom the intention of him that put it in order, as Tullius says (*De Nat. Deorum* ii), quoting Aristotle [Cleanthes]. Secondly, this is clear from a consideration of Divine goodness, which, as we have said above (Q. 44, A. 4; Q. 65, A. 2), was the cause of the production of things in existence. For as *it belongs to the best to produce the best*, it is not fitting that the supreme goodness of God should produce things without giving them their perfection. Now a thing's ultimate perfection consists in the attainment of its end. Therefore it belongs to the Divine goodness, as it brought things into existence, so to lead them to their end: and this is to govern.[50]

Reply Obj. 1.   A thing moves or operates for an end in two ways. First, in moving itself to the end, as man and other rational creatures; and such things have knowledge of their end, and of the means to the end. Secondly, a thing is said to move or operate for an end, as though moved or directed by another thereto, as an arrow directed to the target by the archer, who knows the end unknown to the arrow. Wherefore, as the movement of the arrow towards a definite end shows clearly that it is directed by someone with knowledge, so the unvarying course of natural things which are without knowledge, shows clearly[51] that the world is governed by some reason.

---

[50] The two arguments supplement each other. The first is from observation of order in nature and is an argument from analogy: if we saw order in part of nature (e.g., a house), we would conclude it had some intelligent designer and governor; why should not the same apply to the universe as a whole? The second is a deductive argument from what has already been proved about God. Thus the divine government is shown both from the nature of the governed and from the nature of the Governor.

[51] The "argument from design" is the "clearest" or most popular and understandable of all arguments for a divine Mind. The argument requires an initial act of understanding, or intellectual intuition, like understanding

Reply Obj. 2. In all created things there is a stable element, at least primary matter; and something belonging to movement, if under movement we include operation. And things need governing as to both: because even that which is stable, since it is created from nothing, would return to nothingness were it not sustained by a governing hand, as will be explained later (Q. 104, A. 1).

Reply Obj. 3. The natural necessity inherent in those beings which are determined to a particular thing, is a kind of impression from God, directing them to their end; as the necessity whereby an arrow is moved so as to fly towards a certain point is an impression from the archer, and not from the arrow. But there is a difference, inasmuch as that which creatures receive from God is their nature, while that which natural things receive from man in addition to their nature is somewhat violent. Wherefore, as the violent necessity in the movement of the arrow shows the action of the archer, so the natural necessity of things shows the government of Divine Providence.

SECOND ARTICLE

Whether the End of the Government of the World Is Something outside the World?

On the contrary, It is written (Prov 16:4): *The Lord hath made all things for Himself.* But God is outside the entire order of the universe. Therefore the end of all things is something extrinsic to them.

I answer that, As the end of a thing corresponds to its beginning, it is not possible to be ignorant of the end of things if we know their

---

the wind in moving leaves, or intuiting happiness in a smile. The skeptic who seriously wonders whether a stone hut on a desert island was perhaps formed by chance storms will not be persuaded by it. But given this initial commonsensical intuition, the logical force of the argument is just as strong, if not stronger, in light of modern scientific data, than it was in the Middle Ages. Cf., for example, the "Anthropic Principle": if the universe had been a trillionth of a degree hotter or colder during the first few seconds after the "Big Bang", no human life could ever have evolved.

beginning. Therefore, since the beginning of all things is something outside the universe, namely God, it is clear from what has been expounded above (Q. 44, AA. 1, 2), that we must conclude that the end of all things is some extrinsic good. This can be proved by reason. For it is clear that good has the nature of an end; wherefore, a particular end of anything consists in some particular good; while the universal end of all things is the Universal Good; Which is good of Itself by virtue of Its Essence, Which is the very essence of goodness; whereas a particular good is good by participation. Now it is manifest that in the whole created universe there is not a good which is not such by participation. Wherefore that good which is the end of the whole universe must be a good outside the universe. . . .

THIRD ARTICLE

Whether the World Is Governed by One?

Objection 1. It would seem that the world is not governed by one.[52] For we judge the cause by the effect. Now, we see in the government of the universe that things are not moved and do not operate uniformly, but some contingently and some of necessity in variously different ways. Therefore the world is not governed by one.

Objection 2. Further, things which are governed by one do not act against each other, except by the incapacity or unskillfulness of the ruler; which cannot apply to God. But created things agree not together, and act against each other; as is evident in the case of contraries. Therefore the world is not governed by one.

Objection 3. Further, in nature we always find what is the better. But it *is better that two should be together than one* (Qo 4:9). Therefore the world is not governed by one, but by many.

On the contrary, We confess our belief in one God and one Lord,

---

[52] There seem to be fairly good reasons for polytheism, which nearly the entire world seems to have believed for most of the time it has lived on this planet. Perhaps we moderns dismiss it too automatically, by social fashion rather than by reason.

according to the words of the Apostle (1 Cor 8:6): *To us there is but one God, the Father . . . and one Lord*: and both of these pertain to government. For to the Lord belongs dominion over subjects; and the name of God is taken from Providence as stated above (Q. 13, A. 8). Therefore the world is governed by one.

I answer that, We must of necessity say that the world is governed by one. For since the end of the government of the world is that which is essentially good, which is the greatest good; the government of the world must be the best kind of government. Now the best government is government by one.[53] The reason of this is that government is nothing but the directing of the things governed to the end; which consists in some good. But unity belongs to the idea of goodness, as Boëthius proves (*De Consol.* iii. 11) from this, that, as all things desire good, so do they desire unity; without which they would cease to exist. For a thing so far exists as it is one. Whence we observe that things resist division, as far as they can; and the dissolution of a thing arises from some defect therein.[54] Therefore the intention of a ruler over a multitude is unity, or peace. Now the proper cause of unity is one. For it is clear that several cannot be the cause of unity or concord, except so far as they are united. Furthermore, what is one in itself is a more apt and a better cause of unity than several things united. Therefore a multitude is better governed by one than by several. From this it follows that the government of the world, being the best form of government, must be by one. This is expressed by the Philosopher (*Metaph.* xii, Did. xi. 10): *Things refuse to be ill governed; and multiplicity of authorities is a bad thing, therefore there should be one ruler.*

Reply Obj. 1. Movement is *the act of a thing moved, caused by the mover.* Wherefore dissimilarity of movements is caused by diversity of things moved, which diversity is essential to the perfection of the universe (Q. 47, AA. 1, 2; Q. 48, A. 2), and not by a diversity of governors.

---

[53] St. Thomas is not making a *political* statement here. In fact, he thinks the best political regime is the "mixed regime" of a democratic constitutional monarchy. We cannot project human political structures or needs onto God. The universe is not a democracy.

[54] Note how very frequently St. Thomas appeals to common sense empirical observations to establish his metaphysical points.

Reply Obj. 2. Although contraries do not agree with each other in their proximate ends, nevertheless they agree in the ultimate end, so far as they are included in the one order of the universe.

Reply Obj. 3. If we consider individual goods, then two are better than one. But if we consider the essential good, then no addition is possible. . . .

FIFTH ARTICLE

Whether All Things Are Subject to the Divine Government?

Objection 3. Further, what can govern itself needs not to be governed by another. But the rational creature can govern itself; since it is master of its own act, and acts of itself; and is not made to act by another, which seems proper to things which are governed. Therefore all things are not subject to the Divine government.

On the contrary, Augustine says (*De Civ. Dei* v. 11): *Not only heaven and earth, not only man and angel, even the bowels of the lowest animal, even the wing of the bird, the flower of the plant, the leaf of the tree, hath God endowed with every fitting detail of their nature.* Therefore all things are subject to His government.

I answer that, For the same reason is God the ruler of things as He is their cause, because the same gives existence as gives perfection; and this belongs to government. Now God is the cause not indeed only of some particular kind of being, but of the whole universal being, as proved above (Q. 44, AA. 1, 2). Wherefore, as there can be nothing which is not created by God, so there can be nothing which is not subject to His government. This can also be proved from the nature of the end of government. For a man's government extends over all those things which come under the end of his government. Now the end of the Divine government is the Divine goodness; as we have shown (A. 2). Wherefore, as there can be nothing that is not ordered to the Divine goodness as its end, as is clear from what we have said above (Q. 44, A. 4; Q. 65, A. 2), so it is impossible for anything to escape from the Divine government.

Foolish therefore was the opinion of those who said that the corruptible lower world, or individual things, or that even human affairs, were not subject to the Divine government. These are represented as saying, *God hath abandoned the earth* (Ezek 9:9). . . .

Reply Obj. 3. The rational creature governs itself by its intellect and will, both of which require to be governed and perfected by the Divine intellect and will. Therefore above the government whereby the rational creature governs itself as master of its own act, it requires to be governed by God.[55]

SIXTH ARTICLE

Whether All Things Are Immediately Governed by God?

I answer that, In government there are two things to be considered; the design of government, which is providence itself; and the execution of the design. As to the design of government, God governs all things immediately; whereas in its execution, He governs some things by means of others.

The reason of this is that as God is the very essence of goodness, so everything must be attributed to God in its highest degree of goodness. Now the highest degree of goodness in any practical order, design, or knowledge (and such is the design of government) consists in knowing the individuals acted upon; as the best physician is not the one who can only give his attention to general principles, but who can consider the least details; and so on in other things. Therefore we must say that God has the design of the government of all things, even of the very least.[56]

But since things which are governed should be brought to perfection by government, this government will be so much the better in the degree the things governed are brought to perfection. Now it is a greater perfection for a thing to be good in itself and also the cause of goodness in others, than only to be good in itself. Therefore God so governs things that He makes some of them to be causes of others in government; as a master, who not only imparts knowledge to his pupils, but gives also the faculty of teaching others. . . .

---

[55] Creaturely "free will" does not mean freedom from the divine government, but freedom from natural necessity.

[56] Contrast the view of Plato, Aristotle, and Plotinus, who thought that God would pollute the purity of His knowledge by concerning Himself with particulars.

SEVENTH ARTICLE

Whether Anything Can Happen outside the Order of the Divine Government?

Objection 1. It would seem possible that something may occur outside the order of the Divine government. For Boëthius says (*De Consol.* iii) that *God disposes all for good.* Therefore, if nothing happens outside the order of the Divine government, it would follow that no evil exists.

Objection 2. Further, nothing that is in accordance with the pre-ordination of a ruler occurs by chance. Therefore, if nothing occurs outside the order of the Divine government, it follows that there is nothing fortuitous and casual.

Objection 3. Further, the order of Divine Providence is certain and unchangeable; because it is in accordance with the eternal design. Therefore, if nothing happens outside the order of the Divine government, it follows that all things happen by necessity, and nothing is contingent; which is false. Therefore it is possible for something to occur outside the order of the Divine government.

On the contrary, It is written (Esther 13:9): *O Lord, Lord, almighty King, all things are in Thy power, and there is none that can resist Thy will.*

I answer that, It is possible for an effect to result outside the order of some particular cause; but not outside the order of the universal cause. The reason of this is that no effect results outside the order of a particular cause, except through some other impeding cause; which other cause must itself be reduced to the first universal cause; as indigestion may occur outside the order of the nutritive power by some such impediment as the coarseness of the food, which again is to be ascribed to some other cause, and so on till we come to the first universal cause. Therefore as God is the first universal cause, not of one genus only, but of all being in general, it is impossible for anything to occur outside the order of the Divine government; but from the very fact that from one point of view something seems to evade the order of Divine providence considered in regard to one particular cause, it must necessarily come back to that order as regards some other cause.[57]

---

[57] The practical religious consequences of this theoretical theological

Reply Obj. 1. There is nothing wholly evil in the world, for evil is ever founded on good, as shown above (Q. 48, A. 3).[58] Therefore something is said to be evil through its escaping from the order of some particular good. If it wholly escaped from the order of the Divine government, it would wholly cease to exist.

Reply Obj. 2. Things are said to be fortuitous as regards some particular cause from the order of which they escape. But as to the order of Divine providence, *nothing in the world happens by chance*, as Augustine declares (QQ. 83, qu. 24).

Reply Obj. 3. Certain effects are said to be contingent as compared to their proximate causes, which may fail in their effects; and not as though anything could happen entirely outside the order of Divine government. The very fact that something occurs outside the order of some proximate cause, is owing to some other cause, itself subject to the Divine government. . . .

---

point in the area of the foundation for faith and trust in God's providence are obvious.

[58] This does not *detract* from the commonsensical perception that some things are really evil, or from the reality or seriousness of these evils, but it *adds* a surrounding metaphysical context of being, therefore goodness. Evil is a parasite on good, its host.

Question 104

The Special Effects of the Divine Government

FIRST ARTICLE

Whether Creatures Need to Be Kept in Being by God?

Objection 2. Further, God is more powerful than any created agent. But a created agent, even after ceasing to act, can cause its effect to be preserved in being; thus the house continues to stand after the builder has ceased to build; and water remains hot for some time after the fire has ceased to heat. Much more, therefore, can God cause His creature to be kept in being, after He has ceased to create it. . . .

On the contrary, It is written (Heb 1:3): *Upholding all things by the word of His power.*

I answer that, Both reason and faith bind us to say that creatures are kept in being by God. To make this clear, we must consider that a thing is preserved by another in two ways. First, indirectly, and accidentally; thus a person is said to preserve anything by removing the cause of its corruption, as a man may be said to preserve a child, whom he guards from falling into the fire. In this way God preserves some things, but not all, for there are some things of such a nature that nothing can corrupt them, so that it is not necessary to keep them from corruption. Secondly, a thing is said to preserve another *per se* and directly, namely, when what is preserved depends on the preserver in such a way that it cannot exist without it. In this manner all creatures need to be preserved by God. For the being of every creature depends on God, so that not for a moment could it subsist, but would fall into nothingness were it not kept in being by the operation of the Divine power, as Gregory says (*Moral.* xvi).

This is made clear as follows: Every effect depends on its cause, so far as it is its cause. But we must observe that an agent may be the cause of the *becoming* of its effect, but not directly of its *being*. This may be seen both in artificial and in natural things: for the builder causes the house in its *becoming*, but he is not the direct cause of its *being*.[59] . . .

Therefore as the becoming of a thing cannot continue when that action of the agent ceases which causes the *becoming* of the effect: so neither can the *being* of a thing continue after that action of the agent has ceased, which is the cause of the effect not only in *becoming* but also in *being*. This is why hot water retains heat after the cessation of the fire's action; while on the contrary, the air does not continue to be lit up, even for a moment, when the sun ceases to act upon it, because . . . since it has no root in the air, the light ceases with the action of the sun.

Now every creature may be compared to God, as the air is to the sun which enlightens it. For as the sun possesses light by its nature, and as the air is enlightened by sharing the sun's nature; so God alone is Being by virtue of His own Essence, since His Essence is His existence; whereas every creature has being by participation, so that its essence is not its existence. Therefore, as Augustine says (*Gen. ad lit.* iv. 12): *If the ruling power of God were withdrawn from His creatures, their nature would at once cease, and all nature would collapse.*[60] . . .

---

[59] What Aristotle meant by the efficient cause was only the cause of *becoming*, not of *being*; the cause which imposes a form on matter, not the cause of the very *existence* of the substance or of its matter. For Aristotle believed matter was eternal, not created. In St. Thomas' biblical universe, God created matter itself, and therefore is the cause of the very being of the universe. This gives a new existential meaning to efficient causality and to the very notion of being, as Gilson has shown (cf. *Being and Some Philosophers*).

[60] God is not like a parent who bears a child, or a carpenter who makes a table, but like a mind which conceives a thought, or a lower rung on a ladder which supports the rest of the ladder: the cause is presently active and must be at every moment in order for the effect to continue to be. The practical religious consequences of this vision of intimate divine immanence and presence should be evident. (Cf. also Article 3.)

Reply Obj. 2. God cannot grant to a creature to be preserved in being after the cessation of the Divine influence: as neither can He make it not to have received its being from Himself. For the creature needs to be preserved by God in so far as the being of an effect depends on the cause of its being. So that there is no comparison with an agent that is not the cause of *being* but only of *becoming*. . . .

THIRD ARTICLE

Whether God Can Annihilate Anything?

I answer that, Some have held that God, in giving existence to creatures, acted from natural necessity. Were this true, God could not annihilate anything, since His nature cannot change. But, as we have said above (Q. 19, A. 4), such an opinion is entirely false, and absolutely contrary to the Catholic faith, which confesses that God created things of His own free-will, according to Psalm 134:6: *Whatsoever the Lord pleased, He hath done.* Therefore that God gives existence to a creature depends on His will; nor does He preserve things in existence otherwise than by continually pouring out existence into them, as we have said. Therefore, just as before things existed, God was free not to give them existence, and not to make them; so after they have been made, He is free not to continue their existence; and thus they would cease to exist; and this would be to annihilate them. . . .

FOURTH ARTICLE

Whether Anything Is Annihilated?

I answer that, Some of those things which God does in creatures occur in accordance with the natural course of things; others happen miraculously, and not in accordance with the natural order, as will be explained (Q. 105, A. 6). Now whatever God wills to do according to the natural order of things may be observed from their nature; but those things which occur miraculously, are ordered for the manifestation of grace, according to the Apostle, *To each one is given the manifestation of the Spirit, unto profit* (1 Cor 12:7); and subsequently he mentions, among others, the working of miracles.

Now the nature of creatures shows that none of them is annihilated. For, either they are immaterial, and therefore have no potentiality to non-existence; or they are material, and then they continue to exist, at least in matter, which is incorruptible, since it is the subject of generation and corruption.[61] Moreover, the annihilation of things does not pertain to the manifestation of grace; since rather the power and goodness of God are manifested by the preservation of things in existence. Wherefore we must conclude by denying absolutely that anything at all will be annihilated. . . .

---

[61] A material *thing* can be corrupted (destroyed) naturally, but matter itself cannot, for the corruption of one substance (e.g., the death of a tree) means that the former form (tree) reverts to formless prime matter and takes a different form (e.g., leaf mold).

Question 105

Of the Change of Creatures by God

SECOND ARTICLE

Whether God Can Move a Body Immediately?

I answer that, It is erroneous to say that God cannot Himself produce all the determinate effects which are produced by any created cause. Wherefore, since bodies are moved immediately by created causes, we cannot possibly doubt that God can move immediately any bodies whatever.[62]. . .

THIRD ARTICLE

Whether God Moves the Created Intellect Immediately?

On the contrary, The teacher moves the intellect of the one taught. But it is written (Ps 93:10) that God *teaches man knowledge.* Therefore God moves the human intellect.[63]. . .

---

[62] It is a strange prejudice that will admit God but not miracles, for it means limiting the Creator even more than creatures in the moving of bodies. (Cf. I, 105, 6.)

[63] To move or change someone's mind is not to remove its freedom, of course. *Teaching* is not the same as determining (or even "conditioning" unfreely). When the sun determines the air to be bright, the air is passive and unable to resist. But when a teacher influences a student's mind by teaching truth, the student must actively grasp the truth in order either to agree with it or to disagree and resist. The same is true of moving another's will (Article 4).

FOURTH ARTICLE

Whether God Can Move the Created Will?

I answer that, As the intellect is moved by the object and by the Giver of the power of intelligence, as stated above (A. 3), so is the will moved by its object, which is good, and by Him who creates the power of willing. . . . Now the potentiality of the will extends to the universal good; for its object is the universal good; just as the object of the intellect is universal being. But every created good is some particular good; God alone is the universal good. Whereas He alone fills the capacity of the will, and moves it sufficiently as its object. . . .

FIFTH ARTICLE

Whether God Works in Every Agent?

Objection 2. Further, the same work cannot proceed at the same time from two sources; as neither can one and the same movement belong to two movable things. Therefore if the creature's operation is from God operating in the creature, it cannot at the same time proceed from the creature; and so no creature works at all. . . .

I answer that, Some have understood God to work in every agent in such a way that no created power has any effect in things, but that God alone is the immediate cause of everything wrought; for instance, that it is not fire that gives heat, but God in the fire, and so forth. But this is impossible. First, because the order of cause and effect would be taken away from created things: and this would imply lack of power in the Creator: for it is due to the power of the cause, that it bestows active power on its effect.[64] Secondly, because the active powers which are seen to exist in things, would be bestowed on things to no purpose, if these wrought nothing through them. Indeed, all things created would seem, in a way, to be purposeless, if they lacked an operation proper to them; since the

---

[64] Note that the misdirected urge to give God more glory and power by denying the efficacy of creatures really detracts from God—like refusing to admit a ruler's representatives.

purpose of everything is its operation. For the less perfect is always for the sake of the more perfect: and consequently as the matter is for the sake of the form, so the form which is the first act, is for the sake of its operation, which is the second act;[65] and thus operation is the end of the creature. We must therefore understand that God works in things in such a manner that things have their proper operation. . . .

Reply Obj. 2. One action does not proceed from two agents of the same order. But nothing hinders the same action from proceeding from a primary and a secondary agent. . . .

SIXTH ARTICLE

Whether God Can Do Anything outside the Established Order of Nature?[66]

Objection 3. Further, God established the order of nature. Therefore if God does anything outside the order of nature, it would seem that He is changeable; which cannot be said.

On the contrary, Augustine says (*Contra Faust.* xxvi. *ibid.*): *God sometimes does things which are contrary to the ordinary course of nature.*

I answer that, From each cause there results a certain order to its effects, since every cause is a principle; and so, according to the multiplicity of causes, there results a multiplicity of orders, subjected one to the other, as cause is subjected to cause. Wherefore a higher cause is not subjected to a cause of a lower order; but conversely. An example of this may be seen in human affairs. On the father of a family depends the order of the household; which order is contained in the order of the city; which order again

---

[65] The "first act" (actuality) of any creature is its own form or essence. The "second act" (actuality) is its activity, or operation. As matter is potential to form and "for" form, first act is potential to and "for" second act. Though "action" is logically one of the nine "accidents", activity is not accidental to the fulfillment of a creature's being.

[66] With his characteristic balance and refutation of two opposite errors, St. Thomas turns now from the deniers of nature to the deniers of supernature. The first error would make everything a miracle; the second would make nothing a miracle.

depends on the ruler of the city; while this last order depends on that of the king, by whom the whole kingdom is ordered.

If therefore we consider the order of things depending on the first cause, God cannot do anything against this order; for, if He did so, He would act against His foreknowledge, or His will, or His goodness. But if we consider the order of things depending on any secondary cause, thus God can do something outside such order; for He is not subject to the order of secondary causes; but, on the contrary, this order is subject to Him, as proceeding from Him, not by a natural necessity, but by the choice of His own will; for He could have created another order of things. Wherefore God can do something outside this order created by Him, when He chooses, for instance by producing the effects of secondary causes without them, or by producing certain effects to which secondary causes do not extend. So Augustine says (*Contra Faust.* xxvi. *ibid.*): *God acts against the wonted course of nature, but by no means does He act against the supreme law; because He does not act against Himself.*[67]. . .

Reply Obj. 3. God fixed a certain order in things in such a way that at the same time He reserved to Himself whatever he intended to do otherwise than by a particular cause. So when He acts outside this order, He does not change.

SEVENTH ARTICLE

Whether Whatever God Does outside the Natural Order Is Miraculous?

On the contrary, Augustine says (*Contra Faust.* xxvi. 3): *Where God does anything against that order of nature which we know and are accustomed to observe, we call it a miracle.*

I answer that, The word *miracle* is derived from *admiration,* which arises when an effect is manifest, whereas its cause is hidden; as when a man sees an eclipse without knowing its cause, as the Philosopher says in the beginning of his *Metaphysics.* Now the cause of a manifest effect may be known to one, but unknown to others. Wherefore a thing is wonderful to one man, and not at all to

---

[67] Thus miracles too fit into the ultimate order and plan of creation,

others: as an eclipse is to a rustic, but not to an astronomer. Now a miracle is so called as being full of wonder; as having a cause absolutely hidden from all: and this cause is God. Wherefore those things which God does outside those causes which we know, are called miracles.[68] . . .

---

though they are exceptions to the proximate order of nature.

[68] "Wonder" here means (1) surprise, (2) questioning, desiring to know the cause, and (3) admiration. (1) leads to (2) and (2) leads to (3). Whether a given event is a miracle depends not on whether it arouses wonder in anyone, but on whether the cause is a supernatural act of God.

FIVE

Anthropology:
Body and Soul

Question 75

Of Man Who Is Composed of a Spiritual and a Corporeal Substance: and in the First Place, concerning What Belongs to the Essence of the Soul

Having treated of the spiritual and of the corporeal creature, we now proceed to treat of man, who is composed of a spiritual and corporeal substance. We shall treat first of the nature of man, and secondly of his origin. Now the theologian considers the nature of man in relation to the soul; but not in relation to the body, except in so far as the body has relation to the soul. Hence the first object of our consideration will be the soul. And since Dionysius (*Ang. Hier.* xi) says that three things are to be found in spiritual substances—essence, power, and operation—we shall treat first of what belongs to the essence of the soul; secondly, of what belongs to its power; thirdly, of what belongs to its operation.

Concerning the first, two points have to be considered; the first is the nature of the soul considered in itself; the second is the union of the soul with the body. . . .

FIRST ARTICLE

Whether the Soul Is a Body?

On the contrary, Augustine says (*De Trin.* vi. 6) that the soul *is simple in comparison with the body, inasmuch as it does not occupy space by its bulk.*[1]

---

[1] We can conceive, or intellectualize, or understand the concept of soul, but we cannot *imagine* "soul" because our imagination is inescapably

243

I answer that, To seek the nature of the soul, we must premise that the soul is defined as the first principle [source] of life in those things which live: for we call living things *animate* [*i.e.*, having a soul], and those things which have no life, *inanimate*. Now life is shown principally by two actions, knowledge and movement. The philosophers of old,[2] not being able to rise above their imagination, supposed that the principle of these actions was something corporeal: for they asserted that only bodies were real things; and that what is not corporeal is nothing: hence they maintained that the soul is something corporeal. This opinion can be proved to be false in many ways; but we shall make use of only one proof, based on universal and certain principles, which shows clearly that the soul is not a body.

It is manifest that not every principle of vital action is a soul, for then the eye would be a soul, as it is a principle of vision; and the same might be applied to the other instruments of the soul: but it is the *first* principle of life, which we call the soul. Now, though a body may be a principle of life, as the heart is a principle of life in an animal, yet nothing corporeal can be the first principle of life. For it is clear that to be a principle of life, or to be a living thing, does not belong to a body as such; since, if that were the case, every body would be a living thing, or a principle of life. Therefore a body is competent to be a living thing or even a principle of life, as *such* a body. Now that it is actually such a body, it owes to some principle which is called its act. Therefore the soul, which is the first principle of life, is not a body, but the act of a body.[3] . . .

---

spatial; and souls, though in time, are not in space. If the soul were in space, we would lose part of our soul when we got a haircut.

[2] The pre-Socratics. St. Thomas would consider modern materialism a reversion to a very primitive philosophy.

[3] The argument is so simple that it may seem obscure to the sophisticated mind. The point is that there exist dead bodies as well as living bodies, and the difference between them is not a bodily entity or organ (the dead cow's body is still udderly complete), but is the difference between the presence or absence of the soul, the source of life.

SECOND ARTICLE

Whether the Human Soul Is Something Subsistent[4]

I answer that, It must necessarily be allowed that the principle of intellectual operation which we call the soul, is a principle both incorporeal and subsistent. For it is clear that by means of the intellect man can have knowledge of all corporeal things. Now whatever knows certain things cannot have any of them in its own nature; because that which is in it naturally would impede the knowledge of anything else. Thus we observe that a sick man's tongue being vitiated by a feverish and bitter humor, is insensible to anything sweet, and everything seems bitter to it. Therefore, if the intellectual principle contained the nature of a body it would be unable to know all bodies. Now every body has its own determinate nature. Therefore it is impossible for the intellectual principle to be a body. It is likewise impossible for it to understand by means of a bodily organ; since the determinate nature of that organ would impede knowledge of all bodies; as when a certain determinate color is not only in the pupil of the eye, but also in a glass vase, the liquid in the vase seems to be of that same color.

Therefore the intellectual principle which we call the mind or the intellect has an operation *per se* apart from the body. Now only that which subsists can have an operation *per se*. For nothing can operate but what is actual: wherefore a thing operates according as it is; for which reason we do not say that heat imparts heat, but that what is hot gives heat. We must conclude, therefore, that the human soul, which is called the intellect or the mind, is something incorporeal and subsistent. . . .

---

[4] Subsistence is the existence of a substance. For St. Thomas, the soul is both a substance and a form (the form of the body, or the form of the substance of which the body is the matter). (Cf. I, 76, 1.) As a substance, it can exist of itself without the body. As the form of the body, it is the very life of the body.

THIRD ARTICLE

Whether the Souls of Brute Animals Are Subsistent?[5]

I answer that, The ancient philosophers made no distinction between sense and intellect, and referred both to a corporeal principle, as has been said (A. 1). Plato, however, drew a distinction between intellect and sense; yet he referred both to an incorporeal principle, maintaining that sensing, just as understanding, belongs to the soul as such. From this it follows that even the souls of brute animals are subsistent. But Aristotle held that of the operations of the soul, understanding alone is performed without a corporeal organ. On the other hand, sensation and the consequent operations of the sensitive soul are evidently accompanied with change in the body; thus in the act of vision, the pupil of the eye is affected by a reflection of color: and so with the other senses. Hence it is clear that the sensitive soul has no *per se* operation of its own, and that every operation of the sensitive soul belongs to the composite. Wherefore we conclude that as the souls of brute animals have no *per se* operations they are not subsistent. For the operation of anything follows the mode of its being. . . .

FOURTH ARTICLE

Whether the Soul Is Man?

On the contrary, Augustine (*De Civ. Dei* xix. 3) commends Varro as holding *that man is not a mere soul, nor a mere body; but both soul and body.*

I answer that, The assertion *the soul is man,* can be taken in two senses. First, that man is a soul; though this particular man, Socrates, for instance, is not a soul, but composed of soul and body. I say this, forasmuch as some held that the form alone belongs to the species; while matter is part of the individual, and

---

[5] The modern question about "animal rights" is decided here by an ontological difference in kind, not just in performance or behavioral I.Q.: human souls, being intellectual, are subsistent (and therefore immortal); animal souls are not.

not of the species. This cannot be true; for to the nature of the species belongs what the definition signifies; and in natural things the definition does not signify the form only, but the form and the matter. Hence in natural things the matter is part of the species; not, indeed, signate matter,[6] which is the principle of individuality; but the common matter. For as it belongs to the notion of this particular man to be composed of this soul, of this flesh, and of these bones; so it belongs to the notion of man to be composed of soul, flesh, and bones; for whatever belongs in common to the substance [essence] of all the individuals contained under a given species, must belong also to the substance of the species.

It may also be understood in this sense, that this soul is this man; and this could be held if it were supposed that the operation of the sensitive soul were proper to it, apart from the body; because in that case all the operations which are attributed to man would belong to the soul only; and whatever performs the operations proper to a thing, is that thing; wherefore that which performs the operations of a man is man. But it has been shown above (A. 3) that sensation is not the operation of the soul only. Since, then, sensation is an operation of man, but not proper to him, it is clear that man is not a soul only, but something composed of soul and body.—Plato, through supposing that sensation was proper to the soul, could maintain man to be a soul making use of the body. . . .

FIFTH ARTICLE

Whether the Soul Is Composed of Matter and Form?

I answer that, The soul has no matter. We may consider this question in two ways. First, from the notion of a soul in general; for it belongs to the notion of a soul to be the form of a body. . . .

Secondly, we may proceed from the specific notion of the

---

[6] I.e., matter "signed by" quantity, the matter which multiplies a single universal form into different substances (e.g., "dog" into many dogs). "Common matter" is the matter that is part of the definition, essence, substance, or nature. "Flesh" is part of human *nature*; "*this* flesh" is the "signate matter" which is part of this *individual*.

human soul, inasmuch as it is intellectual. For it is clear that whatever is received into something is received according to the condition of the recipient. . . . If the intellectual soul were composed of matter and form, the forms of things would be received into it as individuals, and so it would only know the individual:[7] just as it happens with the sensitive powers which receive forms in a corporeal organ; since matter is the principle by which forms are individualized. It follows, therefore, that the intellectual soul, and every intellectual substance which has knowledge of forms absolutely, is exempt from composition of matter and form. . . .

SIXTH ARTICLE

Whether the Human Soul Is Incorruptible?

Objection 1. It would seem that the human soul is corruptible. For those things that have a like beginning and process seemingly have a like end. But the beginning, by generation, of men is like that of animals, for they are made from the earth. And the process of life is alike in both; because *all things breathe alike, and man hath nothing more than the beast*, as it is written (Qo 3:19). Therefore, as the same text concludes, *the death of man and beast is one, and the condition of both is equal*. But the souls of brute animals are corruptible. Therefore, also, the human soul is corruptible. . . .

I answer that, We must assert that the intellectual principle which we call the human soul is incorruptible. For a thing may be corrupted in two ways—*per se* [by itself] and accidentally. Now it is impossible for any substance to be generated or corrupted accidentally, that is, by the generation or corruption of something else. For generation and corruption belong to a thing, just as existence belongs to it, which is acquired by generation and lost by

---

[7] A concrete, individual *receiver* requires a concrete, individual *reception*; and a concrete, individual *reception* requires a concrete, individual *thing received*, like a guest received into a house or a sardine into a can. A can could not receive the universal form "sardineness", or sardine nature; but an immaterial *mind* can.

corruption. Therefore, whatever has existence *per se* cannot be generated or corrupted except *per se*;[8] while things which do not subsist, such as accidents and material forms, acquire existence or lose it through the generation or corruption of composite things. Now it was shown above (AA. 2, 3) that the souls of brutes are not self-subsistent, whereas the human soul is; so that the souls of brutes are corrupted, when their bodies are corrupted; while the human soul could not be corrupted unless it were corrupted *per se*.

This, indeed, is impossible, not only as regards the human soul, but also as regards anything subsistent that is a form alone [without matter]. For . . . it is impossible for a form to be separated from itself; and therefore it is impossible for a subsistent form to cease to exist.[9]

. . . Moreover we may take a sign of this from the fact that everything naturally aspires to existence after its own manner. Now, in things that have knowledge, desire ensues upon knowledge. The senses indeed do not know existence, except under the conditions of *here* and *now*, whereas the intellect apprehends existence absolutely, and for all time; so that everything that has an intellect naturally desires always to exist. But a natural desire cannot be in vain.[10] Therefore every intellectual substance is incorruptible.

---

[8] I.e., whatever has its own act of existence (i.e., whatever is a substance rather than an accident). Accidents (like the whiteness of a seagull) and merely material forms (like the nature of a seagull) can be generated or corrupted by the generation or corruption of the substance in which they inhere (the actual seagull); but a substance (e.g., one seagull) is not generated or corrupted by the generation or corruption of another substance (another seagull).

[9] Corruption takes place by a form being separated from its matter (e.g., the soul being separated from its body). This man, this composite matter-form substance, is corruptible. But the soul, as a form without matter, is not corruptible thus.

[10] St. Thomas was too natural, healthy, and sane to consider seriously the possibility that some people might not share this desire to exist. He was also too natural, healthy, and sane to consider seriously the possibility that the universe is fundamentally meaningless, that it produces in us desires which correspond to no real possible satisfaction at all. No one has ever seen nature producing desires for nonexistent objects. The empirical

Reply Obj. 1. Solomon reasons thus in the person of the foolish, as expressed in the words of Wisdom 2. Therefore the saying that man and animals have a like beginning in generation is true of the body; for all animals alike are made of earth. But it is not true of the soul. For the souls of brutes are produced by some power of the body; whereas the human soul is produced by God. To signify this, it is written as to other animals: *Let the earth bring forth the living soul* (Gen 1:24): while of man it is written (*ibid.* 2:7) that *He breathed into his face the breath of life.* [11] And so in the last chapter of Ecclesiastes (12:7) it is concluded: *(Before) the dust return into its earth from whence it was; and the spirit return to God Who gave it.* Again the process of life is alike as to the body, concerning which it is written (Qo 3:19): *All things breathe alike,* and (Wis 2:2), *The breath in our nostrils is smoke.* But the process is not alike of the soul; for man is intelligent, whereas animals are not. Hence it is false to say: *Man has nothing more than beasts.* Thus death comes to both alike as to the body, but not as to the soul. . . .

SEVENTH ARTICLE

Whether the Soul Is of the Same Species As an Angel? [12]

Objection 3. Further, it seems that the soul does not differ from an angel except in its union with the body. But as the body is outside the essence of the soul, it seems that it does not belong to its species. Therefore the soul and angel are of the same species.

---

evidence for "no natural desire is in vain" is 100 percent, and the evidence for its contrary is 0 percent (consider all known natural desires: to eat, drink, sleep, wake, live, walk, copulate, socialize, know, love, be loved, etc.).

[11] This is the fundamental ontological basis for human dignity, intrinsic value, and moral responsibility, viz., that the human soul is God-given, not slime-evolved, and its nature is spiritual ("made in the image of God"). Bodies could have evolved, but not souls.

[12] It is a strangely popular notion that after death we become angels. This change of species is, of course, impossible. For one thing, there is a resurrection of the body. For another, even the temporarily disembodied

On the contrary, Things which have different natural operations are of different species. But the natural operations of the soul and of an angel are different; since, as Dionysius says (*Div. Nom.* vii), *Angelic minds have simple and blessed intelligence, not gathering their knowledge of Divine things from visible things.* Subsequently he says the contrary to this of the soul. Therefore the soul and an angel are not of the same species. . . .

Reply Obj. 3. The body is not of the essence of the soul; but the soul by the nature of its essence can be united to the body, so that, properly speaking, not the soul alone, but the *composite*, is the species. And the very fact that the soul in a certain way requires the body for its operation, proves that the soul is endowed with a grade of intellectuality inferior to that of an angel, who is not united to a body.

---

soul, after bodily death and before the general resurrection at the end of time, is a spirit of a different species than an angel, for two reasons: (1) as St. Thomas notes here, human souls know by sensation and reasoning, while angels are purely intuitive; and (2) human souls are essentially forms of bodies, and therefore incomplete without their bodies, while angels have no tendency to inform bodies.

Question 76

Of the Union of Body and Soul

FIRST ARTICLE

*Whether the Intellectual Principle Is United to
the Body As Its Form?*[13]

Objection 6. Further, whatever exists in a thing by reason of its nature exists in it always. But to be united to matter belongs to the form by reason of its nature; because form is the act of matter, not by an accidental quality, but by its own essence; otherwise matter and form would not make a thing substantially one, but only accidentally one. Therefore a form cannot be without its own proper matter. But the intellectual principle, since it is incorruptible, as was shown above (Q. 75, A. 6), remains separate from the body,

---

[13] St. Thomas is balancing and synthesizing the Platonic insight that the soul is immortal and subsistent, thus validating the soul's survival of the body's death, with the Aristotelian insight that the soul is the form of the body, thus validating our sense of personal psychosomatic, hylomorphic unity. Having established the Platonic point in Question 75, he establishes the Aristotelian point in Question 76.

St. Thomas here opposes:

1. the Platonic doctrine according to which the soul is only *accidentally* united to the body, since it is a substance in itself (cf. Objection 1);

2. the doctrine of "the plurality of forms", according to which man had three souls (forms): vegetative, sensitive, and rational; and the highest was *not* the form of the body (cf. first paragraph of "*I answer that*");

3. Latin Averroism, according to which the first active cause of human intellectual activity was not each man's own intellectual soul but a kind of collective cosmic mind, the lowest of the angelic movers of heavenly bodies (cf. second paragraph of "*I answer that*" and Article 2).

after the dissolution of the body. Therefore the intellectual principle is not united to the body as its form.

On the contrary, According to the Philosopher, *Metaph.* viii (Did. vii. 2), difference is derived from the form. But the difference which constitutes man is *rational*, which is applied to man on account of his intellectual principle. Therefore the intellectual principle is the form of man.

I answer that, We must assert that the intellect which is the principle of intellectual operation is the form of the human body. For that whereby primarily anything acts is a form of the thing to which the act is to be attributed: for instance, that whereby a body is primarily healed is health, and that whereby the soul knows primarily is knowledge; hence health is a form of the body, and knowledge is a form of the soul. The reason is because nothing acts except so far as it is in act; wherefore a thing acts by that whereby it is in act. Now it is clear that the first thing by which the body lives is the soul. And as life appears through various operations in different degrees of living things, that whereby we primarily perform each of all these vital actions is the soul. For the soul is the primary principle of our nourishment, sensation, and local movement; and likewise of our understanding. Therefore this principle by which we primarily understand, whether it be called the intellect or the intellectual soul, is the form of the body. This is the demonstration used by Aristotle (*De Anima* ii. 2).

But if anyone says that the intellectual soul is not the form of the body he must first explain how it is that this action of understanding is the action of this particular man; for each one is conscious that it is himself who understands. . . .

Reply Obj. 6. To be united to the body belongs to the soul by reason of itself, as it belongs to a light body by reason of itself to be raised up. And as a light body remains light, when removed from its proper place, retaining meanwhile an aptitude and an inclination for its proper place; so the human soul retains its proper existence when separated from the body, having an aptitude and a natural inclination to be united to the body.

SECOND ARTICLE

Whether the Intellectual Principle Is Multiplied According to the Number of Bodies? [14]

Objection 1. It would seem that the intellectual principle is not multiplied according to the number of bodies, but that there is one intellect in all men. For an immaterial substance is not multiplied in number within one species. But the human soul is an immaterial substance; since it is not composed of matter and form, as was shown above (Q. 75, A. 5). Therefore there are not many human souls in one species. But all men are of one species. Therefore there is but one intellect in all men. . . .

I answer that, It is absolutely impossible for one intellect to belong to all men. . . . If there is one intellect, no matter how diverse may be all those things of which the intellect makes use as instruments, in no way is it possible to say that Socrates and Plato are otherwise than one understanding man. [15]. . . If there were one intellect for all men, the diversity of phantasms which are in this

---

[14] Philosophers in the thirteenth century were confronted with this teaching of a single intellect in all men, which came from the Arabic commentators on Aristotle, especially Averroes. The idea that there is a single collective intellect is obviously contrary to Christian faith (and also to individual moral responsibility), but it seemed to be backed by the authority of the world's greatest philosopher, Aristotle. This situation obviously threatened the synthesis or marriage between Christianity and philosophy, faith and reason, the fundamental enterprise of medieval Christian philosophy. St. Thomas responded (1) by refuting the idea rationally (here), and (2) by writing a commentary on Aristotle's *De Anima* ("On the Soul"), working with a more accurate new translation, translated directly into Latin from newly discovered Greek originals rather than through Arabic intermediaries, a translation produced by his friend William of Moerbeke. In his commentary St. Thomas showed that Averroes, who was working with an Arabic translation of a Syriac translation of a lost Greek original, had not correctly interpreted Aristotle's text, especially the key passage in Book 3, chapter 5.

[15] Note how St. Thomas instinctively perceives the impossibility of this idea, however popular, and appeals first of all to the simplest and most commonsensical refutation of it. He also does not neglect to refute it more

one and that one would not cause a diversity of intellectual operation in this man and that man.[16] It follows, therefore, that it is altogether impossible and unreasonable to maintain that there exists one intellect for all men.

Reply Obj. 1. Although the intellectual soul, like an angel, has no matter from which it is produced, yet it is the form of a certain matter; in which it is unlike an angel. Therefore, according to the division of matter, there are many souls of one species; while it is quite impossible for many angels to be of one species.[17]. . .

THIRD ARTICLE

Whether Besides the Intellectual Soul There Are in Man Other Souls Essentially Different from One Another?

On the contrary, It is said in the book *De Ecclesiasticis Dogmatibus* xv: *Nor do we say that there are two souls in one man, as James and other Syrians write; one, animal, by which the body is animated, and which is mingled with the blood; the other, spiritual, which obeys the reason; but we say that it is one and the same soul in man, that both gives life to the body by being united to it, and orders itself by its own reasoning.*

I answer that, Plato held that there were several souls in one body, distinct even as to organs, to which souls he referred the different vital actions, saying that the nutritive power is in the liver, the concupiscible in the heart, and the power of knowledge in the brain. Which opinion is rejected by Aristotle (*De Anima* ii. 2), with regard to those parts of the soul which use corporeal organs; for this reason, that in those animals which continue to live when they

---

technically and carefully. Rarely do we find a philosopher who combines common sense simplicity with scholarly sophistication.

[16] For intellection depends on its data, viz., sense images ("phantasms") (cf. I, 84, especially Article 7); and in one individual, a diversity of phantasms does not cause a diversity of acts of intellection (I know the same object via many images).

[17] Each angel is its own species, or is the sole member of its species. Each angel is a totally unique individual, since angels have no matter and matter is the source of individuation within a species (since the form is one).

have been divided, in each part are observed the operations of the soul, as sense and appetite. Now this would not be the case if the various principles of the soul's operations were essentially different, and distributed in the various parts of the body. But with regard to the intellectual part, he seems to leave it in doubt whether it be *only logically* distinct from the other parts of the soul, *or also locally*.

The opinion of Plato might be maintained if, as he held, the soul were supposed to be united to the body, not as its form, but as its motor. For it involves nothing unreasonable that the same movable thing be moved by several motors; and still less if it be moved according to its various parts. If we suppose, however, that the soul is united to the body as its form, it is quite impossible for several essentially different souls to be in one body. . . . [For] an animal would not be absolutely one, in which there were several souls. For nothing is absolutely one except by one form. . . . Against those who hold that there are several souls in the body, he [Aristotle] asks (*De Anima* i. 5), *what contains them?*—that is, what makes them one? It cannot be said that they are united by the one body; because rather does the soul contain the body and make it one, than the reverse.[18]

. . . We must therefore conclude that in man the sensitive soul, the intellectual soul, and the nutritive soul are numerically one soul. . . .

FOURTH ARTICLE

Whether in Man There Is Another Form Besides the Intellectual Soul?

On the contrary, Of one thing there is but one substantial being. But the substantial form gives substantial being. Therefore of one

---

[18] For the soul "the first principle of life", unites the diverse organs and bodily functions as no inorganic (not-alive, not-ensouled) compound can.

The words of a book (which are its matter) are grammatically and thematically unified only by the book's theme or point (which is its form). Thus the form (theme) unifies and contains the matter (words) rather than vice versa. The same is true of man's soul and body.

thing there is but one substantial form. But the soul is the substantial form of man. Therefore it is impossible for there to be in man another substantial form besides the intellectual soul.

I answer that, If we suppose that the intellectual soul is not united to the body as its form, but only as its motor, as the Platonists maintain, it would necessarily follow that in man there is another substantial form, by which the body is established in its being as movable by the soul. If, however, the intellectual soul be united to the body as its substantial form, as we have said above (A. 1), it is impossible for another substantial form besides the intellectual soul to be found in man.[19]. . .

FIFTH ARTICLE

Whether the Intellectual Soul Is Properly United to Such a Body?

Objection 1. It would seem that the intellectual soul is improperly united to such a body. For matter must be proportionate to the form. But the intellectual soul is incorruptible. Therefore it is not properly united to a corruptible body. . . .

Objection 4. Further, what is susceptible of a more perfect form should itself be more perfect. But the intellectual soul is the most perfect of souls. Therefore since the bodies of other animals are naturally provided with a covering, for instance, with hair instead of clothes, and hoofs instead of shoes; and are, moreover, naturally provided with arms, as claws, teeth, and horns; it seems that the intellectual soul should not have been united to a body which is imperfect as being deprived of the above means of protection.

---

[19] Cf. note 13. St. Thomas here refuses to compromise man's psychosomatic unity, any more than he would compromise the soul's substantial independence and immortality. He has the Augustinian habit of holding two apparently contradictory (but not *really* contradictory) teachings together without compromising either, without abandoning or weakening one for the other. There are many other examples: faith and reason, freedom and predestination, creatures' autonomy and total dependence on their Creator.

On the contrary, The Philosopher says (*De anima* ii. 1), that *the soul is the act of a physical organic body having life potentially.*

I answer that, Since the form is not for the matter, but rather the matter for the form, we must gather from the form the reason why the matter is such as it is; and not conversely.[20] Now the intellectual soul, as we have seen above (Q. 55, A. 2) in the order of nature, holds the lowest place among intellectual substances; inasmuch as it is not naturally gifted with the knowledge of truth, as the angels are; but has to gather knowledge from individual things by way of the senses, as Dionysius says (*Div. Nom.* vii). But nature never fails in necessary things: therefore the intellectual soul had to be endowed not only with the power of understanding, but also with the power of feeling. Now the action of the senses is not performed without a corporeal instrument. Therefore it behooved the intellectual soul to be united to a body fitted to be a convenient organ of sense. . . .

Reply Obj. 1. Perhaps someone might attempt to answer this by saying that before sin the human body was incorruptible. This answer does not seem sufficient; because before sin the human body was immortal not by nature, but by a gift of Divine grace; otherwise its immortality would not be forfeited through sin, as neither was the immortality of the devil.[21]

---

[20] This principle—explaining matter by form, explaining empirical details by unifying purpose, explaining the lower and lesser by the higher and greater—perhaps better than any one other single notion distinguishes the classical and medieval notion of reason and explanation from the modern, which tends to the opposite, i.e., to reductionism (e.g., thought is *only* cerebral biochemistry, love is *only* lust, man is *only* a clever ape, etc.). Modern reductionism really begins in the fourteenth century with "Ockham's Razor" and Ockham's most important application of that principle, viz., Nominalism, the doctrine that universality is *only* linguistic, not real; that only names (*nomina*), not forms, are universal.

St. Thomas here explains the union of body and soul from the viewpoint of the needs of the soul, since the body is for the soul, not vice versa, and it is to be explained in terms of the soul, not vice versa, as the setting of a play is explained in terms of its theme, not vice versa.

[21] A good example of how a deductive argument without empirical evidence can still be reasonable. (The skeptic will ask how we could ever

Therefore we answer otherwise by observing that in matter two conditions are to be found; one which is chosen in order that the matter be suitable to the form; the other which follows by force of the first disposition. The artisan, for instance, for the form of the saw chooses iron adapted for cutting through hard material; but that the teeth of the saw may become blunt and rusted, follows by force of the matter itself. So the intellectual soul requires a body of equable complexion, which, however, is corruptible by force of its matter. If, however, it be said that God could avoid this, we answer that in the formation of natural things we do not consider what God might do; but what is suitable to the nature of things, as Augustine says (*Gen. ad lit.* ii. 1). God, however, provided in this case by applying a remedy against death in the gift of grace. . . .

Reply Obj. 4. The intellectual soul as comprehending universals, has a power extending to the infinite; therefore it cannot be limited by nature to certain fixed natural notions, or even to certain fixed means whether of defence or of clothing, as is the case with other animals, the souls of which are endowed with knowledge and power in regard to fixed particular things. Instead of all these, man has by nature his reason and his hands, which are *the organs of organs* (*De Anima* iii), since by their means man can make for himself instruments of an infinite variety, and for any number of purposes. . . .

EIGHTH ARTICLE

Whether the Whole Soul Is in Each Part of the Body?

Objection 4. Further, all the powers of the soul are rooted in the essence of the soul. If, therefore, the whole soul be in each part of the body, it follows that all the powers of the soul are in each part of the body; thus the sight will be in the ear, and hearing in the eye, and this is absurd. . . .

On the contrary, Augustine says (*De Trin.* vi. 6), that *in each body the whole soul is in the whole body, and in each part is entire.*

---

know whether the human body before the Fall was mortal, immortal by nature, or immortal by grace.)

I answer that, As we have said, if the soul were united to the body merely as its motor, we might say that it is not in each part of the body, but only in one part through which it would move the others. But since the soul is united to the body as its form, it must necessarily be in the whole body, and in each part thereof. . . . A proof of which is, that on the withdrawal of the soul, no part of the body retains its proper action. . . .

Reply Obj. 4. Some of the powers of the soul are in it according as it exceeds the entire capacity of the body, namely, the intellect and the will; whence these powers are not said to be in any part of the body. Other powers are common to the soul and body; wherefore each of these powers need not be wherever the soul is, but only in that part of the body which is adapted to the operation of such a power. . . .

Question 77

Of Those Things Which Belong to the Powers of the Soul in General

SECOND ARTICLE

Whether There Are Several Powers of the Soul?

I answer that, Of necessity we must place several powers in the soul. To make this evident, we observe that, as the Philosopher says (*De Coelo* 2:12), [1] the lowest order of things cannot acquire perfect goodness, but they acquire a certain imperfect goodness, by few movements; and [2] those which belong to a higher order acquire perfect goodness by many movements; and [3] those yet higher acquire perfect goodness by few movements; and [4] the highest perfection is found in those things which acquire perfect goodness without any movement whatever. Thus [1] he is least of all disposed of health, who can only acquire imperfect health by means of a few remedies; [2] better disposed is he who can acquire perfect health by means of many remedies; and [3] better still, he who can by few remedies; [4] best of all is he who has perfect health without any remedies. We conclude, therefore, that [1] things which are below man acquire a certain limited goodness; and so they have a few determinate operations and powers. [2] But man can acquire universal and perfect goodness, because he can acquire beatitude. Yet he is in the last degree, according to his nature, of those to whom beatitude is possible; therefore the human soul requires many and various operations and powers. [3] But to angels a smaller variety of powers is sufficient. [4] In God there is no power or action beyond His own Essence.

There is yet another reason why the human soul abounds in a variety of powers;—because it is on the confines of spiritual and corporeal creatures; and therefore the powers of both meet together in the soul.[22]. . .

EIGHTH ARTICLE

*Whether All the Powers Remain in the Soul
When Separated from the Body?*

I answer that, As we have said already (AA. 5, 6, 7), all the powers of the soul belong to the soul alone as their principle. But some powers belong to the soul alone as their subject; as the intelligence and the will. These powers must remain in the soul, after the destruction of the body. But other powers are subjected in the composite; as all the powers of the sensitive and nutritive parts. Now accidents cannot remain after the destruction of the subject.[23] Wherefore, the composite being destroyed, such powers do not remain actually; but they remain virtually[24] in the soul, as in their principle or root. . . .

---

[22] In both these two reasons, St. Thomas, as usual, thinks in terms of "the great chain of being", or cosmic hierarchy. He does not view man, the soul, its powers, or its actions in isolation, but in cosmic context. Man is the highest corporeal creature and the lowest spiritual creature. He is rational–animal, incarnate–spirit, between ape and angel. Confusing man with either angels or animals is endemic in the history of philosophy. Platonism, Gnosticism, Cartesian rationalism, and German Idealism are examples of the former tendency; materialism and empiricism of the latter.

[23] I.e., by natural power alone. In the Eucharist, the accidents (appearances) of bread and wine remain while the substance (essence) is changed (transubstantiated) into the Body and Blood of Christ, according to Catholic dogma. This is philosophically possible only by supernatural power. It is a miracle, but not a contradiction, or a metaphysical impossibility.

[24] I.e., they could be restored to the soul, for the soul is still a human soul, even without its body. "Virtually" is stronger than "potentially" and weaker than "actually". A duck with a broken wing is *actually* grounded, *virtually* airborne, and *potentially* roasted.

Question 78

Of the Specific Powers of the Soul

We next treat of the powers of the soul specifically. The theologian, however, has only to inquire specifically concerning the intellectual and appetitive powers, in which the virtues reside. And since the knowledge of these powers depends to a certain extent on the other powers, our consideration of the powers of the soul taken specifically will be divided into three parts: first, we shall consider those powers which are a preamble to the intellect; secondly, the intellectual powers; thirdly, the appetitive powers.

FIRST ARTICLE

Whether There Are to Be Distinguished Five Genera of Powers in the Soul?

On the contrary, The Philosopher says (*De Anima* ii. 3), *The powers are the vegetative, the sensitive, the appetitive, the locomotive, and the intellectual.*

I answer that, There are five genera of powers of the soul, as above numbered. . . . The reason of this diversity lies in the various souls being distinguished accordingly as the operation of the soul transcends the operation of the corporeal nature in various ways; for the whole corporeal nature is subject to the soul, and is related to it as its matter and instrument. There exists, therefore, an operation of the soul which so far exceeds the corporeal nature that it is not even performed by any corporeal organ; and such is the operation of the *rational soul*. Below this, there is another operation of the soul, which is indeed performed through a corporeal organ, but not through a corporeal quality, and this is the operation of the *sensitive soul*; for though hot and cold, wet and dry, and other such corporeal qualities are required for the work of the senses, yet they are not required in such a way that the operation of the senses takes place by virtue of such qualities; but only for the proper disposition of the organ. The lowest of the operations of the soul is that which is performed by a corporeal organ, and by virtue of a corporeal quality. Yet this transcends the operation of the corporeal nature; because the movements of bodies are caused by an extrinsic principle, while these operations are from an intrinsic principle; for this is common to all the operations of the soul; since every animate thing, in some way, moves itself. Such is the operation of the *vegetative soul*; for digestion, and what follows, is caused instrumentally by the action of heat, as the Philosopher says (*De Anima* ii. 4).[25]

Now the powers of the soul are distinguished generically by their objects. For the higher a power is, the more universal is the object to which it extends, as we have said above (Q. 77, A. 3, *ad* 4). But the object of the soul's operation may be considered in a triple order. For in the soul there is a power the object of which is only the body that is united to that soul; the powers of this genus are called *vegetative*, for the vegetative power acts only on the body to which the soul is united. There is another genus in the powers of the soul [the sensitive] which genus regards a more universal object—namely, every sensible body, not only the body to which the soul is united. And there is yet another genus in the powers of the soul [the rational] which genus regards a still more universal object—namely, not only the sensible body, but all being in universal. Wherefore it is evident that the latter two genera of the soul's powers have an operation in regard not merely to that which is united to them, but also to something extrinsic. Now, since

---

[25] This is the simple essential difference between men, animals, and plants: human life (soul) can reason, sense, and grow; animal life can sense and grow; plant life can only grow.

whatever operates must in some way be united to the object about which it operates, it follows of necessity that this something extrinsic, which is the object of the soul's operation, must be related to the soul in a twofold manner. First, inasmuch as this something extrinsic has a natural aptitude to be united to the soul, and to be by its likeness in the soul. In this way there are two kinds of powers—namely, the *sensitive* in regard to the less common object—the sensible body; and the *intellectual*, in regard to the most common object—universal being.[26] Secondly, forasmuch as the soul itself has an inclination and tendency to the something extrinsic. And in this way there are again two kinds of powers in the soul: one—*the appetitive*—in respect of which the soul is referred to something extrinsic as to an end, which is first in the intention; the other—the *locomotive* power—in respect of which the soul is referred to something extrinsic as to the term of its operation and movement; for every animal is moved for the purpose of realizing its desires and intentions.

The modes of living are distinguished according to the degrees of living things. There are some living things in which there exists only vegetative power, as the plants. There are others in which with the vegetative there exists also the sensitive, but not the locomotive power; such are immovable animals, as shellfish. There are others which besides this have locomotive powers, as perfect animals, which require many things for their life, and consequently movement to seek necessaries of life from a distance. And there are some living things which with these have intellectual power—namely, men. But the appetitive power does not constitute

---

[26] The intellect is by nature capable of knowing anything that is intelligible; and all being is intelligible (in itself, though not necessarily to us: not every being is intelligible at every moment to every mind). There is no curtain of darkness around *being*, only around less-than-omniscient *minds*. So to say that the intellectual soul has universal being as its object, and to say that truth, or intelligibility, is a "transcendental" or universal property of all being as such, are equivalent statements. Some Scholastic philosophers have called this "the principle of intelligibility": that mind and reality, intellect and being, are open to each other. Intelligence and intelligibility are like metaphysical sexuality. Each is made to fit the other.

a degree of living things; because wherever there is sense there is also appetite (*De Anima* ii. 3).[27]

---

[27] Another possible classification, this time of only the two highest kinds of powers of the soul, the intellectual and the sensory, would be as follows: the soul is related to things outside it in two fundamental ways which are always found together, (1) the cognitive and (2) the appetitive. Both on the sensory level (A) and on the intellectual level (B), the soul both (1) *receives* the forms of things outside it, thus *knowing* them by being in-formed ("in-form-ation"), and (2) moves to them, *desires* them as its end. Thus we have (A1) sensory awareness, (A2) sensory appetite, (B1) intellectual awareness, and (B2) intellectual appetite (will).

SIX

Epistemology and Psychology

Question 79

Of the Intellectual Powers

Whether the Intellect Is a Passive Power?[1]

Objection 1. It would seem that the intellect is not a passive power. For everything is passive by its matter, and acts by its form. But the intellectual power results from the immateriality of the intelligent substance. Therefore it seems that the intellect is not a passive power.

Objection 2. Further, the intellectual power is incorruptible, as we have said above (Q. 79, A. 6). But *if the intellect is passive, it is corruptible (De Anima* iii. 5). Therefore the intellectual power is not passive.

Objection 3. Further, the *agent is nobler than the patient,* as Augustine (*Gen. ad lit.* xii. 16) and Aristotle (*De Anima, l.c.*) say. But all the powers of the vegetative part are active; yet they are the lowest among the powers of the soul. Much more, therefore, all the intellectual powers, which are the highest, are active.

On the contrary, The Philosopher says (*De Anima* iii. 4) that *to understand is in a way to be passive.*

I answer that, To be passive may be taken in three ways. Firstly, in its most strict sense, when from a thing is taken something which belongs to it by virtue either of its nature, or of its proper inclination: as when water loses coolness by heating, and as when a man becomes ill or sad.[2] Secondly, less strictly, a thing is said to be

---

[1] "Passive" does not mean "inert" but "receptive". Intellect is both "active" and "passive". "Passive intellect" and "active intellect" do not refer to two intellects but to two *powers* of the intellect.

[2] This assumes that water is naturally cool and that man is naturally

passive, when something, whether suitable or unsuitable, is taken away from it. And in this way not only he who is ill is said to be passive, but also he who is healed; not only he that is sad, but also he that is joyful; or whatever way he be altered or moved. Thirdly, in a wide sense a thing is said to be passive, from the very fact that what is in potentiality to something receives that to which it was in potentiality, without being deprived of anything. And accordingly, whatever passes from potentiality to act, may be said to be passive, even when it is perfected. And thus with us to understand is to be passive. This is clear from the following reason. For the intellect, as we have seen above (Q. 78, A. 1), has an operation extending to universal being.[3] We may therefore see whether the intellect be in act or potentiality by observing first of all the nature of the relation of the intellect to universal being. For we find an intellect whose relation to universal being is that of the act of all being: and such is the Divine intellect, which is the Essence of God, in which originally and virtually, all being pre-exists as in its first cause. And therefore the Divine intellect is not in potentiality, but is pure act. But no created intellect can be an act in relation to the whole universal being; otherwise it would needs be an infinite being. Wherefore every created intellect is not the act of all things intelligible, by reason of its very existence; but is compared to these intelligible things as a potentiality to act.

Now, potentiality has a double relation to act. There is a potentiality which is always perfected by its act: as the matter of the heavenly bodies (Q. 58, A. 1).[4] And there is another potentiality which is not always in act, but proceeds from potentiality to act; as

---

healthy and happy. Medieval hydrology and medieval psychology were both naive by modern standards, the former regrettably and foolishly so, but the latter enviably and wisely so. The simple but startling historical fact that the medieval mind typically assumed that man is by nature happy, while the modern mind typically assumes that unhappiness is our natural condition (see Freud, *Civilization and Its Discontents*), speaks volumes about "progress".

[3] Cf. chap. 5, n. 26 (I, 78, 1).

[4] Medieval science taught that the heavenly bodies were composed of a special, unearthly kind of matter, not one of the four mundane essences (earth, air, fire, water) but the "fifth essence" or "quintessence", which

we observe in things that are corrupted and generated. Wherefore the angelic intellect is always in act as regards those things which it can understand, by reason of its proximity to the first intellect, which is pure act, as we have said above. But the human intellect, which is the lowest in the order of intelligence and most remote from the perfection of the Divine intellect, is in potentiality with regard to things intelligible, and is at first *like a clean tablet on which nothing is written*, as the Philosopher says (*De Anima* iii. 4).[5] This is made clear from the fact that at first we are only in potentiality to understand, and afterwards we are made to understand actually. And so it is evident that with us to understand is *in a way to be passive*; taking passion in the third sense. And consequently the intellect is a passive power.

Reply Obj. 1. This objection is verified of passion in the first and second senses, which belong to primary matter. But in the third sense passion is in anything which is reduced from potentiality to act.

Reply Obj. 2. Passive intellect is the name given by some to the sensitive appetite, in which are the passions of the soul; which appetite is also called *rational by participation*, because it *obeys the reason* (*Ethic.* i. 13). Others give the name of passive intellect to the cogitative power, which is called the *particular reason*. And in each case *passive* may be taken in the two first senses; forasmuch as this so-called intellect is the act of a corporeal organ. But the intellect which is in potentiality to things intelligible, and which for this reason Aristotle calls the *possible* intellect (*De Anima* iii. 4), is not passive except in the third sense: for it is not an act of a corporeal organ. Hence it is incorruptible.

Reply Obj. 3. The agent is nobler than the patient, if the action and the passion are referred to the same thing: but not always, if they refer to different things. Now the intellect is a passive power in regard to the whole universal being: while the vegetative power

---

was unchanging. The mistaken astronomy, making stars too much like angels, does not invalidate the main point, which is a point of psychology.

[5] St. Thomas held this *"tabula rasa"* ("blank tablet") empiricism of Aristotle against Plato's theory of innate ideas and learning by "recollection" (*anamnēsis*). However, it is only an empiricism regarding the temporal *beginning* of human knowledge, not its end.

is active in regard to some particular thing, namely, the body as united to the soul. Wherefore nothing prevents such a passive force being nobler than such an active one.

THIRD ARTICLE

Whether There Is an Active Intellect?

Objection 1. It would seem that there is no active intellect. For as the senses are to things sensible, so is our intellect to things intelligible. But because sense is in potentiality to things sensible, the sense is not said to be active, but only passive. Therefore, since our intellect is in potentiality to things intelligible, it seems that we cannot say that the intellect is active, but only that it is passive. . . .

Objection 3. Further, the likeness of the agent is received into the patient according to the nature of the patient.[6] But the passive intellect is an immaterial power. Therefore its immaterial nature suffices for forms to be received into it immaterially. Now a form is intelligible in act [actually intelligible] from the very fact that it is immaterial.[7] Therefore there is no need for an active intellect to make the species actually intelligible.[8]

On the contrary, The Philosopher says (*De Anima* iii. 5), *As in every nature, so in the soul is there something by which it becomes all things,*[9] *and something by which it makes all things.*[10] Therefore we must admit an active intellect.

---

[6] E.g., a photographic image of a three-dimensional object is a two-dimensional image; a dog's awareness of human speech is merely doggy (sensory, not rational: to them, we only bark funny); and the intellect's understanding of a material thing is not material but spiritual.

[7] For anything immaterial can be received into an intellect, and thus it is intelligible; but matter cannot be so received. There is no *space* in an immaterial intellect to contain matter. A mind can no more hold a stone materially than a stone can hold a mind materially; but a mind can hold the stone "in mind", immaterially.

[8] That is, by actively abstracting the form from the matter so that the form can enter an intellect.

[9] I.e., like a chameleon, or a mirror, it takes upon itself the forms of all things.

[10] I.e., it makes all things intelligible by abstracting their forms.

I answer that, According to the opinion of Plato, there is no need for an active intellect in order to make things actually intelligible. . . . For Plato supposed that the forms of natural things subsisted apart from matter,[11] and consequently that they are intelligible: since a thing is actually intelligible from the very fact that it is immaterial [cf. n. 7]. And he called such forms *species or ideas*; from a participation of which, he said that even corporeal matter was formed, in order that individuals might be naturally established in their proper genera and species: and that our intellect was formed by such participation in order to have knowledge of the genera and species of things.[12] But since Aristotle did not allow that forms of natural things exist apart from matter,[13] and as forms existing in matter are not actually intelligible [cf. n. 7], it follows that the natures or forms of the sensible things which we understand are not actually intelligible.[14] Now nothing is reduced from potentiality to act except by something in act; as the senses are made actual by what is actually sensible. We must therefore assign on the part of the intellect some power to make things actually intelligible, by abstraction of the species from material conditions.[15] And such is the necessity for an active intellect.

Reply Obj. 1. Sensible things are found in act outside the soul; and hence there is no need for an active sense. Wherefore . . . in the sensitive part all are passive: but in the intellectual part, there is something active and something passive. . . .

Reply Obj. 3. If the agent pre-exist, it may well happen that its likeness is received variously into various things, on account of

---

[11] The "Platonic Ideas", or "Platonic Forms".

[12] I.e., both Fido and my idea of a dog participate, or share, or reflect the same Platonic essence or Idea (dogginess), as both the physical object seen and the seeing eye reflect sunlight; the first, objectively and physically, the second, subjectively and mentally.

[13] Aristotle agreed with Plato that forms existed objectively, but disagreed with Plato's separation (*chorismōs*) of the forms from matter. He brought Plato's forms home from Heaven to earth.

[14] They are *potentially* intelligible.

[15] E.g., when we know the nature of a dog, we mentally separate, or abstract, the form of the dog (both the essential form, dogginess, and accidental forms like shagginess or brownness) from the concrete matter which these forms inform to make Fido. Only the forms can enter the mind.

their dispositions. But if the agent does not pre-exist, the disposition of the recipient has nothing to do with the matter. Now the intelligible in act[16] is not something existing in nature; if we consider the nature of things sensible, which do not subsist apart from matter. And therefore in order to understand them, the immaterial nature of the passive intellect would not suffice but for the presence of the active intellect, which makes things actually intelligible by way of abstraction.

FOURTH ARTICLE

Whether the Active Intellect Is Something in the Soul?[17]

Objection 1. It would seem that the active intellect is not something in the soul. For the effect of the active intellect is to give light for the purpose of understanding. But this is done by something higher than the soul: according to John 1:9, *He was the true light that enlighteneth every man coming into this world.* Therefore the active intellect is not something in the soul.

Objection 2. Further, the Philosopher (*De Anima* iii. 5) says of the active intellect, *that it does not sometimes understand and sometimes not understand.* But our soul does not always understand: sometimes it understands, and sometimes it does not understand. Therefore the active intellect is not something in our soul. . . .

Objection 4. Further, . . . nothing can be in potentiality and in act with regard to the same thing. If, therefore, the passive intellect, which is in potentiality to all things intelligible, is something in the soul, it seems impossible for the active intellect to be also something in our soul. . . .

---

[16] I.e., forms that are actually (and presently) intelligible (able to enter an intellect) because they are already abstracted from matter. Plato thought these already-separate forms existed; St. Thomas did not (except in the mind of God).

[17] The Arabian commentators on Aristotle, especially Averroës "*The Commentator*", had presented Aristotle as teaching that the active intellect was a single, unitary cosmic mind outside the individual human soul. St. Thomas refutes this in Article 5. Cf. Chap. 5, n. 14 (I, 76, 2).

I answer that, The active intellect, of which the Philosopher speaks, is something in the soul. In order to make this evident, we must observe that above the intellectual soul of man we must needs suppose a superior intellect, from which the soul acquires the power of understanding. For what is such by participation, and what is mobile, and what is imperfect always requires the pre-existence of something essentially such, immovable and perfect.[18] Now the human soul is called intellectual by reason of a participation in intellectual power; a sign of which is that it is not wholly intellectual but only in part. Moreover it reaches to the understanding of truth by arguing, with a certain amount of reasoning and movement. Again it has an imperfect understanding; both because it does not understand everything, and because, in those things which it does understand, it passes from potentiality to act. Therefore there must needs be some higher intellect, by which the soul is helped to understand.

Wherefore some held that this intellect, substantially separate, is the active intellect, which by lighting up the phantasms as it were, makes them to be actually intelligible. But, even supposing the existence of such a separate active intellect, it would still be necessary to assign to the human soul some power participating in that superior intellect, by which power the human soul makes things actually intelligible.[19] Just as in other perfect natural things, besides the universal active causes, each one is endowed with its proper powers derived from those universal causes: for the sun alone does not generate man,[20] but in man is the power of begetting man: and in like manner with other perfect animals. Now among these lower

---

[18] Acorns, eggs, and children come from oaks, chickens, and adults. St. Thomas has a definite answer to "which comes first, the chicken or the egg?"—not historically and biologically, but in terms of final causality, or teleology. The chicken comes first. A chicken is not just one egg's way of making more eggs.

[19] This sentence is St. Thomas' essential argument against the Averroist doctrine. Notice how simple and commonsensical it is (as usual).

[20] According to medieval science, heat is necessary for the generation of all life, and all heat comes from the sun; therefore the sun is the remote cause of all biological generation. The example is only an illustration, not the basis or premise of the argument.

things nothing is more perfect than the human soul. Wherefore we must say that in the soul is some power derived from a higher intellect, whereby it is able to light up the phantasms. And we know this by experience,[21] since we perceive that we abstract universal forms from their particular conditions, which is to make them actually intelligible. Now no action belongs to anything except through some principle formally inherent therein; as we have said above of the passive intellect (Q. 76, A. 1). Therefore the power which is the principle of this action must be something in the soul. For this reason Aristotle (*De Anima* iii. 5) compared the active intellect to light, which is something received into the air: while Plato compared the separate intellect impressing the soul to the sun, as Themistius says in his commentary on *De Anima* iii. But the separate intellect, according to the teaching of our faith, is God Himself, Who is the soul's Creator, and only beatitude; as will be shown later on (Q. 90, A. 3; I–II, Q. 3, A. 7). Wherefore the human soul derives its intellectual light from Him, according to Psalm 4:7, *The light of Thy countenance, O Lord, is signed upon us.*[22]

Reply Obj. 1. That true light enlightens as a universal cause, from which the human soul derives a particular power, as we have explained.

Reply Obj. 2. The Philosopher says those words not of the active intellect, but of the intellect in act,[23] of which he had already said:

---

[21] Note how St. Thomas constantly appeals to experience to test theories. The theory of a single agent intellect for all men, outside the individual soul, arose because its inventors were overly rationalistic—a tendency of many medieval philosophers. Modern thought tends to the opposite extreme of empiricism. St. Thomas avoids both extremes. Note how the syllogism which begins with this (footnoted) sentence has both an empirical premise and a rational premise.

[22] St. Thomas sees the ancient philosophers' groping errors as confused perceptions of the true God, as most main-line medieval Christian thinkers before him did (e.g., Justin Martyr, Clement of Alexandria, St. Augustine). See Gilson, *Reason and Revelation in the Middle Ages*.

[23] The active intellect is the intellect's active power to abstract forms. This power is not always operating. The intellect in act is the intellect's *activity*.

Knowledge in act is the same as the thing.[24] Or, if we refer those words to the active intellect, then they are said because it is not owing to the active intellect that sometimes we do, and sometimes we do not understand, but to the intellect which is in potentiality. . . .

Reply Obj. 4. The intellectual soul is indeed actually immaterial, but it is in potentiality to [receiving] determinate species. On the contrary, phantasms are actual images of certain [determinate] species, but are immaterial in potentiality [not yet actually immaterial]. Wherefore nothing prevents one and the same soul, inasmuch as it is actually immaterial, having one power by which it makes things [species] actually immaterial, by abstraction from the conditions of individual matter [phantasms, or sense images]: which power is called the *active intellect*; and another power, receptive of such species, which is called the *passive intellect* by reason of its being in potentiality to [determination by] such species. . . .

FIFTH ARTICLE

Whether the Active Intellect Is One in All?[25]

Objection 1. It would seem that there is one active intellect in all. For what is separate from the body is not multiplied according to the number of bodies. But the active intellect is *separate*, as the Philosopher says (*De Anima* iii. 5). Therefore it is not multiplied in the many human bodies, but is one for all men. . . .

On the contrary, The Philosopher says (*De Anima* iii, *l.c.*) that the active intellect is as a light. But light is not the same in the various things enlightened. Therefore the same active intellect is not in various men.

I answer that, The truth about this question depends on what we have already said (A. 4). For if the active intellect were not some-

---

[24] I.e., when we actually know a thing (truly), the same form that makes the thing what it is, informs our intellect. St. Thomas (and Aristotle) held an *identity* theory of truth, not a *correspondence* theory of truth.

[25] Cf. note 17.

thing belonging to the soul, but were some separate substance, there would be one active intellect for all men. And this is what they mean who hold that there is one active intellect for all. But if the active intellect is something belonging to the soul, as one of its powers, we are bound to say that there are as many active intellects as there are souls, which are multiplied according to the number of men, as we have said above (Q. 76, A. 2). For it is impossible that one same power belong to various substances.

Reply Obj. 1. The Philosopher proves that the active intellect is separate, by the fact that the passive intellect is separate: because, as he says (*loc. cit.*), *the agent is more noble than the patient.* Now the passive intellect is said to be separate, because it is not the act of any corporeal organ. And in the same sense the active intellect is also called *separate*; but not as a separate substance. . . .

Reply Obj. 3. . . . There is no need for it to be identical in all. Yet it must be derived by all from one principle. And thus the possession by all men in common of the first principles proves the unity of the separate intellect [the divine mind], which Plato compares to the sun; but not the unity of the active intellect, which Aristotle compares to light.[26] . . .

EIGHTH ARTICLE

Whether the Reason Is Distinct from the Intellect?

On the contrary, Augustine says (*Gen. ad lit.* iii. 20) that *that in which man excels irrational animals is reason, or mind, or intelligence, or whatever appropriate name we like to give it.* Therefore, reason, intellect, and mind are one power.

I answer that, Reason and intellect in man cannot be distinct powers. We shall understand this clearly if we consider their respective actions. For to understand is simply to [immediately] apprehend intelligible truth: and to reason is to advance from one thing understood to another, so as to know an intelligible truth [mediately]. And therefore angels who, according to their nature,

---

[26] Note how St. Thomas finds important truth even in his opponents' errors.

possess perfect knowledge of intelligible truth, have no need to advance from one thing to another, but apprehend the truth simply and without mental discussion, as Dionysius says (*Div. Nom.* vii). But man arrives at the knowledge of intelligible truth by advancing from one thing to another; and therefore he is called rational. Reasoning, therefore, is compared to understanding, as movement is to rest, or acquisition to possession; of which one belongs to the perfect, the other to the imperfect. And since movement always proceeds from something immovable, and ends in something at rest,[27] hence it is that human reasoning, by way of inquiry and discovery, advances from certain things simply understood— namely, the first principles; and, again, by way of judgment returns by analysis to first principles, in the light of which it examines what it has found.[28] Now it is clear that rest and movement are not to be referred to different powers, but to one and the same, even in natural things: since by the same nature a thing is moved towards a certain place, and rests in that place. Much more, therefore, by the same power do we understand and reason: and so it is clear that in man reason and intellect are the same power. . . .

NINTH ARTICLE

Whether the Higher and Lower Reason Are Distinct Powers?

I answer that, The higher and lower reason, as they are understood by Augustine, can in no way be two powers of the soul. For he says that *the higher reason is that which is intent on the contemplation and consultation of things eternal*,[29] forasmuch as in contemplation it

---

[27] This is not a principle of (bad) physics but of (good) logic. No *physical* cause or effect is immovable. But no movement can be *defined* without two terms—its beginning and its end—and those terms cannot be part of the movement, themselves moving. You do not steal a moving second base from a moving first base.

[28] E.g., a syllogism presupposes the Law of Non-contradiction and uses it to check the validity of the argument, to be certain that the conclusion follows necessarily: it would be *self-contradictory* to affirm the premises and deny the conclusion of a valid argument.

[29] Eternal truths like "being is not nonbeing" or "good is to be done".

sees them in themselves, and in consultation it takes its rules of action from them. But he calls the lower reason that which *is intent on the disposal of temporal things.* Now these two—namely, eternal and temporal—are related to our knowledge in this way, that one of them is the means of knowing the other. For by way of discovery, we come through knowledge of temporal things to that of things eternal, according to the words of the Apostle (Rom 1:20), *The invisible things of God are clearly seen, being understood by the things that are made*: while by way of judgment, from eternal things already known, we judge of temporal things, and according to laws of things eternal we dispose of temporal things.[30]

But it may happen that the medium and what is attained thereby belong to different habits: as the first indemonstrable principles belong to the habit of intellect; whereas the conclusions which we draw from them belong to the habit of science. And so it happens that from the principles of geometry we draw a conclusion in another science—for example, perspective. But the power of the reason is such that both medium and term belong to it. For the act of the reason is, as it were, a movement from one thing to another. But the same movable thing passes through the medium and reaches the end. Wherefore the higher and lower reasons are one and the same power. But according to Augustine they are distinguished by the functions of their actions, and according to their various habits: for wisdom is attributed to the higher reason, science to the lower. . . .

ELEVENTH ARTICLE

Whether the Speculative and Practical Intellects Are Distinct Powers?

I answer that, The speculative and practical intellects are not distinct powers. The reason of which is that, as we have said above (Q. 77, A. 3), what is accidental to the nature of the object of a

---

[30] Note the completeness and balance here: St. Thomas neither subordinates the empirical and inductive movement to the rational and deductive, nor vice versa, but unites them as inhaling and exhaling are united, or as systole and diastole are united. Contrast both Rationalism and Empiricism.

power, does not differentiate that power; for it is accidental to a thing colored to be man, or to be great or small; hence all such things are apprehended by the same power of sight. Now, to a thing apprehended by the intellect, it is accidental whether it be directed to operation or not, and according to this the speculative and practical intellects differ. For it is the speculative intellect which directs what it apprehends, not to operation, but to the consideration of truth; while the practical intellect is that which directs what it apprehends to operation. And this is what the Philosopher says (*De Anima* iii, *loc. cit.*); that *the speculative differs from the practical in its end*. Whence each is named from its end: the one speculative, the other practical—*i.e.*, operative. . . .

TWELFTH ARTICLE

Whether Synderesis Is a Special Power of the Soul Distinct from the Others?

I answer that, Synderesis is not a power but a habit; though some held that it is a power higher than reason; while others [cf. Alexander of Hales, *Sum. Theol.* II, Q. 73] said that it is reason itself, not as reason, but as a nature. In order to make this clear we must observe that, as we have said above (A. 8), man's act of reasoning, since it is a kind of movement, proceeds from the understanding of certain things—namely, those which are naturally known without any investigation on the part of reason, as from an immovable principle, —and ends also at the understanding, inasmuch as by means of those principles naturally known, we judge of those things which we have discovered by reasoning. Now it is clear that, as the speculative reason argues about speculative things, so that practical reason argues about practical things. Therefore we must have, bestowed on us by nature, not only speculative principles, but also practical principles. Now the first speculative principles bestowed on us by nature do not belong to a special power, but to a special habit, which is called *the understanding of principles*, as the Philosopher explains (*Ethic.* vi. 6). Wherefore the first practical principles, bestowed on us by nature, do not belong to a special power, but to a special natural habit, which we call *synderesis*. Whence *synderesis* is said to incite to good, and to murmur at evil, inasmuch as through first principles we proceed to discover, and judge of what we have discovered. It is therefore clear that *synderesis* is not a power, but a natural habit.[31] . . .

THIRTEENTH ARTICLE

Whether Conscience Be a Power?

I answer that, Properly speaking conscience is not a power, but an act. This is evident both from the very name and from those things which in the common way of speaking are attributed to conscience. For conscience, according to the very nature of the word, implies the relation of knowledge to something: for conscience may be resolved into *cum alio scientia, i.e.,* knowledge applied to an individual case.[32] But the application of knowledge to something is done by some act. Wherefore from this explanation of the name it is clear that conscience is an act.

The same is manifest from those things which are attributed to conscience. For conscience is said to witness, to bind, or incite, and also to accuse, torment, or rebuke. And all these follow the application of knowledge or science to what we do: which application

---

[31] N.b.: St. Thomas does not commit what G. E. Moore calls "the naturalistic fallacy" of deducing "ought" conclusions from "is" premises only. Rather, he holds that we naturally know self-evident first principles in both the theoretical ("is") and practical ("ought") orders, and we use these to judge conclusions in both orders. "Synderesis" is the habit of both (1) knowing first practical principles and of (2) inciting to good and "murmuring" against evil. It is the *habit* that corresponds to "conscience" as the *act*. The modern meaning of "conscience", when full, embraces both. (When empty, it means mere blind feeling.) I.e., our "conscience" includes St. Thomas' "synderesis" (Article 12) and "conscience" (Article 13). See last paragraph of Article 13.

[32] N.b.: nearly all ancient philosophers see "conscience" as an act of *knowing*, which inherently intends an object, not a mere feeling, which does not. The Sophists and Epicureans were the only two schools of ancient or medieval philosophy which held what today is called "the emotive theory of value" (in effect, reducing conscience to a subjective feeling).

is made in three ways. One way in so far as we recognize that we have done or not done something; *Thy conscience knoweth that thou hast often spoken evil of others* (Qo 7:22), and according to this, conscience is said to witness. In another way, so far as through the conscience we judge that something should be done or not done; and in this sense, conscience is said to incite or to bind. In the third way, so far as by conscience we judge that something done is well done or ill done, and in this sense conscience is said to excuse, accuse, or torment. Now, it is clear that all these things follow the actual application of knowledge to what we do. Wherefore, properly speaking, conscience denominates an act. But since habit is a principle [source] of act, sometimes the name conscience is given to the first natural habit—namely, *synderesis.* . . .

Question 80

Of the Appetitive Powers in General

Whether the Appetite Is a Special Power of the Soul?

I answer that, It is necessary to assign an appetitive power to the soul. To make this evident, we must observe that some inclination follows every form: for example, fire, by its form, is inclined to rise, and to generate its like.[33] Now, the form is found to have a more perfect existence in those things which participate knowledge than in those which lack knowledge. For in those which lack knowledge, the form is found to determine each thing only to its own being—that is, to its nature. Therefore this natural form is followed by a natural inclination, which is called the natural appetite.[34] But in those things which have knowledge, each one is determined to its own natural being by its natural form, in such a manner that it is nevertheless receptive of the species of other things: for example, sense receives the species of all things sensible, and the intellect, of all things intelligible, so that the soul of man

---

[33] "Inclination" means simply a tendency toward movement. Medieval science often guessed wrongly at the reasons for such common observations, but the observation obviously remains true (flames do tend to rise and to ignite other inflammable objects), and the philosophical principle derived from such observations does not depend on medieval scientific explanations of those observations, which have been refuted, but only on the observed facts, which have not changed. Flames did not die when Aristotelian physics did.

[34] "Appetite" is used here more broadly than in modern English. Heavy objects have an "appetite" too; we call it gravity. Plants have an "appetite" for sunlight (tropism), and for growth, that comes from their nature, not from without.

is, in a way, all things by sense and intellect: and thereby, those things that have knowledge, in a way, approach to a likeness to God, *in Whom* [in whose mind] *all things pre-exist*, as Dionysius says (*Div. Nom.* v).

Therefore, as forms exist in those things that have knowledge in a higher manner and above the manner of natural forms; so must there be in them an inclination surpassing the natural inclination, which is called the natural appetite. And this superior inclination belongs to the appetitive power of the soul, through which the animal is able to desire what it apprehends, and not only that to which it is inclined by its natural form. And so it is necessary to assign an appetitive power to the soul. . . .

Question 81

Of the Power of Sensuality

SECOND ARTICLE

Whether the Sensitive Appetite Is Divided into the Irascible and Concupiscible As Distinct Powers?[35]

I answer that, The sensitive appetite is one generic power, and is called sensuality; but it is divided into two powers, which are species of the sensitive appetite—the irascible and the concupiscible. In order to make this clear, we must observe that in natural corruptible things there is needed an inclination not only to the acquisition of what is suitable and to the avoiding of what is harmful, but also to resistance against corruptive and contrary agencies which are a hindrance to the acquisition of what is suitable, and are productive of harm. . . . There must needs be in the sensitive part two appetitive powers—one through which the soul is simply inclined to seek what is suitable, according to the senses, and to fly from what is hurtful, and this is called the concupiscible: and another, whereby an animal resists these attacks that hinder what is suitable, and inflict harm, and this is called the irascible. . . . The irascible is, as it were, the champion and defender of the concupiscible, when it rises up against what hinders the acquisition of the suitable things which the concupiscible desires, or against what inflicts harm, from which the concupiscible flies. And for this reason all the passions of the irascible appetite rise from the passions of the concupiscible appetite and terminate in them. . . . For

---

[35] These terms ("irascible" and "concupiscible") are used today, though less frequently and popularly, with the same basic meanings, but sometimes more narrowly ("irascible" meaning only "angry" and "concupiscible" meaning only "lustful").

this reason also the quarrels of animals[36] are about things concupiscible—namely, food and sex, as the Philosopher says (*De Animal.* viii). . . .

Whether the Irascible and Concupiscible Appetites Obey Reason?[37]

I answer that, In two ways the irascible and concupiscible powers obey the higher part, in which are the intellect or reason, and the will; first, as to reason, secondly as to the will. . . .

Reply Obj. 2. As the Philosopher says (*Polit.* i. 2): *We observe in an animal a despotic and a politic principle: for the soul dominates the body by a despotic power; but the intellect dominates the appetite by a politic and royal power.* For a power is called despotic whereby a man rules his slaves, who have not the right to resist in any way the orders of the one that commands them, since they have nothing of their own. But that power is called politic and royal[38] by which a man rules over free subjects, who, though subject to the government of the ruler, have nevertheless something of their own, by reason of which they can resist the orders of him who commands. And so, the soul is said to rule the body by a despotic power, because the members of the body cannot in any way resist the sway of the soul,

---

[36] The Philosopher evidently did not live in a culture where cook books and sex books were the two most popular forms of literature.

[37] In answering this question affirmatively, St. Thomas, like all premodern philosophers (except the Hedonists among the Sophists and Epicureans), disagrees with Freud's "pleasure principle" of appetite-determinism. He also disagrees, at the other extreme, with Plato's intellectual determinism, according to which appetites always follow the intellect (we always will the apparent good; evil is only ignorance). As usual, St. Thomas takes the commonsensical middle ground: appetites follow reason naturally, but not necessarily, and usually but not always.

[38] Modern egalitarianism often confuses *royalty* with *despotism*, or even all rule and authority with despotism. (This mentality would misunderstand the entire point of Plato's *Republic*, which culminates in the distinction between the royal and the despotic soul and state [Bk. 9, 587–88].)

but at the soul's command both hand and foot, and whatever member is naturally moved by voluntary movement, are moved at once. But the intellect or reason is said to rule the irascible and concupiscible by a politic power: because the sensitive appetite has something of its own, by virtue whereof it can resist the commands of reason. . . .

Question 82

Of the Will

Whether the Will Desires Something of Necessity?

On the contrary, Augustine says (*De Trin.* xiii. 4) that *all desire happiness with one will.* Now if this were not necessary, but contingent, there would at least be a few exceptions. Therefore the will desires something of necessity.

I answer that, The word *necessity* is employed in many ways.[39] For that which must be is necessary. Now that a thing must be may belong to it by an intrinsic principle—either material, as when we say that everything composed of contraries is of necessity corruptible —or formal, as when we say that it is necessary for the three angles of a triangle to be equal to two right angles. And this is *natural* and *absolute necessity*. In another way, that a thing must be, belongs to it by reason of something extrinsic, which is either the end or the agent. On the part of the end, as when without it the end is not to be attained or so well attained: for instance, food is said to be necessary for life, and a horse is necessary for a journey. This is called *necessity of end*, and sometimes also *utility*. On the part of the agent, a thing must be, when someone is forced by some agent, so that he is not able to do the contrary. This is called *necessity of coercion*.

Now this necessity of coercion is altogether repugnant to the will. For we call that violent which is against the inclination of a thing. But the very movement of the will is an inclination to something. Therefore, as a thing is called natural because it is according to the inclination of nature, so a thing is called voluntary

---

[39] The four kinds of necessity correspond to the "four causes".

because it is according to the inclination of the will.[40] Therefore, just as it is impossible for a thing to be at the same time violent and natural, so it is impossible for a thing to be absolutely coerced or violent, and voluntary.

But necessity of end is not repugnant to the will, when the end cannot be attained except in one way: thus from the will to cross the sea, arises in the will the necessity to wish for a ship.

In like manner neither is natural necessity repugnant to the will. Indeed, more than this, for as the intellect of necessity adheres to the first principles, the will must of necessity adhere to the last end, which is happiness: since the end is in practical matters what the principle is in speculative matters. For what befits a thing naturally and immovably must be the root and principle of all else appertaining thereto, since the nature of a thing is the first in everything, and every movement arises from something immovable. . . .

SECOND ARTICLE

Whether the Will Desires of Necessity, Whatever It Desires?

On the contrary, Augustine says (*Retract.* i. 9) that *it is the will by which we sin and live well*, and so the will extends to opposite things. Therefore it does not desire of necessity all things whatsoever it desires.

I answer that, The will does not desire of necessity whatsoever it desires. In order to make this evident we must observe that as the intellect naturally and of necessity adheres to the first principles, so the will adheres to the last end, as we have said already (A. 1). Now there are some things intelligible which have not a necessary connection with the first principles; such as contingent propositions, the denial of which does not involve a denial of the first principles.

---

[40] N.b.: the natural is closer to the voluntary than to the coerced, for the first two both act by inclination. For nearly all pre-modern thinkers, nature acts more like a person than like a machine (though all three act in different ways). If this is true, then even the very primitive confusion of "Mother Nature" with a person is closer to the truth than the modern confusion of nature with a machine!

And to such the intellect does not assent of necessity. But there are some propositions which have a necessary connection with the first principles: such as demonstrable conclusions, a denial of which involves a denial of the first principles. And to these the intellect assents of necessity, when once it is aware of the necessary connection of these conclusions with the principles; but it does not assent of necessity until through the demonstration it recognizes the necessity of such connection. It is the same with the will. For there are certain individual goods which have not a necessary connection with happiness, because without them a man can be happy: and to such the will does not adhere of necessity. But there are some things which have a necessary connection with happiness, by means of which things man adheres to God, in Whom alone true happiness consists. Nevertheless, until through the certitude of the Divine Vision the necessity of such connection be shown, the will does not adhere to God of necessity, nor to those things which are of God. But the will of the man who sees God in His essence of necessity adheres to God, just as now we desire of necessity to be happy. It is therefore clear that the will does not desire of necessity whatever it desires. . . .

THIRD ARTICLE

Whether the Will Is a Higher Power Than the Intellect?[41]

Objection 1. It would seem that the will is a higher power than the intellect. For the object of the will is good and the end. But the end is the first and highest cause. Therefore the will is the first and highest power.

---

[41] The issue, and the one in the following article, is crucial for the enterprise of a marriage of pagan Greek philosophy with Judeo-Christian biblical revelation, for there seems to be a major contradiction here in that for Plato and Aristotle the central, deepest, and highest part of a man is his mind and its knowledge, while in the Bible it is the heart, or will, and its love which are primary. Cf. William Barrett, *Irrational Man*, chap. 4, "Hebraism and Hellenism". St. Thomas, in his usual careful and balanced way, compromises neither insight, but synthesizes them by perceiving a crucial distinction (in the body of this article).

Objection 2. Further, in the order of natural things we observe a progress from imperfect things to perfect. And this also appears in the powers of the soul: for sense precedes the intellect, which is more noble. Now the act of the will, in the natural order, follows the act of the intellect. Therefore the will is a more noble and perfect power than the intellect.

Objection 3. Further, habits are proportioned to their powers, as perfections [are proportioned] to what they make perfect. But the habit which perfects the will—namely, charity—is more noble than the habits which perfect the intellect: for it is written (1 Cor 13:2): *If I should know all mysteries, and if I should have all faith, and have not charity, I am nothing.* Therefore the will is a higher power than the intellect.

On the contrary, The Philosopher holds the intellect to be the highest power of the soul (*Ethic.* x. 7).

I answer that, The superiority of one thing over another can be considered in two ways: *absolutely* and *relatively.* Now a thing is considered to be such absolutely which is considered such in itself: but relatively as it is such with regard to something else. If therefore the intellect and will be considered with regard to themselves, then the intellect is the higher power. And this is clear if we compare their respective objects to one another. For the object of the intellect is more simple and more absolute than the object of the will; since the object of the intellect is the very idea [essence, form] of appetible [desirable] good; and the appetible good, the idea of which is in the intellect, is the object of the will. Now the more simple and the more abstract [immaterial] a thing is, the nobler and higher it is in itself;[42] and therefore the object of the intellect is higher than the object of the will. Therefore, since the proper nature of a power is in its order to its object, it follows that the intellect in itself and absolutely is higher and nobler than the will. But relatively and by comparison with something else, we find that the will is sometimes higher than the intellect, from the fact that the

---

[42] This is because it more closely resembles God, the standard of perfection. St. Thomas' point may be put this way: the intellect thinks God's very thoughts after Him, however imperfectly, while the will desires the good *things* of which these thoughts are the archetypes and models.

object of the will occurs in something higher than that in which occurs the object of the intellect. Thus for instance, I might say that hearing is relatively nobler than sight, inasmuch as something in which there is sound is nobler than something in which there is color, though color is nobler and simpler than sound. For, as we have said above (Q. 16, A. 1; Q. 27, A. 4), the action of the intellect consists in this—that the idea [form] of the thing understood is in the one who understands; while the act of the will consists in this—that the will is inclined to the thing itself as existing in itself. And therefore the Philosopher says in *Metaph.* vi (Did. v. 2) that *good and evil*, which are objects of the will, *are in things*, but *truth and error*, which are objects of the intellect, *are in the mind*.[43] When, therefore, the thing in which there is good is nobler than the soul itself, in which is the idea understood; by comparison with such a thing, the will is higher than the intellect. But when the thing which is good is less noble than the soul, then even in comparison with that thing the intellect is higher than the will. Wherefore the love of God is better than the knowledge of God; but, on the contrary, the knowledge of corporeal things is better than the love thereof.[44] Absolutely, however, the intellect is nobler than the will.

Reply Obj. 1. The aspect of causality is perceived by comparing one thing to another, and in such a comparison the idea of good is found to be nobler: but truth signifies something more absolute, and extends to the idea of good itself: wherefore even good is something true. But, again, truth is something good: forasmuch as the intellect is a thing, and truth its end. And among other ends this is the most excellent:[45] as also is the intellect among the other powers.

Reply Obj. 2. What precedes in order of generation and time is less perfect: for in one and the same thing potentiality precedes act, and imperfection precedes perfection. But what precedes absolutely and in the order of nature is more perfect: for thus act precedes

---

[43] This does not mean that truth is subjective: cf. I, 16, esp. note 126.

[44] This is the practical "bottom line". It is better to love God than to know God, but it is better to know material things than to love them.

[45] Therefore St. Thomas elsewhere says that the greatest good one can do to his neighbor is to lead him to the truth.

potentiality. And in this way the intellect precedes the will, as the motive power precedes the thing movable, and as the active precedes the passive; for good which is understood moves the will.

Reply Obj. 3. This reason is verified of the will as compared with what is above the soul. For charity is the virtue by which we love God.

Whether the Will Moves the Intellect?

Objection 1. It would seem that the will does not move the intellect. For what moves excels and precedes what is moved, because what moves is an agent, and *the agent is nobler than the patient*, as Augustine says (*Gen. ad lit.* xii. 16), and the Philosopher (*De Anima* iii. 5). But the intellect excels and precedes the will, as we have said above (A. 3). Therefore the will does not move the intellect.

Objection 2. Further, what moves is not moved by what is moved, except perhaps accidentally. But the intellect moves the will, because the good apprehended by the intellect moves without being moved; whereas the appetite moves and is moved.[46] Therefore the intellect is not moved by the will.

Objection 3. Further, we can will nothing but what we understand. If, therefore, in order to understand, the will moves by willing to understand, that act of the will must be preceded by another act of the intellect, and this act of the intellect by another act of the will, and so on indefinitely, which is impossible. Therefore the will does not move the intellect.

On the contrary, Damascene says (*De Fid. Orth.* ii. 26): *It is in our power to learn an art or not, as we list.* But a thing is in our power by the will, and we learn art by the intellect. Therefore the will moves the intellect.

---

[46] I.e., the good known in the intellect moves us as *final* cause, without itself moving, simply by being attractive, like a motionless beautiful woman at a party getting all the attention of the men who move around her. But the will (rational *appetite*) moves as *efficient* cause; this mover moves along with its "movee".

I answer that, A thing is said to move in two ways: First as an end [final cause]; for instance, when we say that the end moves the agent. In this way the intellect moves the will, because the good understood is the object of the will, and moves it as an end. Secondly, a thing is said to move as an agent [efficient cause], as what alters moves what is altered, and what impels moves what is impelled. In this way the will moves the intellect, and all the powers of the soul, as Anselm says (Eadmer, *De Similitudinibus*). The reason is, because wherever we have order among a number of active powers, that power which regards the universal end moves the powers which regard particular ends. And we may observe this both in nature and in things politic.[47] For the heaven, which aims at the universal preservation of things subject to generation and corruption, moves all inferior bodies, each of which aims at the preservation of its own species or of the individual. The king also, who aims at the common good of the whole kingdom, by his rule moves all the governors of cities, each of whom rules over his own particular city. Now the object of the will is good and the end in general, and each power is directed to some suitable good proper to it, as sight is directed to the perception of color, and the intellect to the knowledge of truth. Therefore the will as an agent moves all the powers of the soul to their respective acts, except the natural powers of the vegetative part, which are not subject to our will.

Reply Obj. 1. The intellect may be considered in two ways: as apprehensive of universal being and truth, and as a thing and a particular power having a determinate act. In like manner also the will may be considered in two ways: according to the common nature of its object—that is to say, as appetitive of universal good—and as a determinate power of the soul having a determinate act. If, therefore, the intellect and will be compared with one another according to the universality of their respective objects, then, as we have said above (A. 3), the intellect is simply higher and nobler than the will. If, however, we take the intellect as regards the common nature of its object and the will as a determinate power, then again the intellect is higher and nobler than the will,

---

[47] N.b.: the medieval mind saw connections between these two realms because it saw nature as a sort of *polis*, since God designed and created it, and it saw politics as a natural rather than an artificial thing, since God designed man's nature to be social and political.

because under the notion of being and truth is contained both the will itself, and its act, and its object. Wherefore the intellect understands the will, and its act, and its object, just as it understands other species of things, as stone or wood, which are contained in the common notion of being and truth. But if we consider the will as regards the common nature of its object, which is good, and the intellect as a thing and a special power; then the intellect itself, and its act, and its object, which is truth, each of which is some species of good, are contained under the common notion of good. And in this way the will is higher than the intellect, and can move it. From this we can easily understand why these powers include one another in their acts, because the intellect understands that the will wills, and the will wills the intellect to understand. In the same way good is contained in truth, inasmuch as it is an understood truth, and truth in good, inasmuch as it is a desired good.

Reply Obj. 2. The intellect moves the will in one sense, and the will moves the intellect in another, as we have said above.

Reply Obj. 3. There is no need to go on indefinitely, but we must stop at the intellect as preceding all the rest. For every movement of the will must be preceded by apprehension, whereas every apprehension is not preceded by an act of the will; but the principle of counselling and understanding is an intellectual principle higher than our intellect—namely, God—as also Aristotle says (*Eth. Eudemic.* vii. 14), and in this way he explains that there is no need to proceed indefinitely.[48] . . .

---

[48] See note 18. Not only must there be a first, primary cause rather than infinite regress in each order of causality, but there must also be a primary *kind* of cause, and that is the final cause, "the cause of all the other causes". Since final causes operate only through some intellect, intellect must be prior to will in itself. Intellect always must precede will (which is "*rational appetite*") but will does not always precede intellect. The conclusion seems to be borne out in introspective experience.

Question 83

Of Free-Will

Whether Man Has Free-Will?

Objection 1. It would seem that man has not free-will. For whoever has free-will does what he wills. But man does not what he wills; for it is written (Rom 7:19): *For the good which I will I do not, but the evil which I will not, that I do.* Therefore man has not free-will.

Objection 2. Further, whoever has free-will has in his power to will or not to will, to do or not to do. But this is not in man's power: for it is written (Rom 9:16): *It is not of him that willeth—* namely, to will—*nor of him that runneth—*namely, to run. Therefore man has not free-will.

Objection 3. Further, what is *free is cause of itself,* as the Philosopher says (*Metaph.* i. 2). Therefore what is moved by another is not free. But God moves the will, for it is written (Prov 21:1): *The heart of the king is in the hand of the Lord; whithersoever He will He shall turn it;* and (Phil 2:13): *It is God Who worketh in you both to will and to accomplish.* Therefore man has not free-will. . . .

On the contrary, It is written (Sir 15:14): *God made man from the beginning, and left him in the hand of his own counsel;* and the gloss adds: *That is of his free-will.*

I answer that, Man has free-will: otherwise counsels, exhortations, commands, prohibitions, rewards and punishments would be in vain.[49] In order to make this evident, we must observe that

---

[49] Note how basic, practical, and commonsensical St. Thomas' first argument is. Note also how he connects free will with reason. There is a popular misconception that sees reason as unfree and deterministic, and

some things act without judgment; as a stone moves downwards; and in like manner all things which lack knowledge. And some act from judgment, but not a free judgment; as brute animals. For the sheep, seeing the wolf, judges it a thing to be shunned, from a natural and not a free judgment, because it judges, not from reason, but from natural instinct. And the same thing is to be said of any judgment of brute animals. But man acts from judgment, because by his apprehensive power he judges that something should be avoided or sought. But because this judgment, in the case of some particular act, is not from a natural instinct, but from some act of comparison in the reason, therefore he acts from free judgment and retains the power of being inclined to various things. For reason in contingent matters may follow opposite courses, as we see in dialectic syllogisms and rhetorical [probable] arguments. Now particular operations are contingent, and therefore in such matters the judgment of reason may follow opposite courses, and is not determinate to one. And forasmuch as man is rational is it necessary that man have a free-will.

Reply Obj. 1. As we have said above (Q. 81, A. 3, *ad* 2), the sensitive appetite, though it obeys the reason, yet in a given case can resist by desiring what the reason forbids [cf. n. 37]. This is therefore the good which man does not [do] when he wishes— namely, *not to desire against reason*, as Augustine says (*ibid.*).

Reply Obj. 2. Those words of the Apostle are not to be taken as though man does not wish or does not run of his free-will, but because the free-will is not sufficient thereto unless it be moved and helped by God.

Reply Obj. 3. Free-will is the cause of its own movement, because by his free-will man moves himself to act. But it does not of necessity belong to liberty that what is free should be the first cause of itself, as neither for one thing to be cause of another need it be the first cause. God, therefore, is the first cause, Who moves causes both natural and voluntary. And just as by moving natural causes He does not prevent their acts being natural, so by moving voluntary causes He does not deprive their actions of being voluntary:

---

freedom as irrational and arbitrary. It arises from the nineteenth-century Romantic reaction against eighteenth-century classical rationalism and determinism.

but rather is He the cause of this very thing in them; for He operates in each thing according to its own nature.[50] . . .

Whether Free-Will Is an Appetitive Power?

I answer that, The proper act of free will is choice: for we say that we have a free-will because we can take one thing while refusing another; and this is to choose. Therefore we must consider the nature of free-will, by considering the nature of choice. Now two things concur in choice: one on the part of the cognitive power, the other on the part of the appetitive power. On the part of the cognitive power, counsel is required, by which we judge one thing to be preferred to another: and on the part of the appetitive power, it is required that the appetite should accept the judgment of counsel. Therefore Aristotle (*Ethic.* vi. 2) leaves it in doubt whether choice belongs principally to the appetitive or the cognitive power: since he says that choice is either *an appetitive intellect or an intellectual appetite*. But (*Ethic.* iii, *loc. cit.*) he inclines to its being an intellectual appetite when he describes choice as *a desire proceeding from counsel*. And the reason of this is because the proper object of choice is the means to the end: and this, as such, is in the nature of that good which is called useful: wherefore since good, as such, is the object of the appetite, it follows that choice is principally an act of the appetitive power. And thus free-will is an appetitive power. . . .

Whether Free-Will Is a Power Distinct from the Will?

I answer that, The appetitive powers must be proportionate to the apprehensive powers, as we have said above (Q. 64, A. 2).

---

[50] Note how simply and elegantly St. Thomas solves the thorny problem of reconciling human free will with divine causality. If God's being the first cause of the nature of dogs makes dogs doggy and not un-doggy, then God's being the first cause of human freedom makes freedom free, not un-free. Grace establishes nature rather than removing it.

Now, as on the part of the intellectual apprehension we have intellect and reason, so on the part of the intellectual appetite we have will, and free-will which is nothing else but the power of choice. And this is clear from their relations to their respective objects and acts. For the act of *understanding* implies the simple acceptation of something; whence we say that we understand first principles, which are known of themselves without any comparison. But to *reason*, properly speaking, is to come from one thing to the knowledge of another: wherefore, properly speaking, we reason about conclusions, which are known from the principles. In like manner on the part of the appetite, to *will* implies the simple appetite for something: wherefore the will is said to regard the end, which is desired for itself. But to *choose* is to desire something for the sake of obtaining something else: wherefore, properly speaking, it regards the means to the end. Now, in matters of knowledge, the principles [premises] are related to the conclusion to which we assent on account of the principles: just as, in appetitive matters, the end is related to the means, which is desired on account of the end. Wherefore it is evident that as the intellect is to reason, so is the will to the power of choice, which is free-will. But it has been shown above (Q. 79, A. 8) that it belongs to the same power both to understand and to reason, even as it belongs to the same power to be at rest and to be in movement. Wherefore it belongs also to the same power to will and to choose: and on this account the will and the free-will are not two powers, but one.[51] . . .

51

	Appetitive		Cognitive (Apprehensive)	
	Powers	Acts	Powers	Acts
Simple, Immediate	Will	Willing	Intellect	Understanding
Multiple, Mediate	Free Will	Choosing	Reason	Reasoning

Question 84

How the Soul While United to the Body Understands Corporeal Things beneath It

We now have to consider the acts of the soul in regard to the intellectual and the appetitive powers: for the other powers of the soul do not come directly under the consideration of the theologian. Furthermore, the acts of the appetitive part of the soul come under the consideration of the science of morals; wherefore we shall treat of them in the second part of this work, to which the consideration of moral matters belongs. But the acts of the intellectual part we shall treat now.

In treating of these acts we shall proceed in the following order: First, we shall inquire how the soul understands when united to the body; secondly, how it understands when separated therefrom.

The former of these inquiries will be threefold: (1) How the soul understands bodies which are beneath it; (2) How it understands itself and things contained in itself; (3) How it understands immaterial substances, which are above it. . . .

Under the first head there are eight points of inquiry: (1) Whether the soul knows bodies through the intellect? (2) Whether it understands them through its essence, or through any species? (3) If through some species, whether the species of all things intelligible are naturally innate in the soul? (4) Whether these species are derived by the soul from certain separate immaterial forms? (5) Whether our soul sees in the eternal ideas all that it understands? (6) Whether it acquires intellectual knowledge from the senses? (7) Whether the intellect can, through the species of which it is possessed, actually understand, without turning to the phantasms? (8) Whether the judgment of the intellect is hindered by an obstacle in the sensitive powers?

FIRST ARTICLE

Whether the Soul Knows Bodies through the Intellect?

Objection 3. Further, the intellect is concerned with things that are necessary and unchangeable. But all bodies are mobile and changeable. Therefore the soul cannot know bodies through the intellect.[52]

On the contrary, Science is in the intellect. If, therefore, the intellect does not know bodies, it follows that there is no science of bodies; and thus perishes natural science, which treats of mobile bodies.

I answer that, It should be said in order to elucidate this question, that the early philosophers, who inquired into the natures of things, thought there was nothing in the world save bodies. And because they observed that all bodies are mobile, and considered them to be ever in a state of flux, they were of opinion that we can have no certain knowledge of the true nature of things. For what is in a continual state of flux, cannot be grasped with any degree of certitude, for it passes away ere the mind can form a judgment thereon: according to the saying of Heraclitus, that *it is not possible twice to touch a drop of water in a passing torrent,* as the Philosopher relates (*Metaph.* iv, Did. iii. 5).

After these came Plato, who, wishing to save the certitude of our knowledge of truth through the intellect, maintained that, besides these things corporeal, there is another genus of beings, separate from matter and movement, which beings he called *species* or *ideas,* by participation of which each one of these singular and sensible

---

[52] This is Plato's position. Plato sharply separated knowledge of bodies, which was only sensory and probable, from knowledge of Forms, which was intellectual and certain; for he thought there could be no unchanging and certain knowledge of changing things.

St. Thomas possessed none of the writings of the pre-Socratics except the few quoted fragments in Aristotle, and none of Plato except the *Timaeus.* The works of Aristotle had been only recently and incompletely rediscovered. It is a testimony to the community and integrity of philosophers and historians of philosophy during the sixteen hundred years between the Greeks and St. Thomas that he had such an accurate understanding of their major teachings.

things is said to be either a man, or a horse, or the like. Wherefore he said that sciences and definitions, and whatever appertains to the act of the intellect, are not referred to these sensible bodies, but to those beings immaterial and separate: so that according to this the soul does not understand these corporeal things, but the separate species thereof.[53]

Now this may be shown to be false for two reasons. First, because since those species are immaterial and immovable, knowledge of movement and matter would be excluded from science (which knowledge is proper to natural science), and likewise all demonstration through moving and material causes. Secondly, because it seems ridiculous, when we seek for knowledge of things which are to us manifest, to introduce other beings, which cannot be the substance of those others, since they differ from them essentially: so that granted that we have a knowledge of those separate substances, we cannot for that reason claim to form a judgment concerning these sensible things.

Now it seems that Plato strayed from the truth because, having observed that all knowledge takes place through some kind of similitude, he thought that the form of the thing known must of necessity be in the knower in the same manner as in the thing known.[54] Then he observed that the form of the thing understood is in the intellect under conditions of universality, immateriality, and immobility: which is apparent from the very operation of the intellect, whose act of understanding has a universal extension, and is subject to a certain amount of necessity: for the mode of action

---

[53] This is why only mathematics and philosophy, but not the physical sciences, were taught in Plato's Academy, but physical sciences flourished in Aristotle's Lyceum.

N.b.: in listing two Aristotelian objections to Plato's theory of separate Forms in the next paragraph, St. Thomas is especially concerned to preserve scientific knowledge of nature. The problem is, how can we have truly scientific knowledge—i.e., universal, necessary, and unchanging knowledge—about particular, contingent, and changing things? See Objection 3.

[54] Plato's implicit major premise. Philosophical refutation consists largely in making explicit your opponent's implicit assumptions and then criticizing them.

corresponds to the mode of the agent's form. Wherefore he concluded that the things which we understand must have in themselves an existence under the same conditions of immateriality and immobility.

But there is no necessity for this. For even in sensible things it is to be observed that the form is otherwise in one sensible than in another: for instance, whiteness may be of great intensity in one, and of a less intensity in another: in one we find whiteness with sweetness, in another without sweetness. In the same way the sensible form is conditioned differently in the thing which is external to the soul, and in the senses which receive the forms of sensible things without receiving matter, such as the color of gold without receiving gold.[55] So also the intellect, according to its own mode, receives under conditions of immateriality and immobility, the species of material and mobile bodies: for the received is in the receiver according to the mode of the receiver. We must conclude, therefore, that through the intellect the soul knows bodies by a knowledge which is immaterial, universal, and necessary. . . .

Reply Obj. 3. Every movement presupposes something immovable:[56] for when a change of quality occurs, the substance remains unmoved; and when there is a change of substantial form, matter remains unmoved. Moreover the various conditions of mutable things are themselves immovable; for instance, though Socrates be not always sitting, yet it is an immovable truth that whenever he does sit he remains in one place. For this reason there is nothing to hinder our having an immovable science of movable things.

---

[55] I.e., even the senses perform some abstraction; so, a fortiori, does the intellect.

[56] That is, as an unchanging substratum. Otherwise it could not be truly said that x changes, for x would be in no sense still x after the change. This was Aristotle's solution to the puzzle of motion that bedeviled his predecessors—how can x become y while remaining x?—producing three inadequate pre-Aristotelian solutions: (1) Parmenides: motion is an illusion; (2) Heraclitus: *everything* moves (*panta rhei*); (3) Plato: there are two *separate* realms of reality: unmoving Forms and wholly moving natural substances. Note how each solution was closer to the truth than its predecessors.

SECOND ARTICLE

Whether the Soul Understands Corporeal Things through Its Essence?

On the contrary, Augustine says (*De Trin.* ix. 3) that *the mind gathers knowledge of corporeal things through the bodily senses.* But the soul itself cannot be known through the bodily senses. Therefore it does not know corporeal things through itself.

I answer that, . . . If there be an intellect which knows all things by its essence, then its essence must needs have all things in itself immaterially; thus the early philosophers held that the essence of the soul, that it may know all things, must be actually composed of the principles of all material things. Now this is proper to God, that His Essence comprise all things immaterially, as effects pre-exist virtually in their cause. God alone, therefore, understands all things through His Essence: but neither the human soul nor the angels can do so. . . .

THIRD ARTICLE

Whether the Soul Understands All Things through Innate Species?

Objection 3. Further, no one can answer the truth except concerning what he knows. But even a person untaught and devoid of acquired knowledge, answers the truth to every question if put to him in orderly fashion, as we find related in the *Meno* (xv. *seqq.*) of Plato, concerning a certain individual. Therefore we have some knowledge of things even before we acquire knowledge; which would not be the case unless we had innate species. Therefore the soul understands corporeal things through innate species.[57]

On the contrary, The Philosopher, speaking of the intellect, says (*De Anima* iii. 4) that it is like *a tablet on which nothing is written.*

---

[57] This is Plato's famous doctrine of "innate ideas (species)" and "recollection" of them. The connections among the metaphysical, epistemological, and anthropological teachings of Plato and Aristotle (and St. Thomas) should be obvious from the following summary:

I answer that, Since form is the principle of action, a thing must be related to the form which is the principle of an action, as it is to that action: for instance, if upward motion is from lightness, then that which only potentially moves upwards must needs be only potentially light, but that which actually moves upwards must needs be actually light. Now we observe that man sometimes is only a potential knower, both as to sense and as to intellect. And he is reduced from such potentiality to act;—through the action of sensible objects on his senses, to the act of sensation;—by instruction [by others] or discovery [by oneself], to the act of understanding. Wherefore we must say that the cognitive soul is in potentiality both to the images which are the principles of sensing, and to those [ideas, species, forms] which are the principles of understanding. For this reason Aristotle (*ibid.*) held that the intellect by which the soul understands has no innate species, but is at first in potentiality to all such species.

But since that which has a form actually, is sometimes unable to act according to that form on account of some hindrance, as a light thing may be hindered from moving upwards; for this reason did

	Metaphysics	Epistemology	Anthropology
Plato	Forms exist separately from matter	Innate species and knowledge by recollection	Soul is a substance separate from body
Aristotle and St. Thomas	Forms exist in material substances	No innate species and knowledge by sensation and abstraction	Soul is the form of the body

In this article, St. Thomas places Plato and Aristotle in a dialogue as follows:

1. Objection 3: Plato's theory and his reasons for it.
2. "*On the contrary*" and first paragraph of "*I answer that*": Aristotle's alternative theory, with his reasons for it.
3. Paragraph 2, sentence 1: Plato's reply to Aristotle.
4. The rest of paragraph 2: Aristotle's reply to Plato's reply (3).
5. Reply to Objection 3: Aristotle's reply to Plato's original argument (1).

Plato hold that naturally man's intellect is filled with all intelligible species, but that, by being united to the body, it is hindered from the realization of its act. But this seems to be unreasonable. First, because, if the soul has a natural knowledge of all things, it seems impossible for the soul so far to forget the existence of such knowledge as not to know itself to be possessed thereof: for no man forgets what he knows naturally; that, for instance, the whole is larger than the part, and such like. And especially unreasonable does this seem if we suppose that it is natural to the soul to be united to the body, as we have established above (Q. 76, A. 1): for it is unreasonable that the natural operation of a thing be totally hindered by that which belongs to it naturally. Secondly, the falseness of this opinion is clearly proved from the fact that if a sense be wanting, the knowledge of what is apprehended through that sense is wanting also: for instance, a man who is born blind can have no knowledge of colors. This would not be the case if the soul had innate images of all intelligible things. We must therefore conclude that the soul does not know corporeal things through innate species. . . .

Reply Obj. 3. If questions be put in an orderly fashion they proceed from universal self-evident principles to what is particular. Now by such a process knowledge is produced in the mind of the learner. Wherefore when he answers the truth to a subsequent question, this is not because he had knowledge previously, but because he thus learns for the first time. For it matters not whether the teacher proceed from universal principles to conclusions by questioning or by asserting; for in either case the mind of the listener is assured of what follows by that which preceded.

FOURTH ARTICLE

Whether the Intelligible Species Are Derived by the Soul from Certain Separate Forms? [58]

On the contrary, If this were true we should not need the senses in order to understand. And this is proved to be false especially from

---

[58] Having refuted Plato's epistemology (Article 3), St. Thomas now refutes his metaphysics (Article 4).

the fact that if a man be wanting in a sense, he cannot have any knowledge of the sensibles corresponding to that sense.

I answer that, Some have held that the intelligible species of our intellect are derived from certain separate forms or substances. And this in two ways.[59] For Plato, as we have said (A. 1), held that the forms of sensible things subsist by themselves without matter; for instance, the form of a man which he called *per se* man, and the form or idea of a horse which is called *per se* horse, and so forth. He said therefore that these forms are participated both by our soul and by corporeal matter; by our soul, to the effect of knowledge thereof, and by corporeal matter to the effect of existence: so that, just as corporeal matter by participating the idea of a stone, becomes an individual stone, so our intellect, by participating the idea of a stone, is made to understand a stone. Now participation of an idea takes place by some image of the idea[60] in the participator, just as a model is participated by a copy. So just as he held that the sensible forms, which are in corporeal matter, are derived from the ideas as certain images thereof: so he held that the intelligible species of our intellect are images of the ideas, derived therefrom. And for this reason, as we have said above (A. 1), he referred sciences and definitions to those ideas.

But since it is contrary to the nature of sensible things that their forms should subsist without matter, as Aristotle proves in many ways (*Metaph.* vi), Avicenna (*De Anima* v), setting this opinion aside, held that the intelligible species of all sensible things, instead of subsisting in themselves without matter, pre-exist immaterially

---

[59] The two "ways", or different versions of the doctrine of separate species, are (1) Plato's version, which is (a) stated in paragraph 1 and (b) refuted in paragraph 2, sentence 1; and (2) Avicenna's version, which is
a. stated in the rest of paragraph 2;
b. refuted in paragraph 3;
c. Avicenna's first answer to (b) is given in paragraph 4, sentence 1;
d. St. Thomas' refutation of (c) is given in the rest of paragraph 4;
e. Avicenna's second answer to (b) is given in paragraph 5, sentence 1; and
f. St. Thomas' refutation of (e) is given in the rest of paragraph 5.

[60] "Idea" means not a subjective notion but an objective species, or form. What St. Thomas means by "image of the idea" is what we would mean by an "idea".

in the separate intellects:[61] from the first of which, said he, such species are derived by a second, and so on to the last separate intellect which he called the *active intelligence*, from which, according to him, intelligible species flow into our souls, and sensible species into corporeal matter. And so Avicenna agrees with Plato in this, that the intelligible species of our intellect are derived from certain separate forms; but these Plato held to subsist of themselves, while Avicenna placed them in the *active intelligence*. They differ, too, in this respect, that Avicenna held that the intelligible species do not remain in our intellect after it has ceased actually to understand, and that it needs to turn [to the active intellect] in order to receive them anew. Consequently he does not hold that the soul has innate knowledge, as Plato, who held that the participated ideas remain immovably in the soul.

But in this opinion no sufficient reason can be assigned for the soul being united to the body. For it cannot be said that the intellectual soul is united to the body for the sake of the body: for neither is form for the sake of matter, nor is the mover for the sake of the moved, but rather the reverse. Especially does the body seem necessary to the intellectual soul for the latter's proper operation, which is to understand; since as to its being the soul does not depend on the body. But if the soul by its very nature had an inborn aptitude for receiving intelligible species through the influence of only certain separate principles, and were not to receive them from the senses, it would not need the body in order to understand: wherefore to no purpose would it be united to the body.[62]

But if it be said that our soul needs the senses in order to understand, through being in some way awakened by them to the consideration of those things, the intelligible species of which it receives from the separate principles: even this seems an insufficient explanation. For this awakening does not seem necessary to the soul, except in as far as it is overcome by sluggishness, as the Platonists expressed it, and by forgetfulness, through its union with the body: and thus the senses would be of no use to the intellectual soul except for the purpose of removing the obstacle

---

[61] Angels, the lowest of which was supposedly the mover of the moon in its orbit and the single separate "active intellect" for all men. See I, 79, 4 and 5 for St. Thomas' refutation of this teaching.

[62] N.b.: The unproved (because universally-believed in medieval times)

which the soul encounters through its union with the body. Consequently the reason of the union of the soul with the body still remains to be sought.

And if it be said with Avicenna, that the senses are necessary to the soul, because by them it is roused to turn to the *active intelligence* from which it receives the species: neither is this a sufficient explanation. Because if it is natural for the soul to understand through species derived from the *active intelligence*, it follows that at times the soul of an individual wanting in one of the senses can turn to the active intelligence, either from the inclination of its very nature, or through being roused by another sense, to the effect of receiving the intelligible species of which the corresponding sensible species are wanting. And thus a man born blind could have knowledge of colors; which is clearly untrue. We must therefore conclude that the intelligible species, by which our soul understands, are not derived from separate forms. . . .

FIFTH ARTICLE

Whether the Intellectual Soul Knows Material Things in the Eternal Types?[63]

Objection 3. Further, the eternal types are nothing else but ideas, for Augustine says (QQ. 83, *qu.* 46) that *ideas are permanent types existing in the Divine mind.* If therefore we say that the intellectual soul knows all things in the eternal types, we come back to the opinion of Plato who said that all knowledge is derived from them.

On the contrary, Augustine says (*Confess.* xii. 25): *If we both see*

---

commonsense assumption of this argument is that no real thing is without purpose, or end (final cause).

[63] St. Thomas is not merely an Aristotelian but also an Augustinian, and thus a (Christian) Platonist. (See Robert Henle, S.J., *The Platonism of St. Thomas.*) In fact, he accepts Plato's most cherished and central idea, the real existence of separate Forms, or "eternal types"—but only in the Mind of God, not in nature. Following St. Augustine, he gives these metaphysical orphans their home.

that what you say is true, and if we both see that what I say is true, where do we see this, I pray?[64] *Neither do I see it in you, nor do you see it in me: but we both see it in the unchangeable truth which is above our minds.* Now the unchangeable truth is contained in the eternal types. Therefore the intellectual soul knows all true things in the eternal types.

I answer that, As Augustine says (*De Doctr. Christ.* ii. 11): *If those who are called philosophers said by chance anything that was true and*

---

[64] The simple question Augustine asks here is surprisingly profound and puzzling: How do we changing knowers know unchanging Truth? How to account for "a priori knowledge" such as "$2 + 3 = 5$" or "the whole is greater than the part" or "evil should not be done"? The explanations boil down to six:

1. Empiricism (e.g., Hume), which tries to derive such knowledge from sense experience alone. This cannot account for its necessity and eternity, and it leads to skepticism.

2. Platonic or Cartesian rationalism, with its theory of "innate ideas". This theory seems easily refuted by experience; see Article 3 here, and also Locke's arguments at the beginning of his *Essay on Human Understanding*.

3. Kant's "Copernican revolution in philosophy", which attempts to mediate between (1) and (2) and combine their good points. However, it really combines their bad points, viz., (1) an even more severe restriction on our knowledge of things in themselves, or objective reality, than empiricism, and (2) a theory of the innate divinity of mind (the "transcendental ego") that goes beyond rationalism. Rationalism's mind still humbly discovers its object, but Kantianism's mind, like the divine mind, determines its object.

4. Aristotelian modified empiricism, which answers Augustine's question *proximately* by the doctrines of hylomorphism in metaphysics (unchanging forms exist in changing material substances) and abstraction in epistemology (we know unchanging forms by abstracting them from matter), but does not answer the question *ultimately* (the First Cause of forms).

5. St. Augustine's Christian Platonism, which answers the question ultimately (the divine Mind is the First Cause of intelligibility) but not proximately (how do *we* know them? Does "divine illumination" mean we read God's mind?).

6. St. Thomas, who answers the question both proximately and ultimately by combining Aristotelianism (hylomorphism and abstraction) with Augustinianism (exemplarism and illumination).

*consistent with our faith, we must claim it from them as from unjust
possessors. For some of the doctrines of the heathens are spurious imita-
tions or superstitious inventions, which we must be careful to avoid when
we renounce the society of the heathens.* [65] Consequently whenever
Augustine, who was imbued with the doctrines of the Platonists,
found in their teaching anything consistent with faith, he adopted
it: and those things which he found contrary to faith he amended.
Now Plato held, as we have said above (A. 4), that the forms of
things subsist of themselves apart from matter; and these he called
ideas, by participation of which he said that our intellect knows all
things: so that just as corporeal matter by participating the idea of a
stone becomes a stone, so our intellect, by participating the same
idea, has knowledge of a stone. But since it seems contrary to faith
that forms of things should subsist of themselves, outside the
things themselves and apart from matter, as the Platonists held,
asserting that *per se* life or *per se* wisdom are creative substances
[gods], as Dionysius relates (*Div. Nom* xi), therefore Augustine
(QQ. 83, *loc. cit.*), for the ideas defended by Plato, substituted the
types of all creatures existing in the Divine mind, according to
which types all things are made in themselves, and are known to
the human soul.

When, therefore, the question is asked: Does the human soul
know all things in the eternal types? we must reply that one thing is
said to be known in another in two ways. First, as in an object itself
known; as one may see in a mirror the images of things reflected
therein. In this way the soul, in the present state of life, cannot see
all things in the eternal types; but the blessed who see God, and all
things in Him, thus know all things in the eternal types. Secondly,
one thing is said to be known in another as in a principle of
knowledge: thus we might say that we see in the sun what we see
by the sun. And thus we must needs say that the human soul knows

---

[65] This apparently closed-minded language masks an open-minded
attitude, both sympathetic and critical, toward pagan philosophy on
Augustine's part, which typified the main-line tradition in medieval
philosophy. (See Gilson, *Reason and Revelation in the Middle Ages*.) The
next sentence summarizes this Augustinian attitude to and use of Plato as
simply and accurately as it has ever been summarized, and it is precisely
St. Thomas' attitude to and use of Aristotle also.

all things in the eternal types, since by participation of these types we know all things. For the intellectual light itself which is in us, is nothing else than a participated likeness of the uncreated light, in which are contained the eternal types. Whence it is written (Ps 4:6, 7), *Many say: Who showeth us good things?* which question the Psalmist answers, *The light of Thy countenance, O Lord, is signed upon us,* as though he were to say: By the seal of the Divine light in us, all things are made known to us.

But since besides the intellectual light which is in us, intelligible species, which are derived from things, are required in order for us to have knowledge of material things; therefore this same knowledge is not due merely to a participation of the eternal types, as the Platonists held, maintaining that the mere participation of ideas sufficed for knowledge. Wherefore Augustine says (*De Trin.* iv. 16): *Although the philosophers prove by convincing arguments that all things occur in time according to the eternal types, were they able to see in the eternal types, or to find out from them how many kinds of animals there are and the origin of each? Did they not seek for this information from the story of times and places?*

But that Augustine did not understand all things to be known in their *eternal types* or in *the unchangeable truth*, as though the eternal types themselves were seen, is clear from what he says (QQ. 83, *loc. cit.*)—viz., that *not each and every rational soul can be said to be worthy of that vision,* namely, of the eternal types, *but only those that are holy and pure,* such as the souls of the blessed.[66]

From what has been said the objections are easily solved.

---

[66] The following three diagrams may be helpful:

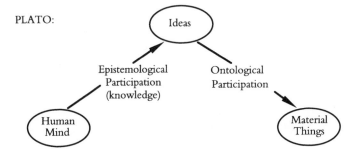

SIXTH ARTICLE

Whether Intellectual Knowledge Is Derived
from Sensible Things?[67]

Objection 2. Further, Augustine says (*Gen. ad lit.* xii. 16): *We must not think that the body can make any impression on the spirit, as though the spirit were to supply the place of matter in regard to the body's action; for that which acts is in every way more excellent than that which it acts on.* Whence he concludes that *the body does not cause its image in the spirit, but the spirit causes it in itself.* Therefore intellectual knowledge is not derived from sensible things.

Objection 3. Further, an effect does not surpass the power of its cause. But intellectual knowledge extends beyond sensible things: for we understand some things which cannot be perceived by the senses. Therefore intellectual knowledge is not derived from sensible things.

ARISTOTLE:

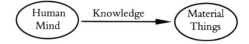

AUGUSTINE
AND
AQUINAS:

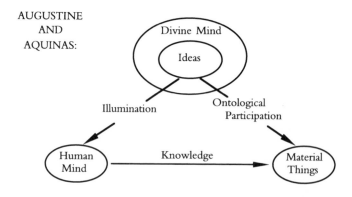

---

[67] Again note St. Thomas' balance: Article 5 (the Platonic–Augustinian point) must be supplemented by Article 6 (the Aristotelian point) and vice versa.

On the contrary, The Philosopher says (*Metaph.* i. 1; *Poster.* ii. 15) that the principle of knowledge is in the senses.

I answer that, On this point the philosophers held three opinions. For Democritus held that *all knowledge is caused by* [material] *images issuing from the bodies we think of and entering into our souls,* as Augustine says in his letter to Dioscorus (cxviii. 4). And Aristotle says (*De Somn. et Vigil.*) that Democritus held that knowledge is caused by a *discharge of images.* And the reason for this opinion was that both Democritus and the other early philosophers did not distinguish between intellect and sense, as Aristotle relates (*De Anima* iii. 3). Consequently, since the sense is affected by the sensible, they thought that all our knowledge is affected by this mere impression brought about by sensible things. Which impression Democritus held to be caused by a discharge of images.

Plato, on the other hand, held that the intellect is distinct from the senses: and that it is an immaterial power not making use of a corporeal organ for its action. And since the incorporeal cannot be affected by the corporeal,[68] he held that intellectual knowledge is not brought about by sensible things affecting the intellect, but by separate intelligible forms being participated by the intellect, as we have said above (AA. 4, 5). Moreover he held that sense is a power operating of itself. Consequently neither is sense, since it is a spiritual power, affected by the sensible: but the sensible organs are affected by the sensible, the result being that the soul is in a way roused to form within itself the species of the sensible. Augustine seems to touch on this opinion (*Gen. ad lit.* xii. 24) where he says that the *body feels not, but the soul through the body, which it makes use of as a kind of messenger, for reproducing within itself what is announced from without.* Thus according to Plato, neither does intellectual knowledge proceed from sensible knowledge, nor sensible knowledge exclusively from sensible things; but these rouse the sensible soul to the sentient act, while the senses rouse the intellect to the act of understanding.

Aristotle chose a middle course.[69] For with Plato he agreed that

---

[68] Plato was right in these three preceding points, but wrong in thinking they necessitated the conclusion that follows the footnote.

[69] As usual. This sentence sums up Aristotle's position vis-à-vis most other philosophers both before him and after him.

intellect and sense are different. But he held that the sense has not its proper operation without the co-operation of the body; so that to feel is not an act of the soul alone, but of the *composite*. And he held the same in regard to all the operations of the sensitive part. Since, therefore, it is not unreasonable that the sensible objects which are outside the soul should produce some effect in the *composite*, Aristotle agreed with Democritus in this, that the operations of the sensitive part are caused by the impression of the sensible on the sense: not by a discharge, as Democritus said, but by some kind of operation. For Democritus maintained that every operation is by way of a discharge of atoms, as we gather from *De Gener.* i. 8. But Aristotle held that the intellect has an operation which is independent of the body's co-operation. Now nothing corporeal can make an impression on the incorporeal. And therefore in order to cause the intellectual operation, according to Aristotle, the impression caused by the sensible does not suffice, but something more noble is required, for *the agent is more noble than the patient*, as he says (*ibid.* 5). Not, indeed, in the sense that the intellectual operation is effected in us by the mere impression of some superior beings, as Plato held; but that the higher and more noble agent which he calls the active intellect, of which we have spoken above (Q. 79, AA. 3, 4), causes the phantasms received from the senses to be actually intelligible, by a process of abstraction.

According to this opinion, then, on the part of the phantasms, intellectual knowledge is caused by the senses. But since the phantasms cannot of themselves affect the passive intellect, and require to be made actually intelligible by the active intellect, it cannot be said that sensible knowledge is the total and perfect cause of intellectual knowledge, but rather that it is in a way the material cause. . . .

Reply Obj. 2. In this passage Augustine speaks not of intellectual but of imaginary knowledge.[70] . . .

Reply Obj. 3. Sensitive knowledge is not the entire cause of intellectual knowledge. And therefore it is not strange that intellectual knowledge should extend further than sensitive knowledge.

---

[70] A charitable but questionable interpretation of Augustine.

SEVENTH ARTICLE

Whether the Intellect Can Actually Understand through the Intelligible Species of Which It Is Possessed, without Turning to the Phantasms [Sense Images]?

Objection 3. There are no phantasms of incorporeal things: for the imagination does not transcend time and space. If, therefore, our intellect cannot understand anything actually without turning to the phantasms, it follows that it cannot understand anything incorporeal. Which is clearly false: for we understand truth, and God, and the angels.

On the contrary, The Philosopher says (*De Anima* iii. 7) that *the soul understands nothing without a phantasm.*

I answer that, In the present state of life in which the soul is united to a passible [movable] body, it is impossible for our intellect to understand anything actually, except by turning to the phantasms. And of this there are two indications. First of all because the intellect, being a power that does not make use of a corporeal organ, would in no way be hindered in its act through the lesion of a corporeal organ, if for its act there were not required the act of some power that does make use of a corporeal organ. Now sense, imagination and the other powers belonging to the sensitive part, make use of a corporeal organ. Wherefore it is clear that for the intellect to understand actually, not only when it acquires fresh knowledge, but also when it applies knowledge already acquired, there is need for the act of the imagination and of the other powers. For when the act of the imagination is hindered by a lesion of the corporeal organ [the brain] for instance, in a case of frenzy; or when the act of the memory is hindered, as in the case of lethargy [or fatigue] we see that a man is hindered from actually understanding things of which he had a previous knowledge. Secondly, anyone can experience this of himself, that when he tries to understand something, he forms certain phantasms to serve him by way of examples, in which as it were he examines what he is desirous of understanding. For this reason it is that when we wish to help someone to understand something, we lay examples before him, from which he forms phantasms for the purpose of understanding.

Now the reason of this is that the power of knowledge is proportioned to the thing known. Wherefore the proper object of the angelic intellect, which is entirely separate from a body, is an intelligible substance separate from a body. Whereas the proper object of the human intellect, which is united to a body, is a quiddity or nature existing in corporeal matter; and through such natures of visible things it rises to a certain knowledge of things invisible. Now it belongs to such a nature to exist in an individual, and this cannot be apart from corporeal matter: for instance, it belongs to the nature of a stone to be in an individual stone, and to the nature of a horse to be in an individual horse, and so forth. Wherefore the nature of a stone or any material thing cannot be known completely and truly, except in as much as it is known as existing in the individual. Now we apprehend the individual through the senses and the [sensory] imagination. And, therefore, for the intellect to understand actually its proper object, it must of necessity turn to the phantasms [sensed or imagined] in order to perceive the universal nature existing in the individual. But if the proper object of our intellect were a separate form; or if, as the Platonists say, the natures of sensible things subsisted apart from the individual; there would be no need for the intellect to turn to the phantasms whenever it understands.[71] . . .

Reply Obj. 3. Incorporeal things, of which there are no phantasms, are known to us by comparison with sensible bodies of which there are phantasms. Thus we understand truth by con-

---

[71] Note how empirical St. Thomas is compared with many philosophers, modern as well as medieval (1) in his conclusion—that in the act of understanding, the intellect always needs the aid of sensory images; (2) in his reasons—*observation* of the intellectual effects of lesions in the physical organs, and the *experience* of learning abstract truths only, or through concrete, imaginable examples; and (3) in the cosmological and anthropological background explanation in paragraph 2, which rejects Platonic "angelism" both in metaphysics and in epistemology (see n. 40). St. Thomas always thinks from the cosmological background of "the great chain of being", on which man is between animals and angels. As Chesterton says, Thomistic man is neither a balloon floating free in the air, nor a mole burrowing in the earth, but a tree, with its roots planted firmly in the earth and its branches reaching up into the heavens. (*St. Thomas Aquinas, The Dumb Ox*—the best book ever written about him.)

sidering a thing of which we possess the truth; and God, as Dionysius says (*Div. Nom.* i), we know as cause, by way of excess and by way of remotion.[72] Other incorporeal substances we know, in the present state of life, only by way of remotion or by some comparison to corporeal things. And, therefore, when we understand something about these things, we need to turn to phantasms of bodies, although there are no phantasms of the things themselves.[73]

---

[72] Cf. Section 3, notes 91 and 93.

[73] Christ's parables are a good example. He knew we could not understand incorporeal, spiritual things like "the Kingdom of God" without sensory images as examples (the Good Samaritan) or analogies (the merchant's pearl, the fishnet, etc.).

Question 85

Of the Mode and Order of Understanding

*Whether Our Intellect Understands Corporeal and
Material Things by Abstraction from Phantasms?*

Objection 1. It would seem that our intellect does not understand
corporeal and material things by abstraction from the phantasms.
For the intellect is false if it understands an object otherwise than as
it really is. Now the forms of material things do not exist as
abstracted from the particular things represented by the phantasms.
Therefore, if we understand material things by abstraction of the
species from the phantasm, there will be error in the intellect.

Objection 2. Further, material things are those natural things
which include matter in their definition. But nothing can be understood apart from that which enters into its definition. Therefore
material things cannot be understood apart from matter. Now
matter is the principle of individualization. Therefore material
things cannot be understood by abstraction of the universal from
the particular, which is the process whereby the intelligible species
is abstracted from the phantasm.[74] . . .

On the contrary, The Philosopher says (*De Anima* iii. 4) that
things are intelligible in proportion as they are separable from matter.
Therefore material things must needs be understood according as
they are abstracted from matter and from material images, namely,
phantasms.

I answer that, As stated above (Q. 84, A. 7), the object of
knowledge is proportionate to the power of knowledge. Now

---

[74] Both these two Objections assume a simple "copy" theory of
knowledge.

there are three grades of the cognitive powers. For one cognitive power, namely, the sense, is the act of a corporeal organ. And therefore the object of every sensitive power is a form as existing in corporeal matter. And since such matter is the principle of individuality, therefore every power of the sensitive part can only have knowledge of the individual.[75] There is another grade of cognitive power which is neither the act of a corporeal organ, nor in any way connected with corporeal matter; such is the angelic intellect, the object of whose cognitive power is therefore a form existing apart from matter: for though angels know material things, yet they do not know them save in something immaterial, namely, either in themselves or in God.[76] But the human intellect holds a middle place:[77] for it is not the act of an organ,[78] yet it is a power of the soul which is the form of the body,[79] as is clear from what we have said above (Q. 76, A. 1). And therefore it is proper to it to know a form existing individually in corporeal matter, but not as existing in this individual matter.[80] But to know what is in individual matter, not as existing in such matter, is to abstract the form from individual matter which is represented by the phantasms. Therefore we must needs say that our intellect understands material things by abstracting from the phantasms; and through material things thus considered we acquire some knowledge of immaterial things, just as, on the contrary, angels know material things through the immaterial.

But Plato, considering only the immateriality of the human intellect, and not its being in a way united to the body, held that the objects of the intellect are separate ideas; and that we understand not by abstraction, but by participating things abstract, as stated above (Q. 84, A. 1).

Reply Obj. 1. Abstraction may occur in two ways: First, by way

---

[75] I.e., we cannot *see* treeness, only trees.

[76] Angels know everything they know, even facts about the material world, by a kind of mental telepathy.

[77] A key principle; again the cosmic hierarchy gives perspective to St. Thomas' Aristotelian "golden mean". (Cf. n. 69 and Chap. 5, n. 22.)

[78] (as the senses are).

[79] (unlike the intellect of an angel).

[80] I.e., not limited to this particular instance.

of composition and division;[81] thus we may understand that one thing does not exist in some other, or that it is separate therefrom. Secondly, by way of simple and absolute consideration;[82] thus we understand one thing without considering the other. Thus for the intellect to abstract one from another things which are not really abstract from one another, does, in the first mode of abstraction, imply falsehood. But, in the second mode of abstraction, for the intellect to abstract things which are not really abstract from one another, does not involve falsehood, as clearly appears in the case of the senses. For if we understood or said that color is not in a colored body, or that it is separate from it, there would be error in this opinion or assertion. But if we consider color and its properties, without reference to the apple which is colored; or if we express in word what we thus understand, there is no error in such an opinion or assertion, because an apple is not essential to color, and therefore color can be understood independently of the apple. Likewise, the things which belong to the species of a material thing, such as a stone, or a man, or a horse, can be thought of apart from the individualizing principles which do not belong to the notion of the species. This is what we mean by abstracting the universal from the particular, or the intelligible species from phantasm; that is, by considering the nature of the species apart from its individual qualities represented by the phantasms. If, therefore, the intellect is said to be false when it understands a thing otherwise than as it is, that is so, if the word *otherwise* refers to the thing understood; for the intellect is false when it understands a thing otherwise than as it is; and so the intellect would be false if it abstracted the species of a stone from its matter in such a way as to regard the species as not existing in matter, as Plato held. But it is not so, if the word *otherwise* be taken as referring to the one who understands. For it is quite true that the mode of understanding, in one who understands, is not the same as the mode of a thing in existing: since the thing understood is immaterially in the one who understands, according

---

[81] This "first way" is a negative *judgment*, the "second act of the mind".

[82] The "second way" is a *concept* abstracted from its individual concrete instances—something within the realm of "the first act of the mind": conception, apprehension, understanding.

to the mode of the intellect, and not materially, according to the mode of a material thing.

Reply Obj. 2. Some have thought that the species of a natural thing is a form only, and that matter is not part of the species [essence]. If that were so, matter would not enter into the definition of natural things. Therefore it must be said otherwise, that matter is twofold: common, and *signate* or individual; common, such as flesh and bone; and individual, as this flesh and these bones. The intellect therefore abstracts the species of a natural thing from the individual sensible matter, but not from the common sensible matter; for example, it abstracts the species of man from *this flesh and these bones*, which do not belong to the species as such, but to the individual (*Metaph.* vii, *Did.* vi. 10), and need not be considered in the species: whereas the species of man cannot be abstracted by the intellect from *flesh and bones*.

Mathematical species, however, can be abstracted by the intellect from sensible matter, not only from individual, but also from common matter; not from common intelligible matter, but only from individual matter. For sensible matter is corporeal matter as subject to sensible qualities, such as being cold or hot, hard or soft, and the like: while intelligible matter is substance as subject to quantity. Now it is manifest that quantity is in substance before other sensible qualities are. Hence quantities, such as number, dimension, and figures, which are the terminations of quantity, can be considered apart from sensible qualities; and this is to abstract them from sensible matter; but they cannot be considered without understanding the substance which is subject to the quantity; for that would be to abstract them from common intelligible matter. Yet they can be considered apart from this or that substance; for that is to abstract them from individual intelligible matter. But some things can be abstracted even from common intelligible matter, such as *being, unity, power, act*, and the like; all these can exist without matter, as is plain regarding immaterial things.[83] Because

---

[83] St. Thomas distinguishes (a) individual sensible matter: this flesh and these bones; (b) common sensible matter: flesh and bones in general; (c) common intelligible matter: quantified substance.

The senses do not abstract from (a) or (b) or (c).

Plato failed to consider the twofold kind of abstraction, as above explained (*ad* 1), he held that all those things which we have stated to be abstracted by the intellect, are abstract in reality. . . .

SECOND ARTICLE

Whether the Intelligible Species Abstracted from the Phantasm Is Related to Our Intellect As That Which Is Understood?[84]

Objection 2. Further, what is actually understood must be in something; else it would be nothing. But it is not in something outside the soul: for, since what is outside the soul is material, nothing therein can be actually understood. Therefore what is actually understood is in the intellect. Consequently it can be nothing else than the aforesaid intelligible species. . . .

The physical sciences abstract from (a) but not from (b) or (c).

The mathematical sciences abstract from (a) and (b) but not from (c).

Metaphysics abstracts from (a) and (b) and (c).

Physics, mathematics, and metaphysics represent the three degrees of abstraction.

[84] This is perhaps the most important article in St. Thomas' epistemology, historically speaking, for it is his alternative to most classical modern epistemology, which in turn is most of classical modern philosophy. Modern epistemology is haunted by the spectre of skepticism and even solipsism because of its constant subjectivistic tendency. This, in turn, stems above all from the "thingification of ideas", the tendency to treat ideas not as intentional *signs* (pure signs, mere signs, "formal signs" in technical Thomistic terminology), but as *things* intended (known) before they intend other things (technically, as "material signs"); not as means (*quo*) of knowing objects, but as objects (*quod*) known. Indeed, this is the very first thesis of Locke's theory of knowledge: "Idea = object of knowledge". St. Thomas takes an alternative path right here at the beginning, defining an idea (or "intelligible species") not as "that which" (*id quod*) is understood, i.e., as an object, but as "that by which" (*id quo*) some objectively real thing is understood. If all we knew primarily and directly were our own ideas, skepticism would be inevitable, eventually; for we would be like prisoners in jail cells, seeing only pictures of the outside world on TV screens and never able to get out of jail and see the real world directly to know whether the TV images are true or false.

On the contrary, The intelligible species is to the intellect what the sensible image is to the sense. But the sensible image is not what is perceived, but rather that by which sense perceives. Therefore the intelligible species is not what is actually understood, but that by which the intellect understands.[85]

I answer that, Some have asserted that our intellectual faculties know only the impression made on them; as, for example, that sense is cognizant only of the impression made on its own organ. According to this theory, the intellect understands only its own impression, namely, the intelligible species which it has received, so that this species is what is understood.[86]

This is, however, manifestly false for two reasons. First, because the things we understand are the objects of science; therefore if what we understand is merely the intelligible species in the soul, it would follow that every science would not be concerned with objects outside the soul, but only with the intelligible species within the soul. . . . Secondly, it is untrue, because it would lead to the opinion of the ancients [the Sophists] who maintained that *whatever seems, is true* [cf. Arist., *Metaph.* iii. 5], and that consequently contradictories are true simultaneously. For if the faculty knows its own impression only, it can judge of that only. Now a thing seems, according to the impression made on the cognitive faculty. Consequently the cognitive faculty will always judge of its own impression as such; and so every judgment will be true: for instance, if taste perceived only its own impression, when anyone

---

[85] The analogy between sense images and ideas ("intelligible species") is not perfect. We cannot by reflection sense the means of our sensing, viz., sense images (see the last half of the last paragraph of the "*I answer that*"); but *ideas*, though not primary objects known, *can* be secondary objects known, reflectively, after some real primary object is known. Sense images, on the other hand, are never sensed even as secondary objects; for the sense image itself has no size, shape, or weight as sensible objects have.

[86] The "intelligible species" is the form, abstracted by the mind from the real substance existing in nature. Thus, according to this semi-subjectivistic, semi-skeptical epistemology St. Thomas is criticizing, we cannot know real things as they really are (what Kant calls "things-in-themselves"). St. Thomas argues that this position would lead to two absurd conclusions (in the next paragraph).

with a healthy taste perceives that honey is sweet, he would judge truly; and if anyone with a corrupt taste perceives that honey is bitter, this would be equally true; for each would judge according to the impression on his taste. Thus every opinion would be equally true; in fact, every sort of apprehension.[87]

Therefore it must be said that the intelligible species is related to the intellect as that by which it understands.[88] . . . But since the intellect reflects upon itself, by such reflection it understands both its own act of intelligence, and the species by which it understands.

---

[87] In other words, "true" means only "true to me". Thus no one is ever *wrong*, for there is no knowledge of objective reality to judge a subjective opinion as failing to conform to it. This is a very popular philosophy among American students: see the first sentence of Alan Bloom's best-seller, *The Closing of the American Mind*. St. Thomas' argument against this relativism is simple and logical: it violates the law of non-contradiction. Another simple argument to the same effect is that if every opinion is equally true, then this opinion is also true: that some opinions are false.

[88] St. Thomas thus implicitly sees ideas as dynamic rather than static, as acts (or instruments) of knowing rather than objects known (except by a second, reflexive act):

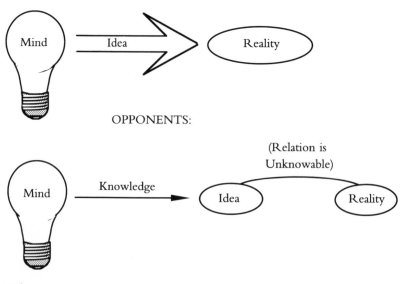

ST. THOMAS:

Mind — Idea → Reality

OPPONENTS:

Mind — Knowledge → Idea   Reality

(Relation is Unknowable)

Thus the intelligible species is that which is understood secondarily; but that which is primarily understood is the object, of which the species is the likeness. . . .

Reply Obj. 2. In these words *the thing actually understood* there is a double implication: the thing which is understood, and the fact that it is understood. In like manner the words *abstract universal* imply two things, the nature of a thing and its abstraction or universality. Therefore the nature itself to which it occurs to be understood, abstracted, or considered as universal, is only in individuals; but that it is understood, abstracted, or considered as universal, is in the intellect. We see something similar to this in the senses. For the sight sees the color of the apple apart from its smell. If therefore it be asked where is the color which is seen apart from the smell, it is quite clear that the color which is seen is only in the apple: but that it be perceived apart from the smell, this is owing to the sight, forasmuch as the faculty of sight receives the likeness of color and not of smell. In like manner humanity understood is only in this or that man; but that humanity be apprehended without conditions of individuality, that is, that it be abstracted and consequently considered as universal, occurs to humanity inasmuch as it is brought under the consideration of the intellect.[89] . . .

Whether Our Intellect Understands by Composition and Division?[90]

I answer that, The human intellect must of necessity understand by composition and division. For since the intellect passes from

---

[89] "Appleness" exists only in individual apples. But the intellect can abstract, or focus on the form alone *without the matter*; thus the form *as known* is universal (for *matter* is what individuates form). Universality is in the mind, not in the world.

[90] I.e., by *judgments*, not just concepts. "Composition" means affirmative judgments, joining (composing) subject and predicate (e.g., "Socrates is a man"); "division" means negative judgments, separating subject and predicate ("Socrates is not a dog").

potentiality to act, it has a likeness to things which are generated, which do not attain to perfection all at once but acquire it by degrees: so likewise the human intellect does not acquire perfect knowledge by the first act of apprehension; but it first apprehends something about its object, such as its quiddity, and this is its first and proper object; and then it understands the properties, accidents, and the various relations of the essence. Thus it necessarily compares one thing with another by composition or division; and from one composition and division it proceeds to another, which is the process of reasoning.[91]

But the angelic and the Divine intellect, like all incorruptible things, have their perfection at once from the beginning. Hence the angelic and the Divine intellect have the entire knowledge of a thing at once and perfectly; and hence also in knowing the quiddity of a thing they know at once whatever we can know by composition, division, and reasoning. Therefore the human intellect knows by composition, division, and reasoning. But the Divine and the angelic intellect know, indeed, composition, division, and reasoning, not by the process itself, but by understanding the simple essence. . . .

SIXTH ARTICLE

Whether the Intellect Can be False?

Objection 1. It would seem that the intellect can be false; for the Philosopher says (*Metaph.* vi, Did. v. 4) that *truth and falsehood are in*

---

[91] Thus "the three acts of the mind" are (1) understanding a quiddity, form, essence, nature, or "whatness" (e.g., redness, or justice) by "simple apprehension" (which is not yet either true or false); (2) judgment, composing or dividing two such concepts (judgments alone are either true or false); and (3) reasoning, proceeding from one judgment as premise to another as conclusion. Acts of reasoning are not either true or false; they are logically valid (if the conclusion necessarily follows from the premises) or invalid (if it does not).

St. Thomas' point here is that it is proper to man to progress to truth in stages, *through* conceiving and reasoning *to* the knowledge of the truth of a judgment; while the angels and God know intuitively and immediately, at once, not through this temporal process.

the mind. But the mind and intellect are the same, as is shown above (Q. 79, A. 1). Therefore falsehood may be in the mind. . . .

On the contrary, Augustine says (QQ. 83, *qu.* 32), that *everyone who is deceived, does not rightly understand that wherein he is deceived.* And the Philosopher says (*De Anima* iii. 10), that *the intellect is always true.* [92]

I answer that, . . . every faculty, as such, is *per se* directed to its proper object. . . . Hence, so long as the faculty exists, its judgment concerning its own proper object does not fail. Now the proper object of the intellect is the *quiddity* of a material thing; and hence, properly speaking, the intellect is not at fault concerning this quiddity; whereas it may go astray as regards the surroundings of the thing . . . , in referring one thing to another, as regards composition or division, or also in the process of reasoning. . . . Also in regard to those propositions, which are understood as soon as the terms thereof are understood, the intellect cannot err, as in the case of first principles from which arises infallible truth. . . .

The intellect, however, may be accidentally deceived in the quiddity of composite things, not by the defect of its organ, for the intellect is a faculty that is independent of an organ; but on the part of the composition affecting the definition, when, for instance, the definition of a thing is false in relation to something else, as the definition of a circle applied to a triangle; [93] or when a definition is false in itself [94] as involving the composition of things incompatible; as, for instance, to describe anything as *a rational winged animal.* Hence as regards simple objects not subject to composite definitions we cannot be deceived unless, indeed, we understand nothing whatever about them, as is said *Metaph.* ix. (Did. viii. 10).

Reply Obj. 1. The Philosopher says that falsehood is in the intellect in regard to composition and division. . . . But in the

---

[92] St. Thomas does not mean that there are no false judgments or opinions in our intellect, but that there are no "false forms", or *false concepts.* The intellect either does not understand a form, or it does understand it. Not understanding it is ignorance, not falsehood. Falsehood appears only in judgment. (And even among judgments, some *cannot* be false or deceive us, viz., "first principles", self-evident truths like "$2 + 3 = 5$" or "there cannot be more in an effect than in its causes".)

[93] Definitions are propositions (x is y), therefore they can be false.

[94] I.e., self-contradictory.

absolute consideration of the quiddity of a thing, and of those things which are known thereby, the intellect is never deceived. . . .

SEVENTH ARTICLE

Whether One Person Can Understand One and the Same Thing Better Than Another Can?[95]

On the contrary, Experience shows that some understand more profoundly than do others; as one who carries a conclusion to its first principles and ultimate causes understands it better than the one who reduces it only to its proximate causes.

I answer that, A thing being understood more by one than by another may be taken in two senses. First, so that the word *more* be taken as determining the act of understanding as regards the thing understood; and thus, one cannot understand the same thing more than another, because to understand it otherwise than as it is, either better or worse, would entail being deceived, and such a one would not understand it, as Augustine argues (*loc. cit*). In another sense the word *more* can be taken as determining the act of understanding on the part of him who understands; and so one may understand the

---

[95] The conclusion of the last Article may seem much too dogmatic and overconfident: is our knowledge in the realm of the "first act of the mind" ("simple apprehension") *perfect*? No indeed; but the defect in our apprehension is not a lack of *truth* but either a lack of clarity and distinctness (if the concept is vague or confused) or a lack of depth, profundity, fullness, or adequacy. The latter lack is *always* present; St. Thomas goes so far as to say that we never fully understand the essence of anything, not even a flea.

This point is in contrast to Descartes, who at the beginning of his *Discourse on Method* maintains that "good sense", or reason, is equal in all men. However, Descartes there redefines "reason" to mean only reaso*n*ing (the third act of the mind) and not understanding (the first act of the mind). Obviously, we all have the same logic software in our mental computers; but we do not have the same understanding of our data. (Computers, by the way, have *no* understanding of their data at all, any more than books do; they just store it, retrieve it, and relate it logically to other data.)

same thing better than someone else, through having a greater power of understanding: just as a man may see a thing better with his bodily sight, whose power is greater, and whose sight is more perfect. The same applies to the intellect in two ways. First, as regards the intellect itself, which is more perfect. For it is plain that the better the disposition of a body, the better the soul allotted to it; which clearly appears in things of different species: and the reason thereof is that act and form are received into matter according to matter's capacity: thus because some men have bodies of better disposition, their souls have a greater power of understanding, wherefore it is said (*De Anima* ii. 9), that *it is to be observed that those who have soft flesh are of apt mind.* [96] Secondly, this occurs in regard to the lower powers of which the intellect has need in its operation: for those in whom the imaginative, cogitative and memorative powers are of better disposition, are better disposed to understand. [97] . . .

---

[96] This is certainly not meant as a racist or discriminatory judgment, only as a sense observation. It may be argued that the reason why people with coarse flesh have coarse minds is merely the accidental circumstance that they have calluses from hard manual labor which has given them no leisure for education. Yet the principle of psychosomatic unity would seem to lend some credence to St. Thomas' explanation for the correlation between sensitive flesh and sensitive mind (and, as a corollary, between their absences). In any case, the issue is peripheral, not crucial.

[97] This is the philosophical basis for the Montessori method of early childhood education; training our senses, imagination, and memory aids the later training of the intellect. (Plato had already discovered this, in the *Republic*.)

Question 86

What Our Intellect Knows
in Material Things

FIRST ARTICLE

Whether Our Intellect Knows Singulars?

On the contrary, The Philosopher says (*Phys.* i. 5), that *the universal is known by reason; and the singular is known by sense.*

I answer that, Our intellect cannot know the singular in material things directly and primarily. The reason of this is that the principle of singularity in material things is individual matter, whereas our intellect, as we have said above (Q. 85, A. 1), understands by abstracting the intelligible species from such matter. Now what is abstracted from individual matter is the universal. Hence our intellect knows directly the universal only. But indirectly, and as it were by a kind of reflection, it can know the singular, because, as we have said above (Q. 85, A. 7), even after abstracting the intelligible species, the intellect, in order to understand, needs to turn to the phantasms in which it understands the species, as is said *De Anima* iii. 7. Therefore it understands the universal directly through the intelligible species, and indirectly the singular represented by the phantasm. And thus it forms the proposition, *Socrates is a man.* . . .

SECOND ARTICLE

Whether Our Intellect Can Know the Infinite?

Objection 1. It would seem that our intellect can know the infinite. For God excels all infinite things. But our intellect can know God, as we have said above (Q. 12, A. 1). Much more, therefore, can our intellect know all other infinite things. . . .

I answer that, Since a faculty and its object are proportional to each other, the intellect must be related to the infinite, as is its object, which is the quiddity of a material thing. Now in material things the infinite does not exist actually, but only potentially, in the sense of one succeeding another, as is said *Phys.* iii. 6. Therefore infinity is potentially in our mind through its considering successively one thing after another: because never does our intellect understand so many things, that it cannot understand more. . . .

Reply Obj. 1. As we have said above (Q. 7, A. 1), God is called infinite, because He is a form unlimited by matter; whereas in material things, the term *infinite* is applied to that which is deprived of any formal term.[98] . . .

---

[98] E.g., the number series, or space, or time—you can always add more. God is *actually* infinite, complete; infinity in matter (and also in the human intellect, which is proportioned to material things as its natural object) is only potential, deprived of its term, or end (viz., actual, completed infinity).

Question 87

How the Intellectual Soul
Knows Itself and All Within Itself

THIRD ARTICLE

Whether Our Intellect Knows Its Own Act?

Objection 1. It would seem that our intellect does not know its own act. For what is known is the object of the knowing faculty. But the act differs from the object. Therefore the intellect does not know its own act.

Objection 2. Further, whatever is known is known by some act. If, then, the intellect knows its own act, it knows it by some act, and again it knows that act by some other act; this is to proceed indefinitely, which seems impossible. . . .

I answer that, . . . there is an intellect, namely, the Divine, which is Its own act of intelligence; so that in God the understanding of His intelligence, and the understanding of His Essence, are one and the same act, because His Essence is His act of understanding. But there is another intellect, the angelic, which is not its own act of understanding, as we have said above (Q. 79, A. 1), and yet the first object of that act is the angelic essence. . . . And there is yet another, namely, the human intellect, which neither is its own act of understanding, nor is its own essence the first object of its act of understanding, for this object is the nature of a material thing. And therefore that which is first known by the human intellect is an object of this kind, and that which is known secondarily is the act by which that object is known; and through the act the intellect itself is known.[99] . . .

---

[99] Contrary to Descartes, who puts the mind's knowledge of itself first, St. Thomas puts it third, after (1) the knowledge of a material thing and

Reply Obj. 1. The object of the intellect is something universal, namely, *being* and *the true*, in which the act also of understanding is comprised. Wherefore the intellect can understand its own act. But not primarily, since the first object of our intellect, in this state of life, is not every being and everything true, but *being* and *true*, as considered in material things, as we have said above (Q. 84, A. 7), from which it acquires knowledge of all other things.

Reply Obj. 2. . . . The act whereby the intellect understands a stone is distinct from the act whereby it understands that it understands a stone; and so on. Nor is there any difficulty in the intellect being thus potentially infinite, as explained above (Q. 86, A. 2). . . .

---

(2) the reflective knowledge of its own act of knowing a material thing. First I know a tree, then I know that I knew a tree, then I know I am a knower. We know nature before we know ourselves. Angels know themselves before they know nature. Descartes asks us to think angelistically.

Question 88

How the Human Soul Knows
What Is above Itself

*Whether the Human Soul in the Present State of Life
Can Understand Immaterial Substances in Themselves?*

I answer that, In the opinion of Plato, immaterial substances are
not only understood by us, but are the objects we understand first
of all. For Plato taught that immaterial subsisting forms, which he
called *Ideas*, are the proper objects of our intellect, and are thus first
and *per se* understood by us; and, further, that material objects are
known by the soul inasmuch as phantasy and sense are mixed up
with the mind. Hence the purer the intellect is, so much the more
clearly does it perceive the intelligible truth of immaterial things.

But in Aristotle's opinion, which experience corroborates, our
intellect in its present state of life has a natural relationship to the
natures of material things; and therefore it can only understand by
turning to the phantasms, as we have said above (Q. 84, A. 7).
Thus it clearly appears that immaterial substances which do not fall
under sense and imagination, cannot first and *per se* be known by
us, according to the mode of knowledge which experience proves
us to have. . . .

THIRD ARTICLE

Whether God Is the First Object Known by the Human Mind?

Objection 1. It would seem that God is the first object known by
the human mind. For that object in which all others are known, and
by which we judge others, is the first thing known to us; as light is

to the eye, and first principles to the intellect. But we know all things in the light of the first truth, and thereby judge of all things, as Augustine says (*De Trin.* xii. 2; *De Vera Rel.* xxxi). Therefore God is the first object known to us. . . .

On the contrary, No man hath seen God at any time (Jn 1:18).

I answer that, Since the human intellect in the present state of life cannot understand even immaterial created substances [angels], much less can it understand the essence of the uncreated substance. Hence it must be said simply that God is not the first object of our knowledge. Rather do we know God through creatures, according to the Apostle (Rom 1:20), *the invisible things of God are clearly seen, being understood by the things that are made:* while the first object of our knowledge in this life is the *quiddity of a material thing*, which is the proper object of our intellect, as appears above in many passages (Q. 84, A. 7; Q. 85, A. 8; Q. 87, A. 2, *ad* 2).

Reply Obj. 1. We see and judge of all things in the light of the first truth, forasmuch as the light itself of our mind, whether natural or gratuitous, is nothing else than the impression of the first truth upon it, as stated above, (Q. 12, A. 2). Hence, as the light itself of our intellect is not the object it understands, but the medium whereby it understands, much less can it be said that God is the first object known by our intellect. . . .

Question 89

Of the Knowledge of the Separated Soul

Whether the Separated Soul Can Understand Anything?

On the contrary, The Philosopher says (*De Anima* i. 1), *If the soul had no proper operation, it could not be separated from the body.* But the soul is separated from the body;[100] therefore it has a proper operation, and above all, that which consists in intelligence. Therefore the soul can understand when it is apart from the body. . . .

---

[100] After the death of the body. Many cases of near-death experiences and out-of-body experiences have confirmed St. Thomas' point here.

Question 90

Of the First Production of Man's Soul

FIRST ARTICLE

Whether the Soul Was Made or Was of God's Substance?

Objection 1. It would seem that the soul was not made, but was God's substance.[101] For it is written (Gen 2:7): *God formed man of the slime of the earth, and breathed into his face the breath of life, and man was made a living soul.* But he who breathes sends forth something of himself. Therefore the soul, whereby man lives, is of the Divine substance. . . .

On the contrary, Augustine (*De Orig. Animae* iii. 15) mentions certain opinions which he calls *exceedingly and evidently perverse, and contrary to the Catholic Faith*, among which the first is the opinion that *God made the soul not out of nothing, but from Himself.*

I answer that, To say that the soul is of the Divine substance involves a manifest improbability. For, as is clear from what has been said (Q. 77, A. 2; Q. 79, A. 2; Q. 84, A. 6), the human soul is sometimes in a state of potentiality to the act of intelligence, acquires its knowledge somehow from things, and has various

---

[101] This is the essential difference between theism and pantheism, between Western and Eastern religions. According to Christianity, Judaism, and Islam, souls are created by God, really distinct from Him and from each other. According to Hinduism and Buddhism, either there is no human soul (Buddha's *anatta* ["no-soul"] doctrine) or all soul is one (*Atman*) and substantially one with Brahman, or God ("*Tat tvam asi*", "Thou art that"). The popular version of this idea in the modern West is that we are all "sparks of the divine fire" or "drops of the divine sea". This idea is often confused with Christianity. Note the adjectives St. Thomas uses to describe this idea in the "*On the contrary*".

powers; all of which are incompatible with the Divine Nature,[102] Which is a pure act, receives nothing from any other, and admits of no variety in itself, as we have proved (Q. 3, AA. 1, 7; Q. 9, A. 1).

This error seems to have originated from two statements of the ancients. For those who first began to observe the nature of things, being unable to rise above their imagination, supposed that nothing but bodies existed. Therefore they said that God was a body,[103] which they considered to be the principle of other bodies. And since they held that the soul was of the same nature as that body which they regarded as the first principle, as is stated in *De Anima* i. 2, it followed that the soul was of the nature of God Himself. According to this supposition, also, the Manichaeans, thinking that God was a corporeal light, held that the soul was part of that light bound up with the body.

Then a further step in advance was made,[104] and some surmised the existence of something incorporeal, not apart from the body, but the form of a body; so that Varro said, *God is a soul governing the world by movement and reason*, as Augustine relates (*De Civ. Dei* vii. 6). So some supposed man's soul to be part of that one soul, as man is a part of the whole world; for they were unable to go so far as to understand the different degrees of spiritual substance, except according to the distinction of bodies.

But, all these theories are impossible, as proved above (Q. 3, AA. 1, 8; and Q. 75, A. 1), wherefore it is evidently false that the soul is of the substance of God.

Reply Obj. 1. The term "breathe" is not to be taken in the material sense; but as regards the act of God, to breathe (*spirare*), is

---

[102] Our potentiality and process and temporality and (at least temporary) ignorance refutes pantheism. The pantheist mystic who believes we are all part of God has never been able to explain why God seems so ignorant of His own identity. He can only call this God's little game, or play (*lila* in Hinduism).

[103] St. Thomas smokes out the root of pantheism: materialistic thinking, as if God were a whole, spread out in space—a fire, a sea, a light, a "stuff"—of which souls could be "parts".

[104] Modern Westerners sometimes think pantheism is the latest stage in progress and enlightenment and sophistication; in fact, historically it is the most primitive and crude state, a regression.

the same as to *make a spirit*. Moreover, in the material sense, man by breathing does not send forth anything of his own substance, but an extraneous thing. . . .

SECOND ARTICLE

Whether the Soul Was Produced by Creation?

On the contrary, It is written (Gen 1:27): *God created man to His own image.* But man is like to God in his soul. Therefore the soul was created.

I answer that, The rational soul can be made only by creation; which, however, is not true of other forms.[105] The reason is because, since to be made is the way to existence, a thing must be made in such a way as is suitable to its mode of existence. Now that properly exists which itself has existence; as it were, subsisting in its own existence. Wherefore only substances are properly and truly called beings; whereas an accident has not existence, but something is [modified] by it, and so far is it called a being; for instance, whiteness is called a being, because by it something is white. Hence it is said in *Metaph.* vii (Did. vi. 1) that an accident should be described as *of something rather than as something.* The same is to be said of all nonsubsistent forms. Therefore, properly speaking, it does not belong to any non-existing form to be made; but such are said to be made through the composite substances being made. On the other hand, the rational soul is a subsistent form, as above explained (Q. 75, A. 2). Wherefore it is competent to be and to be made. And since it cannot be made of pre-existing matter, . . . we must conclude that it cannot exist except by creation. . . .

---

[105] N.b.: St. Thomas is saying here that even though other forms (species) could come into existence by generation (*or* evolution?), souls cannot. Parents generate their children's bodies, but not their souls. Nature *may* evolve new species, but not new souls.

THIRD ARTICLE

Whether the Rational Soul Is Produced by God Immediately?

I answer that, Some have held that angels, acting by the power of God, produce rational souls. But this is quite impossible, and is against faith. For it has been proved that the rational soul cannot be produced except by creation. Now, God alone can create. . . .

Question 93

The End or Term of
the Production of Man

Whether the Image of God Is in Man?

On the contrary, It is written (Gen 1:26): *Let Us make man to Our own image and likeness.*

I answer that, As Augustine says (QQ. 83; qu. 74): *Where an image exists, there forthwith is likeness; but where there is likeness, there is not necessarily an image.* Hence it is clear that likeness is essential to an image; and that an image adds something to likeness —namely, that it is copied from something else. For an *image* is so called because it is produced as an imitation of something else; wherefore, for instance, an egg, however much like and equal to another egg, is not called an image of the other egg, because it is not copied from it.

But equality does not belong to the essence of an image; for as Augustine says (*ibid.*): *Where there is an image there is not necessarily equality*, as we see in a person's image reflected in a glass. Yet this is of the essence of a perfect image; for in a perfect image nothing is wanting that is to be found in that of which it is a copy. Now it is manifest that in man there is some likeness to God, copied from God as from an exemplar; yet this likeness is not one of equality, for such an exemplar infinitely excels its copy. Therefore there is in man a likeness to God; not, indeed, a perfect likeness, but imperfect. And Scripture implies the same when it says that man was made *to* God's likeness; for the preposition *to* signifies a certain approach, as of something at a distance. . . .

SECOND ARTICLE

Whether the Image of God Is to Be Found
in Irrational Creatures?

On the contrary, Augustine says (*Gen. ad lit.* vi. 12): *Man's excellence consists in the fact that God made him to His own image by giving him an intellectual soul, which raises him above the beasts of the field.* Therefore things without intellect are not made to God's image.

I answer that, Not every likeness, not even what is copied from something else, is sufficient to make an image. . . .

. . . Some things are like to God first and most commonly because they exist; secondly, because they live; and thirdly because they know or understand; and these last, as Augustine says (QQ. 83; qu. 51), *approach so near to God in likeness, that among all creatures nothing comes nearer to Him.* It is clear, therefore, that intellectual creatures alone, properly speaking, are made to God's image. . . .

SEVEN

Ethics

FIRST PART OF
THE SECOND PART
Treatise on the Last End

A. Happiness

Question 1

Of Man's Last End[1]

In this matter we shall consider first the last[2] end of human life; and secondly, those things by means of which man may advance towards this end, or stray from the path: for the end is the rule of whatever is ordained to the end. And since the last end of human life is stated to be happiness,[3] we must consider (1) the last end in general; (2) Happiness. . . .

FIRST ARTICLE

Whether It Belongs to Man to Act for an End?

Objection 1. It would seem that it does not belong to man to act for an end. For a cause is naturally first. But an end, in its very name, implies something that is last. Therefore an end is not a cause. But that for which a man acts, is the cause of his action; since this preposition *for* indicates a relation of causality. Therefore it does not belong to man to act for an end. . . .

---

[1] Note the two related but distinct meanings of "end": (1) goal, good, purpose, object-of-desire (*telos*); and (2) term, conclusion, cessation, last-in-time, finish (*finis*). St. Thomas means "end" here in sense (1), for our "last" end is the determinate direction and orientation of all of our life at every moment, not just at the last moment. We love God in life, not just in death.

[2] The *last* end is considered *first* because it determines everything else in life and everything else in the moral science of life. "The end is the rule of whatever is ordained to the end."

[3] "Happiness" (*eudaimonia* in Greek, *felicitas* in Latin) means not merely subjective contentment, or rest of desire, but also real blessedness, the state of possessing the objective good for man. It is contentment, but

I answer that, Of actions done by man those alone are properly called *human*, which are proper[4] to man as man. Now man differs from irrational animals in this, that he is master of his actions. Wherefore those actions alone are properly called human, of which man is master. Now man is master of his actions through his reason and will; whence, too, the free-will is defined as *the faculty and will of reason.* Therefore those actions are properly called human which proceed from a deliberate will. And if any other actions are found in man, they can be called actions *of a man*, but not properly *human* actions, since they are not proper to man as man.—Now it is clear that whatever actions proceed from a power, are caused by that power in accordance with the nature of its object. But the object of the will is the end and the good. Therefore all human actions must be for an end.

Reply Obj. 1. Although the end be last in the order of execution, yet it is first in the order of the agent's intention. And it is this way that it is a cause. . . .

---

contentment in the true good. Like bodily health, it has both a subjective and an objective aspect. The word "happiness" in English usually connotes only subjective satisfaction. Moreover, it connotes something dependent on fortune, or chance ("hap"), something that just "happens", like falling in love, rather than something we work at, like charity.

"The last end of human life is stated to be happiness" because all seek it, and seek it as an end, not as a means to any further end, while they seek all other things as means to this end. No one seeks happiness in order to be rich, or powerful, or wise, but people seek riches, or power, or wisdom because they think these will make them happy, in either the subjective sense or in the objective sense (see above).

[4] *Logically* "proper"—specific, unique—not *morally* "proper" (right). St. Thomas distinguishes a "human act" (*actus humanus*) from an "act of man" (*actus hominis*). A "human act" is specifically human in quality (e.g., reasoning or choosing); the "acts of a man" also include things like sleeping and growing.

SECOND ARTICLE

Whether It Is Proper to the Rational Nature [Alone]
to Act for an End?

On the contrary, The Philosopher proves (*Phys.* ii. 5) that *not only mind but also nature acts for an end.*[5]

I answer that, Every agent, of necessity, acts for an end. For if, in a number of causes ordained to one another, the first be removed, the others must, of necessity, be removed also. Now the first of all causes is the final cause. The reason of which is that matter does not receive form, save in so far as it is moved by an agent; for nothing reduces itself from potentiality to act. But an agent does not move except out of intention[6] for an end. For if the agent were not determinate to some particular effect, it would not do one thing rather than another: consequently in order that it produce a deter-

---

[5] St. Thomas is not saying that nature is in some way conscious. It has no "order of intention". But it does have an "order of execution". Puppies always become dogs, and dogs always have puppies. Heavy bodies on earth always tend to fall, and heat always tends to flow from greater to lesser concentration. There is nothing complex, mysterious, or mystical about the traditional view that nature acts for an end, that there is in nature not only random chance pushing but purposive order pulling from the end, so to speak. It was universal common sense until the seventeenth century and mechanistic physics.

[6] "Intention", like "certitude", is a word which has come to have an exclusively psychological meaning. Just as "certitude" used to mean any determination or definiteness, rational or not, so "intention" meant simply determination to a specific end, conscious or not. St. Thomas' argument is from the order within the four causes: matter needs form to be part of an actual substance; the formal cause needs an efficient cause to move it to inform matter; and an efficient cause needs a final cause to move it to one end rather than another. The reason for this last point is very simple: see the next sentence after the footnote. The argument assumes only the commonsensical "principle of sufficient reason": that there is always a real reason, a real and adequate "why" for everything, including repeated movement to a definite end (stars shine, rabbits reproduce, stones fall, grass grows). Of course efficient causes "push" things, but why do they "push" them *toward determinate ends?*

minate effect, it must, of necessity, be determined to some certain one, which has the nature of an end. And just as this determination is effected, in the rational nature, by the *rational appetite*, which is called the will; so, in other things, it is caused by their natural inclination, which is called the *natural appetite*.[7]

Nevertheless it must be observed that a thing tends to an end, by its action or movement, in two ways: first, as a thing, moving itself to the end,—as man; secondly, as a thing moved by another to the end, as an arrow tends to a determinate end through being moved by the archer, who directs his action to the end. Therefore those things that are possessed of reason, move themselves to an end; because they have dominion over their actions through their free-will, which is the *faculty of will and reason*. But those things that lack reason tend to an end, by natural inclination, as being moved by another and not by themselves; since they do not know the nature of an end as such, and consequently cannot ordain anything to an end, but can be ordained to an end only by another. For the entire irrational nature is in comparison to God as an instrument to the principal agent, as stated above (I. Q. 22, A. 2 *ad* 4; Q. 103, A. 1 *ad* 3).[8] Consequently it is proper to the rational nature to tend to an end, as directing (*agens*) and leading itself to the end: whereas it is proper to the irrational nature to tend to an end, as directed or led by another, whether it apprehend the end, as do irrational animals, or do not apprehend it, as is the case of those things which are altogether void of knowledge.[9] . . .

---

[7] "Appetite" is another word that has narrowed in meaning. For St. Thomas it does not necessarily connote consciousness. Gravity, for instance, is a natural "appetite", but without consciousness. There is obviously an analogy between gravity (unconscious attraction) and love (conscious attraction): cf. the last line of *The Divine Comedy*: "the love that moves the sun and all the stars".

[8] Cf. the fifth "way" in I, 2, 3.

[9] Man knows the good rationally and in general, and therefore has free will to choose among particular goods. Animals know what is good for them in particular (e.g., their food) but do not freely choose it. They cannot will otherwise, against their instincts or natural inclinations: dogs do not fast. Unconscious nature does not know anything, yet it too works in a determinate way toward determinate ends: plants flower, stones fall, neither flies.

THIRD ARTICLE

Whether Human Acts Are Specified[10] *by Their End?*

Objection 1. It would seem that human acts are not specified by their end. For the end is an extrinsic cause. But everything is specified by an intrinsic principle. Therefore human acts are not specified by their end. . . .

On the contrary, Augustine says (*De Mor. Eccl. et Manich.* ii. 13): *According as their end is worthy of blame or praise so are our deeds worthy of blame or praise.*

I answer that, . . . acts are called human, inasmuch as they proceed from a deliberate will. Now the object of the will is the good and the end. And hence it is clear that the principle of human acts, in so far as they are human, is the end. . . . And since, as Ambrose says (*Prolog. super Luc.*), *morality is said properly of man,* moral acts properly speaking receive their species from the end, for moral acts are the same as human acts.

Reply Obj. 1. The end is not altogether extrinsic to the act, because it is related to the act as principle or terminus; and it is just this that is essential to an act, viz., to proceed from something . . . and to proceed towards something.[11] . . .

---

[10] I.e., morally specified, as good or evil. St. Thomas' thesis is not self-evident. Kant, for example, denies that an act's moral worth or goodness comes from its end; he claims it comes only from the actor's intention, or motive. St. Thomas is not saying that human (voluntary, moral) acts are specified *only* by their end; he will mention three (really four) distinct moral determinants in Question 18.

[11] N.b.: the end (*telos*) is not just the last point (*finis*). The last point on a line is not present to all the other points on the line, but the last end (*telos*) of a journey (e.g., home) is present to every step of the journey as its determining, guiding principle, making it this journey rather than that, i.e., a journey *home* rather than somewhere else.

This is also true of death: it is not only extrinsic and future but also intrinsic and present to our life now, which is a "being-towards-death" (Heidegger only develops the idea already latent in St. Thomas' teleology).

FOURTH ARTICLE

Whether There Is One Last End of Human Life? [12]

On the contrary, The Philosopher says (*Metaph.* ii. 2) that *to suppose a thing to be indefinite is to deny that it is good.* [13] But the good is that which has the nature of an end. Therefore it is contrary to the nature of an end to proceed indefinitely. Therefore it is necessary to fix one last end.

I answer that, Absolutely speaking, it is not possible to proceed indefinitely in the matter of ends, from any point of view. [14] For in whatsoever things there is an essential order of one to another, if the first be removed, those that are ordained to the first, must of necessity be removed also. Wherefore the Philosopher proves (*Phys.* viii. 5) that we cannot proceed to infinitude in causes of movement, because then there would be no first mover, without which neither can the others move, since they move only through being moved by the first mover. Now there is to be observed a twofold order in ends,—the order of intention, and the order of execution: and in either of these orders there must be something first. For that which is first in the order of intention, is the principle,

---

[12] The great classical question of the *summum bonum*—what *is* the last end of human life?—presupposes that there is one, that ends are really arranged in a hierarchy. It is this assumption that the modern mind tends to question; it questions St. Thomas' affirmative answer to this question before it questions his answer to the question whether the *summum bonum* is God.

[13] N.b.: St. Thomas does not say *infinity* is incompatible with goodness but that *indefiniteness* is. God is infinite (and good) but not indefinite. The god of pantheism is indefinite and therefore not definitely good as vs. evil. He (or rather, it) is both good and evil, or neither good nor evil, or "beyond good and evil".

[14] Parallel to the argument for the existence of a First, uncaused Cause in the order of efficient causality (I, 2, 3, second "way"), we have the argument in the order of final causality: second (caused) causes necessitate a first (uncaused) cause here too, and "first final cause" means "last end".

Because "second" means "dependent on, or ordered to, the first", order is necessarily hierarchical. Insofar as A is ordered to B, A is for B and teleologically dependent on B. Thus without the end (B), there is no means (A), for "the means" *means* "the means *to the end*".

as it were, moving the appetite; consequently, if you remove this principle, there will be nothing to move the appetite.[15] . . . Now the principle in the intention is the last end. . . . Consequently, . . . if there were no last end, nothing would be desired. . . .

FIFTH ARTICLE

Whether One Man Can Have Several Last Ends?

On the contrary, That in which a man rests as in his last end, is master of his affections, since he takes therefrom his entire rule of life. Hence of gluttons it is written (Phil 3:19): *Whose god is their belly*: viz., because they place their last end in the pleasures of the belly. Now according to Matthew 6:24, *No man can serve two masters*, such, namely, as are not ordained to one another. Therefore it is impossible for one man to have several last ends not ordained to one another.

I answer that, It is impossible for one man's will to be directed at the same time to diverse things, as last ends. . . . Because, since everything desires its own perfection, a man desires for his ultimate end, that which he desires as his perfect and crowning good. Hence Augustine (*De Civ. Dei* xix. 1): *In speaking of the end of good we mean now, not that it passes away so as to be no more, but that it is perfected so as to be complete.* It is therefore necessary for the last end so to fill man's appetite, that nothing is left besides it for man to desire. Which is not possible, if something else be required for his perfection. Consequently it is not possible for the appetite so to tend to two things, as though each were its perfect good. . . .

. . . Therefore, just as of all men there is naturally one last end, so the will of an individual man must be fixed on one last end.[16] . . .

---

[15] Cf. Teilhard de Chardin in *The Divine Milieu*: "The more I consider the matter, the more I see that no one would move his little finger unless motivated, however obscurely, that he was building something definitive: Your kingdom, Lord."

[16] What is true of all men must be true of each man, and what is true objectively and universally ("there *is* one last end") must be true subjectively and individually ("the will of an individual man must be fixed on one last end"). Free choice does not extend to violating the necessary metaphysical principles of our very essence.

Whether Man Wills All, Whatsoever He Wills, for the Last End?

Objection 1. It would seem that man does not will all, what-soever he wills, for the last end. For things ordained to the last end are said to be serious matter, as being useful. But jests are foreign to serious matter. Therefore what man does in jest, he ordains not to the last end.

Objection 2. Further, the Philosopher says at the beginning of his *Metaphysics* (i. 2) that speculative science is sought for its own sake. Now it cannot be said that each speculative science is the last end. Therefore man does not desire all, whatsoever he desires, for the last end.

Objection 3. Further, whoever ordains something to an end, thinks of that end. But man does not always think of the last end in all that he desires or does. Therefore man neither desires nor does all for the last end.

On the contrary, Augustine says (*De Civ. Dei* xix. 1): *That is the end of our good, for the sake of which we love other things, whereas we love it for its own sake.*

I answer that, Man must, of necessity, desire all, whatsoever he desires, for the last end. This is evident for two reasons. First, because whatever man desires, he desires it under the aspect of good. And if he desire it, not as his perfect good, which is the last end, he must, of necessity, desire it as tending to the perfect good, because the beginning of anything is always ordained[17] to its completion; as is clearly the case in effects both of nature and of art. Wherefore every beginning of perfection is ordained to complete perfection which is achieved through [attaining] the last end. Secondly, because the last end stands in the same relation in moving the appetite, as the first mover in other movements. Now it is clear that secondary moving causes do not move save inasmuch as they are moved by the first mover. Therefore secondary objects

---

[17] That is, in objective fact, though not necessarily in subjective, conscious intention. (The point of Objection 3 is true.)

of the appetite do not move the appetite, except as ordained to the first object of the appetite, which is the last end.[18]

Reply Obj. 1. Actions done jestingly are not directed to any external end; but merely to the good of the jester,[19] in so far as they afford him pleasure or relaxation. But man's consummate good is his last end.

Reply Obj. 2. The same applies to speculative science; which is desired as the scientist's good, included in complete and perfect good, which is the ultimate end.[20]

Reply Obj. 3. One need not always be thinking of the last end, whenever one desires or does something: but the virtue of the first intention, which was in respect of the last end, remains in every desire directed to any object whatever,[21] even though one's thoughts be not actually directed to the last end. Thus while walking along the road one needs not to be thinking of the end at every step.

---

[18] The point is commonsensical: we would not put one foot in front of the other unless we wanted to go somewhere.

[19] Wit is a virtue for St. Thomas: "Jokes and plays are words and gestures that are not instructive but merely seek to give lively pleasure. We should enjoy them. They are governed by the virtue of witty gaiety to which Aristotle refers (*Ethics* 1128a1) and which we call pleasantness. A ready-witted man is quick with repartee and turns speech and action to light relief" (II–II, 148, 2). "It is against reason to be burdensome to others, showing no amusement and acting as a wet blanket. Those without a sense of fun, who never say anything ridiculous, and are cantankerous with those who do, these are vicious, and are called grumpy and rude" (II–II, 148, 4) (Thomas Gilby translation).

[20] The last end, our ultimate good (which St. Thomas will prove to be God in Question 2) is not *exclusive* of any natural and proper human good, but inclusive of them all. Cf. Augustine, *Confessions* II, 6, par. 2; Anselm, *Proslogion*, last three chapters.

[21] *How* is the "virtue" (efficacy) of the intention of the last end "in" every desire? ("In" is perhaps the richest word there is, with the most different meanings.) Not merely potentially, but not actually either (certainly not *consciously*). Dietrich von Hildebrand calls this the "super-actual". Karl Rahner calls it the heart's "fundamental option" or orientation.

SEVENTH ARTICLE

Whether All Men Have the Same Last End?

Objection 1. It would seem that all men have not the same last end. For before all else the unchangeable good seems to be the last end of man. But some turn away from the unchangeable good, by sinning. Therefore all men have not the same last end.

Objection 2. Further, man's entire life is ruled according to his last end. If, therefore, all men had the same last end, they would not have various pursuits in life. Which is evidently false.[22]

Objection 3. Further, the end is the term of action. But actions are of individuals. Now although men agree in their specific nature, yet they differ in things pertaining to individuals. Therefore all men have not the same last end.

On the contrary, Augustine says (*De Trin.* xiii. 3) that all men agree in desiring the last end, which is happiness.

I answer that, We can speak of the last end in two ways: first, considering only the [formal] aspect of last end; secondly, considering the thing [content] in which the aspect of last end is realized. So, then, as to the aspect of last end, all agree in desiring the last end: since all desire the fulfilment of their perfection, and it is precisely this fulfilment in which the last end consists, as stated above (A. 5). But as to the thing in which this aspect is realized, all men are not agreed as to their last end: since some desire riches, as their consummate good; some, pleasure; others, something else. Thus to every taste the sweet is pleasant; but to some, the sweetness of wine is most pleasant, to others, the sweetness of honey, or of something similar. Yet that sweet is absolutely the best of all pleasant things, in which he who has the best taste takes most pleasure. In like manner that good is most complete which the man with well-disposed affections desires for his last end.[23]

---

[22] This objection can be interpreted as reflecting a typically modern "pluralism"—"different strokes for different folks"—extended even to a pluralism of last ends. The confusion is between *life* and life*style* ("various pursuits in life"), between end and means, between ultimate and proximate.

[23] Thus the good for man is (1) relative and different for different people with regard to its particular content (some desire riches, some wisdom,

Reply Obj. 1. Those who sin turn from that in which their last end really consists: but they do not turn away from the intention of the last end, which intention they mistakenly seek in other things.[24]

Reply Obj. 2. Various pursuits in life are found among men by reason of the various things in which men seek to find their last end.

Reply Obj. 3. Although actions are of individuals, yet their first principle of action is nature, which tends to one thing, as stated above (A. 5). . . .

---

etc.), (2) absolute and the same for all in its essential form (all desire happiness), and (3) absolute also with regard to the *right* content, what is truly best for all (God). St. Thomas would answer the typically modern relativist's challenge to (3)—"Who's to judge?"—by saying the wise man, with healthy desires, is the rightful judge. Therefore if your desires are not well ordered, you are not just as qualified to judge as he is, as you imply you are with your rhetorical question "Who's to judge?" (Cf. I–II, 2, 1, Reply 1).

[24] Cf. Augustine: "Seek what you seek, but it is not where you seek it." (*Confessions* IV, 12, par. 1). The intention to happiness, fulfillment, and perfection is universal, but the knowledge of where and what it is, is not.

Question 2

Of Those Things in Which Man's Happiness Consists[25]

FIRST ARTICLE

Whether Man's Happiness Consists in Wealth?

Objection 1. It would seem that man's happiness consists in wealth. For since happiness is man's last end, it must consist in that which has the greatest hold on man's affections. Now this is wealth: for it is written (Qo 10:19): *All things obey money.*[26] Therefore man's happiness consists in wealth.

Objection 2. Further, according to Boëthius (*De Consol.* iii), happiness is *a state of life made perfect by the aggregate of all good things.*

---

[25] This Question (2) is the most masterfully condensed summary of the basic answers which philosophers in their writings and people in their lives have always given to the most important question in life, the question of the *summum bonum*, the greatest good, final end, meaning and purpose of life. I have included an unusually large number of footnotes on this Question not because it is obscure but because it is crucially important. Moses, Solomon, Buddha, Krishna, Confucius, Lao-tzu, St. Paul, St. Augustine, Mohammed, Machiavelli, Hobbes, Bacon, Pascal, Kierkegaard, Nietzsche, Sartre, Marx—all sages and pseudo-sages answer this question, and their answer colors and determines the rest of their practical philosophy.

[26] The ancient version of "Everything has a price tag", or even "Every man has his price." N.b.: the arguments of all three objections are only clues; they find some feature common to the *summum bonum* and wealth. As demonstrations, they commit the fallacy of undistributed middle: the *summum bonum* is *x*, wealth is *x*, therefore wealth is the *summum bonum*. The same is true for most of the Objections in subsequent Articles in this Question.

Now money seems to be the means of possessing all things: for, as the Philosopher says (*Ethic.* v. 5), money was invented, that it might be a sort of guarantee for the acquisition of whatever man desires.[27] Therefore happiness consists in wealth.

Objection 3. Further, since the desire for the sovereign good never fails, it seems to be infinite. But this is the case with riches more than anything else; since *a covetous man shall not be satisfied with riches* (Qo 5:9). Therefore happiness consists in wealth.

On the contrary, Man's good consists in retaining happiness rather than in spreading it. But as Boëthius says (*De Consol.* ii), *wealth shines in giving rather than in hoarding: for the miser is hateful, whereas the generous man is applauded.* Therefore man's happiness does not consist in wealth.[28]

I answer that, It is impossible for man's happiness to consist in wealth. For wealth is twofold, as the Philosopher says (*Polit.* i. 3), viz., natural and artificial. Natural wealth is that which serves man as a remedy for his natural wants: such as food, drink, clothing, dwellings, and such like, while artificial wealth is that which is not a direct help to nature, as money, but is invented by the art of man, for the convenience of exchange, and as a measure of things salable.[29]

---

[27] I.e., money is like an umbrella, over everything. Money can buy anything money can buy. Since it is its universality that seems to qualify it as the *summum bonum*, St. Thomas' reply is that its very universality is deceptive. It can buy *only* "anything money can buy" (Reply 2); the umbrella is really too small.

[28] Money, unlike happiness, is good only when spent, not kept. N.b.: the arguments in the "*On the contrary*" sections are not *demonstrations* from cause to effect, but often from effect to cause. The real cause or reason why wealth is not the *summum bonum* is given in the "*I answer that*". The "*On the contrary*" only points to a clue to the fact that wealth is not happiness, but not the real reason or cause.

When St. Thomas says that happiness, unlike wealth, is good when possessed, not when spread, he does not mean that our happiness is not in fact increased when we make others happy, but that the essential meaning of "happiness" is the satisfaction of an individual's desires. These may and should include the desire to make others happy too.

[29] The simple and obvious distinction between natural wealth and artificial wealth (and between natural and artificial anything, such as sex,

Now it is evident that man's happiness cannot consist in natural wealth. For wealth of this kind is sought for the sake of something else, viz., as a support of human nature: consequently it cannot be man's last end, rather is it ordained to man as to its end. Wherefore in the order of nature, all such things are below man, and made for him, according to Psalm 8:8: *Thou hast subjected all things under his feet.*[30]

And as to artificial wealth, it is not sought save for the sake of natural wealth; since man would not seek it except because, by its means, he procures for himself the necessaries of life. Consequently much less can it be considered in the light of the last end.[31] Therefore it is impossible for happiness, which is the last end of man, to consist in wealth.

Reply Obj. 1. All material things obey money, so far as the

---

death, and birth control) is largely forgotten, in practice, in a capitalistic and industrial society. In a society like ours, which gives such prominence to artificial wealth, greed is a very great spiritual danger. For the desire for artificial wealth is unlimited, but the desire for natural wealth, however greedy, is always limited (Reply 3). There is never enough money, but there is often enough food. The good society would foster neither riches (of excess artificial wealth) nor poverty (of needed natural wealth).

[30] Man is an end, things (wealth) are means. For man to serve things is to reverse the order of reality. St. Thomas here assumes that man is an end, not a means. Yet he is not the final end. In Article 7, "*On the contrary*", he says that man is to be loved not for his own sake (as final end) but for God's sake. God is to be adored, man loved, and things used. Two of the commonest and deadliest errors are to adore man, or to use man and love things.

[31] This is a good example of the *a minore* argument: if natural wealth is not the *summum bonum* because it is a mere means, not an end, then how much less can artificial wealth be the *summum bonum*, since it is a mere means to this means (natural wealth).

N.b.: St. Thomas takes the candidates for the *summum bonum* in a deliberate order: from the most foolish and external to the least foolish and most internal. Wealth is the farthest of all from happiness, yet it is the most popular candidate for that exalted office (see Objection 1 and Reply). Pleasure is much closer, since it is at least a *property* of happiness, flowing from it (Article 6, "*I answer that*")—though this is not just bodily pleasure.

multitude of fools is concerned, who know no other than material goods, which can be obtained for money. But we should take our estimation of human goods not from the foolish but from the wise: just as it is for a person, whose sense of taste is in good order, to judge whether a thing is palatable.[32]

Reply Obj. 2. All things salable can be had for money: not so spiritual things, which cannot be sold. Hence it is written (Prov 17:16): *What doth it avail a fool to have riches, seeing he cannot buy wisdom.*

Reply Obj. 3. The desire for natural riches is not infinite: because they suffice for nature in a certain measure. But the desire for artificial wealth is infinite, for it is the servant of disordered concupiscence, which is not curbed, as the Philosopher makes clear (*Polit.* i. 3). Yet this desire for wealth is infinite otherwise than the desire for the sovereign good. For the more perfectly the sovereign good is possessed, the more it is loved, and other things despised: because the more we possess it, the more we know it. Hence it is written, (Sir 24:29): *They that eat me shall yet hunger.* Whereas in the desire for wealth and for whatsoever temporal goods, the contrary is the case: for when we already possess them, we despise them, and seek others:[33] which is the sense of Our Lord's words (Jn 4:13): *Whosoever drinketh of this water,* by which temporal goods are signified, *shall thirst again.* The reason of this is that we realize more their insufficiency when we possess them: and this very fact shows that they are imperfect, and that the sovereign good does not consist therein.[34]

---

[32] St. Thomas' answer to the popular skeptical question, "Who's to say?" (cf. n. 23).

[33] N.b.: the same is true of "sex objects" as of money: they are far less desirable once "attained" than when unattained and desired. The true good is just the opposite. St. Thomas would probably say that our society treats sex like money (as a medium of exchange) and money like sex (for under capitalism, money can reproduce itself in interest [usury], which St. Thomas, like most pre-modern Christian, Jewish, and Muslim thinkers, considered unnatural).

[34] Thus experience is an honest teacher, especially the experience of failure and unhappiness, as Augustine found in his life (cf. *Confessions*) and many find today.

SECOND ARTICLE

Whether Man's Happiness Consists in Honors?[35]

Objection 1. It would seem that man's happiness consists in honors. For happiness or bliss is *the reward of virtue*, as the Philosopher says (*Ethic.* i. 9). But honor more than anything else seems to be that by which virtue is rewarded, as the Philosopher says (*Ethic.* iv. 3). Therefore happiness consists especially in honor.

Objection 2. Further, that which belongs to God and to persons of great excellence seems especially to be happiness, which is the perfect good. But that is honor, as the Philosopher says (*Ethic.* iv. 3). Moreover, the Apostle says (1 Tim 1:17): *To . . . the only God be honor and glory.* Therefore happiness consists in honor.

Objection 3. Further, that which man desires above all is happiness. But nothing seems more desirable to man than honor: since man suffers loss in all other things, lest he should suffer loss of honor.[36] Therefore happiness consists in honor.

On the contrary, Happiness is in the happy. But honor is not in the honored, but rather in him who honors,[37] and who offers deference to the person honored, as the Philosopher says (*Ethic.* i. 5). Therefore happiness does not consist in honor.

I answer that, It is impossible for happiness to consist in honor. For honor is given to a man on account of some excellence in him; and consequently it is a sign and attestation of the excellence that is in the person honored.[38] Now a man's excellence is in proportion, especially, to his happiness, which is man's perfect good; and to its

---

[35] The ancient version of honor ("high marks" from others) is hierarchical—being honored for being *superior*—while the more usual modern version is egalitarian—being accepted as "one of the crowd". But both versions remain subject to the same arguments here.

[36] This Objection, like Objection 1 in Article 1, confuses the *desired* with the *desirable*, or wants with needs.

[37] I.e., honor is external and happiness is internal.

[38] Working for a grade in a course rather than for wisdom is an example of wrongly reversing the sign and the thing signified. Going on a vacation just to take pictures of it is another. Being good just so that people will honor you, or to "get along with people", is a third, very popular form of the same mistake.

parts, *i.e.*, those goods by which he has a certain share of happiness. And therefore honor can result from happiness, but happiness cannot principally consist therein.

Reply Obj. 1. As the Philosopher says (*ibid.*), honor is not that reward of virtue, for which the virtuous work: but they receive honor from men by way of reward, *as from those who have nothing greater to offer*. But virtue's true reward is happiness itself, for which the virtuous work: whereas if they worked for honor, it would no longer be a virtue, but [the vice of] ambition.

Reply Obj. 2. Honor is due to God and to persons of great excellence as a sign of attestation of excellence already existing: not that honor makes them excellent.

Reply Obj. 3. That man desires honor above all else, arises from his natural desire for happiness, from which honor results, as stated above. Wherefore man seeks to be honored especially by the wise, on whose judgment he believes himself to be excellent or happy.[39]

THIRD ARTICLE

Whether Man's Happiness Consists in Fame or Glory?[40]

Objection 1. It would seem that man's happiness consists in glory. For happiness seems to consist in that which is paid to the saints for the trials they have undergone in the world. But this is glory: for the Apostle says (Rom 8:18): *The sufferings of this time are not worthy to be compared with the glory to come, that shall be revealed in us.* Therefore happiness consists in glory.

---

[39] Even in terms of how men *do* behave, much less how they *should* behave, they show that they do not pursue honor as the *summum bonum*, since if they did, it would not matter who gave them the honor. The fact that they want to be honored by the wise, who know the truth, rather than fools, means they want to be honored for being truly happy (i.e., objectively good, blessed, worthy of honor).

[40] Though "honor" and "fame" are similar, they are not identical. We can be honored (by a few) without being famous (to the wider world), or famous without being honored (if the fame is negative or neutral in value). "Fame" here, however, is positive: honor multiplied, quantity added to quality (see "*I answer that*", second sentence).

Objection 2. Further, good is diffusive of itself, as stated by Dionysius (*Div. Nom.* iv.). But man's good is spread abroad in the knowledge of others by glory more than by anything else: since, according to Ambrose [Augustine, *Contra Maxim. Arian.* ii. 13], glory consists *in being well known and praised.* Therefore man's happiness consists in glory [cf. n. 35].

Objection 3. Further, happiness is the most enduring good. Now this seems to be fame or glory; because by this men attain to eternity after a fashion. Hence Boëthius says (*De Consol.* ii): *You seem to beget unto yourselves eternity, when you think of your fame in future time.* Therefore man's happiness consists in fame or glory.

On the contrary, Happiness is man's true good. But it happens that fame or glory is false:[41] for as Boëthius says (*De Consol.* iii), *many owe their renown to the lying reports spread among the people. Can anything be more shameful? For those who receive false fame, must needs blush at their own praise.* Therefore man's happiness does not consist in fame or glory.

I answer that, Man's happiness cannot consist in human fame or glory. For glory consists *in being well known and praised,* as Ambrose [Augustine,—*Contra Maxim. Arian.* ii. 13] says. Now the thing known is related to human knowledge otherwise than to God's knowledge: for human knowledge is caused by the things known, whereas God's knowledge is the cause of the things known.[42] Wherefore the perfection of human good, which is called happiness, cannot be caused by human knowledge: but rather human knowledge of another's happiness proceeds from, and, in a fashion, is caused by, human happiness itself, inchoate or perfect. Consequently man's happiness cannot consist in fame or glory.

On the other hand, man's good depends on God's knowledge as

---

[41] Note the use of "true" and "false" here not as characterizing *propositions* but *realities*, as authentic and inauthentic (cf. I, 16, "*I answer that*").

[42] God caused the universe by knowing it into existence, i.e., by uttering the mental word, according to Genesis. Things exist, and are *what* they are, because God knows them as such (e.g., dogs are doggy because God "thought them up"). Human knowledge is similar in creative art; but in science and in common sense, human knowledge is caused by and conforms to its object: we think "the sky is blue" because the sky *is* blue. This metaphysical principle entails the conclusion that fame cannot

its cause. And therefore man's beatitude depends, as on its cause, on the glory which man has with God;[43] according to Psalm 90:15, 16: *I will deliver him, and I will glorify him; I will fill him with length of days, and I will show him my salvation.*

Furthermore, we must observe that human knowledge often fails, especially in contingent singulars, such as are human acts. For this reason human glory is frequently deceptive. But since God cannot be deceived, His glory is always true; hence it is written (2 Cor 10:18): *He . . . is approved . . . whom God commendeth.*

Reply Obj. 1. The Apostle speaks, then, not of the glory which is with men, but of the glory which is from God, with His Angels. Hence it is written (Mk 8:38): *The Son of Man shall confess him in the glory of His Father, before His angels.*

Reply Obj. 2. A man's good which, through fame or glory, is in the knowledge of many, if this knowledge be true, must needs be derived from good existing in the man himself: and hence it presupposes perfect or inchoate happiness. But if the knowledge be false, it does not harmonize with the thing: and thus good does not exist in him who is looked upon as famous. Hence it follows that fame can nowise make man happy.

Reply Obj. 3. Fame has no stability; in fact, it is easily ruined by false report. And if sometimes it endures, this is by accident. But happiness endures of itself, and for ever.

FOURTH ARTICLE

Whether Man's Happiness Consists in Power?[44]

Objection 1. It would seem that happiness consists in power. For all things desire to become like to God, as to their last end and first beginning. But men who are in power seem, on account of the

cause happiness, since fame is a form of human knowledge, and human knowledge does not cause its object but is caused by it.

[43] This praise and glory from God is an ingredient in supreme happiness (1) because God's knowledge causes reality rather than reflecting it, and (2) because each of the inadequate candidates for happiness is included, transformed, and perfected in true happiness as an ingredient (cf. n. 20).

[44] What modern thinkers usually mean by "freedom" comes under this heading (cf. especially Objection 3).

similarity of power, to be most like to God:[45] hence also in Scripture they are called *gods* (Ex 22:28),—*Thou shalt not speak ill of the gods.* Therefore happiness consists in power.

Objection 2. Further, happiness is the perfect good. But the highest perfection for man is to be able to rule others; which belongs to those who are in power. Therefore happiness consists in power.

Objection 3. Further, since happiness is supremely desirable, it is contrary to that which is before all to be shunned. But, more than aught else, men shun servitude, which is contrary to power. Therefore happiness consists in power.

On the contrary, Happiness is the perfect good. But power is most imperfect. For as Boëthius says (*De Consol.* iii), *the power of man cannot relieve the gnawings of care, nor can it avoid the thorny path of anxiety:* and further on: *Think you a man is powerful who is surrounded by attendants, whom he inspires with fear indeed, but whom he fears still more?*[46] Therefore happiness does not consist in power.

I answer that, It is impossible for happiness to consist in power; and this for two reasons. First because power has the nature of principle, as is stated in *Metaph.* v. 12, whereas happiness has the nature of last end.—Secondly, because power has relation to [is open to either] good and evil: whereas happiness is man's proper and perfect good. Wherefore some happiness might consist in the good use of power, which is by virtue, rather than in power itself.

Now four general reasons may be given to prove that happiness consists in none of the foregoing external goods. First, because, since happiness is man's supreme good, it is incompatible with any evil.[47] Now all the foregoing can be found both in good and in evil men.—Secondly, because, since it is the nature of happiness to *satisfy of itself,* as stated in *Ethic.* i. 7, having gained happiness, man cannot lack any needful good. But after acquiring any one of the foregoing, man may still lack many goods that are necessary to

---

[45] N.b.: we spontaneously think of this attribute before any other, even goodness, for we call Him "*Almighty* God", but use "*Good* God" as a mere expletive!

[46] Cf. Hegel's famous "master-slave dialectic" (the master is really the enslaved) and the maxim "Uneasy lies the head that wears the crown."

[47] Note the difference between (true, objective) *happiness* and mere (subjective) *contentment* here.

him; for instance, wisdom, bodily health, and such like.—Thirdly, because, since happiness is the perfect good, no evil can accrue to anyone therefrom. This cannot be said of the foregoing: for it is written (Qo 5:12) that *riches* are sometimes *kept to the hurt of the owner*; and the same may be said of the other three.—Fourthly, because man is ordained to happiness through principles that are in him; since he is ordained thereto naturally. Now the four goods mentioned above are due rather to external causes, and in most cases to fortune [chance]; for which reason they are called goods of fortune.[48] Therefore it is evident that happiness nowise consists in the foregoing.

Reply Obj. 1. God's power is His goodness:[49] hence He cannot use His power otherwise than well. But it is not so with men. Consequently it is not enough for man's happiness, that he become like God in power, unless he become like Him in goodness also.

Reply Obj. 2. Just as it is a very good thing for a man to make good use of power in ruling many, so is it a very bad thing if he makes a bad use of it.[50] And so it is that power is [open] towards good and evil.

Reply Obj. 3. Servitude is a hindrance to the good use of power: therefore is it that men naturally shun it; not because man's supreme good consists in power.

FIFTH ARTICLE

Whether Man's Happiness Consists in Any Bodily Good?[51]

Objection 1. It would seem that man's happiness consists in bodily goods. For it is written (Sir 30:16): *There is no riches above the*

---

[48] Note how this shallow error is implicitly at the root of the English word "happiness", which derives from "hap" (chance or fortune).

[49] For all of God's attributes are one with each other, since they are all one with His essence (cf. I, 3, 7).

[50] Cf. Lord Acton's maxim, "All power tends to corrupt, and absolute power corrupts absolutely." (Only God is incorruptible.)

[51] *Pleasure* is considered in Article 6, not the Article on "bodily goods" (5), because St. Thomas means by "bodily goods" what is objectively good for the body—essentially, health—rather than subjective feelings of enjoyment.

riches of the health of the body. [52] But happiness consists in that which is best. Therefore it consists in the health of the body. . . .

On the contrary, Man surpasses all other animals in regard to happiness. But in bodily goods he is surpassed by many animals; for instance, by the elephant in longevity, by the lion in strength, by the stag in fleetness. [53] Therefore man's happiness does not consist in goods of the body.

I answer that, It is impossible for man's happiness to consist in the goods of the body; and this for two reasons. First, because, if a thing be ordained to another as to its end, its last end cannot consist in the [mere] preservation of its being. Hence a captain does not intend as a last end, the preservation of the ship entrusted to him, since a ship is ordained to something else as its end, viz., to navigation. [54] Now just as the ship is entrusted to the captain that he may steer its course, so man is given over to his will and reason; according to Sirach 15:14; *God made man from the beginning and left him in the hand of his own counsel.* Now it is evident that man is ordained to something as his end: since man is not the supreme good. [55] Therefore the last end of man's reason and will cannot be the preservation of man's being.

Secondly, because, granted that the end of man's will and reason be the preservation of man's being, it could not be said that the end

---

[52] To quote still another maxim, "If you have your health, you have everything." The plethora of maxims relevant to this Question shows that it is a question most men have thought about; in fact, it is probably the most popular of all the questions philosophers ask, since it is the most practical for everyone.

[53] Thus a trip to the zoo proves that man's *summum bonum* is not bodily good. The argument is extrinsic and does not reveal the real reason, as does the "*I answer that*"; but it is a valid argument. The first premise means we can be more deeply and truly happy than any animal. What ape can fall in love (as distinct from lust), or weep with joy at a symphony? This also shows the difference between happiness and contentment: the lower the animal, the more merely content it is. Slugs are more content than cats, cats than humans.

[54] St. Thomas means by "navigation" not just consulting navigational charts but actually sailing.

[55] Cf. Article 7 for a proof of this point.

of man is some good of the body. For man's being consists in soul and body; and though the being of the body depends on the soul, yet the being of the human soul depends not on the body, as shown above (I, Q. 75, A. 2); and the very body is for the soul, as matter for its form, and the instruments for the man that puts them into motion, that by their means he may do his work. Wherefore all goods of the body are ordained to the goods of the soul, as to their end.[56] Consequently happiness, which is man's last end, cannot consist in goods of the body.

Reply Obj. 1. Just as the body is ordained to the soul, as its end, so are external goods ordained to the body itself. And therefore it is with reason that the good of the body is preferred to external goods, which are signified by *riches*, just as the good of the soul is preferred to all bodily goods.[57] . . .

SIXTH ARTICLE

Whether Man's Happiness Consists in Pleasure?

Objection 1. It would seem that man's happiness consists in pleasure. For since happiness is the last end, it is not desired for something else, but other things for it. But this answers to pleasure more than to anything else: *for it is absurd to ask anyone what is his motive in wishing to be pleased* (*Ethic.* x. 2). Therefore happiness consists principally in pleasure and delight [cf. n. 35]. . . .

Objection 3. Further, since desire is for good, it seems that what all desire is best. But all desire delight;[58] both wise and foolish, and

---

[56] Contrast Hobbes, or any materialist, for whom the reverse is true: the soul is a mere servant to the body. Hobbes says that reason is "the scout for the senses".

[57] The eight Articles here are arranged in a hierarchical order, a scale of values, which is not merely St. Thomas' personal preference. Such an objective hierarchy is a practical necessity to all intelligent moral choices, for most choices are not between a good and an evil but between two competing goods.

[58] Cf. II–II, 35, 4, Reply 2: "No one can live without delight, and that is why a man deprived of spiritual joy goes over to carnal pleasures" (Gilby translation).

even irrational creatures. Therefore delight is the best of all. Therefore happiness, which is the supreme good, consists in pleasure.

On the contrary, Boëthius says (*De Consol.* iii): *Any one that chooses to look back on his past excesses, will perceive that pleasures* [typically] *have a sad ending: and if they can render a man happy, there is no reason why we should not say that the very beasts are happy too.*[59]

I answer that, Because bodily delights are more generally known, *the name of pleasure has been appropriated to them* (*Ethic.* vii. 13), although other delights excel them:[60] and yet happiness does not consist in them. Because in every thing, that which pertains to its essence is distinct from its proper accident: thus in man it is one thing that he is [by essence] a mortal rational animal, and another that he [by proper (universal and necessary) accident] is a risible [able to laugh] animal. We must therefore consider that every delight is a proper accident resulting from happiness, or from some part of happiness; since the reason that a man is delighted is that he has some fitting good, either in reality, or in hope, or at least in memory. Now a fitting good, if indeed it be the perfect good, is precisely man's happiness: and if it is imperfect, it is a share of happiness, either proximate, or remote, or at least apparent. Therefore it is evident that neither is delight, which results from the perfect good, the very essence of happiness, but something resulting therefrom as its proper accident.[61] . . .

---

[59] Another indication of how far the ancients were from the moderns on happiness: if *eudaimonia*, or *makarios* (in Greek), or *felicitas*, or *beatitudo* (in Latin) meant mere feelings of contentment, this argument would be unintelligible.

[60] As Plato pointed out (*Republic*, Bk. 9), all who have experienced both the greatest bodily delights and the greatest spiritual delights testify to the same results of this dual experiment: that the soul can experience far greater pleasure than the body. (It can experience far greater suffering, too.) All who doubt this simply prove they lack the experience and are in no position to judge.

[61] The essence is the cause of the accident, and the cause cannot be identical with the effect. *Because* a triangle is a three-sided enclosed plane figure, it must have 180 degrees in its interior angles. *Because* man is a rational animal, he can laugh, pray, sing, etc. And *because* a man really possesses his fitting good, his end, he is pleased and rejoices. Pleasure is

Reply Obj. 1. . . . Delight . . . is nothing else than the appetite's rest in good: thus . . . just as good is desired for itself, so delight is desired for itself and not for anything else, if the preposition *for* denote the final cause. But if it denote the formal . . . cause, thus delight is desirable for something else, *i.e.*, for the good, which is the object of that delight, and . . . gives it its form: for the reason that delight is desired is that it is rest in the thing desired. . . .

Reply Obj. 3. All desire delight in the same way as they desire good: and yet they desire delight by reason of the good and not conversely, as stated above (Reply 1). Consequently it does not follow that delight is the supreme and essential good, but that every delight results from some good, and that some delight results from that which is the essential and supreme good.

SEVENTH ARTICLE

Whether Some Good of the Soul Constitutes Man's Happiness?

Objection 3. Further, perfection is something belonging to that which is perfected. But happiness is a perfection of man. Therefore happiness is something belonging to man. But it is not something belonging to the body, as shown above (A. 5). Therefore it is something belonging to the soul; and thus it consists in goods of the soul.

On the contrary, As Augustine says (*De Doctr. Christ.* i. 22), *that which constitutes the life of happiness is to be loved for its own sake.* But man is not to be loved for his own sake, but whatever is in man is to be loved for God's sake.[62] Therefore happiness consists in no good of the soul.

I answer that, As stated above (Q. 1, A. 8), the end is twofold:

---

caused by the good, or part of the good, or a remembered or anticipated good, or an apparent good; therefore pleasure is not the good itself. We have found a proper effect of the *summum bonum*—it will always cause joy—but we have not yet found the *summum bonum* itself.

[62] St. Thomas does not mean man is a means to be used rather than an end to be loved, but that the ultimate reason man is to be loved is not himself but God. For God is (1) man's exemplary formal cause: man is made in God's image. One loves the image because of the original, not

namely, the thing itself, which we desire to attain, and the use, namely, the attainment or possession of that thing. If, then, we speak of man's last end, as to the thing itself which we desire as last end, it is impossible for man's last end to be the soul itself or something belonging to it. Because the soul, considered in itself, is as something existing in potentiality: for it becomes knowing actually, from being potentially knowing; and actually virtuous, from being potentially virtuous. Now since potentiality is for the sake of act as for its fulfilment, that which in itself is in potentiality cannot be the last end. Therefore the soul itself cannot be its own last end.[63] . . .

But if we speak of man's last end, as to the attainment or possession thereof, or as to any use whatever of the thing itself desired as an end, thus does something of man, in respect of his soul, belong to his last end: since man attains happiness through his soul. Therefore the thing itself which is desired as end, is that which constitutes happiness, and makes man happy; but the attainment of this thing is called happiness. Consequently we must say that happiness is something belonging to the soul; but that which constitutes happiness is something outside the soul. . . .

Reply Obj. 3. Happiness itself, since it is a perfection of the soul, is an inherent good of the soul; but that which constitutes happiness, viz., which makes man happy, is something outside his soul, as stated above.

EIGHTH ARTICLE

Whether Any Created Good Constitutes Man's Happiness?

Objection 3. Further, man is made happy by that which lulls [satisfies] his natural desire. But man's natural desire does not reach out to a good surpassing his capacity.[64] Since then man's capacity

---

vice versa. And (2) God is man's first efficient cause, his Creator. (3) God is also man's final cause, *summum bonum*, or ultimate end, not vice versa.

[63] If the soul were its own end, this would be as if a moving arrow were its own target.

[64] St. Thomas, following St. Augustine, disagrees with this premise

does not include that good which surpasses the limits of all creation, it seems that man can be made happy by some created good.[65] Consequently some created good constitutes man's happiness.

On the contrary, Augustine says (*De Civ. Dei* xix. 26): *As the soul is the life of the body, so God is man's life of happiness: of Whom it is written: "Happy is that people whose God is the Lord"* (Ps 143:15).

I answer that, It is impossible for any created good to constitute man's happiness. For happiness is the perfect good, which lulls [satisfies] the appetite altogether; else it would not be the last end, if something yet remained to be desired. Now the object of the will, *i.e.,* of man's appetite, is the universal good; just as the object of the intellect is the universal true. Hence it is evident that naught can lull man's will, save the universal good.[66] This is to be found, not in any creature, but in God alone; because every creature has goodness by participation. Wherefore God alone can satisfy the will of man, according to the words of Psalm 102:5: *Who satisfieth thy desire with good things.* Therefore God alone constitutes man's happiness. . . .

Reply Obj. 3. Created good is not less than that good of which man is capable, as of something intrinsic and inherent to him: but it is less than the good of which he is capable, as of an object, and which is infinite. And the participated good which is in an angel, and in the whole universe, is a finite and restricted good.

(cf. *Confessions* 1, 1: "Thou hast made us for Thyself, and our hearts are restless till they rest in Thee"). Whether it is to be called a natural desire or a supernatural desire, there is in us an inherent desire for God.

[65] Another maxim: "Know then thyself; presume not God to scan. The proper study of mankind is man" (Alexander Pope, *An Essay on Man*). C. S. Lewis replies, "The proper study of mankind is everything."

[66] N.b.: St. Thomas does not say universal *goodness*, but the universal *good*. God might be called a "concrete universal" rather than either an abstract universal or a concrete particular.

Question 3

What Is Happiness?

Whether Happiness Is an Operation [Activity]*?*

On the contrary, The Philosopher says (*Ethic.* i. 13) that *happiness is an operation according to perfect virtue.*

I answer that, In so far as man's happiness is something created, existing in him, we must needs say that it is an operation. For happiness is man's supreme perfection. Now each thing is perfect in so far as it is actual; since potentiality without act is imperfect. Consequently happiness must consist in man's last act. But it is evident that operation is the last act of the operator, wherefore the Philosopher calls it *second act* (*De Anima* ii. 1): because that which has a form can be potentially operating, just as he who knows is potentially considering. And hence it is that in other things, too, each one is said to be *for its operation* (*De Caelo* ii. 3). Therefore man's happiness must of necessity consist in an operation. . . .

Whether Happiness Is an Operation of the Sensitive Part, or of the Intellective Part Only?

I answer that, A thing may belong to happiness in three ways: (1) essentially, (2) antecedently, (3) consequently. Now the operation of sense cannot belong to happiness essentially. For man's happiness consists essentially in his being united to the Uncreated Good, Which is his last end, as shown above (A. 1): to Which man cannot be united by an operation of his senses. Again, in like

376

manner, because, as shown above (Q. 2, A. 5), man's happiness does not consist in goods of the body, which goods alone, however, we attain through the operation of the senses.

Nevertheless the operations of the senses can belong to happiness, both antecedently and consequently: antecedently, in respect of imperfect happiness, such as can be had in this life, since the operation of the intellect demands a previous operation of the sense;—consequently, in that perfect happiness which we await in heaven; because at the resurrection, *from the very happiness of the soul*, as Augustine says (*Ep. ad Dioscor.*) *the body and the bodily senses will receive a certain overflow.*[67] . . .

Reply Obj. 3. In perfect happiness the entire man is perfected, in the lower part of his nature, by an overflow from the higher. But in the imperfect happiness of this life, it is otherwise; we advance from the perfection of the lower part to the perfection of the higher part.[68]

FOURTH ARTICLE

Whether, If Happiness Is in the Intellective Part, It Is an Operation of the Intellect or of the Will?

Objection 2. Further, happiness is the supreme good. But good is the object of the will. Therefore happiness consists in an operation of the will. . . .

Objection 4. Further, if happiness be an operation, it must needs be man's most excellent operation. But the love of God, which is an act of the will, is a more excellent operation than knowledge, which is an operation of the intellect, as the Apostle declares (1 Cor 13). Therefore it seems that happiness consists in an act of the will. . . .

On the contrary, Our Lord said (Jn 17:3): *This is eternal life: that*

---

[67] Even now, great happiness of soul often "flows over" into the body: cf. the radiant face of someone in love.

[68] A very important practical principle for all education, especially in the spiritual life.

they may know Thee, the only true God. Now eternal life is the last end, as stated above (A. 2 *ad* 1). Therefore man's happiness consists in the knowledge of God, which is an act of the intellect.[69]

I answer that, As stated above (Q. 2, A. 6) two things are needed for happiness: one, which is the essence of happiness: the other, that is, as it were, its proper accident, *i.e.,* the delight connected with it. I say, then, that as to the very essence of happiness, it is impossible for it to consist in an act of the will. For it is evident from what has been said (AA. 1, 2; Q. 2, A. 7) that happiness is the attainment of the last end. But the attainment of the end does not consist in the very act of the will. For the will is directed to the end, both absent, when it desires it; and present, when it is delighted by resting therein. Now it is evident that the desire itself of the end is not the attainment of the end, but is a movement towards the end: while delight comes to the will from the end being present; and not conversely, is a thing made present, by the fact that the will delights in it. Therefore, that the end be present to him who desires it, must be due to something else than an act of the will.[70]

This is evidently the case in regard to sensible ends. For if the acquisition of money were through an act of the will, the covetous man would have it from the very moment that he wished for it. But at that moment it is far from him; and he attains it, by grasping it in

---

[69] Note how St. Thomas means something more broad and solid by "intellect" than is usually meant today: something that can know a person, not just a concept or an argument.

[70] Here is St. Thomas' argument against voluntarism (the primacy of the will) in regard to the *summum bonum*. It does not deny the truth of the strongest Christian reason for voluntarism, viz., that it is better to love God than to know God (Objection 4, sentence 2—this is true). But the very essence of happiness, the very attaining of God, the glue that sticks us to God, must be knowledge. Deep knowledge, more-than-conceptual knowledge, knowledge not only *about* but *of* and even *into* God, but knowledge nevertheless. The role of the will is to cause it, to motivate it, to move us there by loving God, and then, once there, to rejoice in Him. Thus the will is just as *important* as the intellect, and just as valuable, since loving God is a *greater* good than knowing God; but the essential moment of bliss is knowing God (Jn 17:3). The same may be said of the closest earthly analogy to it, married love: the will's love brings you there and enjoys the knowledge (intimacy) once there, but the essential moment of union and the essence of bliss is "knowing" the beloved (cf. Gen 4:1).

his hand, or in some like manner; and then he delights in the money got. And so it is with an intelligible end. For at first we desire to attain an intelligible end; we attain it, through its being made present to us by an act of the intellect; and then the delighted will rests in the end when attained.

So, therefore, the essence of happiness consists in an act of the intellect: but the delight that results from happiness pertains to the will. In this sense Augustine says (*Conf.* x. 23) that happiness is *joy in truth*, because, to wit, joy itself is the consummation of happiness. . . .

Reply Obj. 2. The will's first object is not its [own] act: just as neither is the first object of the sight, vision, but a[n] [objectively real] visible thing. Wherefore, from the very fact that happiness belongs to the will, as the will's first object, it follows that it does not belong to it as its [own] act. . . .

Reply Obj. 4. Love ranks above knowledge in moving, but knowledge precedes love in attaining: for *naught is loved save what is known*, as Augustine says (*De Trin.* x. 1). Consequently we first attain an intelligible end by an act of the intellect; just as we first attain a sensible end by an act of sense. . . .

FIFTH ARTICLE

Whether Happiness Is an Operation of the Speculative [Contemplative] *or of the Practical Intellect?*

I answer that, Happiness consists in an operation of the speculative rather than of the practical intellect. This is evident for three reasons. First because if man's happiness is an operation, it must needs be man's highest operation. Now man's highest operation is that of his highest power in respect of its highest object: and his highest power is the intellect, whose highest object is the Divine Good. . . .

Secondly, it is evident from the fact that contemplation [of Truth] is sought principally for its own sake. But the act of the practical intellect is not sought for its own sake but for the sake of action: and these very actions are ordained to some end. Consequently it is evident that the last end cannot consist in the active life, which pertains to the practical intellect.

Thirdly, it is again evident, from the fact that in the contemplative life man has something in common with things above him, viz., with God and the angels, to whom he is made like by happiness. But in things pertaining to the active life, other animals also have something in common with man, although imperfectly.

Therefore the last and perfect happiness, which we await in the life to come, consists entirely in contemplation. But imperfect happiness, such as can be had here, consists first and principally in contemplation, but secondarily, in an operation of the practical intellect directing human actions and passions, as stated in *Ethic.* x. 7, 8. . . .

SIXTH ARTICLE

Whether Happiness Consists in the Consideration of Speculative Sciences?[71]

On the contrary, It is written (Jer 9:23): *Let not the wise man glory in his wisdom:* and this is said in reference to speculative sciences. Therefore man's final happiness does not consist in the consideration of these.

I answer that, As stated above (A. 2 *ad* 4), man's happiness is twofold, one perfect, the other imperfect. And by perfect happiness we are to understand that which attains to the true notion of happiness; and by imperfect happiness that which does not attain thereto, but partakes of some particular likeness of happiness. Thus perfect prudence is in man, with whom is the idea of things to be done; while imperfect prudence is in certain irrational animals, who are possessed of certain particular instincts in respect of works similar to works of prudence.

Accordingly perfect happiness cannot consist essentially in the consideration of speculative sciences. To prove this, we must observe that the consideration of a speculative science does not

---

[71] Though happiness is an operation of the speculative *intellect*, it is not a speculative *science*. It is knowing God (Article 8), not knowing philosophical and theological truths *about* God, for these truths that we can know are severely limited, dependent as they are on sense experience as the beginning of all human knowing.

extend beyond the scope of the principles of that science: since the entire science is virtually contained in its principles. Now the first principles of speculative sciences are received through the senses, as the Philosopher clearly states at the beginning of the *Metaphysics* (i. 1), and at the end of the *Posterior Analytics* (ii. 15). Wherefore the entire consideration of speculative sciences cannot extend farther than knowledge of sensibles can lead. . . .

EIGHTH ARTICLE

Whether Man's Happiness Consists in the Vision of the Divine Essence?

On the contrary, It is written (1 Jn 3:2): *When He shall appear, we shall be like to Him; and* (Vulg., *because*) *we shall see Him as He is.*

I answer that, Final and perfect happiness can consist in nothing else than the vision of the Divine Essence. To make this clear, two points must be observed. First, that man is not perfectly happy, so long as something remains for him to desire and seek: secondly, that the perfection of any power is determined by the nature of its object. Now the object of the intellect is *what a thing is,* i.e., the essence of a thing, according to *De Anima* iii. 6. Wherefore the intellect attains perfection, in so far as it knows the essence of a thing. . . . Consequently, when man knows an effect, and knows that it has a cause, there naturally remains in man the desire to know about that cause, *what it is.* And this desire is one of wonder, and causes inquiry, as is stated in the beginning of the *Metaphysics* (i. 2). For instance, if a man, knowing the eclipse of the sun, consider that it must be due to some cause, and know not what that cause is, he wonders about it, and from wondering proceeds to inquire. Nor does this inquiry cease until he arrive at a knowledge of the essence of the cause.

If therefore the human intellect, knowing the essence of some created effect, knows no more of God than *that He is* . . . it is not yet perfectly happy. Consequently, for perfect happiness the intellect needs to reach the very Essence of the First Cause. And thus it will have its perfection through union with God as with that object, in which alone man's happiness consists, as stated above (AA. 1, 7; Q. 2, A. 8). . . .

Question 4

Of Those Things That Are Required for Happiness

FIRST ARTICLE

Whether Delight Is Required for Happiness?

On the contrary, Augustine says (*Conf.* x. 23) that happiness is *joy in truth.*

I answer that, One thing may be necessary for another in four ways. First, as a preamble and preparation to it: thus instruction is necessary for science. Secondly, as perfecting it: thus the soul is necessary for the life of the body. Thirdly, as helping it from without: thus friends are necessary for some undertaking. Fourthly, as something attendant on it: thus we might say that heat is necessary for fire. And in this way delight is necessary for happiness. For it is caused by the appetite being at rest in the good attained. Wherefore, since happiness is nothing else but the attainment of the Sovereign Good, it cannot be without concomitant delight. . . .

SECOND ARTICLE

Whether in Happiness Vision Ranks before Delight?

On the contrary, The cause is greater than its effect. But vision is the cause of delight. Therefore vision ranks before delight. . . .

FOURTH ARTICLE

Whether Rectitude of the Will Is Necessary for Happiness?

On the contrary, It is written (Mt 5:8): *Blessed are the clean of heart; for they shall see God:* and (Heb 12:14): *Follow peace with all men, and holiness, without which no man shall see God.*

I answer that, Rectitude of the will is necessary for Happiness both antecedently and concomitantly. Antecedently, because rectitude of the will consists in being duly ordered to the last end. Now the end in comparison to what is ordained to the end is as form compared to matter. Wherefore, just as matter cannot receive a form, unless it be duly disposed thereto, so nothing gains an end, except it be duly ordained thereto. And therefore none can obtain Happiness, without rectitude of the will.[72] Concomitantly, because as stated above (Q. 3, A. 8), final Happiness consists in the vision of the Divine Essence, Which is the very essence of goodness. So that the will of him who sees the Essence of God, of necessity, loves, whatever he loves, in subordination to God;[73] just as the will of him who sees not God's Essence, of necessity, loves whatever he loves, under that common notion of good which he knows. And this is precisely what makes the will right. Wherefore it is evident that Happiness cannot be without a right will. . . .

---

[72] N.b.: the connection between morality and happiness, and between morality and the knowledge of God's essence, is not extrinsic and artificial, as if God chose to make a "deal" with us, to *make* happiness or knowledge of Him dependent on our good will; but the connection is intrinsic and necessary. The reason God insists so uncompromisingly on morality is because He knows it is the only way we can possibly be happy. This is also the main point and conclusion of the greatest non-Christian book in the history of philosophy, Plato's *Republic*: that justice (virtue) is always more profitable (happifying) than injustice.

[73] This is why there can be no evil in Heaven, yet no one's will is compelled. Once we see God face to face, we simply will not disobey "the first and greatest commandment" and love anything else before Him.

Whether the Body Is Necessary for Man's Happiness?

Objection 3. Further, Happiness is the perfection of man. But the soul, without the body, is not man. Therefore Happiness cannot be in the soul separated from the body.

Objection 4. Further, according to the Philosopher (*Ethic.* vii. 13) *the operation of bliss*, in which operation happiness consists, is *not hindered.* But the operation of the separate soul is hindered; because, as Augustine says (*Gen. ad lit.*, xii. 35) the soul *has a natural desire to rule the body, the result of which is that it is held back,*[74] *so to speak, from tending with all its might to the heavenward journey*, *i.e.*, to the vision of the Divine Essence. Therefore the soul cannot be happy without the body.

Objection 5. Further, Happiness is the sufficient good and lulls desire. But this cannot be said of the separated soul; for it yet desires to be united to the body, as Augustine says (*ibid.*). Therefore the soul is not happy while separated from the body. . . .

On the contrary, It is written (Rev 14:13): *Happy* (Douay,—*blessed*) *are the dead who die in the Lord.*

I answer that, Happiness is twofold; the one is imperfect and is had in this life; the other is perfect, consisting in the vision of God. Now it is evident that the body is necessary for the happiness of this life. For the happiness of this life consists in an operation of the intellect, either speculative or practical. And the operation of the intellect in this life cannot be without a phantasm [sense image], which is only in a bodily organ, as was shown in the First Part (Q. 84, AA. 6, 7). Consequently that happiness which can be had in this life, depends, in a way, on the body.

But as to perfect Happiness, which consists in the vision of God, some have maintained that it is not possible to the soul separated from the body; and have said that the souls of saints, when separated from their bodies, do not attain to that Happiness until the Day of Judgment, when they will receive their bodies back again. And this is shown to be false, both by authority and by

---

[74] That is, by the temporary absence of its body between the time of bodily death and the general resurrection at the end of the world.

reason. By authority, since the Apostle says (2 Cor 5:6): *While we are in the body, we are absent from the Lord;* and he points out the reason of this absence, saying: *For we walk by faith and not by sight.* Now from this it is clear that so long as we walk by faith and not by sight, bereft of the vision of the Divine Essence, we are not present to the Lord. But the souls of the saints, separated from their bodies, are in God's presence; wherefore the text continues: *But we are confident and have a good will to be absent . . . from the body, and to be present with the Lord.* Whence it is evident that the souls of the saints, separated from their bodies, *walk by sight*, seeing the Essence of God, wherein is true Happiness.

Again this is made clear by reason. For the intellect needs not the body, for its operation, save on account of the phantasms, wherein it looks on the intelligible truth, as stated in the First Part (Q. 84, A. 7). Now it is evident that the Divine Essence cannot be seen by means of phantasms, as stated in the First Part (Q. 12, A. 3). Wherefore, since man's perfect Happiness consists in the vision of the Divine Essence, it does not depend on the body. Consequently, without the body the soul can be happy.

We must, however, notice that something may belong to a thing's perfection in two ways. First, as constituting the essence thereof; thus the soul is necessary for man's perfection. Secondly, as necessary for its well-being:[75] thus, beauty of body and keenness of perfection belong to man's perfection. Wherefore though the body does not belong in the first way to the perfection of human Happiness, yet it does in the second way. . . .

Reply Obj. 3. Happiness belongs to man in respect of his intellect: and, therefore, since the intellect remains, it can have Happiness. Thus the teeth of an Ethiopian, in respect of which he is said to be white, can retain their whiteness, even after extraction.[76]

---

[75] Flourishing or fullness of all its proper accidents. An essence can be present even when some of its proper accidents are hindered (e.g., a rose with unopened petals, or even a rose bush with its flowers cut off).

[76] What modern theologian would use the extracted teeth of an Ethiopian to solve the problem of the disembodied soul's happiness? St. Thomas elsewhere uses the biology of worms as an analogy to explain the relation among the Persons in the Trinity! Cf. C. S. Lewis' wonderful description of the medieval mind: "High abstractions jostled the earthiest particulars

Reply Obj. 4. One thing is hindered by another in two ways. First, by way of opposition; thus cold hinders the action of heat: and such a hindrance to operation is repugnant to Happiness. Secondly, by way of some kind of defect, because, to wit, that which is hindered has not all that is necessary to make it perfect in every way: and such a hindrance to operation is not incompatible with Happiness, but prevents it from being perfect in every way. And thus it is that separation from the body is said to hold the soul back from tending with all its might to the vision of the Divine Essence. For the soul desires to enjoy God in such a way that the enjoyment also may overflow into the body, as far as possible. And therefore, as long as it enjoys God, without the fellowship of the body, its appetite is at rest in that which it has, in such a way, that it would still wish the body to attain to its share.

Reply Obj. 5. The desire of the separated soul is entirely at rest, as regards the thing desired; since, to wit, it has that which suffices its appetite. But it is not wholly at rest, as regards the desirer, since it does not possess that good in every way that it would wish to possess it. Consequently, after the body has been resumed [by resurrection], Happiness increases not in intensity, but in extent.[77] . . .

. . . they talked more readily than we about large universals such as death, change, causation, friendship, or salvation; but also about pigs, loaves, boots and boats. The mind darted more easily to and fro between that mental heaven and earth; the cloud of middle generalizations hanging between the two was then much smaller. Hence, as it seems to us, both the naivete and the energy of their writing. . . . They talk something like angels and something like sailors and stable boys, never like civil servants or writers of leading articles" (*The Discarded Image*).

[77] The happiness or unhappiness of two people or two billion people cannot be greater in intensity (quality) for being multiplied by two or by two billion, but it is multiplied in extent (quantity). Thus the pain of the whole world is not greater in quality than the pain of one man.

We want both qualitative and quantitative increase in happiness. Even if we are completely happy, we want our families and friends to be completely happy, too. Similarly, even when the separated soul is completely happy itself, it still desires its body to share in its happiness. Cf. Buddha's "Bodhisattva" vow even after he was totally enlightened "not to rest until the very grass is enlightened".

SIXTH ARTICLE

Whether Perfection of the Body Is Necessary for Happiness?[78]

Objection 1. It would seem that perfection of the body is not necessary for man's perfect Happiness. For perfection of the body is a bodily good. But it has been shown above (Q. 2) that Happiness does not consist in bodily goods. Therefore no perfect disposition of the body is necessary for man's Happiness.

Objection 2. Further, man's Happiness consists in the vision of the Divine Essence, as shown above (Q. 3, A. 8). But the body has no part in this operation, as shown above (A. 5). Therefore no disposition of the body is necessary for Happiness.

Objection 3. Further, the more the intellect is abstracted from the body, the more perfectly it understands. But Happiness consists in the most perfect operation of the intellect. Therefore the soul should be abstracted from the body in every way.[79] Therefore, in no way is a disposition of the body necessary for Happiness.

On the contrary, Happiness is the reward of virtue; wherefore it is written (Jn 13:17): *You shall be blessed, if you do them.* But the reward promised to the saints is not only that they shall see and enjoy God, but also that their bodies shall be well-disposed; for it is written (Is 66:14): *You shall see and your heart shall rejoice, and your bones shall flourish like a herb.* Therefore good disposition of the body is necessary for Happiness.

I answer that, If we speak of that happiness which man can acquire in this life, it is evident that a well-disposed body is of necessity required for it. For this happiness consists, according to the Philosopher (*Ethic.* i. 13) in *an operation according to perfect virtue;* and it is clear that man can be hindered, by indisposition of the body, from every operation of virtue.[80]

---

[78] Notice again St. Thomas' balance between the thesis of Article 5 and that of 6. The body is not necessary for the essence of happiness (5), yet its perfection is necessary for perfect happiness (6).

[79] This was probably the fundamental argument of Neoplatonic and Gnostic philosophers. Even Augustine often makes this Platonic point. It is true existentially—this body often does get in the way—but not essentially—the body is for the soul's good, not for its harm or punishment.

[80] St. Thomas does not mean that someone who is ugly or poor or

But speaking of perfect Happiness, some have maintained that no disposition of body is necessary for Happiness; indeed, that it is necessary for the soul to be entirely separated from the body. Hence Augustine (*De Civ. Dei* xxii. 26) quotes the words of Porphyry who said that *for the soul to be happy, it must be severed from everything corporeal*. But this is unreasonable. For since it is natural to the soul to be united to the body; it is not possible for the perfection of the soul to exclude its natural perfection.

Consequently, we must say that perfect disposition of the body is necessary, both antecedently and consequently, for that Happiness which is in all ways perfect.—Antecedently, because, as Augustine says (*Gen. ad lit.* xii. 35), *if the body be such, that the governance thereof is difficult and burdensome, like unto flesh which is corruptible and weighs upon the soul, the mind is turned away from that vision of the highest heaven*. Whence he concludes that, *when this body will no longer be "natural", but "spiritual," then will it be equalled to the angels, and that will be its glory, which erstwhile was its burden.*—Consequently, because from the Happiness of the soul there will be an overflow on to the body, so that this too will obtain its perfection. Hence Augustine says (*Ep. ad Dioscor.*) that *God gave the soul such a powerful nature that from its exceeding fulness of happiness the vigor of incorruption overflows into the lower nature.*

Reply Obj. 1. Happiness does not consist in bodily good as its object: but bodily good can add a certain charm and perfection to Happiness.

Reply Obj. 2. Although the body has no part in that operation of the intellect whereby the Essence of God is seen, yet it might prove a hindrance thereto. Consequently, perfection of the body is necessary, lest it hinder the mind from being lifted up.

Reply Obj. 3. The perfect operation of the intellect requires indeed that the intellect be abstracted from this corruptible body

---

deformed or retarded cannot be virtuous or happy, but that (1) *complete happiness in this life* includes "the bloom on the rose" of bodily happiness, and that (2) it is hard to contemplate God while you have a migraine headache. Aristotle, St. Augustine, and St. Thomas all realized, as Plato did not, how intimately the body can influence the mind (cf. first quotation from Augustine in "*I answer that*", paragraph 3).

which weighs upon the soul; but not from the spiritual body, which will be wholly subject to the spirit. . . .

Whether Any External Goods Are Necessary for Happiness?

Objection 1. It would seem that external goods also are necessary for Happiness. For that which is promised the saints for reward, belongs to Happiness. But external goods are promised the saints; for instance, food and drink, wealth and a kingdom: for it is said (Lk 22:30); *That you may eat and drink at My table in My kingdom:* and (Mt 6:20): *Lay up to yourselves treasures in heaven:* and (Mt 25:34): *Come, ye blessed of My Father, possess you the kingdom.* Therefore external goods are necessary for Happiness.

Objection 2. Further, according to Boëthius (*De Consol.* iii): happiness is *a state made perfect by the aggregate of all good things.* But some of man's goods are external, although they be of least account, as Augustine says (*De Lib. Arb.* ii. 19). Therefore they too are necessary for Happiness. . . .

I answer that, For imperfect happiness, such as can be had in this life, external goods are necessary, not as belonging to the essence of happiness, but by serving as instruments to happiness, which consists in an operation of virtue, as stated in *Ethic.* i. 13. For man needs in this life, the necessaries of the body, both for the operation of contemplative virtue,[81] and for the operation of active virtue,[82] for which latter he needs also many other things by means of which to perform its operations.

On the other hand, such goods as these are nowise necessary for perfect Happiness, which consists in seeing God. The reason of this is that all suchlike external goods are requisite either for the support of the animal body; or for certain operations which belong to human life, which we perform by means of the animal body: whereas that perfect Happiness which consists in seeing God, will

---

[81] It is difficult to contemplate with a damaged brain.

[82] It is difficult to be magnanimous with your material goods if you have none!

be either in the soul separated from the body, or in the soul united to the body then no longer animal but spiritual. Consequently these external goods are nowise necessary for that Happiness, since they are ordained to the animal life.—And since, in this life, the felicity of contemplation, as being more God-like,[83] approaches nearer than that of action to the likeness of that perfect Happiness, therefore it stands in less need of these goods of the body as stated in *Ethic* x. 8.

Reply Obj. 1. All those material promises contained in Holy Scripture, are to be understood metaphorically, inasmuch as Scripture is wont to express spiritual things under the form of things corporeal, in order *that from things we know, we may rise to the desire of things unknown,* as Gregory says (*Hom.* xi. *in Ev.*).[84] Thus food and drink signify the delight of Happiness: wealth, the sufficiency of God for man; the kingdom, the lifting up of man to union with God.

Reply Obj. 2. These goods that serve for the animal life, are incompatible[85] with that spiritual life wherein perfect Happiness consists. Nevertheless in that Happiness there will be the aggregate of all good things, because whatever good there be in these things, we shall possess it all in the Supreme Fount of goodness. . . .

EIGHTH ARTICLE

Whether the Fellowship of Friends Is Necessary for Happiness?

Objection 3. Further, charity is perfected in Happiness. But charity includes the love of God and of our neighbor. Therefore it seems that fellowship of friends is necessary for Happiness.

On the contrary, It is written (Wis 7:11): *All good things came to me*

---

[83] Cf. Gandhi: "God is not in strength but in truth." "Contemplation", of course, does not mean navel-gazing but understanding, seeing with the inner eye.

[84] Cf. I, 1, 10.

[85] St. Thomas' point is not a Gnostic or Manichean attack on material goods, but simply that we will not need money or cars or even food or sex for our resurrected bodies in Heaven. Yet all that we desire *in* these earthly goods, we will find in God, their inventor and source (cf. Reply 1).

together with her, i.e., with divine wisdom, which consists in contemplating God. Consequently nothing else is necessary for Happiness.

I answer that, If we speak of the happiness of this life, the happy man needs friends, as the Philosopher says (*Ethic.* ix. 9), . . . for the purpose of a good operation, viz., that he may do good to them; that he may delight in seeing them do good; and again that he may be helped by them in his good work. . . .

But if we speak of perfect Happiness which will be in our heavenly Fatherland, the fellowship of friends is not essential to Happiness; since man has the entire fulness of his perfection in God.[86] But the fellowship of friends conduces to the well-being of Happiness. Hence Augustine says (*Gen. ad lit.* viii. 25) that *the spiritual creatures receive no other interior aid to happiness than the eternity, truth, and charity of the Creator. But if they can be said to be helped from without, perhaps it is only by this that they see one another and rejoice in God, at their fellowship.* . . .

Reply Obj. 3. . . . If there were but one soul enjoying God, it would be happy, though having no neighbor to love. But supposing one neighbor to be there, love of him results from perfect love of God.[87] Consequently, friendship is, as it were, concomitant with perfect Happiness.

---

[86] If this were not true, God would not be God. If we needed something in addition to God for our happiness, God would be a partial and particular good, not the total universal and infinite good. Thomas' thesis may shock the humanist, but it is logically necessary: God alone is enough, or else God is not God.

[87] One reason why loving God is the first and greatest commandment and loving neighbor is the second, is that true love of God will always spill over, so to speak, into love of neighbor, but not necessarily vice versa. God will always send you to your neighbor, but your neighbor will not always send you to God.

Question 5

Of the Attainment of Happiness

Whether Man Can Attain Happiness?[88]

I answer that, Happiness is the attainment of the Perfect Good. Whoever, therefore, is capable of the Perfect Good can attain Happiness. Now, that man is capable of the Perfect Good, is proved both because his intellect can apprehend the universal and perfect good, and because his will can desire it. And therefore man can attain Happiness.[89]—This can be proved again from the fact that man is capable of seeing God, as stated in the First Part (Q. 12, A. 1): in which vision, as we stated above (Q. 3, A. 8) man's perfect Happiness consists. . . .

SECOND ARTICLE

Whether One Man Can Be Happier Than Another?

Objection 3. Further, since Happiness is *the perfect and sufficient good* (*Ethic.* i. 7) it brings rest to man's desire. But his desire is not at rest, if he yet lacks some good that can be got. And if he lack

---

[88] The answer is far from obvious, not only to modern pessimists like Freud (cf. *Civilization and Its Discontents*) and Sartre (cf. *Nausea*), but to ancient sages like Ecclesiastes ("vanity of vanities") and perhaps even to Aristotle, who in *Ethics* I, 10 seems to vacillate uncertainly between pessimism ("Call no man happy until he is dead") and optimism, because he vacillates between partial reliance on the goods of fortune, and detachment from them *à la* Socrates.

[89] The assumption is that what we naturally know, we naturally desire,

nothing that he can get, there can be no still greater good. Therefore either man is not happy; or, if he be happy, no other Happiness can be greater.

On the contrary, It is written (Jn 14:2): *In My Father's house there are many mansions;* which, according to Augustine (*Tract.* lxvii. *in Joan.*) signify *the diverse dignities of merits in the one eternal life.* [90] But the dignity of eternal life [the degree of] which is given according to merit, is Happiness itself. Therefore there are diverse degrees of Happiness, and Happiness is not equally in all.

I answer that, As stated above (Q. 1, A. 8; Q. 2, A. 7), Happiness implies two things, to wit, the last end itself, *i.e.,* the Sovereign Good; and the attainment or enjoyment of that same Good. As to that Good itself, Which is the object and cause of Happiness, one Happiness cannot be greater than another, since there is but one Sovereign Good, namely, God, by enjoying Whom, men are made happy.—But as to the attainment [degree of penetration into] or enjoyment of this Good, one man can be happier than another; because the more a man enjoys this Good the happier he is. Now, that one man enjoys God more than another, happens through his being better disposed or ordered to the enjoyment of Him. And in this sense one man can be happier than another. [91] . . .

Reply Obj. 3. None of the Blessed lacks any desirable good; since they have the Infinite Good Itself, Which is *the good of all good,* as Augustine says (*Enarr. in* Ps cxxxiv). But one is said to be happier than another, by reason of diverse participation of the same good. . . .

---

and what we naturally desire, it is possible for us to attain. Nature never gives desires to any creature without giving a corresponding attainable object. Fish do not desire to fly or birds to swim; men do not desire to hatch eggs, or birds to philosophize.

[90] We attain Heaven by God's grace, but we attain our place or level in Heaven (our degree of ability to participate in grace) by merit, by the works of love, which dig in us a deeper place for more of God to fill.

[91] The gas tank of every heavenly car is totally filled with the highest octane gasoline, but some cars have bigger tanks than others.

THIRD ARTICLE

Whether One Can Be Happy in This Life?

On the contrary, It is written (Job 14:1): *Man born of a woman, living for a short time, is filled with many miseries.* But Happiness excludes misery. Therefore man cannot be happy in this life.

I answer that, A certain participation of Happiness can be had in this life: but perfect and true Happiness cannot be had in this life.[92] This may be seen from a twofold consideration.

First, from the general notion of happiness. For since happiness is a *perfect and sufficient good*, it excludes every evil, and fulfils every desire. But in this life every evil cannot be excluded. For this present life is subject to many unavoidable evils: to ignorance on the part of the intellect, to inordinate affection on the part of the appetite, and to many penalties on the part of the body; as Augustine sets forth in *De Civ. Dei* xix. 4. Likewise neither can the desire for good be satiated in this life. For man naturally desires the good, which he has, to be abiding. Now the goods of the present life pass away; since life itself passes away, which we naturally desire to have, and would wish to hold abidingly, for man naturally shrinks from death. Wherefore it is impossible to have true Happiness in this life.[93]

---

[92] The reason why St. Thomas gives a primarily negative answer to this question, with a qualification—a "yes" only regarding "a certain participation in happiness"—rather than a primarily positive answer with a qualification like "but of course this is not perfect happiness", is because he judges the imperfect by the perfect rather than vice versa. After all, Christ did not say, "Pray, 'Thy Kingdom come . . . in Heaven as on earth.' " Like us in our own deepest hearts, made in God's image, St. Thomas is a perfectionist, an idealist.

[93] Of all the arguments in the *Summa* this would seem to be (1) the most obviously conclusive, since its premises are verified in everyone's experience every day, yet (2) the one most Americans resist most "religiously" and feel the most scandalized and threatened by. The value of this terrible truism of Thomas' is that it heads us off from the desperate optimism of hunting for Heaven on earth, which has always brought about enormous misery, both individually and socially, while its traditional "pessimism" ("I never promised you a rose garden") can produce a joyful detachment,

Secondly, from a consideration of the specific nature of Happiness, viz., the vision of the Divine Essence, which man cannot obtain in this life, as was shown in the First Part (Q. 12, A. 11). Hence it is evident that none can attain true and perfect Happiness in this life. . . .

FOURTH ARTICLE

Whether [True] *Happiness Once Had Can Be Lost?*

Objection 1. It would seem that Happiness can be lost. For Happiness is a perfection. But every perfection is in the thing perfected according to the mode of the latter. Since then man is, by his nature, changeable, it seems that Happiness is participated by man in a changeable manner. And consequently it seems that man can lose Happiness.

Objection 2. Further, Happiness consists in an act of the intellect; and the intellect is subject to the will. But the will can be directed to opposites. Therefore it seems that it can desist from the operation whereby man is made happy: and thus man will cease to be happy.

Objection 3. Further, the end corresponds to the beginning.[94] But man's Happiness has a beginning, since man was not always happy. Therefore it seems that it has an end.

On the contrary, It is written (Mt 25:46) of the righteous that *they shall go . . . into life everlasting*, which, as above stated (A. 2), is the Happiness of the saints. Now what is eternal ceases not. Therefore Happiness cannot be lost.

I answer that, If we speak of imperfect happiness, such as can be had in this life, in this sense it can be lost. This is clear of contemplative happiness, which is lost either by forgetfulness, for

---

as in the lines of the poet Dunbar: "Man, please thy Maker and be merry/And for this world give not a cherry."

[94] This is the fundamental premise of Buddha's metaphysics, which he calls "the pure and spotless eye of the *dharma* [doctrine]", viz., that "whatever is an arising thing, that also is a ceasing thing." Unless Christianity is false, it is a false premise; for the human soul, the resurrected body, and man's happiness constitute the exception to this rule: they have a beginning (in time) but no end (in eternity).

instance, when knowledge is lost through sickness; or again by certain occupations, whereby a man is altogether withdrawn from contemplation.

This is also clear of active happiness: since man's will can be changed so as to fall to vice from the virtue, in whose act that happiness principally consists.[95] If, however, the virtue remain unimpaired, outward changes can indeed disturb such like happiness, in so far as they hinder many acts of virtue; but they cannot take it away altogether, because there still remains an act of virtue, whereby man bears these trials in a praiseworthy manner.—And since the happiness of this life can be lost, a circumstance that appears to be contrary to the nature of happiness, therefore did the Philosopher state (*Ethic.* i. 10) that some are happy in this life, not simply [absolutely], but *as men*, whose nature is subject to change.

But if we speak of that perfect Happiness which we await after this life, it must be observed that Origen (*Peri Archon.* ii 3), following the error of certain Platonists, held that man can become unhappy after the final Happiness.

This, however, is evidently false, for two reasons. First, from the general notion of happiness. For since happiness is the *perfect and sufficient good*, it must needs set man's desire at rest and exclude every evil. Now man naturally desires to hold to the good that he has, and to have the surety of his holding: else he must of necessity be troubled with the fear of losing it, or with the sorrow of knowing that he will lose it. Therefore it is necessary for true Happiness that man have the assured opinion of never losing the good that he possesses. If this opinion be true, it follows that he never will lose happiness: but if it be false, it is in itself an evil that he should have a false opinion: because the false is the evil of the intellect, just as the true is its good, as stated in *Ethic.* vi. 2. Consequently he will no longer be truly happy, if evil be in him.

Secondly, it is again evident if we consider the specific nature of Happiness. For it has been shown above (Q. 3, A. 8) that man's perfect Happiness consists in the vision of the Divine Essence.

---

[95] That happiness in this life is primarily "an activity of the soul in accordance with virtue" rather than any of the goods of fortune is shown by Aristotle in the *Ethics* and Plato in the *Republic*, for virtue is to the soul as health is to the body.

Now it is impossible for anyone seeing the Divine Essence, to wish not to see It.[96] Because every good that one possesses and yet wishes to be without, is either insufficient, something more sufficing being desired in its stead; or else has some inconvenience attached to it, by reason of which it becomes wearisome. But the vision of the Divine Essence fills the soul with all good things, since it unites it to the source of all goodness; hence it is written (Ps 16:15): *I shall be satisfied when Thy glory shall appear;* and (Wis 7:11): *All good things came to me together with her, i.e.,* with the contemplation of wisdom. In like manner neither has it any inconvenience attached to it; because it is written of the contemplation of wisdom (Wis 8:16): *Her conversation hath no bitterness, nor her company any tediousness.* It is thus evident that the happy man cannot forsake Happiness of his own accord. Moreover, neither can he lose Happiness, through God taking it away from him. Because, since the withdrawal of Happiness is a punishment, it cannot be enforced by God, the just Judge, except for some fault; and he that sees God cannot fall into a fault, since rectitude of the will, of necessity, results from that vision as was shown above (Q. 4, A. 4).—Nor again can it be withdrawn by any other agent. Because the mind that is united to God is raised above all other things: and consequently no other agent can sever the mind from that union. Therefore it seems unreasonable that as time goes on, man should pass from happiness to misery, and *vice versa;* because such like vicissitudes of time can only be for such things as are subject to time and movement.

Reply Obj. 1. Happiness is consummate perfection, which excludes every defect from the happy. And therefore whoever has happiness has it altogether unchangeably: this is done by the Divine power, which raises man to the participation of eternity which transcends all change.

Reply Obj. 2. The will can be directed to opposites, in things which are ordained to the end; but it is ordained, of natural necessity, to the last end.[97] This is evident from the fact that man is unable not to wish to be happy.

---

[96] This is why there can be no evil and no motive for evil in Heaven.

[97] That is, formally, but not materially. We are not necessarily ordained to, but free to choose, diverse means to the ultimate end of happiness; and we are also free to choose among different interpretations of happiness, or

Reply Obj. 3. Happiness has a beginning owing to the condition of the participator: but it has no end by reason of the [eternal] condition of the good, the participation of which makes man happy. Hence the beginning of happiness is from one cause, its endlessness is from another.

FIFTH ARTICLE

Whether Man Can Attain Happiness by His Natural Powers?

Objection 1. It would seem that man can attain Happiness by his natural powers. For nature does not fail in necessary things. But nothing is so necessary to man as that by which he attains the last end. Therefore this is not lacking to human nature. Therefore man can attain Happiness by his natural powers. . . .

I answer that, Imperfect happiness that can be had in this life, can be acquired by man by his natural powers, in the same way as virtue, in whose operation it consists: on this point we shall speak further on (Q. 63). But man's perfect Happiness, as stated above (Q. 3, A. 8), consists in the vision of the Divine Essence. Now the vision of God's Essence surpasses the nature not only of man, but also of every creature, as was shown in the First Part (Q. 12, A. 4). . . .

Reply Obj. 1. Just as nature does not fail man in necessaries, although it has not provided him with weapons and clothing, as it provided other animals, because it gave him reason and hands, with which he is able to get these things for himself; so neither did it fail man in things necessary, although it gave him not the wherewithal to attain Happiness: since this it could not do. But it did give him free-will, with which he can turn to God, that He may make him happy.[98] . . .

---

material contents to happiness (I–II, 2). Our desire for happiness formally, on the other hand, is not a free choice, but a necessity of our nature (cf. Article 8 and the argument in the last sentence of this Reply). Even a grumpy person gets happiness out of being grumpy, a masochist gets happiness from pain, and a suicide is seeking to escape from an unhappy life, not from a happy one.

[98] Thus nature provides (1) the *desire* for perfect happiness and (2) one

EIGHTH ARTICLE

Whether Every Man Desires Happiness?

I answer that, Happiness can be considered in two ways. First according to the general notion of happiness: and thus, of necessity, every man desires happiness. For the general notion of happiness consists in the perfect good, as stated above (AA. 3, 4). But since good is the object of the will, the perfect good of a man is that which entirely satisfies his will. Consequently to desire happiness is nothing else than to desire that one's will be satisfied. And this everyone desires. Secondly we may speak of Happiness according to its specific notion, as to that in which it consists. And thus all do not know Happiness; because they know not in what thing the general notion of happiness is found.[99] And consequently, in this respect, not all desire it. . . .

---

of the means (free will) to attain it, but not (3) the exercise of this free will in choice (this is our doing, not nature's), nor the three following factors that come only from God, viz., (4) the supernatural revelation of God, which is in practice necessary for many or most men, at least, to attain happiness (see I, 1, 1 *"I answer that"*), (5) the real object (God Himself) in which happiness consists, and (6) the efficient cause needed to attain this object, viz., divine grace.

[99] Cf. St. Augustine: "Seek what you seek, but it is not where you seek it" (*Confessions* IV, 12, par. 1).

B. *Willing*

Question 6

Of the Voluntary and the Involuntary

Since therefore Happiness is to be gained by means of certain acts, we must in due sequence consider human acts, in order to know by what acts we may obtain Happiness, and by what acts we are prevented from obtaining it.[100] But because operations and acts are concerned with things singular, consequently all practical knowledge is incomplete unless it take account of things in detail. The study of Morals, therefore, since it treats of human acts, should consider first the general principles; and secondly matters of detail.

In treating of the general principles, the points that offer themselves for our consideration are—(1) human acts themselves; (2) their principles. Now of human acts some are proper to man; others are common to man and animals. And since Happiness is man's proper good, those acts which are proper to man have a closer connection with Happiness than have those which are common to man and the other animals. First, then, we must consider those acts which are proper to man; secondly, those acts which are common to man and the other animals, and are called Passions. The first of these points offers a twofold consideration: (1) What makes a human act? (2) What distinguishes human acts?

And since those acts are properly called human, which are voluntary, because the will is the rational appetite, which is proper to man; we must consider acts in so far as they are voluntary.

First, then, we must consider the voluntary and involuntary in general; secondly, those acts which are voluntary, as being elicited by the will, and as issuing from the will immediately; thirdly, those acts which are voluntary, as being commanded by the will, which issue from the will through the medium of the other powers.

---

[100] How utterly practical! Such knowledge is nothing less than the science of life, "the one thing needful" (Lk 10:42).

And because voluntary acts have certain circumstances, according to which we form our judgment concerning them, we must first consider the voluntary and the involuntary, and afterwards, the circumstances of those acts which are found to be voluntary or involuntary. . . .

Whether There Is Anything Voluntary in Human Acts?

I answer that, There must needs be something voluntary in human acts. In order to make this clear, we must take note that . . . if a thing has no knowledge of the end . . . the principle of acting or being moved for an end is not in that thing, but in something else, by which the principle of its action towards an end is imprinted on it. Wherefore such like things are not said to move themselves, but to be moved by others. But those things which have a knowledge of the end are said to move themselves because there is in them a principle by which they not only act but also act for an end. And consequently . . . the movements of such things are said to be voluntary: for the word *voluntary* implies that their movements and acts are from their own inclination. Hence it is that, according to the definitions of Aristotle, Gregory of Nyssa, and Damascene, the voluntary is defined not only as [1] having *a principle within* the agent, but also as [2] implying *knowledge*. Therefore, since man especially [2] knows the end of his work, and [1] moves himself, in his acts especially is the voluntary to be found. . . .

FOURTH ARTICLE

Whether Violence Can Be Done to the Will?

Objection 1. It would seem that violence can be done to the will. For everything can be compelled by that which is more powerful. But there is something, namely, God, that is more powerful than the human will. Therefore it can be compelled, at least by Him.[101] . . .

---

[101] This is a fundamental premise of Calvinism. What it forgets is that grace, however infinitely powerful, deals with nature according to its

I answer that, The act of the will is twofold: one is its immediate act, as it were, elicited by it, namely, *to wish*; the other is an act of the will commanded by it, and put into execution by means of some other power, such as *to walk* and *to speak*, which are commanded by the will to be executed by means of the motive power.

As regards the commanded acts of the will, then, the will can suffer violence, in so far as violence can prevent the exterior members from executing the will's command. But as to the will's own proper act, violence cannot be done to the will.[102]

The reason of this is that the act of the will is nothing else than an inclination proceeding from the interior principle of knowledge: just as the natural appetite is an inclination proceeding from an interior principle without knowledge. Now what is compelled or violent is from an exterior principle. Consequently it is contrary to the nature of the will's own act, that it should be subject to compulsion and violence: just as it is also contrary to the nature of a natural inclination or movement. For a stone may have an upward movement from violence, but that this violent movement be from its natural inclination is impossible. In like manner a man may be dragged by force: but it is contrary to the very notion of violence, that he be thus dragged of his own will.

Reply Obj. 1. God Who is more powerful than the human will, can move the will of man, according to Proverbs 21:1: *The heart of the king is in the hand of the Lord; whithersoever He will He shall turn it.* But if this were by compulsion, it would no longer be by an act of the will, nor would the will itself be moved, but something else against the will.[103] . . .

---

nature, and that even omnipotence does not extend to contradictions such as a human will being simultaneously voluntary (uncompelled) and compelled (involuntary).

[102] This thesis is not as controversial as it seems. It is true almost by definition, for when we are compelled, it is *against* our will. An important corollary is that free will can never be taken from us, for it is part of our very essence. "Stone walls do not a prison make, nor iron bars a cage" (for the will). Many prisoners discovered this inner, inviolable freedom only in prison (Dostoyevski, Sartre, Solzhenitsyn, Valladaros).

[103] Thus God's grace can move us without removing our free will. If my moving and influencing you does not necessarily lessen your freedom

FIFTH ARTICLE

Whether Violence Causes Involuntariness?

I answer that, Violence is directly opposed to the voluntary, as likewise to the natural.[104] For the voluntary and the natural have this in common, that both are from an intrinsic principle; whereas violence is from an extrinsic principle. And for this reason, just as in things devoid of knowledge, violence effects something against nature: so in things endowed with knowledge, it effects something against the will. Now that which is against nature is said to be *unnatural*; and in like manner that which is against the will is said to be *involuntary*. Therefore violence causes involuntariness. . . .

SIXTH ARTICLE

Whether Fear Causes Involuntariness Simply?

I answer that, As the Philosopher says (*Ethic.* iii) and likewise Gregory of Nyssa in his book on Man (Nemesius, *loc. cit.*), such things as are done through fear *are of a mixed character*, being partly voluntary and partly involuntary. For that which is done through fear, considered in itself, is not voluntary; but it becomes voluntary in this particular case, in order, namely, to avoid the evil feared. . . . That which is done through fear, is voluntary, inasmuch as it is here and now, that is to say, in so far as, under the circumstances, it hinders a greater evil which was feared; thus the throwing of the cargo into the sea becomes voluntary during the storm, through fear of the danger. . . .

(does reading a book like this make you less free, or more?), why should God's grace do so? Not all moving is violent. E.g., beauty in the object moves the will as final cause, and charity in the willing subject moves the will as efficient cause without lessening freedom.

[104] Thus there are three distinct kinds of acts: natural, voluntary (free), and violent.

SEVENTH ARTICLE

Whether Concupiscence[105] *Causes Involuntariness?*

On the contrary, Damascene says (*De Fide Orthod.* ii. 24): *The involuntary act deserves mercy or indulgence, and is done with regret.* But neither of these can be said of that which is done out of concupiscence. Therefore concupiscence does not cause involuntariness.

I answer that, Concupiscence does not cause involuntariness, but on the contrary makes something to be voluntary. For a thing is said to be voluntary, from the fact that the will is moved to it. Now concupiscence inclines the will to desire the object of concupiscence. Therefore the effect of concupiscence is to make something to be voluntary rather than involuntary. . . .

EIGHTH ARTICLE

Whether Ignorance Causes Involuntariness?

On the contrary, Damascene (*loc. cit.*) and the Philosopher (*Ethic.* iii. 1) say that *what is done through ignorance is involuntary.*

I answer that, If ignorance causes involuntariness, it is in so far as it deprives one of knowledge, which is a necessary condition of voluntariness, as was declared above (A. 1). But it is not every ignorance that deprives one of this knowledge. . . . Ignorance is *consequent* to the act of the will, in so far as ignorance itself is voluntary: and this happens in two ways. . . . First, because the act of the will is brought to bear on the ignorance: as when a man wishes not to know, that he may have an excuse for sin, or that he may not be withheld from sin; according to Job 21:14: *We desire not the knowledge of Thy ways.* And this is called *affected ignorance.* —Secondly, ignorance is said to be voluntary, when it regards that which one can and ought to know. . . . And ignorance of this kind

---

[105] Concupiscence is unregulated, disordered passion. We should distinguish *concupiscence* from *the concupiscible desires*, just as we should distinguish wrath (*ira*) from the irascible desires ("the flight or fight response"). The former (concupiscence and wrath) are evil, the latter are merely psychological raw material for good or evil.

happens, either when one does not actually consider what one can and ought to consider . . . or when one does not take the trouble to acquire the knowledge which one ought to have; in which sense, ignorance of the general principles of law, which one ought to know, is voluntary, as being due to negligence.—Accordingly, if in either of these ways, ignorance is voluntary, it cannot cause involuntariness simply. Nevertheless it causes involuntariness in a certain respect, inasmuch as it precedes the movement of the will towards the act, which movement would not be, if there were knowledge. Ignorance is *antecedent* to the act of the will, when it is not voluntary, and yet is the cause of man's willing what he would not will otherwise. Thus a man may be ignorant of some circumstance of his act, which he was not bound to know, the result being that he does that which he would not do, if he knew of that circumstance; for instance, a man, after taking proper precaution, may not know that someone is coming along the road, so that he shoots an arrow and slays a passer-by. Such ignorance causes involuntariness simply. . . .

Question 8

Of the Will, in Regard to What It Wills

We must now consider the different acts of the will; and in the first place, those acts which belong to the will itself immediately, as being elicited by the will; secondly, those acts which are commanded by the will.

Now the will is moved to the end, and to the means to the end; we must therefore consider—(1) Those acts of the will whereby it is moved to the end; and (2) those whereby it is moved to the means. . . .

FIRST ARTICLE

Whether the Will Is of Good Only?

I answer that, . . . In order that the will tend to anything, it is requisite, not that this be good in very truth, but that it be apprehended as good. Wherefore the Philosopher says (*Phys.* ii. 3) that *the end is a good, or an apparent good.*[106] . . .

---

[106] Thus the crucial importance of prudence, or practical moral wisdom, which distinguishes between real and apparent goods. St. Thomas connects the intellectual virtues with the moral virtues much more closely (through prudence) than typically modern moral philosophies do.

Question 9

Of That Which Moves the Will

Whether the Will Is Moved by the Intellect?

Objection 3. Further, the same is not mover and moved in respect of the same thing. But the will moves the intellect; for we exercise the intellect when[ever] we will. Therefore the intellect does not move the will. . . .

Reply Obj. 3. The will moves the intellect as to the exercise of its act.[107] . . . But as to the determination of the act, which the act derives from the object, the intellect moves the will.[108] . . . It is therefore evident that the same is not mover and moved in the same respect.

SECOND ARTICLE

Whether the Will Is Moved by the Sensitive Appetite?

Objection 3. Further, as is proved in *Phys.* viii. 5, the mover is not moved by that which it moves, in such a way that there be reciprocal motion. But the will moves the sensitive appetite, inasmuch as the sensitive appetite obeys the reason. Therefore the sensitive appetite does not move the will.[109]

---

[107] That is, as efficient cause.

[108] That is, as formal cause.

[109] This argument has a specious plausibility, but St. Thomas is not swayed by it, because of his tendency to stay as close as possible to experience, to tailor his philosophical clothes to experience's body, not vice versa. We experience the will being moved by the appetite, even

On the contrary, It is written (James 1:14): *Every man is tempted by his own concupiscence, being drawn away and allured.* But man would not be drawn away by his concupiscence, unless his will were moved by the sensitive appetite, wherein concupiscence resides. Therefore the sensitive appetite moves the will. . . .

Reply Obj. 3. As the Philosopher says (*Polit.* i. 2), the reason, in which resides the will,[110] moves, by its command, the irascible and concupiscible powers, not, indeed, *by a despotic sovereignty*, as a slave is moved by his master, but by a *royal and politic sovereignty*, as free men are ruled by their governor, and can nevertheless act counter to his commands.[111] Hence both irascible and concupiscible can move counter to the will: and accordingly nothing hinders the will from being moved by them at times. . . .

FIFTH ARTICLE

Whether the Will Is Moved by a Heavenly Body?

I answer that, . . . Some have maintained that heavenly bodies have an influence on the human will, in the same way as some exterior agent moves the will, as to the exercise of its act.—But this

---

though this argument seems to prove it cannot happen, just as we experience motion even though Parmenides and Zeno seem to prove it cannot really happen. Even Augustine occasionally tended to this Platonic doctrine of a one-way vertical causality from reason to will and from will to appetite, and to the correlative Platonic tendency to place reason above experience, especially in his theory that sensation could not be due to the lower and lesser thing (body) causing effects on the higher and greater thing (soul), therefore sense images must have come not from the sense but from the soul working them up out of its own inner substance on the occasion of it perceiving that something was going on in the senses, which it perpetually watched with a "vital attention". However, Augustine vividly knew from his own experience that the passions could move the will and also the reason, and that evil was not due only to ignorance, as Plato taught.

[110] Note how much broader the term "reason" was to pre-modern philosophers than it is in modern usage.

[111] The soul, on the other hand, rules the body "despotically", for it is the very life of the body. The body has no will or life or principle of action of its own apart from the soul; corpses do nothing.

is impossible. For the *will*, as stated in *De Anima* iii. 9, *is in the reason*. Now the reason is a power of the soul, not bound to a bodily organ: wherefore it follows that the will is a power absolutely incorporeal and immaterial. But it is evident that no body can act on what is incorporeal, but rather the reverse: because things incorporeal and immaterial have a power more formal and more universal than any corporeal things whatever.[112] Therefore it is impossible for a heavenly body to act directly on the intellect or the will. . . .

---

[112] The principle is evident to common sense upon a moment's reflection: how could a stone crush a ghost or an angel? Our body cannot *move* our reason, only *obey* it or *disobey* it, or impair its exercise. But reason can move the body, and does, in all conscious acts. Body moves thought only to prevent thought (e.g., a bit of bone pressing on the brain, or a passion distracting our attention), but thought moves body to direct and perfect the body's own acts, like an author using language. The same argument that shows the will to be free of compulsion from heavenly bodies (ancient astrological fatalism) shows it to be free of compulsion from earthly bodies as well (modern psychological determinism).

Question 13

Of Choice, Which Is an Act of the Will with Regard to the Means[113]

FIRST ARTICLE

Whether Choice Is an Act of Will or of Reason?

I answer that, The word choice implies something belonging to the reason or intellect, and something belonging to the will: for the Philosopher says (*Ethic.* vi. 2) that choice is either *intellect influenced by appetite or appetite influenced by intellect.* . . .

SECOND ARTICLE

Whether Choice Is to Be Found in Irrational Animals?

Objection 3. Further, according to *Ethic.* vi. 12, *it is from prudence that a man makes a good choice of means.* But prudence [practical wisdom] is found in irrational animals: hence it is said in the beginning of *Metaph.* (i. 1) that *those animals which, like bees, cannot hear sounds, are prudent by instinct.* We see this plainly, in wonderful cases of sagacity manifested in the works of various animals, such as bees, spiders, and dogs. For a hound in following a stag, on coming to a crossroad, tries by scent whether the stag has passed by the first or the second road: and if he find that the stag has not passed there, being thus assured, takes to the third road without trying the scent; as though he were reasoning by way of exclusion, arguing that the stag must have passed by this way, since he did not

---

[113] I.e., not with regard to the end (happiness), for the will is not free to choose contrary to its own natural, essential, necessary end.

pass by the others, and there is no other road.[114] Therefore it seems that irrational animals are able to choose.

On the contrary, Gregory of Nyssa [Nemesius, *De Nat. Hom.* xxxiii] says that *children and irrational animals act willingly but not from choice.* Therefore choice is not in irrational animals.

I answer that, Since choice is the taking of one thing in preference to another, it must of necessity be in respect of several things that can be chosen. Consequently, in those things which are altogether determinate to one, there is no place for choice. Now the difference between the sensitive appetite and the will is that, as stated above (Q. 1, A. 2 *ad* 3), the sensitive appetite is determinate to one particular thing, according to the order of nature;[115] whereas the will, although determinate to one thing in general, viz., the good, according to the order of nature, is nevertheless indeterminate in respect of particular goods. Consequently choice belongs properly to the will, and not to the sensitive appetite, which is all that irrational animals have. Wherefore irrational animals are not competent to choose. . . .

Reply Obj. 3. As stated in *Phys.* iii. 3 *movement is the act of the movable, caused by a mover.* Wherefore the power of the mover appears in the movement of that which it moves. Accordingly, in all things moved by reason, the order of reason which moves them is evident, although the things themselves are without reason: for an arrow through the motion of the archer goes straight towards the target, as though it were endowed with reason to direct its course. The same may be seen in the movements of clocks and all engines put together by the art of man. Now as artificial things are in comparison to human art, so are all natural things in comparison to the Divine art.[116] And accordingly order is to be seen in things

---

[114] Note the remarkably close observation of nature—a feature of medieval philosophers not usually acknowledged by current conventional clichés.

[115] "Sensitive appetite" includes what we would call "animal instinct". It is determined to one particular action, e.g., a given species of bird will always build its nest in the same way.

[116] St. Thomas is not saying, as Descartes would say later, that animals are mere automata, like clocks, but that although they have sensitive appetite, they do not have reason and will, therefore they cannot direct

moved by nature, just as in things moved by reason, as is stated in *Phys.* ii. And thus it is that in the works of irrational animals we notice certain marks of sagacity, in so far as they have a natural inclination to set about their actions in a most orderly manner through being ordained by the Supreme art. For which reason, too, certain animals are called prudent or sagacious; and not because they reason or exercise any choice about things. This is clear from the fact that all that share in one nature, invariably act in the same way.

Whether Choice Is Only of the Means,
or Sometimes Also of the End?

On the contrary, The Philosopher says (*Ethic.* iii. 2) that *volition is of the end, but choice of the means.*

I answer that, As already stated (A. 1 *ad* 2), choice results from the decision or judgment which is, as it were, the conclusion of a practical syllogism. Hence that which is the conclusion of a practical syllogism, is the matter of choice. Now in practical things the end stands in the position of a principle, not of a conclusion, as the Philosopher says (*Phys.* ii. 9). Wherefore the end, as such, is not a matter of choice.[117] . . .

Whether Man Chooses of Necessity or Freely?

Objection 1. It would seem that man chooses of necessity. For the end stands in relation to the object of choice, as the principle of that which follows from the principles, as declared in *Ethic.* vii. 8. But

---

themselves to their end by choice, but are directed by their Designer through the "wisdom" of their natural instincts. The organs of the human body show a similar "wisdom" that is their own and not their own.

[117] I.e., every choice presupposes, as a prior premise, the end or good sought by means of the choice. We can no more choose our final end than

conclusions follow of necessity from their principles. Therefore man is moved of necessity from [willing] the end to the choice [of the means]. . . .

I answer that, Man does not choose of necessity. . . . The perfect good alone, which is Happiness, cannot be apprehended by the reason as an evil, or as lacking in any way.[118] Consequently man wills Happiness of necessity, nor can he will not to be happy, or to be unhappy. Now since choice is not of the end, but of the means, as stated above (A. 3); it is not of the perfect good, which is Happiness, but of other particular goods. Therefore man chooses not of necessity, but freely.

Reply Obj. 1. The conclusion does not always of necessity follow from the principles, but only when the principles cannot be true if the conclusion is not true. In like manner, the end does not always necessitate in man the choosing of the means, because the means are not always such that the end cannot be gained without them; or, if they be such, they are not always considered in that light.[119] . . .

---

we can prove our first principles such as the law of non-contradiction, for we must always presuppose them. The consequences of this technical, logical point are enormous from a practical and religious point of view: it means that God, our final end, is not avoidable, not an "option" like a movie or a meal, not something for "religious people" (whoever they are), but "the only game in town" (or, as C. S. Lewis puts it, "the only fruit [good] this universe can grow—the only fruit any possible universe can grow").

[118] Thus, in Heaven, when this perfect good (God) is seen clearly, it will be impossible to choose evil. But here, our ignorance of or our ability to doubt the identity of our supreme good (happiness) with God makes possible our choosing evil as our apparent good. Plato is half right: evil is not *only* ignorance, but it must *include* ignorance.

[119] A necessary demonstration is one in which the truth of the premises and the truth of the conclusion are inseparable. Most arguments are not necessary demonstrations but arguments from probability or fittingness. A necessary good is one in which the good of the end and the good of the means are inseparable (e.g., when a life raft is the only way to save yourself from drowning). Like necessary demonstrations, this is relatively rare; most goods are not necessarily connected with the *summum bonum*, or known to be so connected; therefore they are matters to be chosen.

C. Good and Evil

Question 18

Of the Good and Evil of
Human Acts, in General

FIRST ARTICLE

Whether Every Human Action Is Good,
or Are There Evil[120] *Actions?*

I answer that, We must speak of good and evil in actions as of
good and evil in things: because such as everything is, such is the
act that it produces. Now in things, each one has so much good as it
has being: since good and being are convertible, as was stated in the
First Part (Q. 5, AA. 1, 3). But God alone has the whole plenitude
of His Being in a certain unity: whereas every other thing has its
proper fulness of being in a certain multiplicity. Wherefore it
happens with some things, that they have being in some respect,
and yet they are lacking in the fulness of being due to them. Thus
the fulness of human being requires a compound of soul and body,
having all the powers and instruments of knowledge and movement: wherefore if any man be lacking in any of these, he is lacking
in something due to the fulness of his being. So that as much as he
has of being, so much has he of goodness: while so far as he is
lacking in the fulness of his being, so far is he lacking in goodness,
and is said to be evil: thus a blind man is possessed of goodness

---

[120] "Evil" is meant here not only in the narrow and specific sense of
moral evil, but as the opposite of any good. St. Thomas does not believe
that evil is a being, but that it is *in* beings. He does not believe that
multiplicity and finitude are evil in themselves, as the Gnostics and
Manichees taught, but that finitude and multiplicity make evil *possible*. A
tree is not evil for not being God, but a tree, unlike God, can be diseased,
and disease is evil for a tree.

inasmuch as he lives; and of evil, inasmuch as he lacks sight. . . . We must therefore say that every action has goodness, in so far as it has being: whereas it is lacking in goodness, in so far as it is lacking in something that is due to its fulness of being; and thus it is said to be evil:[121] for instance if it lacks the quantity determined by reason, or its due place, or something of the kind. . . .

SECOND ARTICLE

Whether the Good or Evil of a Man's Action Is Derived from Its Object?[122]

Objection 1. It would seem that the good or evil of an action is not derived from its object. For the object of any action is a thing. But *evil is not in things, but in the sinner's use of them*, as Augustine says (*De Doctr. Christ.* iii. 12). Therefore the good or evil of a human action is not derived from its object. . . .

On the contrary, It is written (Hos 9:10): *They became abominable as those things which they loved.* Now man becomes abominable to God on account of the malice of his action. Therefore the malice of his action is according to the evil objects that man loves. And the same applies to the goodness of his action.

I answer that, as stated above (A. 1) the good or evil of an action, as of other things, depends on its fulness of being or its lack of that fulness [cf. n. 121]. Now the first thing that belongs to the fulness of being seems to be that which gives a thing its species. And just as a natural thing has its species from its form, so an action has its

---

[121] St. Thomas means by "being" not merely "existence" (for evil acts *exist*) but also essence, including proper form and order to the end.

[122] N.b.: St. Thomas does not say that an act is made good or evil *only* by its object. He will add "circumstances" (situation) and "end" (intention) as two more moral determinants in the next two articles. Thus an act is good if and only if it (1) has the right object (i.e., is the right kind of act, good by its own nature), (2) is done with the right intention, and (3) in the right circumstances. (Any act is also *ontologically* good; even a murderer's bullet must be a *good* shot. Cf. Article 1 and Article 4, "*I answer that*".) Moral legalism concentrates only on factor 1, moral subjectivism only on factor 2, and moral relativism only on factor 3.

species from its object, as movement from its term.[123] And there-fore, just as the primary goodness of a natural thing is derived from its form, which gives it its species, so the primary goodness of a moral action is derived from its suitable object: hence some call such an action *good in its genus*; for instance, *to make use of what is one's own*. And just as, in natural things, the primary evil is when a generated thing does not realize its specific form (for instance, if instead of a man, something else be generated);[124] so the primary evil in moral actions is that which is from the object, for instance, *to take what belongs to another*. And this action is said to be *evil in its genus*, genus here standing for species, just as we apply the term *mankind* to the whole human species.

Reply Obj. 1. Although external things are good in themselves, nevertheless they have not always a due proportion to this or that action. And so, inasmuch as they are considered as objects of such actions, they have not the quality of goodness.[125] . . .

THIRD ARTICLE

Whether Man's Action Is Good or Evil from a Circumstance?

Objection 1. It would seem that an action is not good or evil from a circumstance. For circumstances stand around (*circumstant*) an action, as being outside it, as stated above (Q. 7, A. 1). But *good and evil are in things themselves*, as is stated in *Metaph.* vi. 4. Therefore an action does not derive goodness or malice from a circumstance. . . .

Objection 3. Further, that which belongs to a thing, in respect of its substance, is not ascribed to it in respect of an accident. But good and evil belong to an action in respect of its substance; because an action can be good or evil in its genus, as stated above (A. 2). Therefore an action is not good or bad from a circumstance.

---

[123] I.e., the answer to the question, "What kind (species) of action is this?" comes from the object aimed at by the action itself (e.g., batting a ball, learning a fact, coveting the possession of another's property).

[124] That is, a genetic monstrosity.

[125] They are ontologically good in themselves, but they are morally not good for the actor; they are the wrong objects of willing (e.g., another man's wife or property).

On the contrary, The Philosopher says (*Ethic.* ii. 3) that a virtuous man acts as he should, and when he should, and so on in respect of the other circumstances. Therefore, on the other hand, the vicious man, in the matter of each vice, acts when he should not, or where he should not, and so on with the other circumstances. Therefore human actions are good or evil according to circumstances.

I answer that, In natural things, it is to be noted that the whole fulness of perfection due to a thing, is not from the mere substantial form, that gives it its species; since a thing derives much from supervening accidents, as man does from shape, color, and the like; and if any one of these accidents be out of due proportion, evil is the result. So it is with action. For the plenitude of its goodness does not consist wholly in its species, but also in certain additions which accrue to it by reason of certain accidents: and such are its due circumstances. Wherefore if something be wanting that is requisite as a due circumstance the action will be evil.

Reply Obj. 1. Circumstances are outside an action, inasmuch as they are not part of its essence; but they are in an action as accidents thereof. Thus, too, accidents in natural substances are outside the essence. . . .

Reply Obj. 3. Since good and being are convertible; according as being is predicated of substance and of accident, so is good predicated of a thing both in respect of its essential being, and in respect of its accidental being; and this, both in natural things and in moral actions.[126]

FOURTH ARTICLE

Whether a Human Action Is Good or Evil from Its End?

Objection 1. It would seem that the good and evil in human actions are not from the end. For Dionysius says (*Div. Nom.* iv) that *nothing acts with a view to evil.*[127] If therefore an action were

---

[126] Note how frequently St. Thomas appeals to metaphysics to ground ethics, and how he relates everything to *being.*

[127] An end must be a good, else it would not be an end. If the end were in no way attractive, it could not attract an action to it; only the desirable can be desired. We are speaking here about all agents in nature, not just man, for all act for an end: cf. I, 44, 4.

good or evil from its end, no action would be evil. Which is clearly false. . . .

I answer that, . . . A fourfold goodness may be considered in a human action. First, that which, as an action, it derives from its genus; because as much as it has of action and being so much has it of goodness, as stated above (A. 1). Secondly, it has goodness according to its species; which is derived from its suitable object. Thirdly, it has goodness from its circumstances, in respect, as it were, of its accidents. Fourthly, it has goodness from its end, to which it is compared as to the cause of its goodness.

Reply Obj. 1. The good in view of which one acts is not always a true good; but sometimes it is a true good, sometimes an apparent good. And in the latter event, an evil action results from the end in view. . . .

SIXTH ARTICLE

Whether an Action Has the Species of Good or Evil from Its End? [128]

I answer that, Certain actions are called human, inasmuch as they are voluntary, as stated above (Q. 1, A. 1). Now, in a voluntary action, there is a twofold action, viz., the interior action of the will, and the external action: and each of these actions has its object. The end is properly the object of the interior act of the will: while the object of the external action, is that on which the action is brought to bear. Therefore just as the external action takes its species from the object on which it bears:[129] so the interior act of the will takes its species from the end, as from its own proper object.[130]

---

[128] Cf. I–II, 20, 1. St. Thomas has just summed up his whole teaching on what makes an act good or evil in four points, in the previous Article. Now he points out the primacy of intention and the interior act of will (Kant's insight) without denying (as Kant did) the other three factors (Article 4). Of course, he learned this primacy not from Kant but from Christ (cf. Mt 5:8, 21–22, 27–28; Mk 7:1–23; 12:30; Lk 6:45).

[129] The external deed commanded by the will is defined essentially by its object, i.e., by what is done.

[130] I.e., the will is specified as good or evil depending on its object, on what is willed, i.e., what is intended.

Now that which is on the part of the will is formal in regard to that which is on the part of the external action: [131] because the will uses the limbs to act as instruments; nor have external actions any measure of morality, save in so far as they are voluntary. Consequently the species of a human act is considered formally with regard to the end, but materially with regard to the object of the external action. [132] Hence the Philosopher says (*Ethic.* v. 2) that *he who steals that he may commit adultery, is, strictly speaking, more adulterer than thief.* . . .

EIGHTH ARTICLE

Whether Any Action Is Indifferent [Neither Good nor Evil] *in Its Species?*

Objection 2. Further, human actions derive their species from their end or object, as stated above (A. 6; Q. 1, A. 3). But every end and every object is either good or bad. Therefore every human action is good or evil according to its species. None, therefore, is indifferent in its species.

On the contrary, Augustine says (*De Serm. Dom. in Mont.* ii. 18), that *there are certain deeds of a middle kind, which can be done with a good or evil mind, of which it is rash to form a judgment.* Therefore some actions are indifferent according to their species.

I answer that, . . . if the object of an action includes something in accord with the order of reason, it will be a good action according to its species; for instance, to give alms to a person in want. On the other hand, if it includes something repugnant to the order of reason, it will be an evil act according to its species; for instance, to steal, which is to appropriate what belongs to another. But it may

---

[131] I.e., the will's good or evil determines the external act which is willed as good or evil. The will gives moral form to the act.

[132] I.e., whether a human (voluntary) act is good or evil depends mainly on the end, for the end gives the deed its moral form (nature); but it also depends on the external object, which is its matter. A good deed needs good matter *and* good form; a good deed *and* a good intention; a good external act of the body *and* a good internal act of the will. But the internal is prior: see the following example.

happen that the object of an action does not include something pertaining to the order of reason; for instance, to pick up a straw from the ground, to walk in the fields, and the like: and such actions are indifferent according to their species.[133] . . .

Reply Obj. 2. Every object or end has some goodness or malice, at least natural to it: but this does not imply moral goodness or malice, which is considered in relation to the reason, as stated above. And it is of this that we are here treating. . . .

Whether an Individual Action Can Be Indifferent?

I answer that, It sometimes happens that an action is indifferent in its species, but considered in the individual it is good or evil. And the reason of this is because a moral action, as stated above (A. 3), derives its goodness not only from its object, whence it takes its species; but also from the circumstances, which are its accidents, as it were; just as something belongs to a man by reason of his individual accidents, which does not belong to him by reason of his species. And every individual action must needs have some circumstance that makes it good or bad, at least in respect of the intention of the end. For since it belongs to the reason to direct; if an action that proceeds from deliberate reason be not directed to the due end, it is, by that fact alone, repugnant to reason, and has the character of evil. But if it be directed to a due end, it is in accord with reason; wherefore it has the character of good. Now it must needs be either directed or not directed to a due end. Consequently every human action that proceeds from deliberate reason, if it be considered in the individual, must be good or bad.[134]

If, however, it does not proceed from deliberate reason, but from some act of the imagination, as when a man strokes his beard,

---

[133] Thus every *human* (rational and voluntary) act is good or evil, but not every *act of man* is.

[134] Therefore most deliberate acts of most people most of the time have positive moral value. Eating, reading, working—these are good by being natural and rightly directed toward a good end.

or moves his hand or foot; such an action, properly speaking, is not moral or human; since this depends on the reason. Hence it will be indifferent, as standing apart from the genus of moral actions. . . .

TENTH ARTICLE

Whether a Circumstance Places a Moral Action in the Species of Good or Evil?

On the contrary, Place is a circumstance. But place makes a moral action to be in a certain species of evil; for theft of a thing from a holy place is a sacrilege. Therefore a circumstance makes a moral action to be specifically good or bad. . . .

ELEVENTH ARTICLE

Whether Every Circumstance That Makes an Action Better or Worse, Places a Moral Action in a Species of Good or Evil?[135]

On the contrary, More and less do not change a species. But more and less is a circumstance of additional goodness or malice. Therefore not every circumstance that makes a moral action better or worse, places it in a species of good or evil.

I answer that, . . . to take what belongs to another in a large or small quantity, does not change the species of the sin. Nevertheless it can aggravate or diminish the sin. The same applies to other evil or good actions. . . .

---

[135] I.e., do circumstances change the morality of an act in degree or in kind ("species")? Answer: sometimes in degree only; sometimes in kind.

Question 19

Of the Goodness and Malice of
the Interior Act of the Will

FIRST ARTICLE

Whether the Goodness of the Will Depends on the Object?

Objection 3. Further, such as a thing is, such does it make a thing
to be. But the object of the will is good, by reason of the goodness
of nature. Therefore it cannot give moral goodness to the will.[136]
Therefore the moral goodness of the will does not depend on the
object. . . .

Reply Obj. 3. Good is presented to the will as its object by the
reason: and in so far as it is in accord with reason, it enters the moral
order, and causes moral goodness in the act of the will: because the
reason is the principle of human and moral acts, as stated above
(Q. 18, A. 5).[137] . . .

THIRD ARTICLE

Whether the Goodness of the Will Depends on Reason?[138]

On the contrary, Hilary says (*De Trin.* x): *It is an unruly will that
persists in its desires in opposition to reason.* But the goodness of the

---

[136] The Objection not only distinguishes, but radically separates, moral
goodness from natural goodness, or ontological goodness, like most
modern moral philosophy.

[137] For St. Thomas, good acts depend on a good will; and good will
depends on reason; reason depends on natural being (its object), and
natural being depends on God (its Creator); therefore the moral goodness
of an act and of the will depends on the ontological goodness of nature and
of God through the mediation of reason (see the next Article).

[138] This affirmation is close to the very essence of classical wisdom. It is

will consists in not being unruly. Therefore the goodness of the will depends on its being subject to reason.

I answer that, As stated above (AA. 1, 2), the goodness of the will depends properly on the object. Now the will's object is proposed to it by reason. Because the good understood is the proportionate object of the will; while sensitive or imaginary good is proportionate not to the will but to the sensitive appetite: since the will can tend to the universal good, which reason apprehends; whereas the sensitive appetite tends only to the particular good, apprehended by the sensitive power. Therefore the goodness of the will depends on reason, in the same way as it depends on the object. . . .

FOURTH ARTICLE

Whether the Goodness of the Will Depends on the Eternal Law?

Objection 1. It would seem that the goodness of the human will does not depend on the eternal law. Because to one thing there is one rule and one measure. But the rule of the human will, on which its goodness depends, is right reason. Therefore the goodness of the will does not depend on the eternal law.

Objection 2. Further, *a measure is homogeneous with the thing measured* (*Metaph.* x. 1). But the eternal law is not homogeneous with the human will. Therefore the eternal law cannot be the measure on which the goodness of the human will depends.

Objection 3. Further, a measure should be most certain. But the eternal law is unknown to us. Therefore it cannot be the measure on which the goodness of our will depends.[139]

---

not as far from Biblical wisdom as many think and write today, because what pre-modern philosophers meant by "reason" was much closer to what Scripture means by "wisdom" than to what modern parlance means by "reason" (which is mere reason*ing*, and often the kind computers can do). It is a momentous sign that we no longer capitalize "reason" or think of it as "naturally apprehending the universal good", as St. Thomas does.

[139] All three Objections try to drive a wedge between the supernatural and theological foundation for morality in the eternal law, and its natural, human foundation. This is another attitude that is much more typical of modern than of medieval thought. St. Thomas, like Scripture, sees the eternal law as very close, as present, not as far removed.

On the contrary, Augustine says (*Contra Faust.* xxii. 27) that *sin is a deed, word or desire against the eternal law.* But malice of the will is the root of sin. Therefore, since malice is contrary to goodness, the goodness of the will depends on the eternal law.

I answer that, Wherever a number of causes are subordinate to one another, the effect depends more on the first than on the second cause: since the second cause acts only in virtue of the first. Now it is from the eternal law, which is the Divine Reason, that human reason is the rule of the human will, from which the human will derives its goodness. Hence it is written (Ps 4:6, 7): *Many say: Who showeth us good things? The light of Thy countenance, O Lord, is signed upon us:* as though to say: "The light of our reason is able to show us good things, and guide our will, in so far as it is the light of [*i.e.,* derived from] Thy countenance." It is therefore evident that the goodness of the human will depends on the eternal law much more than on human reason:[140] and when human reason fails we must have recourse to the Eternal Reason.

Reply Obj. 1. To one thing there are not several proximate measures; but there can be several measures if one is subordinate to the other.

Reply Obj. 2. A proximate measure is homogeneous with the thing measured; a remote measure is not.

Reply Obj. 3. Although the eternal law is unknown to us according as it is in the Divine Mind: nevertheless, it becomes known to us somewhat, either by natural reason which is derived therefrom as its proper image; or by some sort of additional revelation.

FIFTH ARTICLE

Whether the Will Is Evil When It Is at Variance with Erring Reason?

On the contrary, As stated in the First Part (Q. 79, A. 13), conscience is nothing else than the application of knowledge to some action. Now knowledge is in the reason. Therefore when the

---

[140] It does so as the light shed by the full moon on a clear night depends more on the sun, its source, than on the moon, its reflector. What follows

will is at variance with erring reason, it is against conscience. But every such will is evil; for it is written (Rom 14:23): *All that is not of faith—i.e.*, all that is against conscience—*is sin*[141] Therefore the will is evil when it is at variance with erring reason.

I answer that, Since conscience is a kind of dictate of the reason (for it is an application of knowledge to action, as was stated in the First Part, Q. 19, A. 13), to inquire whether the will is evil when it is at variance with erring reason, is the same as to inquire *whether an erring conscience binds.* . . .

. . . Since the object of the will is that which is proposed by the reason, as stated above (A. 3), from the very fact that a thing is proposed by the reason as being evil, the will by tending thereto becomes evil. . . . To believe in Christ is good in itself, and necessary for salvation: but the will does not tend thereto, except inasmuch as it is proposed by the reason. Consequently if it be proposed by the reason as something evil, the will tends to it as to something evil:[142] not as if it were evil in itself, but because it is evil accidentally, through the apprehension of the reason. . . .

. . . When erring reason proposes something as being commanded by God, then to scorn the dictate of reason is to scorn the commandment of God. . . .

---

is the practical difference this fact makes. This, in turn, is true if and only if Objection 3 can be answered and the eternal law can be known.

[141] St. Thomas is saying here that you are always morally obligated to act according to what you believe is true, i.e., according to what your conscience tells you, even when what you believe is in fact false. (For if you *believe* it to be true, you must act as if it is.) Obedience to conscience is a universal and exceptionless moral absolute.

[142] Cf. Kierkegaard's famous passage in the *Concluding Unscientific Postscript* comparing the honest pagan honestly worshipping a false god with a hypocritical Christian worshipping the true God in a false spirit. He asks, "where is there the most truth?" (i.e., goodness). This strong emphasis on individual conscience is often misinterpreted as irrationalism. E.g., many readers of Kierkegaard, and even many writers on him, misinterpret his "truth as subjectivity" as subjective truth and the primacy of feeling over reason. It is not our task here to prove that that is not what Kierkegaard meant, but it *is* our task to be sure that it is not what St. Thomas meant: see the last sentence of the Article.

SIXTH ARTICLE

Whether the Will Is Good When It Abides by Erring Reason?

On the contrary, The will of those who slew the apostles was evil. And yet it was in accord with the erring reason, according to John 16:2: *The hour cometh, that whosoever killeth you, will think that he doth a service to God.* Therefore the will can be evil, when it abides by erring reason.

I answer that, Whereas the previous question is the same as inquiring *whether an erring conscience binds;* so this question is the same as inquiring *whether an erring conscience excuses.*[143] Now this question depends on what has been said above about ignorance. For it was said (Q. 6, A. 8) that ignorance sometimes causes an act to be involuntary, and sometimes not. And since moral good and evil consist in action in so far as it is voluntary, as was stated above (A. 2); it is evident that when ignorance causes an act to be involuntary, it takes away the character of moral good and evil; but not, when it does not cause the act to be involuntary. Again, it has been stated above (Q. 6, A. 8) that when ignorance is in any way willed, either directly or indirectly, it does not cause the act to be involuntary. And I call that ignorance *directly* voluntary, to which the act of the will tends:[144] and that, *indirectly* voluntary, which is due to negligence, by reason of a man not wishing to know what he ought to know, as stated above (Q. 6, A. 8).[145]

If then reason or conscience err with an error that is voluntary, either directly, or through negligence, so that one errs about what one ought to know; then such an error of reason or conscience does not excuse the will, that abides by that erring reason or conscience, from being evil. But if the error arise from ignorance of some circumstance, and without any negligence, so that it cause the act

---

[143] The thesis of this article is needed to balance and supplement that of the previous article. To act wrongly out of ignorance is excusable only if the ignorance itself is involuntary.

[144] E.g., the refusal to attend mentally to the commandment which you know but wish to break.

[145] E.g., not bothering to find out whether a questionable tax deduction is legal or illegal.

to be involuntary, then that error of reason or conscience excuses the will, that abides by that erring reason, from being evil. For instance, if erring reason tell a man that he should go to another man's wife, the will that abides by that erring reason is evil; since this error arises from ignorance of the Divine Law, which he is bound to know. But if a man's reason errs in mistaking another for his wife, and if he wish to give her her right when she asks for it, his will is excused from being evil: because this error arises from ignorance of a circumstance, which ignorance excuses, and causes the act to be involuntary.[146] . . .

EIGHTH ARTICLE

Whether the Degree of Goodness or Malice in the Will Depends on the Degree of Good or Evil in the Intention?

Reply Obj. 2. The goodness of the intention is not the whole cause of a good will. . . .

Reply Obj. 3. The mere malice of the intention suffices to make the will evil: and therefore too, the will is as evil as the intention is evil. But the same reasoning does not apply to goodness.[147] . . .

---

[146] Such an example is perhaps more credible in the Middle Ages, which had no electric lights, than in modern times.

[147] All the morally relevant factors must be good for the act to be good; if any one is evil, the act is evil. A parallel case: all the aesthetically relevant factors must be beautiful if a work of art is to be beautiful; if one factor is ugly, the work is ugly.

Question 20

Of Goodness and Malice
in External Human Actions

FIRST ARTICLE

FIRST ARTICLE

*Whether Goodness or Malice Is First in the Action of the Will,
or in the External Action?*

On the contrary, Augustine says (*Retract.* i. 9) that *it is by the will
that we sin, and that we behave aright.* Therefore moral good and evil
are first in the will.

I answer that, External actions may be said to be good or bad in
two ways. First, in regard to their genus, and the circumstances
connected with them: thus the giving of alms, if the required
conditions be observed, is said to be good. Secondly, a thing is said
to be good or evil, from its relation to the end: thus the giving of
alms for vainglory is said to be evil. Now, since the end is the will's
proper object, it is evident that this aspect of good or evil, which
the external action derives from its relation to the end, is to be
found first of all in the act of the will. . . .

SECOND ARTICLE

*Whether the Whole Goodness and Malice of the External Action
Depends on the Goodness of the Will?* [148]

I answer that, As stated above (A. 1), we may consider a twofold
goodness or malice in the external action: one in respect of due

---

[148] Note again the balance: Article 1 taught the *primacy* of good intention;
Article 2 denies the *adequacy* of good intention alone, and the idea, popular

matter and circumstances; the other in respect of the order to the end. And that which is in respect of the order to the end, depends entirely on the will: while that which is in respect of due matter or circumstances, depends on the reason: and on this goodness depends the goodness of the will, in so far as the will tends towards it.

Now it must be observed, as was noted above (Q. 19, A. 6 *ad* 1), that for a thing to be evil, one single defect suffices, whereas, for it to be good simply, it is not enough for it to be good in one point only, it must be good in every respect. If therefore the will be good, both from its proper object and from its end, it follows that the external action is good. But if the will be good from its intention of the end, this is not enough to make the external action good: and if the will be evil either by reason of its intention of the end, or by reason of the act willed, it follows that the external action is evil. . . .

THIRD ARTICLE

Whether the Goodness and Malice of the External Action Are the Same As Those of the Interior Act?

On the contrary, It was shown above (Q. 18, A. 6) that the act of the will is the form, as it were, of the external action. Now that which results from the material and formal element is one thing. Therefore there is but one goodness of the internal and external act.

I answer that, As stated above (Q. 17, A. 4), the interior act of the will, and the external action, considered morally, are one act. Now it happens sometimes that one and the same individual act has several aspects of goodness or malice, and sometimes that it has but one. Hence we must say that sometimes the goodness or malice of the interior act is the same as that of the external action, and sometimes not. For as we have already said (AA. 1, 2), these two goodnesses or malices, of the internal and external acts, are ordained to one another. . . .

---

today, that "if only you have a good heart, that's all that matters". No one ever preached this morality to his doctor. The *"On the contrary"* of Article 4 simply (but not simplistically) refutes this simplistic (but not simple) error.

FOURTH ARTICLE

Whether the External Action Adds Any Goodness or Malice to That of the Interior Act?

On the contrary, Every agent intends to attain good and avoid evil. If therefore by the external action no further goodness or malice be added, it is to no purpose that he who has a good or an evil will, does a good deed or refrains from an evil deed. Which is unreasonable.

I answer that, If we speak of the goodness which the external action derives from the will tending to the end, then the external action adds nothing to this goodness. . . .

On the other hand, if we speak of the goodness which the external action derives from its matter and due circumstances, . . . it adds to the goodness or malice of the will; because every inclination or movement is perfected by attaining its end or reaching its term. Wherefore the will is not perfect, unless it be such that, given the opportunity, it realizes the operation. But if this prove impossible, as long as the will is perfect, so as to realize the operation if it could; the lack of perfection derived from the external action, is simply involuntary. Now just as the involuntary deserves neither punishment nor reward in the accomplishment of good or evil deeds, so neither does it lessen reward or punishment, if a man through simple involuntariness fail to do good or evil. [149] . . .

FIFTH ARTICLE

Whether the Consequences of the External Action Increase Its Goodness or Malice? [150]

On the contrary, The consequences do not make an action that was evil, to be good; nor one that was good, to be evil. For

---

[149] As usual, St. Thomas' morality reflects common sense. This passage answers Kant's argument (at the beginning of the *Foundations of the Metaphysic of Morals*) against anything but a good will being intrinsically good. Cf. especially the argument in the "*On the contrary*".

[150] Here is St. Thomas' refutation of Utilitarianism. On this point he

instance, if a man give an alms to a poor man who makes bad use of the alms by committing a sin, this does not undo the good done by the giver; and, in like manner, if a man bear patiently a wrong done to him, the wrongdoer is not thereby excused. Therefore the consequences of an action do not increase its goodness or malice.

I answer that, The consequences of an action are either foreseen or not. If they are foreseen, it is evident that they increase the goodness or malice. For when a man foresees that many evils may follow from his action, and yet does not therefore desist therefrom, this shows his will to be all the more inordinate.

But if the consequences are not foreseen, . . . if the consequences follow by accident and seldom, then they do not increase the goodness or malice of the action: because we do not judge of a thing according to that which belongs to it by accident, but only according to that which belongs to it of itself. . . .

---

sides with Kantianism; in the previous Article, he sided with the Utilitarian. He has a habit of synthesizing the insights not only of his predecessors but also of his successors.

Question 21

Of the Consequences of Human Actions by Reason of Their Goodness and Malice

Whether a Human Action Is Right or Sinful,
in So Far As It Is Good or Evil?

I answer that, Evil is more comprehensive than sin, as also is good than right. For every privation of good, in whatever subject, is an evil: whereas sin consists properly in an action done for a certain end, and lacking due order to that end. . . .

Now in those things that are done by the will, the proximate rule is the human reason, while the supreme rule is the Eternal Law. When, therefore, a human action tends to the end, according to the order of reason and of the Eternal Law, then that action is right: but when it turns aside from that rectitude, then it is said to be a sin. Now it is evident from what has been said (Q. 19, AA. 3, 4) that every voluntary action that turns aside from the order of reason and of the Eternal Law, is evil, and that every good action is in accord with reason and the Eternal Law. Hence it follows that a human action is right or sinful by reason of its being good or evil.[151] . . .

---

[151] But not vice versa. All sin is evil, but not all evil is sin. For some evil is in beings lacking reason and will. All righteousness is good, but not all good is righteousness. Diseases are evil but not sinful; apples are good but not righteous.

D. Love

Question 26

Of the Passions of the Soul
in Particular: and First, of Love

SECOND ARTICLE

Whether Love Is a Passion?

Objection 2. Further, love is a kind of union or bond, as Augustine says (*De Trin.* viii. 10). But a union or bond is not a passion, but rather a relation.[152] Therefore love is not a passion. . . .

On the contrary, The Philosopher says (*Ethic.* viii. 5) that *love is a passion.*

I answer that, . . . the first change wrought in the appetite by the appetible object is called *love*, and is nothing else than complacency[153] in that object; and from this complacency results a movement towards that same object, and this movement is *desire*; and lastly, there is rest which is *joy*. Since, therefore, love consists in a change wrought in the appetite by the appetible object, it is evident that love is a passion:[154] properly so called, according as it is in the

---

[152] In terms of the ten categories of Aristotelian logic (substance, quantity, quality, relation, action, passion (reception), time, place, posture, and possession), everything (except God) must be in one and only one of these *summa genera* or most universal generic classes.

[153] Not "complacency" in the sense of undue satisfaction, or sloth, but satisfaction as such: being pleased. Note that for St. Thomas, "from complacency results *desire*". Love includes (1) being pleased with the object, *liking* it; (2) desire for the object, *wanting* it; and (3) joy in the object, *enjoying* it.

[154] The Aristotelian category of "passion" is not necessarily "passionate". It means reception, the "flip side" of action.

concupiscible faculty; in a wider and extended sense, according as it is in the will. . . .

Reply Obj. 2. Union belongs to love in so far as by reason of the complacency of the appetite, the lover stands in relation to that which he loves, as though it were himself or part of himself. Hence it is clear that love is not the very relation of union, but that union is a result of love. Hence, too, Dionysius says that *love is a unitive force* (*Div. Nom.* iv), and the Philosopher says (*Polit.* ii. 1) that union is the work of love. . . .

Whether Love Is the Same As Dilection?

I answer that, We find four words referring in a way, to the same thing: viz., love, dilection, charity and friendship. They differ, however, in this, that *friendship*, according to the Philosopher (*Ethic.* viii. 5), *is like a habit,* whereas *love* and *dilection* are expressed by way of act or passion; and *charity* can be taken either way.

Moreover these three express act in different ways. For love has a wider signification than the others, since every dilection or charity is love, but not vice versa. Because dilection implies, in addition to love, a choice (*electionem*) made beforehand, as the very word denotes: and therefore dilection is not in the concupiscible power, but only in the will, and only in the rational nature.—Charity denotes, in addition to love, a certain perfection of love, in so far as that which is loved is held to be of great price, as the word itself implies [referring to the Latin *carus* (dear)].[155] . . .

---

155 Thus we have:

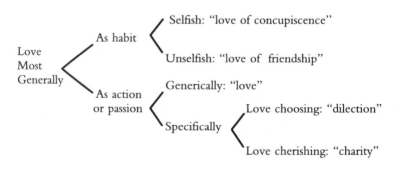

FOURTH ARTICLE

Whether Love Is Properly Divided into
Love of Friendship and Love of Concupiscence?

I answer that, As the Philosopher says (*Rhet.* ii. 4), *to love is to wish good to someone.* Hence the movement of love has a twofold tendency: towards the good which a man wishes to someone—to himself or to another—and towards that [one] to [whom] he wishes some good. Accordingly, man has love of concupiscence [desire] towards the good that he wishes to another, and love of friendship, towards him to whom he wishes good.

Now the members of this division are related as primary and secondary: since that which is loved with the love of friendship is loved simply and for itself; whereas that which is loved with the love of concupiscence, is loved, not simply and for itself, but for something else.[156] For just as that which has existence, is a being simply, while that which exists in another is a relative being; so, because good is convertible with being, the good, which itself has goodness, is good simply; but that which is another's good, is a relative good.[157] Consequently the love with which a thing is loved, that it may have some good, is love simply; while the love, with which a thing is loved, that it may be another's good, is relative love. . . .

---

[156] I.e., as Kant would say, persons are to be loved as ends, and good things as means, as good *for* persons. In the following sentence, note again how St. Thomas relates everything to being.

[157] That is, a good *for* the person.

Question 27

Of the Cause of Love

Whether Good Is the Only Cause of Love?

Objection 3. Further, Dionysius says (*Div. Nom.* iv) that not *the good* only but also *the beautiful is beloved by all*.[158] . . .

Reply Obj. 3. The beautiful is the same as the good, and they differ in aspect only. For since good is what all seek, the notion of good is that which calms[159] the desire; while the notion of the beautiful is that which calms the desire by being seen or known. Consequently those senses chiefly regard the beautiful, which are the most cognitive, viz., sight and hearing, as ministering to reason; for we speak of beautiful sights and beautiful sounds. But in reference to the other objects of the other senses, we do not use the expression *beautiful*, for we do not speak of beautiful tastes, and beautiful odors.[160] Thus it is evident that beauty adds to goodness a relation to the cognitive faculty: so that *good* means that which simply pleases the appetite; while the *beautiful* is something pleasant to apprehend.

---

[158] Cf. Plato's *Symposium*.

[159] I.e., *satisfies*, not *mitigates*.

[160] Actually, the Chinese language, I am told, does have words for beautiful tastes, and a French perfumer would surely speak of "beautiful odors".

SECOND ARTICLE

Whether Knowledge Is a Cause of Love?

Objection 2. Further, to love what we know not seems like loving something more than we know it. But some things are loved more than they are known: thus in this life God can be loved [as He is] in Himself, but cannot be known [as He is] in Himself. Therefore knowledge is not the cause of love. . . .

On the contrary, Augustine proves (*De Trin.* x. 1, 2) that *none can love what he does not know.*

I answer that, As stated above (A. 1), good is the cause of love, as being its object. But good is not the object of the appetite, except as apprehended. And therefore love demands some apprehension of the good that is loved. For this reason the Philosopher (*Ethic.* ix. 5, 12) says that bodily sight is the beginning of sensitive love: and in like manner the contemplation of spiritual beauty or goodness is the beginning of spiritual love. Accordingly knowledge is the cause of love. . . .

Reply Obj. 2. Something [more] is required for the perfection of knowledge, that is not requisite for the perfection of love. For knowledge belongs to the reason, whose function it is to distinguish things which in reality are united,[161] and to unite together, after a fashion, things that are distinct,[162] by comparing one with another. Consequently the perfection of knowledge requires that man should know distinctly all that is in a thing, such as its parts, powers, and properties. On the other hand, love is in the appetitive power, which regards a thing as it is in itself: wherefore it suffices, for the perfection of love, that a thing be loved according as it is known. . . . Hence it is, therefore, that a thing is loved more than it is known; since it can be loved perfectly,[163] even without being perfectly known. . . .

---

[161] Analysis.

[162] Synthesis.

[163] Completely. The "first and greatest commandment", to love God with our whole heart, does not require knowing God completely, for an impossibility cannot be meaningfully commanded.

FOURTH ARTICLE

Whether Any Other Passion of the Soul Is a Cause of Love?

On the contrary, All the other emotions of the soul are caused by love, as Augustine says (*De Civ. Dei* xiv. 7, 9).[164]

I answer that, There is no other passion of the soul that does not presuppose love of some kind. . . .

---

[164] The contrast between St. Thomas' supposed intellectualism and St. Augustine's primacy of love is usually overdone and oversimplified. St. Thomas *includes* St. Augustine's insight here.

Question 28

Of the Effects of Love

Whether Union Is an Effect of Love?

On the contrary, Dionysius says (*Div. Nom.* iv) that every love is a *unitive force.*

I answer that, The union of lover and beloved is twofold. The first is real union; for instance, when the beloved is present with the lover.—The second is union of affection.[165] . . . When a man loves another with the love of friendship, he wills good to him, just as he wills good to himself; wherefore he apprehends him as his other self, in so far, to wit, as he wills good to him as to himself. Hence a friend is called a man's *other self* (*Ethic.* ix. 4), and Augustine says (*Confess.* iv. 6), *Well did one say to his friend: Thou half of my soul.*[166] . . .

SECOND ARTICLE

Whether Mutual Indwelling Is an Effect of Love?

On the contrary, It is written (1 Jn 4:16): *He that abideth in charity abideth in God, and God in him.* . . . For . . . every love makes the beloved to be[167] in the lover, and vice versa.

I answer that, This effect of mutual indwelling may be under-

---

[165] The difference between the Catholic and the classical Protestant theology of the sacraments can be explained in terms of this distinction.

[166] This is why we feel a part of ourselves has died when a friend dies.

[167] Note again the *metaphysical* nature of love, and the metaphysical

stood as referring both to the apprehensive and to the appetitive power. Because, as to the apprehensive power, the beloved is said to be in the lover, inasmuch as the beloved abides in the apprehension of the lover, according to Philippians 1:7, *For that I have you in my heart:* while the lover is said to be in the beloved, according to apprehension, inasmuch as the lover is not satisfied with a superficial apprehension of the beloved, but strives to gain an intimate knowledge of everything pertaining to the beloved, so as to penetrate into his very soul.[168] Thus it is written concerning the Holy Ghost, Who is God's Love, that He *searcheth all things, yea the deep things of God* (1 Cor 2:10).

As the appetitive power, the object loved is said to be in the lover, inasmuch as it is in his affections, by a kind of complacency [cf. n. 153]: causing him either to take pleasure in it, or in its good, when present; or, in the absence of the object loved, by his longing, to tend towards it with the love of concupiscence, or towards the good that he wills to the beloved, with the love of friendship: not indeed from any extrinsic cause [end] (as when we desire one thing on account of another, or wish good to another on account of something else), but because the complacency in the beloved is rooted in the lover's heart. For this reason we speak of love as being *intimate*; and of *the bowels of charity*. On the other hand, the lover is in the beloved, by the love of concupiscence [desire] and by the love of friendship, but not in the same way. For the love of concupiscence is not satisfied with any external or superficial possession or enjoyment of the beloved; but seeks to possess the beloved perfectly, by penetrating into his heart, as it were. Whereas, in the love of friendship, the lover is in the beloved, inasmuch as he reckons what is good or evil to his friend, as being so to himself; and his friend's will as his own, so that it seems as though he felt the good or suffered the evil in the person of his friend. Hence it is proper to friends *to desire the same things, and to grieve and rejoice at the same*, as

---

revolution effected by love: a new mode of being, viz., in-being or with-being (Marcel: *co-esse*).

[168] If we say we love someone, we are interested in knowing everything we can about him or her. The same is true of our love for God. The negative corollary must also be true: disinterest in intellectual intimacy indicates lack of love.

the Philosopher says (*Ethic.* ix. 3 and *Rhet.* ii. 4). Consequently in so far as he reckons what affects his friend as affecting himself, the lover seems to be in the beloved, as though he were become one with him: but in so far as, on the other hand, he wills and acts for his friend's sake as for his own sake, looking on his friend as identified with himself, thus the beloved is in the lover.

In yet a third way, mutual indwelling in the love of friendship can be understood in regard to reciprocal love: inasmuch as friends return love for love, and both desire and do good things for one another.[169] . . .

THIRD ARTICLE

Whether Ecstasy[170] *Is an Effect of Love?*

On the contrary, Dionysius says (*Div. Nom.* iv) that *the Divine love produces ecstasy,* and that *God Himself suffered*[171] *ecstasy through love.* Since therefore according to the same author (*ibid.*), every love is a participated likeness of the Divine Love, it seems that every love causes ecstasy.

I answer that, To suffer ecstasy means to be placed outside oneself.[172] This happens as to the apprehensive power and as to the

---

[169] This whole threefold analysis of mutual indwelling applies, analogically, to all forms of friendship-love, especially to (1) the love among the Persons in the Trinity, (2) the love of Christ for His Church, (3) the "theological virtue" of charity, and (4) marriage.

[170] The primary meaning of this word has been largely forgotten, for we think of "ecstasy" merely as intense pleasure, neglecting the cause of this pleasure, viz., a kind of self-transcendence which is anticipatory of Heaven and of the life of the Persons in the Trinity. "Ecstasy" means literally "standing-outside-yourself" (*ek-stasis*).

[171] In a literal sense, God cannot suffer any passion at all, for He is pure act, without passive potency. But he experiences, or acts, or is, love; and love is inherently ecstatic.

[172] Nothing can be physically and literally outside itself, i.e., outside its surface boundaries (though in trans-Newtonian, Einsteinian physics, it can be said to exist wherever it exercises an effect). But knowledge and desire enable a person to exist not only inside his skin but also in the knowledge and love of another. And, in the words of the song, "love lifts

appetitive power. As to the apprehensive power, a man is said to be placed outside himself, when he is placed outside the knowledge proper to him. This may be due to his being raised to a higher knowledge; thus, a man is said to suffer ecstasy, inasmuch as he is placed outside the connatural apprehension of his sense and reason, when he is raised up so as to comprehend things that surpass sense and reason. . . .—As to the appetitive power, a man is said to suffer ecstasy, when that power is borne towards something else, so that it goes forth out from itself, as it were. . . .

FOURTH ARTICLE

Whether Zeal Is an Effect of Love?

On the contrary, Dionysius says (*Div. Nom.* iv): *God is said to be a zealot;*[173] *on account of his great love for all things.*

I answer that, Zeal, whatever way we take it, arises from the intensity of love. For it is evident that the more intensely a power tends to anything, the more vigorously it withstands opposition or resistance. Since therefore love is *a movement towards the object loved,* as *Augustine says* (QQ. 83, qu. 35), an intense love seeks to remove everything that opposes it.

But this happens in different ways according to love of concupiscence, and love of friendship. For in love of concupiscence he who desires something intensely, is moved against all that hinders his gaining or quietly enjoying the object of his love. It is thus that husbands are said to be jealous of their wives, lest association with others prove a hindrance to their exclusive individual rights. In like manner those who seek to excel, are moved against those who seem to excel, as though these were a hindrance to their excelling. And this is the zeal of envy, of which it is written (Ps 36:1): *Be not emulous of evil doers, nor envy (zelaveris) them that work iniquity.*

---

us up where we belong, where eagles fly over mountains high." Or—the same point in St. Thomas' words—"when he is raised up so as to comprehend things that surpass sense and reason", note that it is *love* that brings us beyond reason. A strange "rationalism"!

[173] Remember this quotation when someone calls you this name: the worst insult that a sophisticated, worldly society can imagine.

On the other hand, love of friendship seeks the friend's good: wherefore, when it is intense, it causes a man to be moved against everything that opposes the friend's good. In this respect, a man is said to be zealous on behalf of his friend, when he makes a point of repelling whatever may be said or done against the friend's good. In this way, too, a man is said to be zealous on God's behalf, when he endeavors, to the best of his means, to repel whatever is contrary to the honor or will of God; according to 1 Kings 19:14: *With zeal I have been zealous for the Lord of hosts*. Again . . . the words of John 2:17: *The zeal of Thy house hath eaten me up*. . . .

Reply Obj. 2. . . . The zeal of envy . . . does not arise, properly speaking, in the case of those things which, in their entirety, can be possessed by many: for no one envies another the knowledge of truth, which can be known entirely by many; except perhaps one may envy another his superiority in the knowledge of it. . . .

FIFTH ARTICLE

Whether Love Is a Passion That Wounds the Lover?

On the contrary, Dionysius says (*Div.* iv) that *everything loves itself with a love that holds it together, i.e.,* that preserves it. Therefore love is not a wounding passion, but rather one that preserves and perfects.

I answer that, . . . Now nothing is hurt by being adapted to that which is suitable to it; rather, if possible, it is perfected and bettered. But if a thing be adapted to that which is not suitable to it, it is hurt and made worse thereby. Consequently love of a suitable good perfects and betters the lover; but love of a good which is unsuitable to the lover, wounds and worsens him. Wherefore man is perfected and bettered chiefly by the love of God: but is wounded and worsened by the love of sin, according to Hosea 9:10: *They became abominable, as those things which they loved.*

. . . Four proximate effects may be ascribed to love: viz., melting, enjoyment, languor, and fervor. Of these the first is *melting*, which is opposed to freezing. For things that are frozen, are . . . hard to pierce. But it belongs to love that the appetite is fitted to receive the good which is loved, inasmuch as the object loved is in the lover, as stated above (A. 2). Consequently the freezing or hardening of the heart is a disposition incompatible with love: while melting denotes a softening of the heart, whereby the heart shows itself to be ready for the entrance of the beloved.—If, then, the beloved is present and possessed, pleasure or enjoyment ensues. But if the beloved be absent, two passions arise: viz., sadness at its absence, which is denoted by *languor* (hence Cicero in *De Tuscul. Quaest.* iii. 11 applies the term *ailment* chiefly to sadness); and an intense desire to possess the beloved, which is signified by *fervor*. . . .

SIXTH ARTICLE

Whether Love Is Cause of All That the Lover Does?[174]

I answer that, Every agent acts for an end, as stated above (Q. 1, A. 2). Now the end is the good desired and loved by each one. Wherefore it is evident that every agent, whatever it be, does every action from love of some kind. . . .

---

[174] In all six of these articles, note how St. Thomas uses some (but not all) of the commonplace sayings of courtly love poetry (much of which was repeated in nineteenth-century Romanticism), but universalizes its application to love as such.

Question 29

Of Hatred

SECOND ARTICLE

Whether Love Is a Cause of Hatred?

On the contrary, Augustine says (*De Civ. Dei* xiv. 7, 9) that all emotions are caused by love. Therefore hatred also, since it is an emotion of the soul, is caused by love.

I answer that, . . . Nothing is hated, save through being contrary to a suitable thing which is loved. And hence it is that every hatred is caused by love. . . .

THIRD ARTICLE

Whether Hatred Is Stronger Than Love?

I answer that, It is impossible for an effect to be stronger than its cause. Now every hatred arises from some love as its cause, as above stated (A. 2). Therefore it is impossible for hatred to be stronger than love absolutely.

But furthermore, love must needs be, absolutely speaking, stronger than hatred. Because a thing is moved to the end more strongly than to the means. Now turning away from evil [hating] is directed as a means to the gaining of good. Wherefore, absolutely speaking, the soul's movement in respect of good [love] is stronger than its movement in respect of evil [hate].

Nevertheless hatred sometimes seems to be stronger than love . . . because hatred is more keenly felt than love.[175] . . .

---

[175] N.b.: St. Thomas does not take feelings as an adequate index to being.

FOURTH ARTICLE

Whether a Man Can Hate Himself?

Objection 1. It would seem that a man can hate himself. For it is written (Ps 10:6): *He that loveth iniquity, hateth his own soul.* But many love iniquity. Therefore many hate themselves.

Objection 2. Further, him we hate, to whom we wish and work evil. But sometimes a man wishes and works evil to himself, *e.g.*, a man who kills himself. Therefore some men hate themselves. . . .

On the contrary, The Apostle says (Eph 5:29) that *no man ever hated his own flesh.*

I answer that, Properly speaking, it is impossible for a man to hate himself. For everything naturally desires good, nor can anyone desire anything for himself, save under the aspect of good. . . . Now to love a man is to will good to him, as stated above (Q. 26, A. 4). Consequently, a man must, of necessity, love himself; and it is impossible for a man to hate himself, properly speaking.

But accidentally it happens that a man hates himself. . . . Now it is clear that man is principally the mind of man. And it happens that some men account themselves as being principally that which they are in their material and sensitive nature. Wherefore they love themselves according to what they take themselves to be, while they hate that which they really are, by desiring what is contrary to reason. . . .

Reply Obj. 2. No man wills and works evil to himself, except he apprehend it under the aspect of good. For even they who kill themselves, apprehend death itself as a good, considered as putting an end to some unhappiness or pain. . . .

FIFTH ARTICLE

Whether a Man Can Hate the Truth?

Objection 1. It would seem that a man cannot hate the truth. For good, true, and being are convertible. But a man cannot hate good. Neither, therefore, can he hate the truth.

Objection 2. Further, *All men have a natural desire for knowledge*, as stated in the beginning of the *Metaphysics* (i. 1). But knowledge is only of truth. Therefore truth is naturally desired and loved. But that which is in a thing naturally, is always in it. Therefore no man can hate the truth. . . .

On the contrary, The Apostle says (Gal 4:16): *I am become your enemy because I tell you the truth.* [176]

I answer that, . . . It may happen in three ways that some particular truth is repugnant or hurtful to the good we love. First, . . . man sometimes hates a particular truth, when he wishes that what is true were not true. [177]—Secondly, according as truth . . . hinders him from gaining the object loved: such is the case of those who wish not to know the truth of faith, that they may sin freely; in whose person it is said (Job 21:14): *We desire not the knowledge of Thy ways.* [178]—Thirdly, a particular truth is hated, as being repugnant, inasmuch as it is in the intellect of another man: as, for instance, when a man wishes to remain hidden in his sin, he hates that anyone should know the truth about his sin. [179] In this respect, Augustine says (*Confess.* x. 23) that men *love truth when it enlightens, they hate it when it reproves.* This suffices for the Reply to the First Objection.

Reply Obj. 2. The knowledge of truth is lovable in itself: hence Augustine says that men love it when it enlightens. But accidentally, the knowledge of truth may become hateful, in so far as it hinders one from accomplishing one's desire. . . .

---

[176] In fact, the *more* someone tells the truth, the more enemies, and the more passionate enemies, he will make. The greatest truth-tellers are usually the most hated and frequently martyred. No politician could be elected who told the truth, the whole truth, and nothing but the truth all the time.

[177] E.g., "you need root canal work."

[178] E.g., "there are no exceptions to the Seventh Commandment."

[179] E.g., our (foolish) reluctance to use the Sacrament of Penance.

E. Virtues

Question 55

Of the Virtues, As to Their Essence

Whether Human Virtue Is a Habit?

Objection 2. Further, Augustine says (*De Lib. Arb.* ii) [*Retract.* ix.; *cf. De Lib. Arb.* ii. 19] that *virtue is good use of free-will.* But use of free-will is an act. Therefore virtue is not a habit,[180] but an act.

Objection 3. Further, we do not merit[181] by our habits, but by our actions: otherwise a man would merit continually, even while asleep. But we do merit by our virtues. Therefore virtues are not habits, but acts. . . .

Reply Obj. 2. Good use of free-will is said to be a virtue . . . because it is that to which virtue is directed as to its proper act. . . .

Reply Obj. 3. We are said to merit by something in two ways. First, as by merit itself, just as we are said to run by running; and thus we merit by acts. Secondly, we are said to merit by something as by the principle [source] whereby we merit, as we are said to run by the motive power; and thus are we said to merit by virtues and habits. . . .

---

[180] A *habit* is not a static routine or rut, but a dynamic tendency to act in a certain determinate way. Virtues are good habits and vices are bad habits.

[181] To "merit" is to deserve justly. If there is justice, there must be merit and demerit, else there could be no *just* rewards and punishments.

Question 57

Of the Intellectual Virtues[182]

We now have to consider the various kinds of virtue: (1) the [natural] intellectual virtues; (2) the [natural] moral virtues; and (3) the [supernatural] theological virtues. . . .

SECOND ARTICLE

Whether There Are Only Three Habits of the Speculative Intellect, Viz., Wisdom, Science and Understanding?

On the contrary, The Philosopher (*Ethic.* vi. 1) reckons these three alone as being intellectual virtues, viz., wisdom, science and understanding.

I answer that, As already stated (A. 1), the virtues of the speculative intellect are those which perfect the speculative intellect for the consideration of truth: for this is its good work. Now a truth is subject to a twofold consideration,—as known in itself, and as known through another [truth]. What is known in itself, is as a *principle,* and is at once understood by the intellect:[183] wherefore

---

[182] The category of "intellectual virtue" has largely disappeared from modern ethics. For the word "virtue" has narrowed to mean moral virtue only. Thus we are surprised to hear St. Thomas speak of understanding, for example as a virtue; for this means that Hitler, and even Satan, have some virtues. But surely intelligence as such is good and valuable and praiseworthy.

[183] When formulated as propositions, these "truths known through themselves" are self-evident propositions such as "good is to be done" or "the whole is greater than the part"; while truths known through other truths are conclusions demonstrated by argument from premises. Such conclusions must be made evident by means of other truths (premises)

the habit that perfects the intellect for the consideration of such truth is called *understanding*, which is the habit of principles.

On the other hand, a truth which is known through another, is understood by the intellect, not at once, but by means of the reason's inquiry. . . . [Reason's two virtues are] *wisdom*, which considers the highest causes, as stated in *Metaph*. i. 1, 2—Wherefore it rightly judges all things and sets them in order, because there can be no perfect and universal judgment that is not based on the first causes—[and] . . . *science*. . . . Wherefore according to the different kinds of knowable matter, there are different habits of scientific knowledge; whereas there is but one wisdom.[184] . . .

FOURTH ARTICLE

Whether Prudence Is a Distinct Virtue from Art?

I answer that, . . . Art is the *right reason* [rational knowledge] *of things to be made*; whereas prudence is the *right reason of things to be done*.[185] Now *making and doing differ*, as stated in *Metaph*. ix., text. 16, in that *making* is an action passing into outward matter, e.g., *to build*, *to saw*, and so forth; whereas *doing* is an action abiding in the agent, e.g., *to see*, *to will*, and the like. Accordingly prudence stands in the same relation to such like human actions, consisting in the use of powers and habits, as art does to outward makings. . . .

---

because they are not self-evident. E.g., we ask whether capital punishment is to be done, and why, but we do not ask whether good is to be done, or why; we just "at once understand".

[184] Wisdom is the knowledge of first causes in all four orders of causality, especially, in ethics, the first *final* cause, or the *summum bonum*. "Science" is the knowledge of second, or proximate, causes, causes proper to specific areas of reality. Second causes are many, therefore there are many sciences. The first cause is one, therefore wisdom, which is the knowledge of the first cause, is one.

[185] "Wisdom" is speculative knowledge (the knowledge of first causes); "prudence" is practical knowledge (the knowledge of what to do); "art" is productive knowledge (the knowledge of what to make).

FIFTH ARTICLE

Whether Prudence Is a Virtue Necessary to Man?

On the contrary, It is reckoned with other virtues necessary for human life, when it is written (Wis 8:7) of Divine Wisdom: *She teacheth temperance and prudence and justice and fortitude,* [186] *which are such things as men can have nothing more profitable in life.*

I answer that, Prudence is a virtue most necessary for human life. For a good life consists in good deeds. Now in order to do good deeds, it matters not only what a man does, but also how he does it; to wit, that he do it from right choice and not merely from impulse or passion. And, since choice is about things in reference to the end, rectitude of choice requires two things; namely, the due end, and something suitably ordained to that due end. Now man is suitably directed to his due end by a virtue which perfects the soul in the appetitive part, the object of which is the good and the end. And to that which is suitably ordained to the due end [i.e., the means] man needs to be rightly disposed by a habit in his reason, because counsel and choice, which are about things ordained to the end, are acts of the reason. Consequently an intellectual virtue is needed in the reason, to perfect the reason, and make it suitably affected towards things ordained to the end; and this virtue is prudence. Consequently prudence is a virtue necessary to lead a good life. . . .

---

[186] The four cardinal virtues, first clearly formulated by Plato. The author of the late, deuterocanonical Book of Wisdom obviously knew Greek philosophy. Plato probably meant by "wisdom" both what St. Thomas called "wisdom" and what St. Thomas called "prudence"; for the true philosopher, according to the *Republic*, is to be trained to know both the world of Forms outside the "cave" of sensation and opinion (and this is "wisdom") and also how to live in that cave ("prudence").

Question 58

Of the Difference between Moral
and Intellectual Virtues

SECOND ARTICLE

Whether Moral Virtue Differs from Intellectual Virtue?

On the contrary, It is stated in *Ethic.* 1, 13 that *there are two kinds of virtue: some we call intellectual; some, moral.*

I answer that, Reason is the first principle of all human acts; and whatever other principles of human acts may be found, they obey reason somewhat, but in various ways. For some obey reason blindly and without any contradiction whatever: such are the limbs of the body, provided they be in a healthy condition, for as soon as reason commands, the hand or the foot proceeds to action. Hence the Philosopher says (*Polit.* i. 3) that *the soul rules the body like a despot,* i.e., as a master rules his slave, who has no right to rebel. Accordingly some held that all the active principles in man are subordinate to reason in this way. If this were true, for man to act well it would suffice that his reason be perfect. Consequently, since virtue is a habit perfecting man in view of his doing good actions, it would follow that it is only in the reason, so that there would be none but intellectual virtues. This was the opinion of Socrates, who said *every virtue is a kind of prudence,* as stated in *Ethic.* vi. 13. Hence he maintained that as long as a man is in possession of knowledge, he cannot sin; and that every one who sins, does so through ignorance.[187]

Now this is based on a false supposition. Because the appetitive faculty obeys the reason, not blindly, but with a certain power of

---

[187] This is also the implicit philosophy of many penologists, sociologists, and psychologists today who believe that education, or psychotherapeutic self-knowledge, is the cure for antisocial behavior.

opposition; wherefore the Philosopher says (*Polit.* i. 3) that *reason commands the appetitive faculty by a politic power*, whereby a man rules over subjects that are free, having a certain right of opposition. Hence Augustine says on Ps. cxviii (*serm.* 8) that *sometimes we understand* [what is right] *while desire is slow, or follows not at all*, in so far as the habits or passions of the appetitive faculty cause the use of reason to be impeded in some particular action. And in this way, there is some truth in the saying of Socrates that so long as a man is in possession of knowledge he does not sin: provided, however, that this knowledge is made to include the use of reason in this individual act of choice.

Accordingly for a man to do a good deed, it is requisite not only that his reason be well disposed by means of a habit of intellectual virtue; but also that his appetite be well disposed by means of a habit of moral virtue. And so moral differs from intellectual virtue, even as the appetite differs from the reason. . . .

THIRD ARTICLE

Whether Virtue Is Adequately Divided into Moral and Intellectual?

I answer that, Human virtue is a habit perfecting man in view of his doing good deeds. Now, in man there are but two principles of human actions, viz., the intellect or reason and the appetite: for these are the two principles of movement in man as stated in *De Anima*, iii, text, 48. Consequently every human virtue must needs be a perfection of one of these principles. Accordingly if it perfects man's speculative or practical intellect in order that his deed may be good, it will be an intellectual virtue: whereas if it perfects his appetite, it will be a moral virtue. It follows therefore that every human virtue is either intellectual or moral. . . .

FOURTH ARTICLE

Whether There Can be Moral without Intellectual Virtue?

Objection 2. Further, by means of intellectual virtue man obtains perfect use of reason. But it happens at times that men are virtuous and acceptable to God, without being vigorous in the use of reason.[188] Therefore it seems that moral virtue can be without intellectual. . . .

On the contrary, Gregory says (*Moral.* xxii) that *the other virtues, unless we do prudently what we desire to do, cannot be real virtues.* But prudence is an intellectual virtue, as stated above (Q. 57, A. 5). Therefore moral virtues cannot be without intellectual virtues.

I answer that, Moral virtue can be without some of the intellectual virtues, viz., wisdom, science, and art; but not without understanding and prudence.[189] Moral virtue cannot be without prudence, because it is a habit of choosing, i.e., making us choose well. Now in order that a choice be good, two things are required. First, that the intention be directed to a due end; and this is done by moral virtue, which inclines the appetitive faculty to the good. . . . Secondly, that man take rightly those things which have reference to the end:[190] and this he cannot do unless his reason counsel, judge and command aright, which is the function of prudence and the virtues annexed to it, as stated above (Q. 57, AA. 5, 6). Wherefore there can be no moral virtue without prudence: and consequently neither can there be without understanding. For it is by the virtue of understanding that we know self-evident principles both in speculative and in practical matters. Consequently just as right reason in speculative matters, in so far as it proceeds from naturally known principles, presupposes the understanding of those principles, so also does prudence, which is the right reason about things to be done.[191] . . .

Reply Obj. 2. A man may be virtuous without having full use of reason as to everything, provided he have it with regard to those things which have to be done virtuously. In this way all virtuous

---

[188] Saints are often simple and unintellectual: cf. 1 Cor 1:26–27.

[189] These are the five intellectual virtues.

[190] I.e., choose the right means.

[191] Empirical evidence for St. Thomas' conclusion is the fact that all saints have understanding (of their end) and prudence (in choosing good means to it), but not all saints have philosophical wisdom, science, or art. Cf. Pascal: "Knowledge of physical science will not console me for ignorance of morality in time of affliction, but knowledge of morality will always console me for ignorance of physical science" (*Pensées* 23).

men have full use of reason. Hence those who seem to be simple, through lack of worldly cunning, may possibly be prudent, according to Matthew 10:16: *Be ye therefore prudent* (Douay,—*wise*) *as serpents, and simple as doves.* . . .

FIFTH ARTICLE

Whether There Can Be Intellectual without Moral Virtue?

I answer that, Other intellectual virtues can, but prudence cannot, be without moral virtue. . . . For the virtuous man judges aright of the end of virtue, because *such as a man is, such does the end seem to him* (*Ethic.* iii. 5).[192] Consequently the right reason about things to be done, viz., prudence, requires man to have moral virtue. . . .

---

[192] I.e., moral virtue has a "feedback" into intellectual virtue: if we *are* good, we will *know* what is good (cf. Mt 5:5; Jn 7:17). Just as a singer understands singing and judges rightly about it, a morally virtuous man understands and judges rightly about moral virtue.

Question 59

Of Moral Virtue in Relation
to the Passions

Whether Moral Virtue Is a Passion?

On the contrary, It is stated in *Ethic.* ii. 5 that *passions are neither virtues*[193] *nor vices.*[194]

I answer that, . . . Passions are not in themselves good or evil. For man's good or evil is something in reference to reason: wherefore the passions, considered in themselves, are referable both to good and to evil, for as much as they may accord or disaccord with reason.[195] . . .

Whether There Can Be Moral Virtue with Passion?

On the contrary, Augustine says (*De Civ. Dei* xiv. 6): *If the will is perverse, these movements,* viz., the passions, *are perverse also: but if it is upright, they are not only blameless, but even praiseworthy.* But nothing praiseworthy is incompatible with moral virtue. Therefore moral virtue does not exclude the passions, but is consistent with them.

I answer that, The Stoics and Peripatetics disagreed on this point, as Augustine relates (*De Civ. Dei* ix. 4). For the Stoics held that the

---

[193] Contrary to pop psychology.
[194] Contrary to Stoicism.
[195] Passions are like horses; reason is like a rider.

soul's passions cannot be in a wise or virtuous man: whereas the Peripatetics, who were founded by Aristotle, as Augustine says (*ibid.*), maintained that the passions are compatible with moral virtue. . . .

. . . Hence Aristotle says (*Ethic.* ii. 3) that *some describe virtue as being a kind of freedom from passion and disturbance; this is incorrect, because the assertion should be qualified:* they should have said virtue is freedom from those passions *that are not as they should be.* . . .

THIRD ARTICLE

Whether Sorrow Is Compatible with Moral Virtue?

On the contrary, Christ was perfect in virtue. But there was sorrow in Him, for He said (Mt 26:38): *My soul is sorrowful even unto death.* Therefore sorrow is compatible with virtue.[196]

I answer that, As Augustine says (*De Civ. Dei* xiv. 8), the Stoics . . . held that no evil can happen to a wise man: for they thought that, just as man's only good is virtue, and bodily goods are no good to man; so man's only evil is vice,[197] which cannot be in a virtuous man. But this is unreasonable. For, since man is composed of soul and body, whatever conduces to preserve the life of the body, is some good to man; yet not his supreme good, because he can abuse it. Consequently the evil which is contrary to this good can be in a wise man, and can cause him moderate sorrow.—Again, although a virtuous man can be without grave sin, yet no man is to be found to live without committing slight sins, according to 1 John 1:8: *If we say that we have no sin, we deceive ourselves.*[198]

. . . Now it pertains to virtue that the sensitive appetite be conformed to reason, as stated above (A. 1, *ad* 2). Wherefore moderated sorrow for an object which ought to make us sorrowful,

---

[196] Note the psychological normalcy and completeness of the Christian ideal man, as contrasted with the partial and limiting nature of most pagan ideals, ancient or modern. Cf. also Article 5.

[197] The Stoics, like nearly all ancient schools of philosophy, claimed they were the true disciples of Socrates, who taught this in *Apology* 41d, 28b.

[198] And it is right to have sorrow for sin, and wrong not to.

is a mark of virtue; as also the Philosopher says (*Ethic.* ii. 6, 7).—Moreover, this proves useful for avoiding evil: since, just as good is more readily sought for the sake of pleasure, so is evil more undauntedly shunned on account of sorrow. . . .

Whether There Can Be Moral Virtue without Passion?

Objection 1. It would seem that moral virtue can be without passion. For the more perfect moral virtue is, the more does it overcome the passions. Therefore at its highest point of perfection it is altogether without passion. . . .

On the contrary, No man is just who rejoices not in just deeds, [199] as stated in *Ethic.* i. 8. But joy is a passion. Therefore justice cannot be without passion: and still less can the other virtues be.

I answer that, If we take the passions as being inordinate emotions, as the Stoics did, it is evident that in this sense perfect virtue is without the passions.—But if by passions we understand any movement of the sensitive appetite, it is plain that moral virtues, which are about the passions as about their proper matter, cannot be without passions. The reason for this is that otherwise it would follow that moral virtue makes the sensitive appetite altogether idle: whereas it is not the function of virtue to deprive the powers subordinate to reason of their proper activities, but to make them execute the commands of reason, by exercising their proper acts. Wherefore just as virtue directs the bodily limbs to their due external acts, so does it direct the sensitive appetite to its proper regulated movements.

Those moral virtues, however, which are not about the passions, but about operations, can be without passions. Such a virtue is justice: because it applies the will to its proper act, which is not a passion. Nevertheless, joy results from the act of justice; at least in

---

[199] Thus there is also an emotional component to virtue: the thoroughly virtuous man has his feelings sanctified too. He not only does good deeds but also rejoices in, is pleased by, and enjoys them.

the will, in which case it is not a passion. And if this joy be increased through the perfection of justice, it will overflow into the sensitive appetite; in so far as the lower powers follow the movement of the higher, as stated above (Q. 17, A. 7; Q. 24, A. 3). Wherefore by reason of this kind of overflow, the more perfect a virtue is, the more does it cause passion.

Reply Obj. 1. Virtue overcomes inordinate passion; it produces ordinate passion. . . .

Question 60

How the Moral Virtues
Differ from One Another

*Whether Moral Virtues about Operations Are Different
from Those That Are About Passions?*

On the contrary, The Philosopher reckons justice to be about
operations; and temperance, fortitude, and gentleness, about
passions (*Ethic.* ii. 3, 7; v. 1, *seqq.*). . . .

Whether There Is Only One Moral Virtue about Operations?

I answer that, All the moral virtues that are about operations
agree in the one general notion of justice, which is in respect of
something due to another. . . . But the thing due is not of the same
kind in all these virtues: for something is due to an equal in one
way, to a superior, in another way, to an inferior, in yet another;
and the nature of a debt differs according as it arises from a contract, a promise, or a favor already conferred. And corresponding
to these various kinds of debt[200] there are various virtues: e.g.,

---

[200] "Debt" connotes to the modern mind something economic, like
"the national debt". But it did not have this cold and limiting connotation
to the medievals. "Debt" means something due, that is, just, appropriate,
and fitting—and this means something harmonious and therefore beautiful,
like music. The debt due to a contract is very different from the debt due
for a favor. The medievals even spoke of lovemaking as "the marriage
debt"!

Religion, whereby we pay our debt to God; *Piety* [respect], whereby we pay our debt to our parents or to our country; *Gratitude*, whereby we pay our debt to our benefactors, and so forth. . . .

Question 61

Of the Cardinal Virtues

Whether There Are Four Cardinal Virtues?

On the contrary, Gregory says (*Moral.* ii): *The entire structure of good works is built on four virtues.*

I answer that, Things may be numbered either in respect of their formal principles, or according to the subjects in which they are: and either way we find that there are four cardinal virtues.[201]

For the formal principle of the virtue of which we speak now is good as defined by reason; which good can be considered in two ways. First, as existing in the very act of reason: and thus we have one principal virtue, called *Prudence* [practical wisdom].—Secondly, according as the reason puts its order into something else; either into operations, and then we have *Justice*; or into passions, and then we need two virtues. For the need of putting the order of reason into the passions is due to their thwarting reason: and this occurs in two ways. First, by the passions inciting to something against reason; and then the passions need a curb, which we call *Temperance* [moderation, self-control]. Secondly, by the passions withdrawing us from following the dictate of reason, *e.g.*, through fear of

---

[201] St. Thomas is very good at this sort of thing: providing a theoretical outline as a background to explain and justify some traditional list. In primitive societies we nearly always find simple numerical lists (The Ten Terrible Things, The Five Treasures, The Twelve Steps of Mystic Initiation, etc.). The Greeks and medievals raised the concept of order to a higher level of abstraction than mere lists. Modernity tends to see all such traditional order as imposed by the mind, largely because of Kant's "Copernican revolution", and as historically relative, largely because of Hegel's historicism.

danger or toil: and then man needs to be strengthened for that which reason[202] dictates, lest he turn back; and to this end there is *Fortitude* [courage].

In like manner, we find the same number if we consider the subjects[203] of virtue. For there are four subjects of the virtue we speak of now: viz., the power which is rational in its essence, and this is perfected by *Prudence*; and that which is rational by participation,[204] and is threefold, the will, subject of *Justice*, the concupiscible [desiring] faculty, subject of *Temperance*, and the irascible [averting] faculty, subject of *Fortitude*. . . .

FOURTH ARTICLE

Whether the Four Cardinal Virtues Differ from One Another?

Objection 1. It would seem that the above four virtues are not diverse and distinct from one another.[205] For Gregory says (*Moral.* xxii. 1): *There is no true prudence, unless it be just, temperate and brave; no perfect temperance, that is not brave, just and prudent; no sound fortitude, that is not prudent, temperate and just; no real justice, without prudence, fortitude and temperance.* But this would not be so, if the above four virtues were distinct from one another: since the different species of one genus do not qualify one another. Therefore the aforesaid virtues are not distinct from one another. . . .

Reply Obj. 1. . . . These four virtues qualify one another by a kind of overflow. For the qualities of prudence overflow on to the

---

[202] Note how St. Thomas' classification of all four virtues is determined by their relation to reason. This is surprising only if we forget that St. Thomas meant by "reason" not just reasoning but also insight into reality, understanding truth.

[203] A *subject* of virtue is that in which virtue inheres, that which *has* the virtue.

[204] I.e., sharing reason by obeying reason, as a flying arrow shares the plan and purpose and intelligence of the archer.

[205] This is Plato's teaching, that all the virtues are one. For him they are unified by wisdom, or prudence, since Plato thought it was impossible to know the true good and not to will it. St. Thomas points out in the Reply that this is a half-truth.

other virtues in so far as they are directed by prudence. And each of the others overflows on to the rest, for the reason that whoever can do what is harder, can do what is less difficult. Wherefore whoever can curb his desires for the pleasures of touch, so that they keep within bounds, which is a very hard thing to do, for this very reason is more able to check his daring in dangers of death, so as not to go too far, which is much easier; and in this sense fortitude is said to be temperate. Again, temperance is said to be brave, by reason of fortitude overflowing into temperance: in so far, to wit, as he whose mind is strengthened by fortitude against dangers of death, which is a matter of very great difficulty, is more able to remain firm against the onslaught of pleasures. . . .

Question 62

Of the Theological Virtues

Whether There Are Any Theological Virtues?

I answer that, Man is perfected by virtue, for those actions whereby he is directed to happiness,[206] as was explained above (Q. 5, A. 7). Now man's happiness is twofold, as was also stated above (*ibid.*, A. 5). One is proportionate to human nature, a happiness, to wit, which man can obtain by means of his natural principles. The other is a happiness surpassing man's nature, and which man can obtain by the power of God alone, by a kind of participation of the Godhead, about which it is written (2 Pet 1:4) that by Christ we are made *partakers of the Divine nature.* And because such happiness surpasses the capacity of human nature, man's natural principles which enable him to act well according to his capacity, do not suffice to direct man to this same happiness. Hence it is necessary for man to receive from God some additional principles,[207] whereby he may be directed to supernatural happiness, even as he is directed to his connatural end, by means of his natural principles, albeit not without the Divine assistance. Such

---

[206] Note the close connection between virtue and happiness for St. Thomas. It is the oldest truism in the world: if you are good you will be happy. Or, in Plato's words (the main thesis of the *Republic*), "justice is always more profitable than injustice". Moral duty is not merely for duty's sake, as in Kant. Nor is it a mere means to the end of pleasure, or enjoyment, as in Utilitarianism. But it is the means to true happiness (cf. n. 3).

[207] "Principles", of course, refer not to abstract formulas but to causally efficacious realities, real sources.

like principles are called *theological virtues*: first, because their object
is God, inasmuch as they direct us aright to God: secondly, because
they are infused[208] in us by God alone: thirdly, because these
virtues are not made known to us, save by Divine revelation,
contained in Holy Writ. . . .

THIRD ARTICLE

*Whether Faith, Hope, and Charity Are Fittingly
Reckoned as Theological Virtues?*

Objection 2. Further, the theological virtues are more perfect
than the intellectual and moral virtues. Now faith is not reckoned
among the intellectual virtues, but is something less than a virtue,
since it is imperfect knowledge. Likewise hope is not reckoned
among the moral virtues, but is something less than a virtue, since
it is a passion. Much less therefore should they be reckoned as
theological virtues. . . .

On the contrary, The Apostle says (1 Cor 13:13): *Now there remain
faith, hope, charity, these three.*

I answer that, As stated above (A. 1), the theological virtues
direct man to supernatural happiness in the same way as by the
natural inclination man is directed to his connatural end. Now the
latter . . . fall[s] short of the order of supernatural happiness,
according to 1 Corinthians 2:9: *The eye hath not seen, nor ear heard,
neither hath it entered into the heart of man, what things God hath
prepared for them that love Him.* Consequently . . . man needed to
receive in addition something supernatural to direct him to a
supernatural end. First, as regards the intellect, man receives certain supernatural principles, which are held by means of a Divine
light: these are the articles of faith, about which is faith.—Secondly,
the will is directed to this end, both as to the movement of
intention, which tends to that end as something attainable,—and
this pertains to hope,—and as to a certain spiritual union, whereby
the will is, so to speak, transformed into that end,—and this
belongs to charity. . . .

---

[208] This does not mean we are not free to accept or refuse them, but that
their source is supernatural and their term is inward.

Reply Obj. 2. Faith and hope imply a certain imperfection: since faith is of things unseen, and hope, of things not possessed. Hence faith and hope in things that are subject to human power, fall short of the notion of virtue. But faith and hope in things which are above the capacity of human nature surpass all virtue that is in proportion to man, according to 1 Corinthians 1:25: *The weakness of God is stronger than men.* . . .

FOURTH ARTICLE

Whether Faith Precedes Hope, and Hope Charity?

On the contrary, The Apostle enumerates them thus (1 Cor 13:13): *Now there remain faith, hope, charity.*

I answer that, Order is twofold: order of generation, and order of perfection. By order of generation, in respect of which matter precedes form, and the imperfect precedes the perfect, in one same subject faith precedes hope, and hope charity, as to their acts. . . . For the movement of the appetite cannot tend to anything, either by hoping or loving, unless that thing be apprehended by the sense or by the intellect. Now it is by faith that the intellect apprehends the object of hope and love. Hence in the order of generation, faith precedes hope and charity. . . .

But in the order of perfection, charity precedes faith and hope: because both faith and hope are quickened by charity, and receive from charity their full complement as virtues. For thus charity is the mother and the root of all the virtues, inasmuch as it is the form of them all.[209] . . .

---

[209] N.b.: charity is not only the greatest virtue but the form, or essence, of all virtues. Faith and hope can be spoken of as aspects of charity, just as hope and charity can be spoken of as aspects of faith.

Question 63

Of the Cause of Virtues[210]

Whether Virtue Is in Us by Nature?

On the contrary, Whatever is in man by nature is common to all men, and is not taken away by sin, since even in the demons natural gifts remain, as Dionysius states (*Div. Nom.* iv). But virtue is not in all men, and is cast out by sin. Therefore it is not in man by nature.

I answer that, . . . With regard to sciences and virtues, some held that they are wholly from within, so that all virtues and sciences would pre-exist in the soul naturally, but that the hindrances to science and virtue, which are due to the soul being weighed down by the body, are removed by study and practice, even as iron is made bright by being polished. This was the opinion of the Platonists.—Others said that they are wholly from without, being due to the inflow of the active intellect, as Avicenna maintained. Others said that sciences and virtues are in us by nature, so far as we are adapted to them, but not in their perfection: this is the teaching of the Philosopher (*Ethic.* ii. 1), and is nearer the truth.

. . . Virtue is natural to man . . . in so far as in man's reason are to be found instilled by nature certain naturally known principles of

---

[210] The question answered by Question 63 is the one that begins Plato's *Meno*: How do we acquire virtue? Meno mentions four possibilities in the first paragraph, which are subsequently delineated by the history of philosophy: (1) teaching (Plato, Confucius), (2) habit (Aristotle, Aquinas), (3) innately, by nature (Rousseau, Lao-tzu), and (4) "some other way", probably *against* nature, by force or artifice (Hobbes, Marx).

both knowledge and action, which are the nurseries[211] of intellectual
and moral virtues, and in so far as there is in the will a natural
appetite for good in accordance with reason. . . .

It is therefore evident that all virtues are in us by nature,
according to aptitude and inchoation, but not according to perfection, except the theological virtues, which are entirely from
without. . . .

---

[211] The metaphor is apt. The virtues, like ourselves, are not born as
adults but as infants, yet born into "nurseries" naturally fit for them.
Actual (perfected) virtue is not innate, but only the "aptitude" for virtue
—something stronger than mere potentiality but weaker than actuality.

Question 64

Of the Mean of Virtue

Whether Moral Virtues Observe the Mean?[212]

Objection 1. It would seem that moral virtue does not observe the mean. For the nature of a mean is incompatible with that which is extreme. Now the nature of virtue is to be something extreme; for it is stated in *De Caelo* i. that *virtue is the limit of power*. Therefore moral virtue does not observe the mean.

Objection 2. Further, the maximum is not a mean. Now some moral virtues tend to a maximum: for instance magnanimity to very great honors, and magnificence to very large expenditure, as stated in *Ethic.* iv. 2, 3. Therefore not every moral virtue observes the mean.

Objection 3. Further, if it is essential to a moral virtue to observe the mean, it follows that a moral virtue is not perfected, but on the contrary corrupted, through tending to something extreme. Now some moral virtues are perfected by tending to something extreme; thus virginity, which abstains from all sexual pleasure, observes the extreme, and is the most perfect chastity: and to give all to the poor is the most perfect mercy or liberality. Therefore it seems that it is not essential to moral virtue that it should observe the mean.

On the contrary, The Philosopher says (*Ethic.* ii. 6) that *moral virtue is a habit of choosing the mean.*

I answer that, As already explained (Q. 55, A. 3), the nature of virtue is that it should direct man to good. Now moral virtue is

---

[212] Aristotle's doctrine of each virtue observing a "golden mean" between two bad extremes (e.g., courage is between cowardice and foolhardiness) is a typically classical rather than Romantic idea.

properly a perfection of the appetitive part of the soul in regard to some determinate matter: and the measure or rule of the appetitive movement in respect of appetible objects is the reason. But the good of that which is measured or ruled consists in its conformity with its rule: thus the good of things made by art is that they follow the rule of art. Consequently, in things of this sort, evil consists in discordance from their rule or measure. Now this may happen either by their exceeding the measure or by their falling short of it; as is clearly the case in all things ruled or measured. Hence it is evident that the good of moral virtue consists in conformity with the rule of reason.—Now it is clear that between excess and deficiency the mean is equality or conformity. Therefore it is evident that moral virtue observes the mean.

Reply Obj. 1. Moral virtue derives goodness from the rule of reason, while its matter[213] consists in passions or operations. If therefore we compare moral virtue to reason, then, if we look at that which it has of reason, it holds the position of one extreme, viz. conformity; while excess and defect take the position of the

---

[213] Passions (feelings) and operations (actions) are virtue's "matter", or raw material, to be shaped, formed, and directed by reason, which provides the form. Virtue's matter is like the keys on a piano. Virtue's form is like the sheet music, which tells you how much and when to play each note. Virtue is not a mean as to its form—you cannot have too much conformity to the rule of right reason—but as to its matter—you can have too much or too little of any passion:

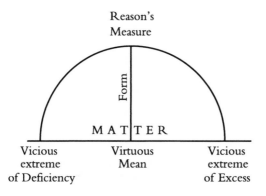

other extreme, viz., deformity. But if we consider moral virtue in respect of its matter, then it holds the position of mean, in so far as it makes the passion conform to the rule of reason. Hence the Philosopher says (*Ethic.* ii. 6) that *virtue, as to its essence, is a mean state,* in so far as the rule of virtue is imposed on its proper matter: *but it is an extreme in reference to the "best" and "the excellent,"* viz., as to its conformity with reason.

Reply Obj. 2. . . . There will be excess, if one tends to this maximum *when* it is not right, or *where* it is not right, or for an undue *end*; and there will be deficiency if one fails to tend thereto *where* one ought, and *when* one ought. This agrees with the saying of the Philosopher (*Ethic.* iv. 3) that *the magnanimous man observes the extreme in quantity, but the mean in the right mode of his action.*

Reply Obj. 3. The same is to be said of virginity and poverty as of magnanimity. For virginity abstains from all sexual matters, and poverty from all wealth, for a right end, and in a right manner, i.e., according to God's word, and for the sake of eternal life. But if this be done in an undue manner, i.e., out of unlawful superstition, or again for vainglory, it will be in excess. And if it be not done when it ought to be done, or as it ought to be done, it is a vice by deficiency: for instance, in those who break their vows of virginity or poverty. . . .

FOURTH ARTICLE

Whether the Theological Virtues Observe the Mean?

Objection 3. Further, hope, which is a theological virtue, is a mean between despair and presumption. Likewise faith holds a middle course between contrary heresies, as Boëthius states (*De Duab. Natur.* vii): thus, by confessing one Person and two natures in Christ, we observe the mean between the heresy of Nestorius, who maintained the existence of two persons and two natures, and the heresy of Eutyches, who held to one person and one nature. Therefore theological virtue observes the mean.

On the contrary, Wherever virtue observes the mean, it is possible to sin by excess as well as by deficiency. But there is no sinning by excess against God, Who is the object of theological virtue. . . .

I answer that, . . . so that never can we love God as much as He ought to be loved, nor believe and hope in Him as much as we should.[214] . . .

Reply Obj. 3. Hope observes the mean between presumption and despair, in relation to us, in so far, to wit, as a man is said to be presumptuous, through hoping to receive from God a good in excess of his condition; or to despair through failing to hope for that which according to his condition he might hope for. But there can be no excess of hope in comparison with God, Whose goodness is infinite.—In like manner faith holds a middle course between contrary heresies, not by comparison with its object, which is God, in Whom we cannot believe too much; but in so far as human opinion itself takes a middle position between contrary opinions, as was explained above.[215]

---

[214] Here St. Thomas bursts out of the Greek, classical, finite mold to a Christian "extremism" or Romanticism.

[215] Insofar as faith's object is doctrines or opinions, the objection holds. But the ultimate object of faith is God, not doctrines, just as the ultimate object of fidelity is one's spouse, not the Seventh Commandment.

Question 65

Of the Connection of Virtues

Whether the Moral Virtues Are Connected with One Another?

On the contrary, Ambrose says on Luke 6:20: *The virtues are connected and linked together,*[216] *so that whoever has one, is seen to have several:* and Augustine says (*De Trin.* vi. 4) that *the virtues that reside in the human mind are quite inseparable from one another:* and Gregory says (*Moral.* xxii. 1) that *one virtue without the other is either of no account whatever, or very imperfect:* and Cicero says (*Quaest. Tusc.* ii): *If you confess to not having one particular virtue, it must needs be that you have none at all.*

I answer that, Moral virtue may be considered either as perfect or as imperfect. An imperfect moral virtue, temperance for instance, or fortitude, is nothing but an inclination in us to do some kind of good deed, whether such inclination be in us by nature or by habituation. If we take the moral virtues in this way, they are not connected: since we find men who, by natural temperament or by being accustomed, are prompt in doing deeds of liberality, but are not prompt in doing deeds of chastity.[217]

But the perfect moral virtue is a habit that inclines us to do a good

---

[216] Plato thought all the virtues were one: prudence (cf. II–II, 58, 2). St. Thomas here sees a half-truth in this error, as he does in most.

[217] Here St. Thomas sees the half-truth in the teaching that perfect virtue is distinct from inclination (though not, as in Kant, unrelated to inclination or even opposed to it). For St. Thomas, inclination is incomplete virtue, and complete virtue not only is aided by good inclinations but also results in "converted" inclinations, so that the more virtuous you are, the more your inclinations enjoy virtue.

deed well; and if we take moral virtues in this way, we must say that they are connected, as nearly all are agreed in saying. . . .

Whether the Moral Virtues Are Better Than the Intellectual Virtues?[218]

Objection 1. It would seem that the moral virtues are better than the intellectual. Because that which is more necessary . . . is better. Now the moral virtues are . . . more necessary for human life. Therefore they are preferable to the intellectual virtues. . . .

I answer that, A thing may be said to be greater or less in two ways: first, simply; secondly, relatively. . . . Hence, speaking simply, that virtue is more excellent, which has the more excellent object. Now it is evident that the object of the reason is more excellent than the object of the appetite: since the reason apprehends things in the universal, while the appetite tends to things themselves, whose being is restricted to the particular. Consequently, speaking simply, the intellectual virtues, which perfect the reason, are more excellent than the moral virtues, which perfect the appetite.

But if we consider virtue in its relation to act, then moral virtue, which perfects the appetite, whose function it is to move the other powers to act, as stated above (Q. 9, A. 1), is more excellent.—And since virtue is so called from its being a principle of action, for it is the perfection of a power, it follows again that the nature of virtue agrees more with moral than with intellectual virtue, though the intellectual virtues are more excellent habits, simply speaking.

Reply Obj. 1. . . . That the moral virtues are more necessary for

---

[218] The question is *not* the concrete one: Who is the better person—which is the better choice—to have a maximum of intellectual virtue with a minimum of moral virtues, or to have a maximum of moral virtues with a minimum of intellectual virtues? (i.e., to be a clever cad or a well-meaning fool); but the abstract question: Which class of virtues is in itself the more ontologically perfect? The answer is: Each, in different ways, like men and women.

human life, proves that they are more excellent, not simply, but relatively. Indeed, the speculative intellectual virtues, from the very fact that they are not referred to something else, as a useful thing is referred to an end, are more excellent. The reason for this is that in them we have a kind of beginning of that happiness which consists in the knowledge of truth.[219] . . .

Whether Justice Is the Chief of the Moral Virtues?

Objection 1. It would seem that justice is not the chief of the moral virtues. For it is better to give of one's own than to pay what is due. Now the former belongs to liberality, the latter to justice. Therefore liberality is apparently a greater virtue than justice. . . .

Reply Obj. 1. The act of liberality needs to be founded on an act of justice, for *a man is not liberal in giving, unless he gives of his own* (*Polit.* ii. 3). Hence there could be no liberality apart from justice, which discerns between *meum* [mine] and *tuum* [yours]: whereas justice can be without liberality. Hence justice is simply greater than liberality, as being more universal, and as being its foundation: while liberality is greater relatively since it is an ornament and an addition to justice.[220] . . .

Whether Wisdom Is the Greatest of the Intellectual Virtues?

I answer that, As stated above (A. 3), the greatness of a virtue, as to its species, is taken from its object. Now the object of wisdom

---

[219] Thus Aristotle teaches that the speculative sciences, whose end is knowledge of the truth for its own sake, are nobler than the practical and productive sciences, whose end is knowledge for the sake of practice (action) or production (making). For knowledge of truth perfects our very essence (consciousness), while practice perfects our life and behavior and production perfects our external world. This is why we attain our greatest happiness and most ultimate perfection from knowing the truth.

[220] Justice is the rose, liberality is the bloom.

surpasses the objects of all the intellectual virtues: because wisdom considers the Supreme Cause, which is God, as stated at the beginning of the *Metaphysics*. And since it is by the cause that we judge of an effect, and by the higher cause that we judge of the lower effects; hence it is that wisdom exercises judgment over all the other intellectual virtues, directs them all, and is the architect of them all. . . .

SIXTH ARTICLE

Whether Charity Is the Greatest of the Theological Virtues?[221]

Objection 1. It would seem that charity is not the greatest of the theological virtues. Because, since faith is in the intellect, while hope and charity are in the appetitive power, it seems that faith is compared to hope and charity, as intellectual to moral virtue. Now intellectual virtue is greater than moral virtue, as was made evident above (Q. 62, A. 3). Therefore faith is greater than hope and charity. . . .

On the contrary, The Apostle says (1 Cor 13:13): *Now there remain faith, hope, charity, these three; but the greatest of these is charity.*

I answer that, As stated above (A. 3), the greatness of a virtue, as to its species, is taken from its object.—Now, since the three theological virtues look at God as their proper object, it cannot be said that any one of them is greater than another by reason of its having a greater object, but only from the fact that it approaches nearer than another to that object; and in this way charity is greater than the others. Because the others, in their very nature, imply a certain distance from the object: since faith is of what is not seen, and hope is of what is not possessed. But the love of charity is of that which is already possessed: since the beloved is, in a manner, in

---

[221] Thus wisdom and charity are the two greatest virtues. This tallies with the teaching of all the great sages in other world traditions, e.g., Buddha's *prajna* (wisdom) and *karuna* (compassion—not quite active charity, but similar), and with the convictions of those who have had out-of-body or near-death experiences and "came back" uniformly convinced that only these two values matter absolutely.

the lover, and, again, the lover is drawn by desire to union with the beloved; hence it is written (1 Jn 4:16): *He that abideth in charity, abideth in God, and God in him.*

Reply Obj. 1. Faith and hope are not related to charity in the same way as prudence to moral virtue; and for two reasons. First, because the theological virtues have an object surpassing the human soul: whereas prudence and the moral virtues are about things beneath man. Now in things that are above man, to love them is more excellent than to know them. Because knowledge is perfected by the known being in the knower: whereas love is perfected by the lover being drawn to the beloved. Now that which is above man is more excellent in itself than in man: since a thing is contained according to the mode of the container. But it is the other way about in things beneath man. [222] Secondly, because prudence moderates the appetitive movements pertaining to the moral virtues, whereas faith does not moderate the appetitive movement tending to God, which movement belongs to the theological virtues: it only shows the object. And this appetitive movement towards its object surpasses human knowledge, according to Ephesians 3:19: *The charity of Christ which surpasseth all knowledge.* . . .

---

[222] I.e., when we know something, we elevate it to our level (we make a material stone into the idea of a stone) or drag it down to our level (we think of God in humanly-limited ways), while when we love something, we elevate ourselves to it (by loving God we become more like God) or lower ourselves to it (by loving idols we become like them: Ps 135:15–18).

Question 71

Of Vice and Sin
Considered in Themselves

SECOND ARTICLE

Whether Vice Is Contrary to Nature?

Objection 3. Further, anything contrary to a nature, is not found in the greater number of individuals possessed of that nature. Now vice is found in the greater number of men; for it is written (Mt 7:13): *Broad is the way that leadeth to destruction, and many there are who go in thereat.* Therefore vice is not contrary to nature.[223] . . .

On the contrary, Augustine says (*De Lib. Arb.* iii. 13): *Every vice, simply because it is a vice, is contrary to nature.*

I answer that, As stated above (A. 1), vice is contrary to virtue. Now the virtue of a thing consists in its being well disposed in a manner befitting its nature, as stated above (A. 1). Hence the vice of any thing consists in its being disposed in a manner not befitting its nature, and for this reason is that thing *vituperated*, which word is derived from *vice* according to Augustine (*De Lib. Arb.* iii. 14).

But it must be observed that the nature of a thing is chiefly the form from which that thing derives its species. Now man derives his species from his rational soul: and consequently whatever is contrary to the order of reason is, properly speaking, contrary to the nature of man, as man, while whatever is in accord with reason,

---

[223] There is a real puzzle here. Every other disease is rare in its species, is exceptional; but sin or vice is statistically "normal". Thus we say, concerning sinful behavior, "it's only normal", or "it's only human", when in fact all sin is *de*humanizing; and we say of popular vices, "it's only natural" when all vice is in fact *un*natural. For we confuse the (ontologically) *natural* with the (statistically) *normal*, the qualitative with the quantitative.

is in accord with the nature of man, as man. Now *man's good is to be in accord with reason, and his evil is to be against reason*, as Dionysius states (*Div. Nom.* iv). Therefore human virtue, which makes a man good, and his work good, is in accord with man's nature, for as much as it accords with his reason: while vice is contrary to man's nature, in so far as it is contrary to the order of reason. . . .

Reply Obj. 3. There is a twofold nature in man, rational nature, and the sensitive nature. And since it is through the operation of his senses that man accomplishes acts of reason, hence there are more who follow the inclinations of the sensitive nature, than who follow the order of reason: because more reach the beginning of a business than achieve its completion. Now the presence of vices and sins in man is owing to the fact that he follows the inclination of his sensitive nature against the order of his reason.[224] . . .

THIRD ARTICLE

Whether Vice Is Worse Than a Vicious Act?

On the contrary, A man is justly punished for a vicious act; but not for a vicious habit, so long as no act ensues. Therefore a vicious action is worse than a vicious habit.

I answer that, A habit stands midway between power and act. Now it is evident that both in good and in evil, act precedes[225] power, as stated in *Metaph.* ix. 19. For it is better to do well than to be able to do well, and in like manner, it is more blameworthy to do evil, than to be able to do evil: whence it also follows that both in goodness and in badness, habit stands midway between power and act. . . . This is also made clear from the fact that a habit is not called good or bad, save in so far as it induces to a good or bad act. . . .

---

[224] This is not offered as an *excuse*. This is only the material-cause explanation for vice. The efficient-cause explanation involves free will, and the final-cause explanation involves an apparent good desired. The formal-cause explanation involves a violation of the natural law and right reason.

[225] Not in time, but in importance.

SIXTH ARTICLE

Whether Sin Is Fittingly Defined As a Word, Deed,
or Desire Contrary to the Eternal Law?

I answer that, As was shown above (A. 1), sin is nothing else than
a bad human act.[226] Now that an act is a human act is due to its
being voluntary, as stated above (Q. 1, A. 1), whether it be
voluntary, as being elicited by the will, e.g. to will or to choose, or
as being commanded by the will, e.g. the exterior actions of speech
or operation. Again, a human act is evil through lacking conformity
with its due measure: and conformity of measure in a thing depends
on a rule, from which if that thing depart, it is incommensurate.
Now there are two rules of the human will: one is proximate . . .
viz. the human reason; the other is the first rule, viz. the eternal
law, which is God's reason, so to speak. Accordingly Augustine
includes two things in the definition of sin; one, pertaining to the
substance of a human act, and which is the matter, so to speak, of
sin, when he says, *word, deed, or desire*; the other, pertaining to the
nature of evil, and which is the form, as it were, of sin, when he
says, *contrary to the eternal law.* . . .

---

[226] St. Thomas here uses "sin" in a broad and not specifically religious
sense, as synonymous with any vicious act, not just in explicit relation to
God and His revealed law.

Question 72

Of the Distinction of Sins

Whether Spiritual Sins Are Fittingly Distinguished from Carnal Sins?

On the contrary, Gregory (*Moral.* xxxi. 17) says that *of the seven capital sins five are spiritual, and two carnal.*

I answer that, As stated above (A. 1), sins take their species from their objects. Now every sin consists in the desire for some mutable good, for which man has an inordinate desire, and the possession of which gives him inordinate pleasure.[227] Now, as explained above (Q. 31, A. 3), pleasure is twofold. One belongs to the soul . . . ; this can also be called spiritual pleasure, e.g. when one takes pleasure in human praise or the like. The other pleasure is bodily or natural, and is realized in bodily touch, and this can also be called carnal pleasure.

Accordingly, those sins which consist in spiritual pleasure, are called spiritual sins; while those which consist in carnal pleasure, are called carnal sins, e.g. gluttony, which consists in the pleasures of the table; and lust, which consists in sexual pleasures. Hence the Apostle says (2 Cor 7:1): *Let us cleanse ourselves from all defilement of the flesh and of the spirit. . . .*

---

[227] St. Thomas is not here locating the sin in the pleasure as such, but in the inordinate (disordered, unreasonable) desire for a lesser good with the kind of desire proper to a greater good.

FOURTH ARTICLE

Whether Sin Is Fittingly Divided into Sin against God, against Oneself, and against One's Neighbor?

On the contrary, Isidore (*De Summo Bono*), in giving the division of sins, says that *man is said to sin against himself, against God, and against his neighbor.*

I answer that, As stated above (Q. 71, AA. 1, 6), sin is an inordinate act. Now there should be a threefold order in man: one in relation to the rule of reason, in so far as all our actions and passions should be commensurate with the rule of reason: another order is in relation to the rule of the Divine law, whereby man should be directed in all things: and if man were by nature a solitary animal, this twofold order would suffice.—But since man is naturally a civic and social animal, as is proved in *Polit.* i. 2, hence a third order is necessary, whereby man is directed in relation to other men among whom he has to dwell. Of these orders the second contains the first and surpasses it. For whatever things are comprised under the order of reason, are comprised under the order of God Himself. Yet some things are comprised under the order of God, which surpass the human reason, such as matters of faith, and things due to God alone. Hence he that sins in such matters, for instance, by heresy, sacrilege, or blasphemy, is said to sin against God. In like manner, the first order includes the third and surpasses it, because in all things wherein we are directed in reference to our neighbor, we need to be directed according to the order of reason. Yet in some things we are directed according to reason, in relation to ourselves only, and not in reference to our neighbor; and when man sins in these matters, he is said to sin against himself, as is seen in the glutton, the lustful, and the prodigal. But when man sins in matters concerning his neighbor, he is said to sin against his neighbor, as appears in the thief and the murderer. . . . For it is evident from what has been said (Q. 62, AA. 1, 2, 3) that by the theological virtues man is directed to God; by temperance and fortitude, to himself; and by justice to his neighbor.[228] . . .

---

[228] In terms of inclusion, (see diagram, next page)

SIXTH ARTICLE

Whether Sins of Commission and Omission Differ Specifically?

On the contrary, Omission and commission are found in the same species of sin. For the covetous man both takes what belongs to others, which is a sin of commission; and gives not of his own to whom he should give, which is a sin of omission. Therefore omission and commission do not differ specifically.[229] . . .

SEVENTH ARTICLE

Whether Sins Are Fittingly Divided into Sins of Thought, Word, and Deed?

On the contrary, Jerome in commenting on Ezekiel 43:23, says: *The human race is subject to three kinds of sin, for when we sin, it is either by thought, or word, or deed.*

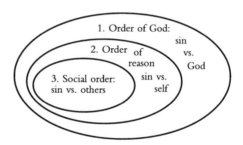

Thus all sins against others are also sins against self, and all sins against self are also sins against God. Ethics traditionally included these three parts; modern ethics tends to concentrate the least on the most important, most ultimate, and most universal part, and to concentrate the most on the least ultimate and universal part, as well as to neglect the middle area, individual character. C. S. Lewis uses the metaphor of a fleet of ships to explain why all three parts are necessary: the sailors need to know (1) the reason they are at sea in the first place, their ultimate goal or mission, (2) how to keep each ship shipshape, and (3) how to cooperate with the other ships in the fleet.

[229] Therefore neither one of these two is necessarily worse than the other.

I answer that, . . . sins are divided into these three, viz., sins of thought, word, and deed, not as into various complete species: for the consummation of sin is in the deed, wherefore sins of deed have the complete species; but the first beginning of sin is its foundation, as it were, in the sin of thought;[230] the second degree is the sin of word, in so far as man is ready to break out into a declaration of his thought; while the third degree consists in the consummation of the deed. Consequently these three differ in respect of the various degrees of sin. Nevertheless it is evident that these three belong to the one complete species of sin, since they proceed from the same motive. For the angry man, through desire of vengeance, is at first disturbed in thought, then he breaks out into words of abuse, and lastly he goes on to wrongful deeds; and the same applies to lust and to any other sin. . . .

---

[230] Therefore St. Paul tells us to "take every thought captive to obey Christ" (2 Cor 10:5), and Buddha tells us that "all that we are is made by our thoughts" (*Dhammapada*, 1, 1).

Question 73

Of the Comparison of
One Sin with Another

Whether All Sins Are Connected with One Another?

I answer that, The intention of the man who acts according to virtue in pursuance of his reason, is different from the intention of the sinner in straying from the path of reason. For the intention of every man acting according to virtue is to follow the rule of reason, wherefore the intention of all the virtues is directed to the same end, so that all the virtues are connected together in the right reason of things to be done, viz. prudence, as stated above (Q. 65, A. 1). But the intention of the sinner is not directed to the point of straying from the path of reason; rather is it directed to tend to some appetible good whence it derives its species.[231] Now these goods, to which the sinner's intention is directed when departing from reason, are of various kinds, having no mutual connection; in fact they are sometimes contrary to one another. Since, therefore, vices and sins take their species from that to which they turn, it is evident that, in respect of that which completes a sin's species, sins are not connected with one another. For sin does not consist in passing from the many to the one, as is the case with virtues, which are connected, but rather in forsaking the one for the many.[232] . . .

---

[231] The sinner does not sin simply because he wants to disobey reason, but because he wants some forbidden or inordinate good.

[232] Thus the saint is simple and single of heart, while the sinner is dissipated and divided. The extreme case of this is damnation: the demon-possessed man says, "My name is Legion, for we are many" (Mk 5:9). Cf.

THIRD ARTICLE

Whether the Gravity of Sins Varies according to Their Objects?

I answer that, As is clear from what has been said (Q. 71, A. 5), the gravity of sins varies in the same way as one sickness is graver than another. . . . Thus a sickness which comes on the human body from the heart, which is the principle of life, or from some neighboring part, is more dangerous. Wherefore a sin must needs be so much the graver, as the disorder occurs in a principle which is higher in the order of reason. Now in matters of action the reason directs all things in view of the end: wherefore the higher the end which attaches to sins in human acts, the graver the sin. Now the object of an act is its end, as stated above (Q. 72, A. 3, *ad* 2); and consequently the difference of gravity in sins depends on their objects. Thus it is clear that external things are directed to man as their end, while man is further directed to God as his end. Wherefore a sin which is about the very substance of man, e.g. murder, is graver than a sin which is about external things, e.g. theft; and graver still is a sin committed directly against God, e.g. unbelief, blasphemy, and the like: and in each of these grades of sin, one sin will be graver than another according as it is about a higher or a lower principle.[233] . . .

FIFTH ARTICLE

Whether Carnal Sins Are of Less Guilt Than Spiritual Sins?

Objection 1. It would seem that carnal sins are not of less guilt than spiritual sins. Because adultery is a more grievous sin than

---

G. K. Chesterton: "There is only one angle at which to stand upright, but many opposite angles at which to fall."

[233] It sounds shocking to the modern humanistic mind that blasphemy or unbelief is more grave than murder. But this conclusion necessarily follows from the reasonable premises that preceded it. A corollary would be that to deter unbelief is an even more important deed than to deter murder, for saving a man's soul is even more important than saving his body.

theft: for it is written (Prov 6:30, 32): *The fault is not so great when a man has stolen, . . . but he that is an adulterer, for the folly of his heart shall destroy his own soul.* Now theft belongs to covetousness, which is a spiritual sin; while adultery pertains to lust, which is a carnal sin. Therefore carnal sins are of greater guilt than spiritual sins.

Objection 2. Further, Augustine says in his commentary on Leviticus [*De Civ. Dei* ii. 4 and iv. 31] that *the devil rejoices chiefly in lust and idolatry.* But he rejoices more in the greater sin. Therefore, since lust is a carnal sin, it seems that the carnal sins are of most guilt.

Objection 3. Further, the Philosopher proves (*Ethic.* vii. 6) that *it is more shameful to be incontinent in lust than in anger.* But anger is a spiritual sin, according to Gregory (*Moral.* xxxi. 17); while lust pertains to carnal sins. Therefore carnal sin is more grievous than spiritual sin.

On the contrary, Gregory says (*Moral.* xxxiii. 11) that carnal sins are of less guilt, but of more shame than spiritual sins.[234]

I answer that, Spiritual sins are of greater guilt than carnal sins: yet this does not mean that each spiritual sin is of greater guilt than each carnal sin; but that, considering the sole difference between spiritual and carnal, spiritual sins are more grievous than carnal sins, other things being equal. Three reasons may be assigned for this. The first is on the part of the subject: because spiritual sins belong to the spirit, to which it is proper to turn to God, and to turn away from Him; whereas carnal sins are consummated in the carnal pleasure of the appetite, to which it chiefly belongs to turn to goods of the body; so that carnal sin, as such, denotes more a *turning to* something, and for that reason, implies a closer cleaving; whereas spiritual sin denotes more a *turning from* something, whence the notion of guilt arises;[235] and for this reason it involves greater guilt.—A second reason may be taken on the part of the person against whom sin is committed: because carnal sin, as such, is against the sinner's own body, which he ought to love less, in the order of charity, than God and his neighbor, against whom he

---

[234] Guilt is before God, and individual; shame is before man, and social.

[235] St. Thomas here sees guilt not as a subjective feeling but as an objective state of a broken relationship with God. Cf. the cartoon in which the condemned prisoner protests to the judge, "But I don't *feel* guilty."

commits spiritual sins, and consequently spiritual sins, as such, are of greater guilt.—A third reason may be taken from the motive, since the stronger the impulse to sin, the less grievous the sin,[236] as we shall state further on (A. 6). Now carnal sins have a stronger impulse, viz. our innate concupiscence of the flesh. Therefore spiritual sins, as such, are of greater guilt.

Reply Obj. 1. Adultery belongs not only to the sin of lust, but also to the sin of injustice, and in this respect may be brought under the head of covetousness, as a gloss observes on Ephesians 5:5, *No fornicator, or unclean, or covetous person*, etc.; so that adultery is so much more grievous than theft, as a man loves his wife more than his chattels [possessions].[237]

Reply Obj. 2. The devil is said to rejoice chiefly in the sin of lust, because it is of the greatest adhesion, and man can with difficulty be withdrawn from it. *For the desire of pleasure is insatiable,* as the Philosopher states (*Ethic.* iii. 12).[238]

Reply Obj. 3. As the Philosopher himself says (*ibid.*), the reason why it is more shameful to be incontinent in lust than in anger, is that lust partakes less of reason; and in the same sense he says (*Ethic.* iii. 10) that *sins of intemperance are most worthy of reproach, because they are about those pleasures which are common to us and irrational animals:* hence, by these sins man is, so to speak, brutalized;[239] for which same reason Gregory says (*loc. cit.*) that they are more shameful. . . .

---

[236] Because it is less rational and deliberate. Cold, calculating sins are the worst. Thus Jesus was most severe with the Pharisees.

[237] St. Thomas sees a great difference in gravity between simple lust and adultery because he judges sins objectively. The modern mind tends to judge more subjectively and psychologically, in terms of states of soul; from this point of view, adultery and lust are the same desire, feeling, or state of consciousness.

[238] A sin that is less objectively grave can still do greater damage to an individual soul because it is more attractive and difficult to overcome, as an alcoholic can be more harmed by the many little drinks which he cannot do without than by some more dangerous but (to him) less addictive drug.

[239] That is, made more like an irrational animal ("brute") and less human.

Question 76

Of the Causes of Sin

FOURTH ARTICLE

Whether Ignorance Diminishes a Sin?

Objection 2. Further, one sin added to another makes a greater sin. But ignorance is itself a sin, as stated above (A. 2). Therefore it does not diminish a sin. . . .

On the contrary, Whatever is a reason for sin to be forgiven, diminishes sin. Now such is ignorance, as is clear from 1 Timothy 1:13: *I obtained . . . mercy . . . because I did it ignorantly.* Therefore ignorance diminishes or alleviates sin.

I answer that, Since every sin is voluntary, ignorance can diminish sin, in so far as it diminishes its voluntariness; and if it does not render it less voluntary, it nowise alleviates the sin. Now it is evident that the ignorance which excuses from sin altogether (through making it altogether involuntary) does not diminish a sin, but does away with it altogether. On the other hand, ignorance which is not the cause of the sin being committed . . . neither diminishes nor increases the sin.

Therefore sin cannot be alleviated by any ignorance, but only by such as is a cause of the sin being committed, and yet does not excuse from the sin altogether. Now it happens sometimes that such . . . ignorance is directly and essentially voluntary, as when a man is purposely ignorant that he may sin more freely, and ignorance of this kind seems rather to make the act more voluntary and more sinful, since it is through the will's intention to sin that he is willing to bear the hurt of ignorance, for the sake of freedom in sinning.[240] Sometimes, however, the ignorance which is the cause of a sin being committed, is not directly voluntary, but indirectly or accidentally, as when a man is unwilling to work hard at his studies, the result being that he is ignorant, or as when a man willfully drinks too much wine, the result being that he becomes drunk and indiscreet, and this ignorance diminishes voluntariness and consequently alleviates the sin.[241] For when a thing is not known to be a sin, the will cannot be said to consent to the sin directly, but only accidentally. . . .

Reply Obj. 2. One sin added to another makes more sins, but it does not always make a sin greater, since, perchance, the two sins do not coincide, but are separate. It may happen, if the first diminishes the second, that the two together have not the same gravity as one of them alone would have; thus murder is a more grievous sin if committed by a man when sober, than if committed by a man when drunk, although in the latter case there are two sins: because drunkenness diminishes the sinfulness of the resulting sin more than its own gravity implies. . . .

---

[240] Thus those who do not admit that certain very obvious sins are sins at all have sinned also against their mind.

[241] N.b.: St. Thomas judges the gravity of sin and virtue not from society's point of view, or from human respectability, but from God's point of view and from the objective nature of things.

Question 74

Of the Subject of Sin

Whether the Will Is a Subject of Sin?

On the contrary, Augustine says (*Retract.* i. 9) that *it is by the will that we sin, and live righteously.*

I answer that, Sin is an act, as stated above (Q. 71, AA. 1, 6). Now some acts pass into external matter, e.g. *to cut* and *to burn*: and such like acts have for their matter and subject, the thing into which the action passes: thus the Philosopher states (*Phys.* iii, text. 18) that *movement is the act of the thing moved, caused by a mover.*—On the other hand, there are acts which do not pass into external matter, but remain in the agent, e.g. *to desire* and *to know*: and such are all moral acts, whether virtuous or sinful. Consequently the proper subject of sin must needs be the power which is the principle of the act. Now since it is proper to moral acts that they are voluntary, as stated above (Q. 1, A. 1; Q. 18, A. 6), it follows that the will, which is the principle of voluntary acts, both of good acts, and of evil acts or sins, is the principle of sins. Therefore it follows that sin is in the will as its subject. . . .

Of the Cause of Sin,
on the Part of the Sensitive Appetite

SECOND ARTICLE

Whether the Reason Can Be Overcome by a Passion,
against Its Knowledge?[242]

Objection 4. Further, whoever knows the universal, knows also
the particular which he knows to be contained in the universal: thus
who knows that every mule is sterile, knows that this particular
animal is sterile, provided he knows it to be a mule, as is clear from
Poster. i., text. 2. Now he who knows something in general, e.g.
that *no fornication is lawful*, knows this general proposition to
contain, for example, the particular proposition, *This is an act of
fornication.* Therefore it seems that his knowledge extends to the
particular.

Objection 5. Further, according to the Philosopher (*Peri Herm.* i.),
words express the thoughts of the mind. Now it often happens that
man, while in a state of passion, confesses that what he has chosen
is an evil, even in that particular case. Therefore he has knowledge,
even in particular.

Therefore it seems that the passions cannot draw the reason
against its universal knowledge; because it is impossible for it to
have universal knowledge together with an opposite particular
judgment.

On the contrary, The Apostle says (Rom 7:23): *I see another law in*

---

[242] Socrates (Plato) argues that it cannot. His position seems very
rational (St. Thomas admits it contains some truth), but experience shows
him to be wrong (cf. the quotation in *"On the contrary"*). St. Thomas will
not let his reason contradict experience, only explain it.

*my members, fighting against the law of my mind, and captivating me in
the law of sin.* Now the law that is in the members is concupiscence,
of which he had been speaking previously. Since then concupiscence
is a passion, it seems that a passion draws the reason counter to its
knowledge.

I answer that, As the Philosopher states (*Ethic.* vii. 2), the opinion
of Socrates was that knowledge can never be overcome by passion;
wherefore he held every virtue to be a kind of knowledge, and
every sin a kind of ignorance. In this he was somewhat right,
because, since the object of the will is a good or an apparent good, it
is never moved to an evil, unless that which is not good appear
good in some respect to the reason; so that the will would never
tend to evil, unless there were ignorance or error in the reason.
Hence it is written (Prov 14:22): *They err that work evil.*

Experience, however, shows that many act contrary to the
knowledge that they have, and this is confirmed by Divine
authority, according to the words of Luke 12:47: *The servant who
knew the will of his lord . . . and did not . . . shall be beaten with many
stripes*, and of James 4:17: *To him . . . who knoweth to do good, and
doth it not, to him it is a sin.* Consequently he was not altogether
right, and it is necessary, with the Philosopher (*Ethic.* vii. 3) to
make a distinction. Because, . . . it must be observed that nothing
prevents a thing which is known habitually from not being considered actually: so that it is possible for a man to have correct
knowledge not only in general but also in particular, and yet not to
consider[243] his knowledge actually: and in such a case it does not
seem difficult for a man to act counter to what he does not actually
consider. . . . Sometimes man fails to consider actually what he
knows habitually, on account of some hindrance supervening, e.g.
some external occupation, or some bodily infirmity; and, in this
way, a man who is in a state of passion, fails to consider in
particular what he knows in general, in so far as the passions hinder
him from considering it. Now it hinders him in three ways. First,

---

[243] For this ("to consider") is an act prompted by the will. When we sin,
our will turns our reason away from considering the truth, and the law,
and the fact that obedience to the law always brings us good and joy in the
end, and turns our reason instead to consider the short-range pleasure in
the evil. Plato did not know or admit that the will could move the reason.

by way of distraction, as explained above (A. 1). Secondly, by way of opposition, because a passion often inclines to something contrary to what man knows in general. Thirdly, by way of bodily transmutation, the result of which is that the reason is somehow fettered so as not to exercise its act freely; even as sleep or drunkenness, on account of some change wrought on the body, fetters the use of reason. That this takes place in the passions is evident from the fact that sometimes, when the passions are very intense, man loses the use of reason altogether: for many have gone out of their minds through excess of love or anger. It is in this way that passion draws the reason to judge in particular, against the knowledge which it has in general. . . .

Reply Obj. 4. He that has knowledge in a universal, is hindered, on account of a passion, from reasoning about that universal, so as to draw the conclusion: but he reasons about another universal proposition suggested by the inclination of the passion, and draws his conclusion accordingly. Hence the Philosopher says (*Ethic.* vii. 3) that the syllogism of an incontinent man has four propositions, two particular and two universal, of which one is of the reason, e.g. No fornication is lawful, and the other, of passion, e.g. Pleasure is to be pursued. Hence passion fetters the reason, and hinders it from arguing and concluding under the first proposition; so that while the passion lasts, the reason argues and concludes under the second.

Reply Obj. 5. Even as a drunken man sometimes gives utterance to words of deep signification, of which, however, he is incompetent to judge, his drunkenness hindering him; so a man who is in a state of passion, may indeed say in words that he ought not to do so and so, yet his inner thought is that he must do it, as stated in *Ethic.* vii. 3.

THIRD ARTICLE

Whether a Sin Committed through Passion,
Should Be Called a Sin of Weakness?

Objection 1. It would seem that a sin committed through passion should not be called a sin of weakness. For a passion is a vehement movement of the sensitive appetite, as stated above (A. 1). Now vehemence of movements is evidence of strength rather than of weakness. Therefore a sin committed through passion, should not be called a sin of weakness. . . .

On the contrary, Cicero (*De Quaest. Tusc.* iv) calls the passions diseases of the soul. Now weakness is another name for disease. Therefore a sin that arises from passion should be called a sin of weakness.

I answer that, The cause of sin is on the part of the soul, in which, chiefly, sin resides. Now weakness may be applied to the soul by way of likeness to weakness of the body. Accordingly, man's body is said to be weak, when it is disabled or hindered in the execution of its proper action, through some disorder of the body's parts, so that the humors and members of the human body cease to be subject to its governing and motive power. Hence a member is said to be weak, when it cannot do the work of a healthy member, the eye, for instance, when it cannot see clearly, as the Philosopher states (*De Hist. Animal.* x. 1). Therefore weakness of the soul is when the soul is hindered from fulfilling its proper action on account of a disorder in its parts. Now as the parts of the body are said to be out of order, when they fail to comply with the order of nature, so too the parts of the soul are said to be inordinate, when they are not subject to the order of reason, for the reason is the ruling power of the soul's parts. Accordingly, when the concupiscible or irascible power is affected by any passion contrary to the order of reason, the result being that an impediment arises in the aforesaid manner to the due action of man, it is said to be a sin of weakness. Hence the Philosopher (*Ethic.* vii. 8) compares the incontinent man to an epileptic, whose limbs move in a manner contrary to his intention.

Reply Obj. 1. Just as in the body the stronger the movement against the order of nature, the greater the weakness, so likewise, the stronger the movement of passion against the order of reason, the greater the weakness of the soul.[244] . . .

---

[244] N.b.: irrationally passionate people are *not* strong people, as they may seem to be.

FOURTH ARTICLE

Whether Self-Love Is the Source of Every Sin?

Objection 1. It would seem that self-love is not the source of every sin. For that which is good and right in itself is not the proper cause of sin. Now love of self is a good and right thing in itself: wherefore man is commanded to love his neighbor as himself (Lev 19:18). Therefore self-love cannot be the proper cause of sin. . . .

Objection 4. Further, as man sins at times through inordinate love of self, so does he sometimes through inordinate love of his neighbor. Therefore self-love is not the cause of every sin.

On the contrary, Augustine says (*De Civ. Dei* xiv. 28) that *self-love, amounting to contempt of God, builds up the city of Babylon.*[245] Now every sin makes man a citizen of Babylon.[246] Therefore self-love is the cause of every sin.

I answer that, . . . every sinful act proceeds from inordinate desire for some temporal good. Now the fact that anyone desires a temporal good inordinately, is due to the fact that he loves himself inordinately; for to wish anyone some good is to love him. Therefore it is evident that inordinate love of self is the cause of every sin.

Reply Obj. 1. Well ordered self-love, whereby man desires a fitting good for himself, is right and natural; but it is inordinate self-love, leading to the contempt of God, that Augustine (*loc. cit.*) reckons to be the cause of sin. . . .

Reply Obj. 4. A friend is like another self (*Ethic.* ix): wherefore the sin which is committed through love for a friend, seems to be committed through self-love. . . .

---

[245] Babylon (the "city of the world") and Jerusalem (the "City of God") are the two "cities", or invisible societies of men, which form the subject of St. Augustine's *The City of God*. He defines a "city" as a society of men united by a common object of their love. Everyone belongs to one or the other of these two cities, because everyone must choose between God and self as the first object of love.

[246] But divine forgiveness, accepted by repentance and faith, makes the sinner a citizen of Jerusalem.

SIXTH ARTICLE

Whether Sin Is Alleviated on Account of a Passion?

On the contrary, The passion of concupiscence is called a temptation of the flesh. But the greater the temptation that overcomes a man, the less grievous his sin, as Augustine states (*De Civ. Dei* iv. 12).

I answer that, Sin consists essentially in an act of the free will, which is a faculty of the will and reason; while passion is a movement of the sensitive appetite. Now the sensitive appetite can be related to the free will, antecedently and consequently. . . .

Accordingly if we take passion as preceding the sinful act, it must needs diminish the sin: because the act is a sin in so far as it is voluntary, and under our control. Now a thing is said to be under our control, through the reason and will: and therefore the more the reason and will do anything of their own accord, and not through the impulse of a passion, the more is it voluntary and under our control. In this respect passion diminishes sin, in so far as it diminishes its voluntariness.

On the other hand, a consequent passion does not diminish a sin, but increases it; or rather it is a sign of its gravity, in so far, to wit, as it shows the intensity of the will towards the sinful act; and so it is true that the greater the pleasure or the concupiscence with which anyone sins, the greater the sin.[247] . . .

EIGHTH ARTICLE

Whether a Sin Committed through Passion Can Be Mortal?

Objection 3. . . . Passion is a hindrance to reason, as explained above (AA. 1, 2). Now it belongs to the reason to turn to God, or to turn away from Him, which is the essence of a mortal sin. Therefore a sin committed through passion cannot be mortal. . . .

I answer that, Mortal sin, as stated above (Q. 72, A. 5), consists in turning away from our last end which is God, which aversion

---

[247] And the greater the pleasure in virtue, the greater the virtue. The two ideas are corollaries to each other.

pertains to the deliberating reason, whose function it is also to direct towards the end. Therefore that which is contrary to the last end can happen not to be a mortal sin, only when the deliberating reason is unable to come to the rescue, which is the case in sudden movements. Now when anyone proceeds from passion to a sinful act, or to a deliberate consent, this does not happen suddenly: and so the deliberating reason can come to the rescue here, since it can drive the passion away, or at least prevent it from having its effect, as stated above: wherefore if it does not come to the rescue, there is a mortal sin; and it is thus, as we see, that many murders and adulteries are committed through passion. . . .

Reply Obj. 3. Passion does not always hinder the act of reason altogether: consequently the reason remains in possession of its free-will, so as to turn away from God, or turn to Him. If, however, the use of reason be taken away altogether, the sin is no longer either mortal or venial.

G. Law

Question 90

Of the Essence of Law

reason = 1st principle of human acts.
reason directs to end.

FIRST ARTICLE

Whether Law Is Something Pertaining to Reason?

YES Law pertains to reason.

I answer that, Law is a rule and measure of acts, whereby man is induced[248] to act or is restrained from acting: for *lex* (law) is derived from *ligare* (to bind), because it binds one to act. Now the rule and measure of human acts is the reason, which is the first principle of human acts, as is evident from what has been stated above (Q. 1, A. 1 *ad* 3); since it belongs to the reason to direct to the end, which is the first principle in all matters of action. . . .

the end.

SECOND ARTICLE

1st principle in practical matters
bliss / happiness

Whether the Law Is Always Something Directed to the Common Good?

I answer that, . . . the first principle in practical matters, which are the object of the practical reason, is the last end: and the last end of human life is bliss or happiness, as stated above (Q. 2, A. 7; Q. 3, A. 1). Consequently the law must needs regard principally the relationship to happiness.[249] Moreover, since every part is ordained

---

[248] I.e., led, moved, commanded. This is something stronger than merely "advised" or "requested" but weaker than "forced" or "necessitated". Law binds morally but not physically. It obligates but it does not necessitate. It appeals to free will to obey or disobey. Free will follows upon reason— where reason is, free will is too—therefore law appeals to reason.

[249] Contrast this with Kant's concept of law, which has nothing to do with happiness, only with duty.

the law must regard some need for happiness in the human life

to the whole, as imperfect to perfect; and since one man is a part of the perfect community,[250] the law must needs regard properly the relationship to universal happiness. Wherefore the Philosopher, in the above definition of legal matters mentions both happiness and the body politic:[251] for he says (*Ethic.* v. 1) that we call those legal matters *just, which are adapted to produce and preserve happiness and its parts for the body politic.* ...

[handwritten: We are all individually part of a whole. We must regard each person's happiness when designing law.]

THIRD ARTICLE

Whether the Reason of Any Man Is Competent to Make Laws?

I answer that, A law, properly speaking, regards first and foremost the order to the common good. Now to order anything to the common good, belongs either to the whole people, or to someone who is the viceregent[252] of the whole people. And therefore the making of a law belongs either to the whole people or to a public personage who has care of the whole people. ...

[handwritten: Viceregent = representative]

FOURTH ARTICLE

Whether Promulgation Is Essential to a Law?

[handwritten: Making known to the public.]

I answer that, As stated above (A. 1), a law is imposed on others by way of a rule and measure. Now a rule or measure is imposed by being applied to those who are to be ruled and measured by it. Wherefore, in order that a law obtain the binding force which is proper to a law, it must needs be applied to the men who have to be

---

[250] Somewhat as the soul is both a substance in its own right and also, as the form of the body, a part of the substance "man", so the individual is a whole in himself and also a part of the larger whole of the community.

[251] I.e., communal, or social. The word "politics" did not have the narrow, specialized, and bureaucratic connotation it has today.

[252] A "vice-regent" is a *representative*. St. Thomas holds that the good state, whether ruled by one, a few, or many, should contain at least an essential element of democracy; even a king reigns for the people's good, not for his own.

ruled by it. Such application is made by its being notified to them by promulgation. Wherefore promulgation is necessary for the law to obtain its force.

Thus from the four preceding articles, the definition of law may be gathered; and it is nothing else than [1] an ordinance [2] of reason [3] for the common good, [4] made by him who has care of the community, [5] and promulgated.[253]

---

[253] There are thus five notes in the definition: the first is the genus, the second the specific difference, the third the final cause, the fourth the efficient cause, and the fifth a necessary property or proper condition. It follows from this definition that if a law is essentially (1) disordered, (2) irrational, (3) harmful, (4) unauthorized, or (5) unknown, it is not a real law, not binding.

Question 91

Of the Various Kinds of Law

FIRST ARTICLE

Whether There Is an Eternal Law?

Handwritten annotation: It Yes, Law is eternal b/c it comes from God (reasoning) Who is eternal

I answer that, As stated above (Q. 90, A. 1 *ad* 2; AA. 3, 4), a law is nothing else but a dictate of practical reason emanating from the ruler who governs a perfect [complete] community. Now it is evident, granted that the world is ruled by Divine Providence, as was stated in the First Part (Q. 22, AA. 1, 2), that the whole community of the universe is governed by Divine Reason. Wherefore the very Idea of the government of things in God the Ruler of the universe, has the nature of a law. And since the Divine Reason's conception of things is not subject to time but is eternal, according to Proverbs 8:23, therefore it is that this kind of law must be called eternal. . . .

SECOND ARTICLE

Whether There Is in Us a Natural Law?

Handwritten annotation: Yes, b/c everyone is made by Him who made eternal law.

On the contrary, A gloss on Romans 2:14: *When the Gentiles, who have not the [Mosaic] law, do by nature those things that are of the law,* comments as follows: *Although they have no written law, yet they have the natural law, whereby each one knows, and is conscious of, what is good and what is evil.*

I answer that, As stated above (Q. 90, A. 1 *ad* 1), law, being a rule and measure, can be in a person in two ways: in one way, as in him that rules and measures; in another way, as in that which is ruled and measured, since a thing is ruled and measured, in so far as it partakes of the rule or measure. Wherefore, since all things subject

503

our consciences are sacred.

to Divine providence are ruled and measured by the eternal law, as was stated above (A. 1); it is evident that all things partake somewhat of the eternal law, in so far as, namely, from its being imprinted on them, they derive their respective inclinations to their proper acts and ends. Now among all others, the rational creature is subject to Divine providence in the most excellent way, in so far as it partakes of a share of providence, by being provident both for itself and for others. Wherefore it has a share of the Eternal Reason, whereby it has a natural inclination to its proper act and end: and this participation of the eternal law in the [very nature of the] rational creature is called the natural law. Hence the Psalmist after saying (Ps 4:6): *Offer up the sacrifice of justice*, as though someone asked what the works of justice are, adds: *Many say, Who showeth us good things?* in answer to which question he says: *The light of Thy countenance, O Lord, is signed upon us:* thus implying that the light of natural reason, whereby we discern what is good and what is evil, which is the function of the natural law, is nothing else than an imprint on us of the Divine light. It is therefore evident that the natural law is nothing else than the rational creature's participation of the eternal law.[254] . . . *the natural law is nothing else than the rational creatures participation of the eternal law.*

our conscience ←

THIRD ARTICLE

Whether There Is a Human Law?

Yes *But it may or may not admit eternal law. which is eternal law. always made by natural law pervaded by s.*

I answer that, As stated above (Q. 90, A. 1, *ad* 2), a law is a dictate of the practical reason. Now it is to be observed that the same procedure takes place in the practical and in the speculative reason: for each proceeds from principles to conclusions, as stated above (*ibid.*). Accordingly we conclude that just as, in the speculative reason, from naturally known indemonstrable principles,[255] we draw the conclusions of the various sciences, the knowledge of

Sacred Conscience ←

---

[254] Thus the voice of conscience (natural reason judging good and evil) is the echo of the voice of God, and is therefore sacred and inviolable.

[255] Self-evident theoretical axioms like the law of non-contradiction. There are also self-evident practical axioms, both general ("Do good, avoid evil") and specific ("Be just"). These are "the precepts of the natural law", which, since it is in our nature, is also naturally *known*, just as first theoretical principles are.

acceptance = good thing
homosexual = bad thing
marriage

[handwritten: human law.]

which is not imparted to us by nature, but acquired by the efforts of reason, so too it is from the precepts of the natural law, as from general and indemonstrable principles, that the human reason needs to proceed to the more particular determination of certain matters. These particular determinations, devised by human reason, are called human laws.[256] . . .

FOURTH ARTICLE

Whether There Was Any Need for a Divine Law?[257]

I answer that, Besides the natural and the human law it was necessary for the directing of human conduct to have a Divine law. And this for four reasons. First, because . . . man is ordained to an end of eternal happiness. . . . Secondly . . . on account of the uncertainty of human judgment. . . . Thirdly, because . . . man is not competent to judge of interior movements, that are hidden. . . . Fourthly, because . . . human law cannot punish or forbid all evil deeds. . . .

FIFTH ARTICLE

Whether There Is But One Divine Law?

On the contrary, The Apostle says (Heb 7:12): *The priesthood being translated, it is necessary that a translation also be made of the law.* But the priesthood is twofold, as stated in the same passage, viz.,

---

[256] "Human law" is "positive law", law posited (made) by man. Moral positivism reduces all moral law to this, denying the eternal law and the natural law. A philosopher could admit the natural law without admitting the eternal law, since one could know the effect without knowing the cause; therefore the argument between legal positivism and natural law does not depend only on whether or not God is admitted. St. Thomas would disagree with Dostoyevski's saying, "If God does not exist, everything is permissible."

[257] The divine law is that part of the eternal law which God made known by special revelation.

505

is there I divine Law?

→ Divine Law is heavenly & earthly
Two-fold = New & Old law (testament)

the Levitical priesthood, and the priesthood of Christ. Therefore the Divine law is twofold, namely the Old Law [covenant, testament] and the New Law.

I answer that, . . . In the first place, it belongs to law to be directed to the common good as to its end, as stated above (Q. 90, A. 2). This good may be twofold. It may be a sensible and earthly good; and to this, man was directly ordained by the Old Law: wherefore, at the very outset of the law, the people were invited to the earthly kingdom of the Chananaeans (Ex 3:8, 17).[258] Again it may be an intelligible and heavenly good: and to this, man is ordained by the New Law. . . .

Secondly, it belongs to the law to direct human acts according to the order of righteousness (A. 4): wherein also the New Law surpasses the Old Law, since it directs our internal acts, according to Matthew 5:20: *Unless your justice abound more than that of the Scribes and Pharisees, you shall not enter into the kingdom of heaven.* Hence the saying that *the Old Law restrains the hand but the New Law controls the mind* (3 *Sentent.*, D. xl). *→ Mind over hand.*

Thirdly, it belongs to the law to induce men to observe its commandments. This the Old Law did by the fear of punishment: but the New Law, by love, which is poured into our hearts by the grace of Christ, bestowed in the New Law, but foreshadowed in the Old.[259] . . .

---

[258] St. Thomas is not implying that the Hebrews knew no higher good than earthly goods. But (1) life after death was not clearly revealed in the Old Testament until quite late, and (2) the distinction between the sensible and the intelligible, body and soul, also became clear only gradually, and late.

[259] The Old Law prophesies that a later, newer law will do this: Jer 31:31–34.

Question 92

Of the Effects of Law

FIRST ARTICLE

Whether an Effect of Law Is to Make Men Good?[260]

Objection 1. It seems that it is not an effect of law to make men good. For men are good through virtue, since virtue, as stated in *Ethic.* ii. 6 is *that which makes its subject good.* But virtue is in man from God alone, because He it is Who *works it in us without us,* as we stated above (Q. 55, A. 4) in giving the definition of virtue. Therefore the law does not make men good.

Objection 2. Further, Law does not profit a man unless he obeys it. But the very fact that a man obeys a law is due to his being good. Therefore in man goodness is presupposed to the law. Therefore the law does not make men good.

Objection 3. Further, Law is ordained to the common good, as stated above (Q. 90, A. 2). But some behave well in things regarding the community, who behave ill in things regarding themselves. Therefore it is not the business of the law to make men good.

Objection 4. Further, some laws are tyrannical, as the Philosopher

---

[260] The question, in contemporary terms, is: Can you legislate morality? St. Thomas answers, Of course! What else is worth legislating? Of course, law cannot *guarantee* moral behavior, since man's will is free to disobey; but it can certainly make a great difference, and make men better. St. Thomas would agree, I think, with Peter Maurin's simple definition of the good society: the good society is a society where it is easy to be good (because of its good laws). But he would also agree with St. Thomas More that "the times (or the society) are never so bad but that a good man can live in them."

507

Law making Tyrants are self-seeking.

says (*Polit.* iii. 6). But a tyrant does not intend the good of his subjects, but considers only his own profit. Therefore law does not make men good.

On the contrary, The Philosopher says (*Ethic.* ii. 1) that the *intention of every lawgiver is to make good citizens.* . . *lawgiver in th*

Reply Obj. 1. Virtue is twofold, as explained above (Q. 63, A. 2), *vi* viz., acquired and infused. Now the fact of being accustomed to an action contributes to both, but in different ways; for it causes the acquired virtue; while it disposes to infused virtue, and preserves and fosters it when it already exists. And since law is given for the *viv* purpose of directing human acts; as far as human acts conduce to *is* virtue, so far does law make men good. Wherefore the Philosopher *prac* says in the second book of the *Politics* (*Ethic.* ii) that *lawgivers make men good by habituating them to good works.*

law makes men good as far as their limited virtue is practical

Reply Obj. 2. It is not always through perfect goodness of virtue that one obeys the law, but sometimes it is through fear of punishment.[261] . . .

Reply Obj. 3. The goodness of any part is considered in comparison with the whole; hence Augustine says (*Conf.* iii) that *unseemly is the part that harmonizes not with the whole.* Since then every man is a part of the state, it is impossible that a man be good, unless he be well proportionate to the common good: nor can the whole be well consistent unless its parts be proportionate to it. Consequently the common good of the state cannot flourish, unless the citizens be virtuous,[262] at least those whose business it is to govern. But it is enough for the good of the community, that the other citizens be so far virtuous that they obey the commands of their rulers. . . . → *Law is to make every part*

every individual part.

good

Reply Obj. 4. A tyrannical law, through not being according to reason, is not a law, absolutely speaking, but rather a perversion of law. . . .

tyrannical law is not law.

---

[261] Objection 2 has a good point: no law is needed in Heaven. Antinomians merely confuse earth with Heaven. Antinomianism is impatience.

[262] Cf. also "*I answer that*". This is *the* most obvious and also *the* most important truth in social science, yet the one most frequently forgotten by many theorists today.

SECOND ARTICLE

Whether the Acts of Law Are Suitably Assigned?

Objection 4. Further, the intention of a lawgiver is to make men good, as stated above (A. 1). But he that obeys the law, merely through fear of being punished, is not good: because *although a good deed may be done through servile fear, i.e., fear of punishment, it is not done well,* as Augustine says (*Contra duas Epist. Pelag.* ii). Therefore punishment is not a proper effect of law.

On the contrary, Isidore says (*Etym.* v. 19): *Every law either permits something, as: "A brave man may demand his reward":* or *forbids something, as: "No man may ask a consecrated virgin in marriage":* or *punishes, as: "Let him that commits a murder be put to death."* . . .

Reply Obj. 4. From becoming accustomed to avoid evil and fulfil what is good, through fear of punishment, one is sometimes led on to do so likewise, with delight and of one's own accord. Accordingly, law, even by punishing, leads men on to being good. [263]

Yes.

---

[263] Another very evident truism of individual and social psychology known by all the ancients and medievals and often forgotten by moderns.

Question 93

Of the Eternal Law

We must now consider each law by itself; and (1) The eternal law; (2) The natural law; (3) The human law; (4) The old law; (5) The new law, which is the law of the Gospel. . . .

SECOND ARTICLE

Whether the Eternal Law Is Known to All?

Objection 1. It would seem that the eternal law is not known to all. Because, as the Apostle says (1 Cor 2:11), *the things that are of God no man knoweth, but the Spirit of God.* But the eternal law is a type [ideal, model, plan] existing in the Divine mind. Therefore it is unknown to all save God alone. . . .

On the contrary, Augustine says (*De Lib. Arb.* i. 6) that *knowledge of the eternal law is imprinted on us.*

I answer that, A thing may be known in two ways: first, in itself; secondly, in its effect, wherein some likeness of that thing is found: thus someone not seeing the sun in its substance, may know it by its rays. So then no one can know the eternal law, as it is in itself, except the blessed who see God in His Essence. But every rational creature knows it in its reflection, greater or less. For every knowledge of truth is a kind of reflection and participation of the eternal law, which is the unchangeable truth, as Augustine says (*De Vera Relig.* xxxi). Now all men know the truth to a certain extent, at least as to the common principles of the natural law: and as to the others, they partake of the knowledge of truth, some more, some less; and in this respect are more or less cognizant of the eternal law.

Reply Obj. 1. We cannot know the things that are of God, as they are in themselves; but they are made known to us in their effects, according to Romans 1:20: *The invisible things of God . . . are clearly seen, being understood by the things that are made.* . . .

THIRD ARTICLE

Whether Every Law Is Derived from the Eternal Law?

Objection 2. Further, nothing unjust can be derived from the eternal law, because, as stated above (A. 2, *Obj.* 2), *the eternal law is that, according to which it is right that all things should be most orderly.* But some laws are unjust, according to Isaiah 10:1: *Woe to them that make wicked laws.* Therefore not every law is derived from the eternal law.

Objection 3. Further, Augustine says (*De Lib. Arb.* i. 5) that *the law which is framed for ruling the people, rightly permits many things which are punished by Divine providence.* But the type of Divine providence is the eternal law, as stated above (A. 1). Therefore not even every good law is derived from the eternal law. . . .

I answer that, . . . Since the eternal law is the plan of government in the Chief Governor, all the plans of government in the inferior governors must be derived from the eternal law. But these plans of inferior governors are all other laws besides the eternal law. Therefore all laws, in so far as they partake of right reason, are derived from the eternal law.[264] Hence Augustine says (*De Lib. Arb.* i. 6) that *in temporal law there is nothing just and lawful, but what man has drawn from the eternal law.* . . .

Reply Obj. 2. Human law has the nature of law in so far as it partakes of right reason; and it is clear that, in this respect, it is derived from the eternal law. But in so far as it deviates from reason, it is called an unjust law, and has the nature, not of law but of violence. Nevertheless even an unjust law, in so far as it retains some appearance of law, though being framed by one who is in power, is derived from the eternal law; since all power is from the Lord God, according to Romans 13:1.

---

[264] In objective fact, not merely in subjective knowledge. St. Thomas is not implying that our knowledge of natural law or human law depends on our knowledge of eternal law explicitly and as such. When an atheist knows that theft is wrong he in fact knows something of the eternal law, but he does not know that it is the eternal law. Note also: "eternal law" is not the same as "divine law". "Eternal law" is not "religious", i.e., specially revealed by Church or Scripture, as is "divine law", both the "Old Law" and the "New Law".

Reply Obj. 3. Human law is said to permit certain things, not as approving of them, but as being unable to direct them. And many things are directed by the Divine law, which human law is unable to direct, because more things are subject to a higher than to a lower cause. Hence the very fact that human law does not meddle with matters it cannot direct, comes under the ordination of the eternal law. It would be different, were human law to sanction what the eternal law condemns. Consequently it does not follow that human law is not derived from the eternal law, but that it is not on a perfect equality with it. . . .

SIXTH ARTICLE

Whether All Human Affairs Are Subject to the Eternal Law?

I answer that, There are two ways in which a thing is subject to the eternal law, as explained above (A. 5): first by partaking of the eternal law by way of knowledge; secondly, by way of action and passion, i.e., by partaking of the eternal law by way of an inward motive principle: and in this second way, irrational creatures are subject to the eternal law, as stated above (*ibid.*). But since the rational nature, [in addition to] that which it has in common with all creatures, has something proper to itself inasmuch as it is rational, consequently it is subject to the eternal law in both ways; because while each rational creature has some knowledge of the eternal law, as stated above (A. 2), it also has a natural inclination to that which is in harmony with the eternal law; for *we are naturally adapted to be the recipients of virtue* (*Ethic.* ii. 1).[265]

[Margin handwritten note: Felt justice!]

---

[265] Note the optimistic view of human nature here. Though fallen and sinful, it retains its essential properties, including its innate inclination to the good that God ordained for it by His eternal law. St. Thomas is sometimes criticized by modern thinkers for being too pessimistic about man's sinful *acts* (e.g., I–II, 77, 8 and the next paragraph here) *and* too optimistic about man's *nature* (e.g., this footnoted paragraph). That is because the typically modern mind is less certain that we have an essence, or that it can be known, or that it can be known to be metaphysically good, and also less certain that sin is as serious as Christianity has traditionally seen it to be; and also because the modern mind tends toward

Both ways, however, are imperfect, and to a certain extent destroyed, in the wicked; because in them the natural inclination to virtue is corrupted by vicious habits, and, moreover, the natural knowledge of good is darkened by passions and habits of sin. But in the good both ways are found more perfect: because in them, besides the natural knowledge of good, there is the added knowledge of faith and wisdom; and again, besides the natural inclination to good, there is the added motive of grace and virtue. . . .

Partaking in eternal law
1 by way of knowledge
2 by way of passion

---

egalitarianism and is uncomfortable with strong value judgments such as the sharp distinction between the wicked and the good in the last paragraph. But this is an ideologically-based opinion: cf. Scott Peck, *People of the Lie*.

Question 94

Of the Natural Law

Whether the Natural Law Contains Several Precepts, or One Only?

On the contrary, The precepts of the natural law in man stand in relation to practical matters, as the first principles to matters of demonstration.[266] But there are several first indemonstrable principles. Therefore there are also several precepts of the natural law.

I answer that, As stated above (Q. 91, A. 3), the precepts of the natural law are to the practical reason, what the first principles of demonstrations are to the speculative reason; because both are self-evident principles. Now a thing is said to be self-evident in two ways: first, in itself; secondly, in relation to us. Any proposition is said to be self-evident in itself, if its predicate is contained in the notion of the subject: although, to one who knows not the definition of the subject, it happens that such a proposition is not self-evident. For instance, this proposition, *Man is a rational being*, is, in its very

---

[266] I.e., they are axioms to which all else is reduced, not from which all else is deduced. The three axioms of logical demonstration are the law of identity ($x = x$), the law of non-contradiction ($x \neq$ non-x), and the law of excluded middle (either x or non-x). From these we cannot deduce anything (e.g., that all men are mortal), but to them we reduce all demonstrations (e.g., "all animals are mortal and all men are animals, therefore all men are mortal" is valid because of these laws). Similarly, from "Do good and avoid evil" and "give each his due" we cannot deduce that defensive war is just and aggression unjust, but "it is just to defend civilians by repelling unjust aggressors" is reduced to and validated by these principles.

nature, self-evident, since who says *man*, says *a rational being*: and yet to one who knows not what a man is, this proposition is not self-evident. Hence it is that, as Boëthius says (*De Hebdom.*), certain axioms or propositions are universally self-evident to all; and such are those propositions whose terms are known to all, as, *Every whole is greater than its part,* and, *Things equal to one and the same are equal to one another.* But some propositions are self-evident only to the wise, who understand the meaning of the terms of such propositions: thus to one who understands that an angel is not a body, it is self-evident that an angel is not circumscriptively in a place: but this is not evident to the unlearned, for they cannot grasp it.

Now a certain order is to be found in those things that are apprehended universally. For that which, before aught else, falls under apprehension, is *being*,[267] the notion of which is included in all things whatsoever a man apprehends. Wherefore the first indemonstrable principle is that *the same thing cannot be affirmed and denied at the same time*, which is based on the notion of *being* and *not-being*: and on this principle all others are based, as is stated in *Metaph.* iv, text. 9. Now as *being* is the first thing that falls under the apprehension simply, so *good* is the first thing that falls under the apprehension of the practical reason, which is directed to action: since every agent acts for an end under the aspect of good. Consequently the first principle in the practical reason is one founded on the notion of good, viz., that *good is that which all things seek after*. Hence this is the first precept of law, that *good is to be done and pursued, and evil is to be avoided*.[268] All other precepts of the natural law are based upon this: so that whatever the practical

---

[267] "Before" not chronologically but logically, and not explicitly but implicitly.

[268] N.b.: for St. Thomas, all ethics is most fundamentally about *goods*; most modern ethics is about rights, obligations, duties, laws, or "values". The significance of the word "good" is that "good" is (1) decidedly metaphysical, (2) objective (unlike "values"), (3) universal (unlike "rights" and "duties"), (4) intellectually known ("naturally apprehended by reason as being good"), and (5) correlative with natural inclination, in accord with human nature. All this contrasts both with "deontological" (Kantian) and "teleological" (Utilitarian) ethics.

reason naturally apprehends as man's good (or evil) belongs to the precepts of the natural law as something to be done or avoided.

Since, however, good has the nature of an end, and evil, the nature of a contrary, hence it is that all those things to which man has a natural inclination, are naturally apprehended by reason as being good, and consequently as objects of pursuit, and their contraries as evil, and objects of avoidance. Wherefore according to the order of natural inclinations, is the order of the precepts of the natural law. Because in man there is first of all an inclination to good in accordance with the nature which he has in common with all substances: inasmuch as every substance seeks the preservation of its own being, according to its nature: and by reason of this inclination, whatever is a means of preserving human life, and of warding off its obstacles, belongs to the natural law. Secondly, there is in man an inclination to things that pertain to him more specially, according to that nature which he has in common with other animals: and in virtue of this inclination, those things are said to belong to the natural law, *which nature has taught to all animals* [*Pandect. Just.* I., tit. i], such as sexual intercourse, education of offspring and so forth. Thirdly, there is in man an inclination to good, according to the nature of his reason, which nature is proper to him: thus man has a natural inclination to know the truth about God, and to live in society: and in this respect, whatever pertains to this inclination belongs to the natural law; for instance, to shun ignorance, to avoid offending those among whom one has to live, and other such things regarding the above inclination.[269] . . .

THIRD ARTICLE

Whether All Acts of Virtue Are Prescribed by the Natural Law?

Objection 2. . . . Every sin is opposed to some virtuous act. If therefore all acts of virtue are prescribed by the natural law, it seems to follow that all sins are against nature: whereas this applies to certain special sins. . . .

---

[269] Thus the natural law is not merely "biologistic", or animal instinct, because (1) natural instinct is only its matter, or substratum, and (2) because

I answer that, . . . If . . . we speak of acts of virtue, considered as virtuous, thus all virtuous acts belong to the natural law. For it has been stated (A. 2) that to the natural law belongs everything to which a man is inclined according to his nature. Now each thing is inclined naturally to an operation that is suitable to it according to its form: thus fire is inclined to give heat. Wherefore, since the rational soul is the proper form of man, there is in every man a natural inclination to act according to reason: and this is to act according to virtue. Consequently, considered thus, all acts of virtue are prescribed by the natural law: since each one's reason naturally dictates to him to act virtuously. . . .

Reply Obj. 2. By human nature we may mean either that which is proper to man—and in this sense all sins, as being against reason, are also against nature, as Damascene states (*De Fide Orthod.* ii. 30): or we may mean that nature which is common to man and other animals; and in this sense, certain special sins are said to be against nature; thus contrary to sexual intercourse, which is natural to all animals, is unisexual lust, which has received the special name of the unnatural crime. . . .

FOURTH ARTICLE

Whether the Natural Law Is the Same in All Men?

On the contrary, Isidore says (*Etym.* v. 4): *The natural law is common to all nations.*

I answer that, As stated above (AA. 2, 3), to the natural law belongs those things to which a man is inclined naturally: and among these it is proper to man to be inclined to act according to reason. Now the process of reason is from the common to the proper, as stated in *Phys.* i. The speculative reason, however, is differently situated in this matter, from the practical reason. For,

---

this substratum is both broader and narrower than man's animal nature: broader because man shares the natural desire for self-preservation with all substances, not just animals, and narrower because the properly human part of the natural law concerns what only reason can know. See also Reply 2 of the next Article.

since the speculative reason is busied chiefly with necessary things, which cannot be otherwise than they are, its proper conclusions, like the universal principles, contain the truth without fail. The practical reason, on the other hand, is busied with contingent matters, about which human actions are concerned: and consequently, although there is necessity in the general principles, the more we descend to matters of detail, the more frequently we encounter defects. Accordingly then in speculative matters truth is the same in all men, both as to principles and as to conclusions: although the truth is not known to all as regards the conclusions, but only as regards the principles which are called common notions. But in matters of action, truth or practical rectitude is not the same for all, as to matters of detail, but only as to the general principles: and where there is the same rectitude in matters of detail, it is not equally known to all.[270]

It is therefore evident that, as regards the general principles whether of speculative or of practical reason, truth or rectitude is the same for all, and is equally known by all. As to the proper conclusions of the speculative reason, the truth is the same for all, but is not equally known to all: thus it is true for all that the three angles of a triangle are together equal to two right angles, although it is not known to all. But as to the proper conclusions of the practical reason, neither is the truth or rectitude the same for all,

---

[270] For the *application* of the unchanging first principles of the natural law to diverse and changing situations is diverse and changing. To sum up,

		First, general principles	Proper conclusions
Speculative Reason	Objectively	True for all equally	True for all equally
	Subjectively	Known by all equally	Known only by some, unequally
Practical (Moral) Reason	Objectively	True for all equally	Not true for all, but for the most part
	Subjectively	Known by all equally	Not known by all, even when true for all

nor, where it is the same, is it equally known by all. Thus it is right and true for all to act according to reason: and from this principle it follows as a proper conclusion, that goods entrusted to another should be restored to their owner. Now this is true for the majority of cases: but it may happen in a particular case that it would be injurious, and therefore unreasonable, to restore goods held in trust; for instance if they are claimed for the purpose of fighting against one's country. And this principle will be found to fail the more, according as we descend further into detail, e.g., if one were to say that goods held in trust should be restored with such and such a guarantee, or in such and such a way; because the greater the number of conditions added, the greater the number of ways in which the principle may fail, so that it be not right to restore or not to restore.[271]

Consequently we must say that the natural law, as to general principles, is the same for all, both as to rectitude and as to knowledge.[272] But as to certain matters of detail, which are conclusions, as it were, of those general principles, it is the same for all in the majority of cases, both as to rectitude and as to knowledge; and yet in some few cases it may fail, both as to rectitude, by reason of certain obstacles (just as natures subject to generation and corruption fail in some few cases on account of some obstacle), and as to knowledge [cf. n. 272], since in some the reason is perverted by passion, or evil habit, or an evil disposition of nature; thus formerly, theft, although it is expressly contrary to the natural law, was not considered wrong among the Germans, as Julius Caesar relates (De Bello Gall. vi). . . .

FIFTH ARTICLE

Whether the Natural Law Can Be Changed?

I answer that, A change in the natural law may be understood in two ways. First, by way of addition. In this sense nothing hinders the natural law from being changed: since many things for the

---

[271] N.b.: St. Thomas, like Jesus, is not the kind of moral absolutist and legalist who denies moral common sense (cf. Mk 2:27).

[272] "Rectitude" = what is objectively right; "as to knowledge" = as to

benefit of human life have been added over and above the natural law, both by the Divine law and by human laws.[273]

Secondly, a change in the natural law may be understood by way of subtraction, so that what previously was according to the natural law, ceases to be so. In this sense, the natural law is altogether unchangeable in its first principles: but in its secondary principles, which, as we have said (A. 4), are certain detailed proximate conclusions drawn from the first principles, the natural law . . . may be changed in some particular cases of rare occurrence, through some special causes hindering the observance of such precepts, as stated above (A. 4). . . .

SIXTH ARTICLE

Whether the Law of Nature Can Be Abolished from the Heart of Man?

On the contrary, Augustine says (*Conf.* ii): *Thy law is written in the hearts of men, which iniquity itself effaces not.* But the law which is written in men's hearts is the natural law. Therefore the natural law cannot be blotted out.

I answer that, As stated above (AA. 4, 5), there belong to the natural law, first, certain most general precepts, that are known to all; and secondly, certain secondary and more detailed precepts,

---

whether all know it. Thus the natural moral law tells what is naturally and usually right (e.g., "pay debts"), just as natural physical law tells us how nature usually behaves (e.g., "birds fly"); but there are exceptions to both when we come to detail. "Do not give a murderer his gun back" is an exception to "Justice means paying what is owed", and dodos are an exception to "birds fly." The natural moral law is also naturally *known*, as is much of natural physical law; yet there are exceptions to both: e.g., in the case of natural moral law, St. Thomas' example of those Germans in Caesar's day who justified theft (or, in our own day, genocide); and in the case of natural physical law, some South Pacific natives believed women got pregnant by sitting under a sacred tree.

[273] E.g., the Beatitudes and the "evangelical counsels" in the New Testament add significantly to the old law; and there is the obligation to vote in a modern democracy, but not in an ancient monarchy.

which are, as it were, conclusions following closely from first principles. As to those general principles, the natural law, in the abstract, can nowise be blotted out from men's hearts. But it[274] is blotted out in the case of a particular action, in so far as reason is hindered from applying the general principle to a particular point of practice, on account of concupiscence or some other passion, as stated above (Q. 77, A. 2).—But as to the other, *i.e.*, the secondary precepts, the natural law can be blotted out from the human heart . . . by vicious customs and corrupt habits, as among some men, theft, and even unnatural vices, as the Apostle states (Rom 1), were not esteemed sinful.[275] . . .

becoming
numb
to sin.

---

[274] I.e., the *knowledge* of the moral law, not the "rectitude" or objective rightness of it.

[275] The greatest harm done by vice is thus its blinding of the reason against even *knowing* good and evil (cf. Jn 7:17). Cf. the blithely self-confident justification of "unnatural vice" today.

Question 95

Of Human Law

FIRST ARTICLE

Whether It Was Useful for Laws to Be Framed by Men?

On the contrary, Isidore says (*Etym.* v. 20): *Laws were made that in fear thereof human audacity might be held in check, that innocence might be safeguarded in the midst of wickedness, and that the dread of punishment might prevent the wicked from doing harm.* But these things are most necessary to mankind. Therefore it was necessary that human laws should be made.

I answer that, As stated above (Q. 63, A. 1; Q. 94, A. 3), man has a natural aptitude for virtue; but the perfection of virtue must be acquired by man by means of some kind of training.[276] Thus we observe that man is helped by industry in his necessities, for instance, in food and clothing. Certain beginnings of these he has from nature, viz., his reason and his hands; but he has not the full complement, as other animals have, to whom nature has given sufficiency of clothing and food. Now it is difficult to see how man could suffice for himself in the matter of this training: since the

---

[276] St. Thomas would disagree with both Rousseau, who says we are born virtuous, and Hobbes, who says we must be compelled by artifice and force to act contrary to our vicious nature (and also with Behaviorists, who deny we *have* an "innate" nature, good or bad). There is a parallel in epistemology: St. Thomas would disagree with both rationalism (Platonic or Cartesian), which teaches that knowledge is innate in us, and Empiricism (Hume), which teaches that knowledge is merely the passive reception and ordering of sense impressions. Rather, we have a natural aptitude for knowledge, and for virtue, but we must freely choose the active work to acquire both. This Article and the following one are so clear that no footnotes seem necessary; and their practical importance is also very clear.

perfection of virtue consists chiefly in withdrawing man from undue pleasures, to which above all man is inclined, and especially the young, who are more capable of being trained. Consequently a man needs to receive this training from another, whereby to arrive at the perfection of virtue. And as to those young people who are inclined to acts of virtue, by their good natural disposition, or by custom, or rather by the gift of God, paternal training suffices, which is by admonitions. But since some are found to be depraved, and prone to vice, and not easily amenable to words, it was necessary for such to be restrained from evil by force and fear, in order that, at least, they might desist from evil-doing, and leave others in peace, and that they themselves, by being habituated in this way, might be brought to do willingly what hitherto they did from fear, and thus become virtuous. Now this kind of training, which compels through fear of punishment, is the discipline of laws. Therefore, in order that man might have peace and virtue, it was necessary for laws to be framed: for, as the Philosopher says (*Polit.* i. 2), *as man is the most noble of animals if he be perfect in virtue, so is he the lowest of all, if he be severed from law and righteousness;* because man can use his reason to devise means of satisfying his lusts and evil passions, which other animals are unable to do. . . .

SECOND ARTICLE

Whether Every Human Law Is Derived from the Natural Law?

Objection 3. Further, the law of nature is the same for all; since the Philosopher says (*Ethic* v. 7) that *the natural just is that which is equally valid everywhere.* If therefore human laws were derived from the natural law, it would follow that they too are the same for all: which is clearly false. . . .

I answer that, As Augustine says (*De Lib. Arb.* i. 5), *that which is not just seems to be no law at all:* wherefore the force of a law depends on the extent of its justice. Now in human affairs a thing is said to be just, from being right, according to the rule of reason. But the first rule of reason is the law of nature, as is clear from what has been stated above (Q. 91, A. 2 *ad* 2). Consequently every human law has just so much of the nature of law, as it is derived from the law of nature. But if in any point it deflects from the law of nature, it is no longer a law but a perversion of law.

But it must be noted that something may be derived from the natural law in two ways: first, as a conclusion from premises, secondly, by way of determination of certain generalities. The first way is like to that by which, in sciences, demonstrated conclusions are drawn from the principles: while the second mode is likened to that whereby, in the arts, general forms are particularized as to details. Thus the craftsman needs to determine the general form of a house to some particular shape. Some things are therefore derived from the general principles of the natural law, by way of conclusions; *e.g.*, that *one must not kill* may be derived as a conclusion from the principle that *one should do harm to no man*: while some are derived therefrom by way of determination; *e.g.*, the law of nature has it that the evil-doer should be punished; but that he be punished in this or that way, is a determination of the law of nature.

Accordingly both modes of derivation are found in the human law. But those things which are derived in the first way, are contained in human law not as emanating therefrom exclusively, but have some force from the natural law also. But those things which are derived in the second way, have no other force than that of human law. . . .

Reply Obj. 3. The general principles of the natural law cannot be applied to all men in the same way on account of the great variety of human affairs: and hence arises the diversity of positive laws among various people. . . .

Question 96

Of the Power of Human Law

*Whether Human Law Should Be Framed for the Community
Rather Than for the Individual?* Yes- A the Majority

On the contrary, The jurist says (*Pandect. Justin.* lib. i, tit. iii, art. ii,
De legibus, etc.) that *laws should be made to suit the majority of
instances; and they are not framed according to what may possibly happen
in an individual case.*

I answer that, Whatever is for an end should be proportionate to
that end. Now the end of law is the common good; because, as
Isidore says (*Etym.* v. 21), that *law should be framed, not for any
private benefit, but for the common good of all the citizens.* Hence human
laws should be proportionate to the common good. Now the
common good comprises many things. Wherefore law should take
account of many things, as to persons, as to matters, and as to
times. Because the community of the state is composed of many
persons, and its good is procured by many actions; nor is it
established to endure for only a short time, but to last for all time by
the citizens succeeding one another, as Augustine says (*De Civ. Dei*
ii. 21; xxii. 6). . . .

SECOND ARTICLE

Whether It Belongs to the Human Law to Repress All Vices?

I answer that, . . . the same thing is not possible to one who has
not a virtuous habit, as is possible to one who has. Thus the same
is not possible to a child as to a full-grown man: for which reason
the law for children is not the same as for adults, since many things

are permitted to children, which in an adult are punished by law or at any rate are open to blame. In like manner many things are permissible to men not perfect in virtue, which would be intolerable in a virtuous man.

Now human law is framed for a number of human beings, the majority of whom are not perfect in virtue. Wherefore human laws do not forbid all vices, from which the virtuous abstain, but only the more grievous vices, from which it is possible for the majority to abstain; and chiefly those that are to the hurt of others, without the prohibition of which human society could not be maintained: thus human law prohibits murder, theft and suchlike.[277] . . .

THIRD ARTICLE

Whether Human Law Prescribes Acts of All the Virtues?

Objection 1. It would seem that human law does not prescribe acts of all the virtues. For vicious acts are contrary to acts of virtue. But human law does not prohibit all vices, as stated above (A. 2). Therefore neither does it prescribe all acts of virtue.

Objection 2. Further, a virtuous act proceeds from a virtue. But virtue is the end of law; so that whatever is from a virtue, cannot come under a precept of law. Therefore human law does not prescribe all acts of virtue.[278]

Objection 3. Further, law is ordained to the common good, as stated above (Q. 90, A. 2). But some acts of virtue are ordained, not to the common good, but to private good. Therefore the law does not prescribe all acts of virtue.

On the contrary, The Philosopher says (*Ethic.* v. 1) that the law *prescribes the performance of the acts of a brave man, . . . and the acts of the temperate man, . . . and the acts of the meek man: and in like manner*

---

[277] St. Thomas' point here has been used to justify legalizing abortion —a use which presumes abortion is a small vice, like overeating, and does not hurt anyone(!).

[278] This is what people mean when they say, "You can't legislate morality." Law cannot enforce virtuous *character*, but it can enforce virtuous *behavior*.

as regards the other virtues and vices, prescribing the former, forbidding the latter.

I answer that, The species of virtues are distinguished by their objects, as explained above (Q. 54, A. 2; Q. 60, A. 1; Q. 62, A. 2). Now all the objects of virtues can be referred either to the private good of an individual, or to the common good of the multitude: thus matters of fortitude may be achieved either for the safety of the state, or for upholding the rights of a friend, and in like manner with the other virtues. But law, as stated above (Q. 90, A. 2), is ordained to the common good. Wherefore there is no virtue whose acts cannot be prescribed by the law. Nevertheless human law does not prescribe concerning all the acts of every virtue: but only in regard to those that are ordainable to the common good,—either immediately, as when certain things are done directly for the common good,—or mediately, as when a lawgiver prescribes certain things pertaining to good order, whereby the citizens are directed in the upholding of the common good of justice and peace.

Reply Obj. 1. Human law does not forbid all vicious acts, by the obligation of a precept, as neither does it prescribe all acts of virtue. But it forbids certain acts of each vice, just as it prescribes some acts of each virtue.

Reply Obj. 2. An act is said to be an act of virtue in two ways. First, from the fact that a man does something virtuous; thus the act of justice is to do what is right, and an act of fortitude is to do brave things: and in this way law prescribes certain acts of virtue. —Secondly an act of virtue is when a man does a virtuous thing in a way in which a virtuous man does it. Such an act always proceeds from virtue: and it does not come under a precept of law, but is the end at which every lawgiver aims.

Reply Obj. 3. There is no virtue whose act is not ordainable to the common good, as stated above, either mediately or immediately.[279]

---

[279] Therefore there are no "victimless crimes". Suicide, for instance, harms your friends, family, and society. Prostitution harms the institution of the family, thus all members of all families. Drugs harm the social body by harming the individual member of the body.

FOURTH ARTICLE

Whether Human Law Binds a Man in Conscience?

Objection 1. It would seem that human law does not bind a man in conscience. For an inferior power has no jurisdiction in a court of higher power. But the power of man, which frames human law, is beneath the Divine power. Therefore human law cannot impose its precept in a Divine court, such as is the court of conscience.

Objection 2. Further, the judgment of conscience depends chiefly on the commandments of God. But sometimes God's commandments are made void by human laws, according to Matthew 15:6: *You have made void the commandment of God for your tradition.* Therefore human law does not bind a man in conscience.

Objection 3. Further, human laws often bring loss of character and injury on man, according to Isaiah 10:1 *et seq.: Woe to them that make wicked laws, and when they write, write injustice; to oppress the poor in judgment, and do violence to the cause of the humble of My people.* But it is lawful for anyone to avoid oppression and violence. Therefore human laws do not bind man in conscience.

On the contrary, It is written (1 Pet 2:19): *This is thankworthy, if for conscience . . . a man endure sorrows, suffering wrongfully.*

I answer that, Laws framed by man are either just or unjust. If they be just, they have the power of binding in conscience, from the eternal law whence they are derived, according to Proverbs 8:15: *By Me kings reign, and lawgivers decree just things. . . .*

On the other hand laws may be unjust in two ways: first, by being contrary to human good, . . . as when an authority imposes on his subjects burdensome laws, conducive, not to the common good, but rather to his own cupidity or vainglory;—or . . . when a man makes a law that goes beyond the power committed to him;—or . . . when burdens are imposed unequally on the community. . . . The like are acts of violence rather than laws; because, as Augustine says (*De Lib. Arb.* i. 5), *a law that is not just, seems to be no law at all.* Wherefore such laws do not bind in conscience, except perhaps in order to avoid scandal[280] or disturbance, for which cause a man should even yield his right, according to Matthew 5:40–41:

---

[280] "Scandal" means not merely *upsetting* people, but harming people morally—e.g., if a drinker leads a teetotaler to drink, which he considers

If a man . . . take away thy coat, let go thy cloak also unto him; and whosoever will force thee one mile, go with him other two.

Secondly, laws may be unjust through being opposed to the Divine good: such are the laws of tyrants inducing to idolatry, or to anything else contrary to the Divine law: and laws of this kind must nowise be observed, because, as stated in Acts 5:29, *we ought to obey God rather than men.*

Reply Obj. 1. As the Apostle says (Rom 13:1, 2), all human power is from God . . . *therefore he that resisteth the power*, in matters that are within its scope, *resisteth the ordinance of God*; so that he becomes guilty according to his conscience.

Reply Obj. 2. This argument is true of laws that are contrary to the commandments of God, which is beyond the scope of (human) power. Wherefore in such matters human law should not be obeyed.[281]

Reply Obj. 3. This argument is true of a law that inflicts unjust hurt on its subjects. The power that man holds from God does not extend to this: wherefore neither in such matters is man bound to obey the law, provided he avoid giving scandal or inflicting a more grievous hurt. . . .

SIXTH ARTICLE

Whether He Who Is Under a Law May Act Beside the Letter of the Law?

On the contrary, . . . we should take account of the motive of the lawgiver, rather than of his very words.

I answer that, . . . Now it happens often that the observance of

---

wrong. "Disturbance" also means more than "bothering people"; it means disturbing the real common good. Jesus and the saints often upset and bothered people.

[281] N.b.: *only* one who believes in a higher law than human law—natural law or eternal law or both—can justify disobedience to human law. Thus a moral positivist, who believes only in man-made ("posited") laws, must logically be a legalist and a status-quo conformist, since human law is the highest thing. The prevailing view, that believers in a natural law and/or an eternal law are conformists and legalists, while unbelievers are bold rebels, is exactly upside down.

some point of law conduces to the common weal in the majority of instances, and yet, in some cases, is very hurtful. Since then the lawgiver cannot have in view every single case, he shapes the law according to what happens most frequently, by directing his attention to the common good. Wherefore if a case arise wherein the observance of that law would be hurtful to the general welfare, it should not be observed. For instance, suppose that in a besieged city it be an established law that the gates of the city are to be kept closed, this is good for public welfare as a general rule: but, if it were to happen that the enemy are in pursuit of certain citizens, who are defenders of the city, it would be a great loss to the city, if the gates were not opened to them: and so in that case the gates ought to be opened, contrary to the letter of the law, in order to maintain the common weal, which the lawgiver had in view.

Nevertheless it must be noted, that if the observance of the law according to the letter does not involve any sudden risk needing instant remedy, it is not competent for everyone to expound what is useful and what is not useful to the state: those alone can do this who are in authority, and who, on account of such like cases, have the power to dispense from the laws. If, however, the peril be so sudden as not to allow of the delay involved by referring the matter to authority, the mere necessity brings with it a dispensation, since necessity knows no law.[282] . . .

---

[282] One is right to break speed laws to get a patient in danger of death to a hospital, without taking time to get police permission first. Jean Valjean, in *Les Miserables*, is justified even in stealing a loaf of bread from the rich to feed his starving family. Moral common sense never takes a beating in St. Thomas.

Question 97

Of Change in Laws

Whether Human Law Should Be Changed in Any Way?

On the contrary, Augustine says (*De Lib. Arb.* i. 6): *A temporal law, however just, may be justly changed in course of time.*

I answer that, As stated above (Q. 91, A. 3), human law is a dictate of reason, whereby human acts are directed. Thus there may be two causes for the just change of human law: one on the part of reason; the other on the part of man whose acts are regulated by law. The cause on the part of reason is that it seems natural to human reason to advance gradually from the imperfect to the perfect. Hence, in speculative sciences, we see that the teaching of the early philosophers was imperfect, and that it was afterwards perfected by those who succeeded them. So also in practical matters: for those who first endeavored to discover something useful for the human community, not being able by themselves to take everything into consideration, set up certain institutions which were deficient in many ways; and these were changed by subsequent lawgivers who made institutions that might prove less frequently deficient in respect of the common weal.[283]

On the part of man, whose acts are regulated by law, the law can be rightly changed on account of the changed condition of man, to whom different things are expedient according to the difference of his condition. An example is proposed by Augustine (*De Lib. Arb.* i. 6): *If the people have a sense of moderation and responsibility, and are most careful guardians of the common weal, it is right to enact a law*

---

[283] The idea of progress was not invented in modern times; the idea of necessary, automatic, universal progress was.

allowing such a people to choose their own magistrates for the government of the commonwealth. But if, as time goes on, the same people become so corrupt as to sell their votes, and entrust the government to scoundrels and criminals; then the right of appointing their public officials is rightly forfeit to such a people, and the choice devolves to a few good men.

SECOND ARTICLE

Whether Human Law Should Always Be Changed, Whenever Something Better Occurs?

I answer that, As stated above (A. 1), human law is rightly changed, in so far as such change is conducive to the common weal. But, to a certain extent, the mere change of law is of itself prejudicial to the common good: because custom avails much for the observance of laws. . . . Consequently, when a law is changed, the binding power of the law is diminished, in so far as custom is abolished. Wherefore human law should never be changed, unless, in some way or other, the common weal be compensated according to the extent of the harm done in this respect. Such compensation may arise either from some very great and very evident benefit conferred by the new enactment; or from the extreme urgency of the case, due to the fact that either the existing law is clearly unjust, or its observance extremely harmful. Wherefore the jurist says [*Pandect. Justin.* lib. i. ff., tit. 4, *De Constit. Princip.*] that *in establishing new laws, there should be evidence of the benefit to be derived, before departing from a law which has long been considered just.* [284]

---

[284] Ambrose Bierce defined a conservative as "one who is enamored of existing evils; a liberal is one who wishes to replace them with new ones." By this definition, St. Thomas is neither (how *can* he not fit into our categories?) but he is farthest from the liberal. "If it's not broken, don't fix it." Common sense again.

INDEX